A Select Bibliography on Economic Development: With Annotations

Other Titles in This Series

Westview Special Studies in Social, Political, and Economic Development

A Select Bibliography on Economic Development: With Annotations
John P. Powelson

This bibliography of more than 2,000 titles contains both books and journal articles, primarily those published since 1970. Most of the entries are annotated. The material is classified according to forty-eight categories, and there is also a list of relevant titles for each major country in Africa, Asia, and Latin America.

John P. Powelson is a program director of the Institute of Behavioral Science and professor of economics at the University of Colorado, Boulder.

A Select Bibliography
on Economic Development:
With Annotations

compiled by John P. Powelson

Westview Press / Boulder, Colorado

Westview Special Studies in Social, Political, and Economic Development

Copyright © 1979 by Westview Press, Inc.

Published in 1979 in the United States of America by
     Westview Press, Inc.
     5500 Central Avenue
     Boulder, Colorado 80301
     Frederick A. Praeger, Publisher

Library of Congress Catalog Card Number: 79-4848
ISBN: 0-89158-497-8

Composition for this book was provided by the author
Printed and bound in the United States of America

Contents

Preface

This bibliography has two purposes: <u>first</u>, to supply a basic reading list, with annotations, for students and researchers in economic development; and <u>second</u>, to provide a general review of principles and issues for those who might want to peruse the annotations. I suggest to my own students that they read whole sections of annotations as part of their basic reading material.

The bibliography exists because I needed it, for my students and myself. Fifteen years ago I began a card collection of books and articles on economic development, from which to prepare the reading lists for my courses. Students with special reading and research requirements began to consult these cards, and I felt the necessity to keep a basic list of titles in a variety of fields related to development.

But what is a field related to development? And is development a separate branch of economics? I will not try to answer these questions, nor to defend my selections (any one of which could be part of "general" economics rather than "development"), except to say that they have worked for me. The categories and items are those that have appeared to me to be of interest to students in economic development. They are broad in coverage, including works on politics, sociology, and history of less developed areas.

Over the years, of course, I have culled the collection. An enormous volume of material is pouring forth in many categories, such that for every title selected, several have to be omitted. While there is no particular cut-off date at the early end, the rejection standards become harder the farther back one goes in time. Therefore, the collection is mainly recent, or materials from the past eight years.

I am indebted to the Journal of Economic Literature (JEL), Foreign Affairs (FA), and Latin America
in Books (University of New Orleans) for supplying
annotations. Annotations written by me are indicated
as (Ed). Those annotations marked (BPA) were taken
from book publishers' or sellers' brochures or from
the jackets of the books concerned (caveat lector!).
Annotations borrowed from elsewhere are usually
abridged, and in the case of BPA, the superlatives
have been deleted.

I am indebted to two colleagues in particular:
William Loehr, who collected many of the titles in
conjunction with writings we are doing together; and
Ragaei El Mallakh, who supplied me with a list of
titles he had collected for his students. My own
students have also been valuable sources and commen-
tators. Finally, I am indebted to Diana Oldsen,
Brian Seitz, Velma Shanahan, and Kris Yoshida for
assistance in collecting and sorting the listings,
and to Jacqueline Myers for the many difficult hours
she spent typing the final copy and humoring me with
my countless revisions and additions.

John P. Powelson

A Student's Guide to Using This Bibliography and Seeking Other Materials

Many students in out-of-the-way areas (such as a university campus in the Rocky Mountains) believe--wrongly, I feel--that they are isolated from source materials, especially from those areas where development events are occurring--in Africa, Asia, and Latin America. Such materials are, however, easily obtained, although sometimes with a bit of delay. First, the United Nations, its specialized agencies, and other international institutions now assemble a wealth of data on less developed countries. Almost all of these are immediately accessible in university libraries. Second, publications of statistical and other materials by governments of less developed countries are now generally available on microfilm, from the following two sources:

The Institute of Developing Economies in Tokyo (Japan) prepares a catalog of Statistical Materials of Developing Countries, which it has collected. This catalog is available in the reference rooms of university libraries in the United States, and the microfilms themselves (copies of which are in the United States) may be ordered through inter-library loan facilities.

The Inter-Documentation Service in Zug (Switzerland) collects the economic development plans of virtually all countries. Once again, these plans, on microfilm, are available in the United States and may be ordered through inter-library loan facilities.

University libraries in the United States (and possibly other countries) ordinarily have inter-library loan facilities, such that if a title is not found in one's own library, it may be quickly borrowed from another. If one library does not subscribe to a journal, a xerox copy of the article wanted may be requested from another. In the United

States, such exchanges normally require two to three weeks, but longer if the materials are not owned by (or have been borrowed from) the library of first request, and others need to be canvassed.

This bibliography opens with a list of periodicals and reports, classified according to those dealing with general development and with specific geographic areas. In each category, there is a subdivision according to whether they are general periodicals, or issues of the United Nations and other international agencies.

By examining the table of contents of this bibliography, readers will acquire a general idea of how titles are classified. Many books and articles belong to more than one category. Where this is the case, each one is entered in one category only, with cross reference in the other(s). Where possible, a title has been classified in the category of prime concern; for example, a title on agrarian reform in Egypt would be classified in "agrarian reform" if it deals mainly with general principles of agrarian reform, and using Egypt only as example. It would be classified under "Egypt" if that were the major subject. In many cases, however, the major subject was not at all clear, and arbitrary selections were made. Therefore, the cross-reference part of each section should be considered an integral part of that section; authors listed in it qualify for inclusion just as much as those whose titles are primarily assigned there.

The cross-reference section is identified by the cachet X-REF. Each category referred to is entered in upper-case letters, followed by authors in lower-case. Where an author reference would normally be capitalized (as in the initials ILO and UN), these appear nevertheless in lower case (e.g., Ilo and Un) so as to avoid confusion. Only one word appears for each author (e.g., a title by Brown, Samuel; Fitch, Reginald; and Jones, Oscar, would appear in the X-REF section under Brown only. In case there is more than one "Brown" title in the section referred to, the reader should have little difficulty discovering which is pertinent.

No cross references appear between titles in over-all areas, such as Africa, and those in specific countries within each area. There are so many such references that the X-REF section would be cluttered. Therefore, readers looking for specific-country references might wish to peruse both the country and area listings.

Among the categories is one entitled, "Miscellaneous." This contains titles on general development, which could not easily be classified elsewhere. Nothing derogatory is intended about a title consigned to "miscellaneous." (One of my own books is there).

Because this is a "select" bibliography, ranging over the field of development and related topics, it could not be exhaustive on any one topic. Students wishing more titles for a specific topic might prepare their own bibliographies in the following way:

1. Consult the books and articles listed in this bibliography. Often these will present their own, further bibliographies.

2. Such bibliographies, of course, contain only works earlier than the book or article in which they are cited. To find later works, consult the Citations Index (usually found in university libraries), to see who has been quoting the author of the book or article already referred to.

3. Consult recent issues of other journals. The present bibliography lists many of the journals in development, published in different countries. The Journal of Economic Literature contains the tables of contents of current issues of some of these journals.

4. Consult the Readers' Guide, or other indices of periodicals normally found in reference rooms of university libraries; also the card catalogs. If the library has an open stack system, find the section in the stacks that deals with the subject on hand, and peruse the titles located in that vicinity.

5. Finally, ask the reference librarian for help.

Abbreviations

BPA	Annotation taken from a book publishers' announcement
CEPAL	Comisión Económica para América Latina (Naciones Unidas)
ECLA	Economic Commission for Latin America (United Nations)
(Ed)	Annotation by editor
(FA)	Annotation from Foreign Affairs
FAO	Food and Agricultural Organization
IDB	Inter-American Development Bank
ISHI	Institute for the Study of Human Issues (Philadelphia, Pennsylvania)
ILO	International Labor Organization
JEL	Annotation by Journal of Economic Literature
K/L	Capital-labor ratio
K/O	Capital-output ratio
LAB	Annotation from Latin America in Books (University of New Orleans)
LTC	Land Tenure Center (University of Wisconsin)
MNC	Multinational Corporation

MNR	Movimiento Nacional Revolucionario (Bolivia)
MTN	Multilateral Trade Negotiations
OAS	Organization of American States
OEA	Organización de Estados Americanos
OECD	Organization of Economic Cooperation and Development
SELA	Sistema Económico Latinoamericano
SSRC	Social Science Research Council
UN	United Nations
UNCTAD	United Nations Conference on Trade and Development
UNESCO	United Nations Educational, Scientific, and Cultural Organization
UNFPA	United Nations Funds for Population Activities
UNITAR	United Nations Institute for Training and Research

A Select Bibliography
on Economic Development:
With Annotations

Periodicals and Reports

DEALING WITH GLOBAL DEVELOPMENT

General

Cultures et Developpement, Louvain, Belgium
Developing Economies, Tokyo, Institute of Asian
  Economic Affairs
Development and Change, The Hague, Institute of
  Social Studies
Development Dialogue, Uppsala, Dag Hammerskjoeld
  Foundation
Development Finance, Kuala Lumpur
Developpement et Civilisations, Paris
IDS Bulletin, Sussex University, Institute of
  Development Studies
International Development Review, Washington,
  Society for International Development
Journal of Developing Areas, Macomb, Illinois,
  Western Illinois University
Journal of Development Economics, Amsterdam
Journal of Development Studies, London
Journal of Energy and Development, Boulder,
  Colorado, University of Colorado
Mondes en Developpement, Paris
Studies in Comparative International Development,
  St. Louis, Washington University
World Development, Oxford
World Development Letter, Washington, D.C.,
  Agency for International Development

United Nations Statistical Office

Commodity Imports
Commodity Trade Statistics
Demographic Yearbook
Monthly Bulletin of Statistics
Statistical Yearbook
Yearbook of International Trade Statistics
Yearbook of National Accounts Statistics

Other United Nations (except those listed under specialized agencies by name, or under countries)

Commission on International Trade: Commodity
  Survey
Commission on International Trade Law: Yearbook
Department of Economic and Social Affairs:
    Progress in Land Reform
    Triennial Report on Water Resources
      Development
Centre for Development Planning, Projections,
  and Policies: World Economic Survey
Conference on Trade and Development (UNCTAD):
    Handbook of International Trade and
      Development Statistics
    Trade in Manufactures of Developing
      Countries, Review
Economic and Social Council, Advisory Committee
  on the Application of Science and Technology
  to Development, Report
UNESCO Statistical Yearbook
Industrial Development Organization (UNIDO):
    Boletin Informativo
    Monographs on Industrial Development
    Industrial Development Survey
    Industrial Implementation Systems

World Bank

Atlas
Economic Development Institute, Report
Issues Papers (issued occasionally)
Publication Summaries (issued separately for impor-
  tant publications)
Sector policy papers (various sectors)
Statement of loans
Trends in Developing Countries: Population,
  economic growth, international capital flow
  and external debt and international trade
World Bank and IDA, Annual report
World Bank Staff Occasional Papers
World Development Report (annual)
World Tables

International Monetary Fund

Annual Report
Balance of Payments Yearbook
Direction of Trade
IMF Survey

2

Report on Exchange Restrictions
Staff Papers
Summary Proceedings of Annual Meeting
Surveys of African Economies (See under: Africa)

Food and Agriculture Organization

Bibliography on Land Tenure
Boletin Mensual de Economia y Estadistica
   Agricolas
Commodity Policy Studies
Commodity Review and Outlook
Commodity Series
Development Paper
Monthly Bulletin of Agricultural Economics
   and Statistics
Production Yearbook
Trade Yearbook
World Food Program Studies
World Grain: Trade Statistics

International Labor Organization

Bulletin of Labor Statistics
International Labor Review
Yearbook of Labor Statistics

Other international organizations

Afro-Asian Organization for Economic Cooperation,
   Cairo
      Basic Information on Afro-Asian Countries
      Afro-Asian Economic Review
Chambre de Commerce et d'Industries pour le
   marche commun eurafricain: Eurafrica et
   tribune du tiers-monde; revue monsuelle de
   cooperation internationale, Brussels, 1957
European Community, Africa, Caribbean, Pacific: The
   Courier (Brussels)
International Congress for the Study of the
   Problems of Developing Areas, Milan:
   Proceedings
Organization for European Economic Cooperation
   and Development, Paris
      Main Economic Indicators
      OECD Observer

DEALING WITH AFRICA

General

Africa Today, Denver, Colorado, University of
Denver
Africa Quarterly, New Delhi, Indian Council for
Africa
Africa Research Bulletin, Exeter, Africa Research
Limited
    (Economic, financial, and technical series;
    and Political, Social, and Cultural Series)
African Affairs, London, Royal African Society
African Development, London
African Economic History Review, Madison,
Wisconsin
African Index, Washington, D.C.
African Review, University of Dar es Salaam,
Political Science Department
African Studies, Johannesburg, University of
Witwatersrand
African Studies Bulletin, New York, African
Studies Association
Africana Bulletin, University of Warsaw
Afrika Spectrum, Hamburg, Deutsches Institut fuer
Afrika-Forschung
Afrique et Asie Modernes, Paris
Afrique Contemporaine, Paris, Centre d'etudes et
de documentation sur l'Afrique et l'outre-mer
Afro-Asian Affairs, London
Annee africaine, University of Bordeaux
Annuaire de l'Afrique du Nord, Universite d'Aix-
Marseille, Centre d'etudes nord-africaines
Asian and African Studies, Jerusalem
Cahiers d'etudes africaines, La Haye-Paris, Ecole
Pratique des Hautes Etudes
Canadian Journal of African Studies, Ottawa,
Committee on African Studies in Canada
Eastern Africa Economic Review, Nairobi, Oxford
East Africa Journal, Nairobi, East African
Institute of Social and Cultural Affairs
Eastern Africa Journal of Rural Development,
Nairobi, Eastern Africa Agricultural Economics
Society and University of Makerere (Kampala)
Internationales Afrika Forum, Munich,
Europaeisches Institut fuer Politiche,
Wirtschaftliche, und Sociale Fragen
Journal of African Studies, Los Angeles, UCLA
African Studies Center
Journal of Asian and African Studies, Leyden

4

Journal of Southern Africa Studies, London,
  Oxford
South African Journal of Economics, Johannesburg,
  Economic Society of South Africa

United Nations Economic Commission for Africa

African Economic Indicators
Demographic Handbook for Africa
Economic Bulletin for Africa
Foreign Trade Newsletter
Foreign Trade Statistics of Africa:
     Series A: Direction of Trade
     Series B: Trade by Commodity
International Economic Assistance to Africa
Planning Newsletter
Quarterly Bulletin of Activities
Quarterly Statistical Bulletin for Africa
Report of Conference of African Statisticians
Report of Sessions of UNECA
Statistical and Economic Information Bulletin
  for Africa
Statistical Newsletter
Statistical Yearbook
Survey of Economic Conditions in Africa
Yearly Statistics of Industrial Production

Other United Nations

Bureau of Economic Affairs: Economic
  Developments in Africa

International Labor Organization

African Regional Conference, Record of
  Proceedings
Africa Newsletter

Other International Agencies

African Development Bank: Annual report
African Institute for Economic Development and
  Planning, Dakar: Series in Economic
  Development and Planning
Banque Internationale pour l'Afrique Occidentale:
  Lettre Economique Africaine, Paris
Organization of African Unity, Economic and
  Social Commission: Proceedings and Report

DEALING WITH ASIA

General

Afrique et Asie Modernes, Paris
Afro-Asian Affairs, London
Asia Quarterly, Brussels, Centre d'Etude du
  Sud-est Asiatique et de l'Extreme-orient
Asian Affairs, London, Journal of the Royal
  Central Asian Society
Asian and African Studies, Jerusalem
Asian Economic Review, Hyderabad, Indian
  Institute of Economics
Asian Economies, Seoul, Research Institute of
  Asian Economics
Asian Finance, Hong Kong, Asian Finance
  Publications
Asian Survey, Berkeley, University of
  California Institute of International Studies
Internationales Asien Forum, Weltforum Verlag
Journal of Asian Studies, Ann Arbor, Association
  for Asian Studies
Journal of Asian and African Studies, Leyden
Journal of Contemporary Asia, London
Journal of Southeast Asian Studies, Singapore,
  McGraw-Hill
Modern Asian Studies, London
Southeast Asia, Carbondale, Illinois, Southern
  Illinois University Center for Vietnamese
  Studies
Southeast Asian Review, London, Royal Society
  for India, Pakistan, and Sri Lanka

United Nations Economic Commission for Asia and the Far East

Asian Industrial Development News
Committee on Industrial and Natural Resources,
  Report
Economic Bulletin for Asia and the Far East
Economic Survey of Asia and the Far East
Foreign Trade Statistics of Asia and the
  Far East
Quarterly Bulletin of Statistics for Asia and
  the Far East
Regional Economic Cooperation Series (each
  volume a distinctive title)
Sample Surveys in the ECAFE Region
Small Industry Bulletin for Asia and the
  Far East
Statistical Newsletter

Statistical Yearbook for Asia and the Far East
Transport and Communication Bulletin for Asia and
   the Far East
Water Resources Journal
Working Party on Economic Development and
   Planning, Report to ECAFE
Working Party on Small-Scale Industries and
   Handicraft Marketing, Report to the Committee
   on Industry and Trade

International Labor Organization

Asian Regional Conference, Record of Proceedings

Other International Agencies

Asian Socialist Conference, Planning Information
   Bureau, Rangoon: Economic Bulletin
Asian Productivity Organization, Tokyo: Asian
   Productivity
Association of Southeast Asia Nations: Report
   of meetings
Southeast Asia Development Advisory Group, New
   York: SEADAG Papers on Problems of Development
   in Southeast Asia

DEALING WITH LATIN AMERICA

General

Economic and Social Survey of Latin America,
   Washington
Inter-American Economic Affairs, Washington,
   Institute of Inter-American Studies
Journal of Inter-American Studies and World
   Affairs, Gainesville, Florida, University of
   Florida, School of Inter-American Studies
Journal of Latin American Studies, Cambridge,
   Cambridge University Press
Latin America Commodities Report, London, Latin
   American Newsletters Ltd.
Latin America Economic Report, London, Latin
   American Newsletters Ltd.
Latin America Political Report, London, Latin
   American Newsletters Ltd.
Latin American Index, Washington, D.C.
Latin American Perspectives, Riverside,
   California
Latin American Report, New Orleans
Latin American Research Review, Austin, Texas

Latin American Urban Research, Gainesville,
   Florida, University of Florida Center for
   Latin American Studies
Trimestre Económico, Mexico

United Nations Economic Commission for Latin America

Economic Bulletin for Latin America
Economic Survey of Latin America
Noticias de la CEPAL
Report
Statistical Bulletin for Latin America
Statistical Yearbook for Latin America

Other United Nations

UN Committee on Economic Cooperation in
   Central America: Report

Inter-American Development Bank

Annual Report
Economic and Social Progress in Latin America:
   annual report
Institute for Latin American Integration:
   annual report

Organization of American States

Informative Bulletin of the Capital Markets
   Program
Informaciones Economicas (Pan American Union,
   Department of Economic and Social Affairs)
Latin America: Problems and Perspectives of
   Economic Development (Pan American Union,
   Department of Economic and Social Affairs)

Other International Agencies

Centro Latinoamericano de Economía Humana,
   Montevideo: Cuadernos Latinoamericanos de
   Economia Humana
Instituto Interamericano de Ciencias, Bogota:
   Desarrollo Rural en las Americas
Inter-American Council of Commerce and Production,
   Montevideo: Boletín Informativo

Topics

Agrarian Reform

X-REF: BOLIVIA: Burke, Clark, Heath, Heyduck, BRAZIL: Cehelsky, Cline, Kutcher, COLOMBIA: Adams, Dorner, Egginton, CHILE: Barraclough, Kaufman, Lehman, Steenland, Thiesenhusen, ECUADOR: Redclift, CHINA: Lippitt, Wong, EGYPT: Radwan, ETHIOPIA: Cohen, HAITI: Lacerte, INDIA: Jannuzi, Joshi, Minhas, Mishra, IRAN: Aresvik, Katouzian, Lambton, KENYA: Clayton, Harbeson, KOREA: Morrow, MEXICO: Wilkie, NIGERIA: Famoriyo, Parsons, PAKISTAN: Herring, Khan, PARAGUAY: Arnold, PERU: Ford, Handelman, Tullis, PHILIPPINES: Koone, Medina, PUERTO RICO: Bergad, SRI LANKA: Gold, TAIWAN: Koo, TANZANIA: Feldman, van Hekken, TECHNOLOGY: Uchendu

Abdel-Fadil, Mahmoud, DEVELOPMENT, INCOME DISTRIBU-
TION AND SOCIAL CHANGE IN RURAL EGYPT (1952-
1970): A Study in the Political Economy of
Agrarian Transition, Occasional Paper 45, New
York, Cambridge University Press, 1975. Analyzes and assesses the progress of agrarian transition in Egypt between 1952 and 1970. Surveys
the basic changes occurring as a result of the
major land reform changes in 1952 and 1961, affecting land ownership, size of holdings, and
conditions of tenure. No index. (JEL)

Alexander, Robert J., AGRARIAN REFORM IN LATIN
AMERICA, New York, Macmillan Publishing Co.,
Inc., London, Collier Macmillan Publishers,
1974, ed., Samual L. Baily and Ronald T.
Hyman.

Alier, Juan Martinez, HACIENDAS, PLANTATIONS AND
COLLECTIVE FARMS, London, Frank Cass, 1977.
This book examines the economic and political
motivation of both landlords and peasants in
two contrasting situations, Cuban plantations

9

and Peruvian highland haciendas. It also analyses trends in agrarian change, including land reform. (BPA)

Barraclough, Solon, ed., AGRARIAN STRUCTURE IN LATIN AMERICA, Lexington, Massachusetts, Toronto, London, Lexington Books, D. C. Heath and Company, 1973.

Berry, R. Albert, LAND REFORM AND THE AGRICULTURAL INCOME DISTRIBUTION, Economic Growth Center, Discussion Paper No. 184, New Haven, Connecticut, Yale University, 1972.

Chao, Kang, ECONOMIC EFFECTS OF LAND REFORMS IN TAIWAN, JAPAN, AND MAINLAND CHINA: A Comparative Study, Madison, Wisconsin, The Land Tenure Center, University of Wisconsin-Madison.

Cohen, J. M.; Goldsmith, A. A.; and Mellor, J. W., REVOLUTION AND LAND REFORM IN ETHIOPIA: PEASANT ASSOCIATIONS, LOCAL GOVERNMENT AND RURAL DEVELOPMENT, Occasional Papers No. 6, Ithaca, New York, Cornell University Rural Development Committee.

Dorner, Peter and Kanel, Don, THE ECONOMIC CASE FOR LAND REFORM: EMPLOYMENT, INCOME DISTRIBUTION AND PRODUCTIVITY, Madison, Wisconsin, Land Tenure Center, University of Wisconsin LTC reprint No. 74, 1971.

Dorner, Peter, LAND REFORM AND ECONOMIC DEVELOPMENT, Harmondsworth, England, Penguin, 1972.

Dorner, Peter, ed., LAND REFORM IN LATIN AMERICA: ISSUES AND CASES, Madison, Wisconsin, University of Wisconsin-Madison, 1971.

Duncan, Kenneth; Rutledge, Ian; and Harding, Colin, LAND AND LABOUR IN LATIN AMERICA: Essays on the Development of Agrarian Capitalism in the Nineteenth and Twentieth Centuries, Cambridge Latin American Studies 26, New York, Cambridge University Press, 1977. The papers in this book examine in detail the different forms of agrarian capitalist development in Latin America in the nineteenth and twentieth century. The main theme concerns the problems and contradictions of the numerous and different attempts to create a uniform class of wage-earning landless laborers out of such groups as peasants, tenants, sharecroppers and free communities of subsistence cultivators. (BPA)

Dunning, Harrison C., LAND REFORM IN ETHIOPIA: A Case Study in Non-development, Madison, Wisconsin, Land Tenure Center, University of Wisconsin LTC reprint No. 97, 1970.

Eckstein, Alexander, "Land Reform and Economic Development," World Politics, Vol. VII, p. 650.

Foland, F. M., "Agrarian Unrest in Asia and Latin America," World Affairs, Vol. 2, Nos. 4 & 5, April-May 1974.

Food and Agriculture Organization of the United Nations, Documentations Center, LAND REFORM: ANNOTATED BIBLIOGRAPHY, Rome, 1971. Author and subject index, FAO publications and documents, 1945 to April, 1970. (Document DC/SP.20; ESR/MI SC/71/3)

Food and Agricultural Organization of the United Nations, special committee on agrarian reform, REPORT: SUMMARY, Rome, 1971. (FAO document C/71/22)

Gersovitz, Mark, DISTRIBUTION AND PRODUCTION IMPLICATIONS OF LAND REFORM, Economic Growth Center, Discussion Paper No. 194, New Haven, Connecticut, Yale University, December 1973.

Griffin, Keith. LAND CONCENTRATION AND RURAL POVERTY, London, Macmillan, 1976. Focuses on distribution of land ownership in developing countries. (BPA)

International Bank for Reconstruction and Development, LAND REFORM, Washington, D.C., World Bank, 1974.

ILO, AGRARIAN REFORM AND RURAL POVERTY, Egypt, 1952-75, Geneva, 1977. This study attempts to appraise the impact on rural Egypt of a quarter of a century of agrarian reform. (BPA)

ILO, POVERTY AND LANDLESSNESS IN RURAL ASIA, Geneva, 1977. An important new study focusing on the problems of inequality of landownership and income distribution and calling for a wider distribution of productive assets as an essential

11

component of development strategy. There are 11
research studies covering seven Asian countries
including China. (BPA)

Ip, P. C. and Stahl, C. W., "Systems of Land Tenure,
Allocative Efficiency, and Economic Development,"
American Journal of Agricultural Economics, Vol.
60, No. 1, February 1978, pp. 19-28. This paper
discusses comparative efficiency of resource
allocation under alternative forms of land tenure, sharecropping, fixed rental, wage cultivation, and owner cultivation. (JEL)

Jones, E. L. and Woolf, S. J., eds., AGRARIAN CHANGE
AND ECONOMIC DEVELOPMENT: THE HISTORICAL
PROBLEMS, London, Methuen; New York, Barnes and
Noble, 1969. Contains an introductory essay by
the editors, and six papers resulting from a
seminar at the University of Reading (England)
in early 1968. (JEL)

King, Russell, LAND REFORM: A World Survey, University of Leicester, September 1977. Dr. King
surveys the human and rural environments of the
Third World, studying causes, changes, and the
current and possible developments relating to
recent land reforms. He examines land reform
not only as a political, economic, and social
phenomenon, but presents its general themes and
principles within its spatial framework in Latin
America, Asia, Africa, and the Middle East. His
work serves well as both a synthesis and a source
book. (BPA) One of the best recent surveys of
agrarian reform throughout the world. (Ed)

Klein, Sidney, THE PATTERN OF LAND TENURE REFORM IN
EAST ASIA AFTER WORLD WAR II, New York, Bookman
Associates, 1958.

Land Tenure Center, LAND TENURE AND AGRARIAN REFORM
IN AFRICA AND THE NEAR EAST: An Annotated
Bibliography, Madison, Wisconsin, Land Tenure
Center Library, University of Wisconsin,
November 1977.

Landsberger, Henry A., ed., LATIN AMERICAN PEASANT
MOVEMENTS, Ithaca, New York and London, Cornell
University Press, 1969.

Ledesma, Antonio J., LAND REFORM PROGRAMS IN EAST AND SOUTHEAST ASIA: A Comparative Approach, Madison, Wisconsin, Land Tenure Center, University of Wisconsin LTC reprint No. 69, November 1976.

Lehmann, David, AGRARIAN REFORM AND AGRARIAN REFORMISM: Studies of Peru, Chile, China and India, London, Faber & Faber, 1974.

Lehmann, David, ed., LANDLORDS AND GOVERNMENTS: AGRARIAN REFORM IN THE THIRD WORLD, New York, Holmes and Meier Publishers, 1974.

Lin, Sein, LAND REFORM IMPLEMENTATION, A Comparative Perspective, Hartford, Connecticut, John C. Lincoln Institute, 1974.

Lin, Sein, ed., READINGS IN LAND REFORM, Taipei, Taiwan, Good Friends Press in Taipei, financed by Lincoln Institute of Land Policy, Inc., Cambridge, Massachusetts, 1970.

Mitchell, Clyde C., LAND REFORM IN ASIA: A Case Study, Washington, D.C., National Planning Association, 1952.

Montgomery, John D., ALLOCATION OF AUTHORITY IN LAND REFORM PROGRAMS: A Comparative Study of Administrative Processes and Outputs, New York, The Agricultural Development Council, Inc., March 1974.

Olson, Gary L., U.S. FOREIGN POLICY AND A THIRD WORLD PEASANT: Land Reform in Asia and Latin America, New York, Praeger, 1974.

Paige, Jeffrey M., AGRARIAN REVOLUTION: Social Movements and Export Agriculture in the Underdeveloped World, New York, The Free Press, 1975.

Parsons, Kenneth; Penn, Raymond; J.; and Raup, Philip M., eds., "Land Tenure," Journal of Economic Abstracts, March 1968.

Querol, Mariano N., LAND REFORM IN ASIA, Manila, Philippines, Solidaridad Publishing House, 1974. An elementary exposition, addressed to unsophisticated readers, containing valuable information on agrarian reforms in Asia, by countries. (Ed)

13

Shaw, Paul R., LAND TENURE AND THE RURAL EXODUS IN CHILE, COLOMBIA, COSTA RICA, AND PERU, Latin American Monographs, Second Series, No. 19, Gainesville, Florida: The University Presses of Florida for the Center for Latin American Studies, University of Florida, 1976. Rural migration to cities in Latin America has meant that in several countries one-fourth to one-third of the national population lives in the capital city. In this study all the complicated multiple-regression techniques used, and refined graphic analyses made, serve to demonstrate the crying need for land redistribution that would overcome the gross inequalities and inequities of the minifundio-latifundio complex. (LAB)

Sinha, J. N., "Agrarian Reforms and Employment in Densely Populated Agrarian Economies," International Labour Review, Vol. 108, No. 5, November 1973.

Smith, Theodore Reynolds, EAST ASIAN AGRARIAN REFORM: JAPAN, REPUBLIC OF KOREA, TAIWAN, AND THE PHILIPPINES, Hartford, Connecticut, John C. Lincoln Institute, 1972.

Stavenhagen, Rodolfo, ed., AGRARIAN PROBLEMS AND PEASANT MOVEMENTS IN LATIN AMERICA, Garden City, New York, Anchor Books, Doubleday & Company, Inc., 1970.

Sternberg, M. J., "Agrarian Reform and Employment: Potentials and Problems," International Labour Review, Vol. 103, No. 5, May 1971.

Tai, Hung-Chao, LAND REFORM AND POLITICS: A Comparative Analysis, Berkeley, University of California Press, 1974.

Thiesenhusen, William C., "WHAT NEXT?", Madison, Wisconsin, Land Tenure Center, University of Wisconsin LTC reprint No. 132, December 1977.

Tuma, Elias H., TWENTY-SIX CENTURIES OF AGRARIAN REFORM: A Comparative Analysis, Berkeley and Los Angeles, The University of California Press, 1965.

Uchendu, Victor C., THE IMPACT OF CHANGING AGRICUL-
    TURAL TECHNOLOGY ON AFRICAN LAND TENURE,
    Madison, Wisconsin, Land Tenure Center, Univer-
    sity of Wisconsin LTC reprint No. 71, 1970.

United Nations, PROGRESS IN LAND REFORM, Fifth
    Report, New York, United Nations, 1970.

United Nations, PROGRESS IN LAND REFORM, Sixth
    Report, New York, United Nations, 1976.

U.S. Agency for International Development, Office of
    Agriculture and Fisheries, LAND REFORM: A
    Collected List of References for A.I.D. Tech-
    nicians, Washington, D.C., A.I.D. Bibliography
    Series: Agriculture, #4, 1970.

U.S. Department of State, LAND REFORM--A World
    Challenge, Washington, D.C., U.S. Government
    Printing Office, 1952.

University of Wisconsin, Land Tenure Center,
    AGRARIAN REFORM IN LATIN AMERICA: An Annotated
    Bibliography, Madison, Wisconsin, University of
    Wisconsin, Land Tenure Center, Land Economics
    Monograph Series No. 5, 1975. This massive
    bibliography contains more than 5,000 annotated
    entries covering virtually all the materials--
    books, journal articles, pamphlets, unpublished
    reports, etc.--relating to land tenure and
    reform in Latin America which exist on the
    University of Wisconsin-Madison campus. (BPA)

Walinsky, Louis J., AGRARIAN REFORM AS UNFINISHED
    BUSINESS: The Selected Papers of Wolf
    Ladejinsky, New York, Oxford University Press,
    1977. A splendid testament to the life's work
    of Wolf Ladejinsky, a man who combined a pas-
    sionate dedication to democracy with a mission
    to alleviate rural poverty in the Third World.
    Few other men in this century have understood
    as well as Ladejinsky the political importance
    of land. For anyone interested in agrarian
    reform this is essential reading. (FA)

Warriner, D., "Employment and Income Aspects of
    Recent Agrarian Reforms in the Middle East,"
    International Labour Review, Vol. 101, No. 6,
    June 1970.

World Bank, AGRICULTURAL LAND SETTLEMENT, A World
    Bank Issues Paper, January 1978.

World Bank, LAND REFORM, Sector Policy Paper, May
    1975.

Agricultural Credit

X-REF: ASIA: Kato, BRAZIL: Adams, COLOMBIA: Mc-
Pherson, Thirsk, INDIA: Baker, UGANDA: Hunt,
ZAMBIA: Wilson

Abbott, J. C., "Credit Institutions and Their Impact
    on Agricultural Development in Africa," Monthly
    Bulletin of Agricultural Economics and
    Statistics, Vol. 23, 7-15.

Adams, Dale W.; Davis, Harlan; and Bettis, Lee, "Is
    Inexpensive Credit a Bargain for Small Farmers?
    The Recent Brazilian Experience," Inter-American
    Economic Affairs, Vol. 26, No. 1, Spring 1972.

Agency for International Development, AGRICULTURAL
    CREDIT AND RURAL SAVINGS, A Selected List of
    References for A.I.D. Technicians, Washington,
    D.C., A.I.D. Bibliography Series, Agriculture
    No. 7, December 1, 1972.

Agency for International Development, AGRICULTURAL
    CREDIT AND RURAL SAVINGS: II, Washington,
    D.C., A.I.D. Bibliography Series, Agriculture
    No. 8, January 1976.

Baker, C. B. and Bhargava, Vinay K., "Financing
    Small-Farm Development in India," Australian
    Journal of Agricultural Economics, Vol. 18,
    No. 2, August 1974, 101-118.

Baum, Warren C., "Agricultural Credit and the Small
    Farmer," Finance and Development, Vol. 13,
    No. 2, June 1976.

Caplin, Lionel, "The Multiplication of Social Ties:
    The Strategy of Credit Transactions in East
    Nepal," Economic Development and Cultural
    Change, Vol. 20, July 1972, 691-702.

Donald, Gordon, CREDIT FOR SMALL FARMERS IN DEVELOP-
ING COUNTRIES, Boulder, Colorado, Westview Press,
1976. Prepared for the Agency for International
Development, this is the most comprehensive review of the field, both in its statistical data
and the scope of its analysis. It explores a
wide range of aspects, including a number of innovative approaches and assessments of more traditional views. (BPA)

Firth, Raymond and Yamey, B. S., eds., CAPITAL,
SAVING AND CREDIT IN PEASANT SOCIETIES: Studies
from Asia, Oceania, the Caribbean, and Middle
America, Chicago, Aldine Publishing Company,
1964.

Ghosal, S. N., "Farm Financing by Commercial Banks:
A Strategy," Prajnan, Vol. 2, No. 4, October-
December 1973, 499-506.

Howse, C. J., "Agricultural Development without
Credit," Agricultural Administration, Vol. 1,
1974, 259-262.

Jodha, N. S., "Land-Based Credit Policies and
Investment Prospects for Small Farmers,"
Economic and Political Weekly, Vol. 6,
September 1971, A143-A148.

Kato, Yuzuru, "Sources of Loanable Funds of Agricultural Credit Institutions in Asia,"
Developing Economies, Vol. 10, 1972, 126-140.

Ladman, Jerry R., "A Model of Credit Applied to the
Allocation of Resources in a Case Study of a
Sample of Mexican Farms," Economic Development
and Cultural Change, Vol. 22, June 1974,
279-301.

Ladman, Jerry R., "Some Empirical Evidence in
Unorganized Rural Credit Markets," The Canadian
Journal of Economics, Vol. 19, November 1971,
61-66.

Lele, Uma J., ROLE OF CREDIT AND MARKETING FUNCTIONS
IN AGRICULTURAL DEVELOPMENT, Washington, D.C.,
International Economic Association, September
4, 1972.

Lipton, M., "Agricultural Finance and Rural Credit in Poor Countries," World Development, Vol. 4, No. 7, July 1976.

McPherson, W. W. and Schwartz, Michael, CROP INPUT PRODUCTIVITY AND AGRICULTURAL CREDIT ON THE NORTH COAST OF COLOMBIA, Economics Report 56, December, 1973.

World Bank, AGRICULTURAL CREDIT, Sector Policy Paper, May 1975.

Agricultural Development

X-REF: AFRICA: Adams, Amann, Cleaver, Krishna, ASIA: Rao, Yamada, BRAZIL: Knight, CHINA: American, Juo, Myers, Stavis, COLOMBIA: Berry, GUATEMALA: Fletcher, INDIA: Agarwal, Frankel, IRAN: Aresvik, JAPAN: Ohkawa, Voelkner, JORDAN: Aresvik, KENYA: Heyer, MEXICO: Baring, Wellhausen, PAKISTAN: Khan, PANAMA: Merrill, PARAGUAY: Arnold, PERU: Coutu, Lewellen, SRI LANKA: Ganewatte, Gooneratne, TECHNOLOGY: Street, Uchendu, THAILAND: Inukai, URUGUAY: Brannon, VENEZUELA: Heaton, ZAMBIA: Dodge

Abbott, J. C. and Creupelandt, H. C., AGRICULTURAL MARKETING BOARDS: THEIR ESTABLISHMENT AND OPERATION, FAO Marketing Guide No. 5, 1974.

Abercrombie, K. C., "Incomes and Their Distribution in Agriculture and the Rest of the Economy," Monthly Bulletin of Agricultural Economics and Statistics, Vol. 16, No. 6, June 1967, 1-8.

Adams, Dale W., and Coward, E. Walter, SMALL-FARMER DEVELOPMENT STRATEGIES: A Seminar Report, The Agricultural Development Council, Inc., July 1972.

Agarwal, N. L. and Kumawat, R. K., "Green Revolution and Capital and Credit Requirements of the Farmers in Semiarid Region of Rajasthan," Indian Journal of Agricultural Economics, Vol. 29, No. 1, 1974, 67-75.

Agribusiness Council, AGRICULTURAL INITIATIVE IN THE THIRD WORLD: A Report on the Conference: Science and Agribusiness in the Seventies, Lexington, Massachusetts, Lexington Books, 1975.

18

In this volume, sponsored by the Agribusiness
Council, contributors report how, through
investments and well-defined agriculture
research, private investors and business firms
can help developing countries meet their
responsibilities for increasing their own food
production and decreasing their population
growth. (BPA)

Aldington, T. J. and Smith, L. D., THE MARKETING OF
RICE IN KENYA, Institute for Development Studies
Discussion Paper No. 74, November 1968.

Amann, Victor R., ed., AGRICULTURAL EMPLOYMENT AND
LABOUR MIGRATION IN EAST AFRICA, Kampala,
Uganda, Makerere University, 1974.

Bell, C., "The Acquisition of Agricultural Tech-
nology: Its Determinants and Effects,"
Journal of Development Studies, Vol. 9, No. 1,
October 1972.

Biggs, Huntley H. and Tinnermeier, Ronald L., ed.,
SMALL FARM AGRICULTURAL DEVELOPMENT PROBLEMS,
Fort Collins, Colorado State University, 1974.

Bird, Richard M., TAXING AGRICULTURAL LAND IN DEVEL-
OPING COUNTRIES, Cambridge, Massachusetts,
Harvard University Press, 1974.

Brown, Lester R., SEEDS OF CHANGE: The Green Revolution and Development in the 1970's, New York,
Praeger (for the Overseas Development Council),
1970. Succinct and readable account of the
contemporary revolution in agriculture by a
former official of the Department of Agriculture. Optimistic in tone, it stresses the
problems resulting from increased productivity
and makes proposals for dealing with some of
them. (FA)

Carroll, Thomas F., "Peasant Cooperation in Latin
America" from P. M. Worsley, ed., TWO BLADES OF
GRASS, Manchester, Manchester University Press,
1971.

Clayton, E. S., "A Note on Farm Mechanisation and
Employment in Developing Countries," International Labour Review, Vol. 110, No. 1, July
1974.

19

Clayton, E. S., "Mechanization and Employment in East African Agriculture," International Labour Review, Vol. 105, No. 4, April 1972.

Cochrane, Willard W., AGRICULTURAL DEVELOPMENT PLANNING: Economic Concepts, Administrative Procedures, and Political Process, New York and London, Praeger, Praeger Special Studies in International Economics and Development, 1974. The author provides a survey of the state of knowledge regarding agricultural development, an outline of national development planning, a review of the role of the agricultural sector in national planning, and an examination of planning and implementation problems within agriculture. (JEL)

Dorner, Peter, ed., COOPERATIVE AND COMMUNE, Madison, University of Wisconsin Press, 1977. Designed to integrate international knowledge of cooperative-collective farming, this information will serve policy-makers in their attempts to formulate programs for approaching agrarian issues in their countries and will provide the teacher and student of development with a detailed account of a wide range of experiences and hypotheses for research. Cooperative farming in several countries is covered. (BPA)

Farmer, B. H., GREEN REVOLUTION?, Boulder, Colorado, Westview Press, 1977. This volume, a report on the impact of Green Revolution technology on rice farming in India and Sri Lanka, suggests that diversity, as a basic characteristic of agricultural enterprise, is costly to ignore. (BPA)

Gerken, Egbert, LAND PRODUCTIVITY AND THE EMPLOYMENT PROBLEM OF RURAL AREAS, New Haven, Connecticut, Yale University, Economic Growth Center, Discussion Paper No. 176, 1973.

Gittinger, J. Price, ECONOMIC ANALYSIS OF AGRICULTURAL PROJECTS, Baltimore and London, The Johns Hopkins University Press, 1972.

Griffin, Keith, THE POLITICAL ECONOMY OF AGRARIAN CHANGE, Cambridge, Massachusetts, Harvard University Press, 1974. This is a study of the economic, social, and political consequences of the "green revolution" in Asia and Latin America.

20

The "green revolution" has not resulted in greater agricultural production per capita or reduced
malnutrition. Rather, the indirect and measurable effects have been more significant--the
market oriented crop system, the growth of agricultural labor, the increased power of landowners, the declining share of wages. (BPA)

Hayami, Yujiro and Ruttan, Vernon W., AGRICULTURAL
DEVELOPMENT: AN INTERNATIONAL PERSPECTIVE,
Baltimore, Maryland, Johns Hopkins Press, 1971.
This very interesting inquiry into productivity
in agriculture, based on American and Japanese
experience, stresses the importance of economic
incentives plus the organization of governmental research. The implications for less-
developed countries are explored with emphasis
on the need for markets that accurately reflect
requirements. (FA)

Hayami, Y. and Ruttan, V. W., "Agricultural Productivity Differences Among Countries," American
Economic Review, Vol. LX, No. 5, December 1970.

Hayami, Y. and Ruttan, V. W., "Factor Prices and
Technical Change in Agricultural Development:
The United States and Japan, 1880-1960,"
Journal of Political Economy, September-October
1970. This study attempts to test a hypothesis
of the induced bias in technical change against
the historical data of U.S. and Japanese agricultural development for 1880-1960. (JEL)

Hazell, P. B. R., and Scandizzo, P. L., FARMERS'
EXPECTATIONS, RISK AVERSION, AND MARKET EQUI-
LIBRIUM UNDER RISK, World Bank Reprint Series,
No. 37, Reprinted from American Journal of
Agricultural Economics, 59, February 1977.

Ho, Samuel P. S., AGRICULTURAL TRANSFORMATION UNDER
COLONIALISM: The Case of Taiwan, New Haven,
Connecticut, Yale University, Economic Growth
Center Paper No. 122, 1968.

Hopkins, Raymond F.; Puchala, Donald J.; and Talbot,
Ross B., eds., FOOD, POLITICS, AND AGRICULTURAL
DEVELOPMENT. Case Studies in the Public Policy
of Rural Modernization, Boulder, Colorado,
Westview Press, 1979. This collection of studies on the politics of agricultural development
in key countries and regions of Asia and Africa

21

focuses on the political forces. They substantiate the assertion that political rather than technical factors hold the key to improved agriculture and economic development; they emphasize the need for steady and significant increase in food production in the developing countries themselves. (BPA)

Hunter, Guy, MODERNIZING PEASANT SOCIETIES: A Comparative Study in Asia and Africa, New York and London, Oxford University Press for the Institute of Race Relations, 1969. Broad, economically non-technical study of developmental problems facing the peasant societies of Asia and tropical Africa. Modernization of these societies is discussed in terms of the economic, social and political factors, and the central theme of the book is that "growth takes place as a long chain of small related sequences each of which determines the possibilities of the next. Few quantitative data. Index. (JEL)

Hymer, S. and Resnick, S., "A Model of an Agrarian Economy with Nonagricultural Activities," American Economic Review, Vol. LIX, No. 4, Part 1, September 1969. One of the early articles recognizing the relationship between farming and non-farm production in the total life of farmers in less developed countries. (Ed)

ILO, MECHANISATION AND EMPLOYMENT IN AGRICULTURE: Case Studies from Four Continents, Geneva, 1974. In this volume an attempt is made to discover how the twin advantages of increased output and higher employment can be secured through selective mechanisation. (BPA)

Johnston, Bruce F. and Kilby, Peter, AGRICULTURE AND STRUCTURAL TRANSFORMATION: Economic Strategies in Late-Developing Countries, New York, London and Toronto, Oxford University Press, 1975.

Johnson, D. Gale, WORLD AGRICULTURE IN DISARRAY, New York, St. Martin's Press, 1973. A leading American expert digs deeply into the national farm policies of the industrial countries to show their costs, effects and contradictions. His proposals for national and international measures to improve trade and production deal with

22

long-run conditions rather than current fears
of global shortage. (FA)

Krishna, K. G. V., "Smallholder Agriculture in Africa,
Constraints and Potential," The Annals, Vol.
432, July 1977, 12-25.

Mellor, John W., THE ECONOMICS OF AGRICULTURAL
DEVELOPMENT, Ithaca, New York, Cornell University Press, 1966.

Mitra, Ashok, TERMS OF TRADE AND CLASS RELATIONS,
London, Frank Cass, 1977. The author finds
that the key problem in the whole process of
economic development is the relationship of
agriculture and industry; the most important
manifestation of that relationship is the terms
of trade between the two sectors. (BPA)

Morgan, W. B., AGRICULTURE IN THE THIRD WORLD: A
SPATIAL ANALYSIS, Boulder, Colorado, Westview
Press, 1978. The book covers practically all
aspects of Third World agriculture and analyzes
the prospects for agricultural improvement, with
an emphasis on agricultural economy and spatial
organization. Innovations and improvement are
shown as closely related to specific locations.
(BPA)

Morss, E.; Hatch, J.; Mickelwait, D.; and Sweet, C.,
STRATEGIES FOR SMALL FARMER DEVELOPMENT: An
Empirical Study of Rural Development Projects
in The Gambia, Ghana, Kenya, Lesotho, Nigeria,
Bolivia, Colombia, Ecuador, Mexico, Paraguay
and Peru, Boulder, Colorado, Westview Press,
1977. This study uncovers and documents the
vital link between development project success
and a sustained and early effort to win the
commitment of the small farmer himself to working with the project. (BPA)

Owen, W. F., "The Developmental Squeeze on Agriculture," American Economic Review, Vol. LVI, No. 1,
March 1966.

Owen, Wyn F., TWO RURAL SECTORS: Their Character-
istics and Roles in the Development Process,
Bloomington, Indiana, Indiana University,
Occasional Papers, International Development
Research Center, March 1971.

Poleman, Thomas T., and Freebairn, Donald K., eds.,
     FOOD, POPULATION AND EMPLOYMENT: The Impact of
     the Green Revolution, New York, Washington,
     and London, Praeger Publishers, 1973.

The Puebla Project, SEVEN YEARS OF EXPERIENCE: 1967-
     1973, Analysis of a Program to Assist Small
     Subsistence Farmers to Increase Crop Production
     in a Rainfed Area of Mexico, The International
     Maize and Wheat Improvement Center, 1973.

Rao, V. K. R. V., GROWTH WITH JUSTICE IN ASIAN
     AGRICULTURE: An Exercise in Policy Formula-
     tion, Geneva, United Nations Research Institute
     for Social Development, 1974.

Reynolds, Lloyd G., ed., AGRICULTURE IN DEVELOPMENT
     THEORY, New Haven, Connecticut and London,
     Yale University Press, 1975.

Rice, E. B., EXTENSION IN THE ANDES, Cambridge,
     Massachusetts; MIT Press, 1975. Agricultural
     specialists will welcome this detailed account
     of the history and development of extension
     services in 12 Latin American countries during
     the 30-year period ending in 1971. (FA)

Ruttan, Vernon, "Planning Technological Advance in
     Agriculture: The Case of Rice Production in
     Taiwan, Thailand and the Philippines." Chapter
     3 of: Solo, Robert A. and Rogers, Everett M.,
     INDUCING TECHNOLOGICAL CHANGE FOR ECONOMIC
     GROWTH AND DEVELOPMENT, Ann Arbor, Michigan
     State University Press, 1972.

Schultz, T. W., ECONOMIC GROWTH AND AGRICULTURE,
     New York, 1968.

Schultz, T. W., TRANSFORMING TRADITIONAL AGRICULTURE,
     New Haven, Connecticut: Yale University Press,
     1964.

Scientific American, "Food and Agriculture,"
     Scientific American Inc., Vol. 235, No. 3,
     September 1976.

Shanin, Teodor, ed., PEASANTS AND PEASANT SOCIETIES,
     Great Britain, C. Nicholls & Company Ltd., 1971.

Sharma, A. C., "Impact of Farm Size and Mechanisation on Human and Animal Power on Ludhiana Farms," Economic Affairs, Vol. 19, No. 9, September 1974.

Shaw, Robert d'A., JOBS AND AGRICULTURAL DEVELOPMENT: A Study of the effects of a New Agricultural Technology on Employment in Poor Nations, Washington, D.C., Overseas Development Council, 1970.

Stevens, Robert D., ed., TRADITION AND DYNAMICS IN SMALL-FARM AGRICULTURE: Economic Studies in Asia, Africa, and Latin America, Iowa State University Press, 1977. Discusses problems of increasing food production on the 100 million small farms in the developing nations of Asia, Africa, and Latin America. Aims to increase understanding of the technical, economic, and social decisions faced by small farmers. (BPA)

Thiesenhusen, William C., GREEN REVOLUTION IN LATIN AMERICA: Income Effects, Policy Decisions, Madison, University of Wisconsin, LTC reprint No. 83, 1972.

Thornbecke, E., "Sector Analysis and Models of Agriculture in Developing Countries," Food Res. Inst. Stud., 1973, Vol. 12, No. 1, 73-89. The purpose of the article is twofold. First, it offers a selective typology of agriculture sector models in developing countries and, secondly, it reviews the requirements of various users of sector analysis such as national ministries and international donor agencies.(JEL)

Uchendu, Victor C., "The Impact of Changing Agricultural Technology on African Land Tenure," Journal of Developing Areas, Vol. 4, July 1970, 477-485.

U.S. Agency for International Development, SPRING REVIEW ON SMALL FARMERS, Washington, D.C., 1974. A compilation of papers by the U.S. foreign aid agency to assist in its development of policy toward small farmers in less developed countries. (Ed)

Valdes, Alberto, ed., ECONOMICS AND THE DESIGN OF
    SMALL-FARMER TECHNOLOGY, Ames, Iowa State Uni-
    versity Press, 1978. Sixteen contributors ex-
    plain how economists in cooperation with biolo-
    gists can contribute to the design of new tech-
    nologies for small farmers. The essays are
    divided into three parts: (1) methodological
    aspects; (2) design of technology; (3) tech-
    nology, rural development, and welfare. (BPA)

Vallianatos, E. G., FEAR IN THE COUNTRYSIDE: The
    Control of Agricultural Resources in the Poor
    Countries by Nonpeasant Elites, Cambridge,
    Massachusetts, Ballinger, 1976. Uneven and
    argumentative--the word "must" is a constant
    refrain--but with fascinating historical mater-
    ial on Western attitudes toward colonial agri-
    culture. (FA)

Weeks, J., "Uncertainty, Risk, and Wealth and Income
    Distribution in Peasant Agriculture," Journal of
    Development Studies, Vol. 7, No. 1, October
    1970.

Weitz, Raanan, FROM PEASANT TO FARMER: A REVOLU-
    TIONARY STRATEGY FOR DEVELOPMENT, New York,
    Columbia University Press, 1971. An Israeli
    specialist stresses people, organization, com-
    munity-building and cooperation as elements in
    making agriculture a key to development. (FA)

Wharton, Clifton R., Jr., ed., SUBSISTENCE AGRICUL-
    TURE AND ECONOMIC DEVELOPMENT, Chicago, Aldine,
    1970. Fourteen theoretical, historical, and
    empirical papers presented to a 1965 Conference
    at the East-West Center in Honolulu. Part I
    considers "The Subsistence Farmer, Agrarian
    Cultures, and Peasant Societies"; Part II is
    "The Economic Behavior of Subsistence Farmers";
    Part III, "Theories of Change and Growth": Part
    IV, "Developing Subsistence Agriculture"; and
    Part V is on "Research Priorities. Index. (JEL)

World Bank, FORESTRY, Sector Policy Paper, February
    1978.

Yamada, Saburo, A COMPARATIVE ANALYSIS OF ASIAN
    AGRICULTURAL PRODUCTIVITIES AND GROWTH PATTERNS,
    Asian Productivity Organization, 1975.

Yudelman, Montague and Howard, Frederic, AGRICULTURAL
    DEVELOPMENT AND ECONOMIC INTEGRATION IN LATIN
    AMERICA, Inter-American Development Bank, April
    1969.

Yudelman, Montague, THE INTER-AMERICAN DEVELOPMENT
    BANK AND AGRICULTURAL DEVELOPMENT IN LATIN
    AMERICA, Inter-American Development Bank, July
    1966.

Commodities

X-REF: COLOMBIA: Bird, CUBA: Brunner, MALAYSIA:
Thoburn, TRADE: Maizels, FOREIGN AID: Frank.

Adams, F. G. and Klein, S., STABILIZING WORLD COM-
    MODITY MARKETS: Analysis, Practice, and
    Policy, Lexington, Massachusetts, Lexington
    Books. This book develops a model of world
    commodity markets. It also considers the
    theoretical, economic, political, and institu-
    tional aspects of commodity policy and analyzes
    integrated commodity stabilization programs.(BPA)

Behrman, Jere R., INTERNATIONAL COMMODITY AGREEMENTS:
    An Evaluation of the UNCTAD Integrated Commodity
    Programme, Monograph No. 9 NIEO Series, Washing-
    ton, D.C., Overseas Development Council, 1977.
    This study presents an empirical analysis of the
    likely costs and benefits of the UNCTAD-proposed
    common fund for the financing of buffer stocks.
    (BPA)

Bidwell, Percy W., RAW MATERIALS: A Study of Ameri-
    can Policy, New York, Harper and Brothers, 1958.

Bosson, Rex, and Varon, Bension, "The Mining Industry
    and the Developing Countries," The World Bank,
    1977.

Brook, Ezriel M. & Grilli, Enzo R., "Commodity Price
    Stabilization and the Developing World,"
    Finance and Development, Vol. 14, No. 1,
    March 1977.

Brown, C. P., PRIMARY COMMODITY CONTROL, New York,
    Oxford University Press, 1975. Ties together
    literature on subject, viewing it from per-
    spective of developing nations. (BPA)

Comptroller-General of the U.S., "Government Documents: Foreign Aid Provided Through the Operations of the U.S. Sugar Act and the International Coffee Agreement," Inter-American Economic Affairs, Vol. 23, No. 3, Winter 1969.

Coquin, Michel, "Cocoa: A New International Agreement," Developing Country Topics in The Courier, No. 35, January-February 1976, pp. 51-52.

Fisher, Bart S., THE INTERNATIONAL COFFEE AGREEMENT: A Study in Coffee Diplomacy, New York, Praeger, 1972. A clearly argued and well-informed analysis of that rara avis, a durable commodity agreement. (FA)

Fox, William, TIN: The Working of a Commodity Agreement, London, Mining Journal Books, 1974. This valuable book--probably the only account of a commodity agreement by one who played a key part in administering it for many years--has great current interest. While discreet, Mr. Fox is quite frank about mistakes and conflicts of views and restrained in his assessment of the buffer stocks, export controls and other devices of the tin agreements. (FA)

Frank, Isaiah, "Toward a New Framework for International Commodity Policy," Finance and Development, Vol. 13, No. 2, June 1976.

Girvan, Norman, CORPORATE IMPERIALISM: Conflict and Expropriation, White Plains, New York, Sharpe, 1977. Nationalization of raw materials is not enough if it leaves producing countries tied into the international economy, says this Jamaican economist after reviewing the history of bauxite in the Caribbean and copper in Chile. Along with "dependent industrialization" it leads to the "cooptation of economic nationalism." Only a socialist reorientation of life in developing countries will free them from corporate imperialism, he concludes. (FA)

Hanson, Simon G., "The Success of the International Coffee Agreement: How the State Department Deceived the Congress," Inter-American Economic Affairs, Vol. 21, No. 2, Autumn 1967.

Hveem, Helge, THE POLITICAL ECONOMY OF THIRD WORLD PRODUCER ASSOCIATIONS, Oslo, Universitetsforlaget, 1978, (New York, Columbia University Press, distributer). A Norwegian scholar marshals a great deal of material about the production, trade, processing and corporate control of raw materials with the aim of helping developing countries organize better cartels, or at least use their bargaining power more effectively. (FA)

Law, Alton D., "Coffee: Structure, Control and Development," Inter-American Economic Affairs, Vol. 27, No. 1, Summer 1973.

Law, Alton D., "Stabilization of Prices of Primary Products: A Review Article," Inter-American Economic Affairs, Vol. 24, No. 3, Winter 1970.

Mason, Edward S., CONTROLLING WORLD TRADE: Cartels and Commodity Agreements, New York and London, McGraw-Hill Book Company, Inc., 1946.

McNicol, David L., COMMODITY AGREEMENTS AND PRICE STABILIZATION, Lexington, Massachusetts, Lexington Books, 1978. Nice exposition of the strengths and weaknesses of different kinds of commodity arrangements. The worst results come from expecting them to do too many things at once. (FA)

Payer, Cheryl, ed., COMMODITY TRADE OF THE THIRD WORLD, New York, Halsted Press, 1976. "...High commodity prices are no answer in themselves to the problems of poverty in the Third World and may even contribute to its exacerbation." A collapse of the world market would also not help. The editor's conclusions are buttressed by seven case studies showing how hard it is to generalize about commodities. A good book. (FA)

Pearson, Scott R. and Cownie, John, COMMODITY EXPORTS AND AFRICAN ECONOMIC DEVELOPMENT, Lexington, Massachusetts, Lexington Books, 1974. This rather technical study is more useful for the specific information it offers on eight African economies than for its highly qualified generalizations about such developmental desiderata as generation of employment, construction of infrastructure, diversification of exports. (FA)

29

Rangarajan, L. N., COMMODITY CONFLICT, London,
    Croom Helm/Ithaca, New York, Cornell University
    Press, 1978. In the most comprehensive book on
    commodities to be published in recent years, an
    Indian diplomat concentrates his generally well-
    balanced analysis on the many conflicting inter-
    ests involved in their production, processing
    and trade. He is very critical of the programs
    advanced by UNCTAD and the Group of 77 and
    puts forward a proposal for a framework agree-
    ment within which a variety of commodity agree-
    ments can be negotiated to further a number of
    the purposes of producing and consuming
    countries. (FA)

Reutlinger, Shlomo, A SIMULATION MODEL FOR EVALUATING
    WORLDWIDE BUFFER STOCKS OF WHEAT, World Bank
    Reprint Series, Number 34, 1976.

Ridker, Ronald G., CHANGING RESOURCE PROBLEMS OF THE
    FOURTH WORLD, Baltimore, Maryland, Johns
    Hopkins University Press, 1976. The contributors
    assess the consequences of increases in the
    price of food and fertilizers, metals and
    minerals, and oil for Fourth World countries--
    "The poorest of the poor." (BPA)

Singh, Shamsher, "The International Dialogue on
    Commodities," World Bank Reprint Series,
    Number 39, reprinted from Resources Policy,
    June, 1976.

Singh, de Vries, Hulley, and Young, COFFEE, TEA, AND
    COCOA: Market Prospects and Development
    Lending, World Bank, 1977.

Varon, Bension and Takeuchi, Kenji, "Developing
    Countries and Non-Fuel Minerals," Foreign
    Affairs, Vol. 52, No. 3, April 1974.

Debt

Aronson, Jonathan David, ed., DEBT AND THE LESS
    DEVELOPED COUNTRIES, Boulder, Colorado, West-
    view Press, 1979. Authors from economics, po-
    litical science, sociology, and government dis-
    cuss debt in the international system and its
    relevance to development, exploring both posi-
    tive and negative impacts of debt on developing

countries. In the final section, they look on interactions between debtors and creditors when loans begin to sour. (BPA)

Avramovic, Dragoslav, ECONOMIC GROWTH AND EXTERNAL DEBT, Baltimore, Maryland, Johns Hopkins Press, (1964) 1970.

Goodman, Stephen H., ed., FINANCING AND RISK IN DEVELOPING COUNTRIES, New York, Praeger, 1978. Discussing lending by U.S. banks in Third World Countries, this volume examines the current debt situation in developing countries, and prospects for the future international exposure and risk management are discussed and techniques for assessing country credit risk are outlined. (BPA)

Smith, Gordon W., THE EXTERNAL PUBLIC DEBT PROSPECTS OF THE NON-OIL-EXPORTING DEVELOPING COUNTRIES, No. 10, NIEO Series, Washington, D.C., Overseas Development Council, 1977. Applies statistical models to data for the major debtor nations in order to determine which are dangerously close to default and finds only a limited number of countries to be in a "danger zone." (BPA)

World Bank, WORLD DEBT TABLES (issued periodically), Washington, D.C.

Dependency Theory, Imperialism, and Marxism

X-REF: AFRICA: Harris, BRAZIL: Ianni, Roett, CARIBBEAN: Beckford, Palmer, CHINA: de Vylder, Moran, COSTA RICA: De Witt, CUBA: Benjamin, Ritter, TRADE: Green, VENEZUELA: Liss, Michelena, ZAMBIA: Anglin, Shaw.

Amin, Samil, IMPERIALISM AND UNEQUAL DEVELOPMENT, New York, Monthly Review Press, 1977.

Baran, Paul A., THE POLITICAL ECONOMY OF GROWTH, New York and London, Modern Reader Paperbacks, 1957.

Beckford, George L., PERSISTENT POVERTY: Underdevelopment in Plantation Economies of the Third World, New York, and London, Oxford University Press, 1972.

31

Best, Michael H., "Uneven Development and Dependent
    Market Economies," American Economic Review,
    Vol. 66, No. 2, May 1976, pp. 136-141.

Caporaso, James A., ed., "Dependence and Dependency
    in the Global System," International Organiza-
    tion, Winter 1978. An entire issue of this re-
    view is devoted to articles on dependency, in-
    cluding a general review of the concept; sugges-
    tions leading toward precision in dependency;
    dependency and multinational corporations;
    asymmetrical bargaining; and dependency in the
    Andean Group, Black Africa, and Mexico. (Ed)

Cardoso, Fernando Henrique, "The Consumption of De-
    pendency Theory in the United States," Latin
    American Research Review, Vol. XII, No. 3, 1977.

Cecena, Jose Luis, EL CAPITALISMO MONOPOLISTA Y LA
    ECONOMIA MEXICANA, Cuadernos Americanos,
    Mexico, 1963.

Chilcote, Ronald H. "A Question of Dependency,"
    Latin American Research Review, Vol. XIII, No. 2,
    1978.

Chilcote, Ronald H. and Edelstein, Joel C., eds.,
    LATIN AMERICA: The Struggle with Dependency and
    Beyond, Cambridge: Schenkman, 1974. Lengthy
    studies of the historical sources and current
    characteristics of dependency and underdevelop-
    ment in Guatemala, Mexico, Argentina, Brazil,
    Chile, and Cuba, with a left-leaning perspec-
    tive. (FA)

Clarkson, Stephen, THE SOVIET THEORY OF DEVELOPMENT:
    India and the Third World in Marxist-Leninist
    Scholarship, Toronto, University of Toronto
    Press, 1978. Based on research in Paris, New
    York, the Soviet Union and India, this book
    provides an insight into how Soviet thinkers
    understand crucial problems in development such
    as planning in mixed economies, foreign aid
    coming from socialist and capitalist donors,
    agrarian reform, and the class struggle...neither
    hostile nor uncritical. (BPA)

Dos Santos, Theotonio, "The Structure of Dependence,"
    The American Economic Review, Vol. LX, No. 2,
    May 1970.

Erb, Guy F. and Kallab, Valeriana, eds., BEYOND
DEPENDENCY: The Developing World Speaks Out.
Praeger Special Studies in International
Economics and Development, New York, Praeger in
cooperation with the Overseas Development
Council, 1975. The papers, organized in four
sections, discuss the major internal and
external changes needed to give a more effective
and equitable interdependence, review the main
issues involved, analyze the current position of
developing countries in historical perspective,
and establish some elements of a possible bargain between rich and poor countries. (JEL)

Frank, Andre Gunder, CAPITALISM AND UNDERDEVELOPMENT
IN LATIN AMERICA, New York and London, Modern
Reader Paperbacks, 1967. Historical studies of
Chile and Brazil.

Frank, Andre Gunder, LATIN AMERICA: UNDERDEVELOPMENT
OR REVOLUTION: Essays on the Development of
Underdevelopment and the Immediate Enemy, New
York, Monthly Review Press, 1969. Many of
these twenty-five essays have been published
previously. The theme is "underdevelopment in
Latin America is the result of the colonial
structure of world capitalist development....As
a result, the development of underdevelopment
[sic] will continue in Latin America until its
people free themselves from this structure the
only way possible, by violent revolutionary
victory over their own bourgeoisie and over
imperialism." No index. (JEL)

Frank, Andre Gunder, ON CAPITALIST UNDERDEVELOPMENT,
Bombay; New York; London and Hong Kong, Oxford
University Press, 1975. Underdevelopment is
seen as a result of the historical process of
capitalist development, an outgrowth of colonization processes undertaken by the developed
nations. The bulk of the essay is a historical
analysis of the genesis of capitalism, its relation to feudalism, and its colonial aspects.
(JEL)

Hodges, Donald C., THE LEGACY OF CHE GUEVARA: A
Documentary Study, New York, Thames and Hudson,
1977. Excerpts of speeches, articles, and similar sources are assembled to illustrate the
history of the Guevarist movement, its princi-

33

ples and conflicts, and its impact on and relationship with other radical approaches. (FA)

Jenkins, Rhys O., DEPENDENT INDUSTRIALIZATION IN
LATIN AMERICA: The Automotive Industry in
Argentina, Chile, and Mexico, New York, Praeger,
1976. Analyzes the often negative impact of
multinational corporate investment on the development of the automotive industries of three
Latin American nations from the late 1950s to
the present. Finds that subsidiaries of MNCs
have achieved dominance in this industry by
taking advantage of their parent companies'
superior financial, managerial, and technical
resources, and to the disadvantage of the
indigenous industries. (BPA)

Kahl, Joseph A., MODERNIZATION, EXPLOITATION AND
DEPENDENCY IN LATIN AMERICA, New Brunswick, New
Jersey, Transaction Books, 1976.

Lall, S., "Is 'Dependence' a Useful Concept in
Analysing Underdevelopment?," World Development,
Vol. 3, Nos. 11 and 12, November/December 1975.

Marx, Karl, CAPITAL AND THE COMMUNIST MANIFESTO, New
York, The Modern Library, 1932.

Rhodes, Robert I., ed., IMPERIALISM AND UNDERDE-
VELOPMENT: A READER, New York, Monthly Review
Press, 1970. A collection of 18 essays organized into three sections. The first essays
examine imperialism and underdevelopment, both
at a general level and by offering case-studies
of various aspects of development, such as the
contributions of agriculture and mining to
development. Part III is concerned with "politics, class conflict, and underdevelopment."
Bibliography; no index. (JEL)

Sloan, John W., "Dependency Theory and Latin American
Development: Another Key Fails to Open the
Door," Inter-American Economic Affairs, Vol. 31,
No. 3, Winter 1977.

Stein, Stanley J. and Stein, Barbara H., THE COLONIAL
HERITAGE OF LATIN AMERICA, ESSAYS ON ECONOMIC
DEPENDENCE IN PERSPECTIVE, New York, Oxford
University Press, 1970.

Tancer, Shoshana B., ECONOMIC NATIONALISM IN LATIN
    AMERICA: The Quest for Economic Independence,
    New York, Praeger, 1976.

Uri, Pierre, DEVELOPMENT WITHOUT DEPENDENCE, Praeger
    Special Studies in International Economics and
    Development, New York and London, Praeger for
    the Atlantic Institute for International
    Affairs, 1976. Discusses control of population
    growth, the role and necessary scale of official
    foreign aid, stabilization of the raw materials
    market so as to assist consumers and producers
    alike, and the types of industries the develop-
    ing countries should strive to build as a part
    of a rational world division of labor.
    Examines the control and regulation of multi-
    national corporations and, focusing on Latin
    America, the extent to which regional coopera-
    tion can be developed. Recommends that develop-
    ment planning be based on future population
    growth and distribution. (BPA)

Desertification

Glantz, Michael H., ed., DESERTIFICATION, Boulder,
    Colorado, Westview Press, 1977. This collection
    of articles focuses on a primary form of such
    destruction: desertification--the creation of
    desert-like conditions in arid or semiarid
    regions either by changes in climate patterns
    or by human mismanagement. (BPA)

Glantz, Michael H., THE POLITICS OF NATURAL DISASTER:
    The Case of the Sahel Drought, New York, Praeger,
    1976. To sum up the collected wisdom of the
    political scientists, public health experts,
    climatologists and agronomists assembled here:
    both coordination--between donors and recipi-
    ents--and balance--in ecological planning--are
    essential to save the Sahel and its people. (FA)

Economic Integration

X-REF: AFRICA: Cosgrove, Mutharika, Robana, Smock,
AGRICULTURAL DEVELOPMENT: Yudelman, CARIBBEAN:
Crassweller, Demas, CENTRAL AMERICA: Cline, McClel-
land, Cohen, Shaw, Willmore, Wunia, EAST AFRICA:

35

Hazlewock, IMPORT SUBSTITUTION: Ayza, INDUSTRIAL
DEVELOPMENT: Carnoy, LATIN AMERICA: Council,
Ffrench, Grunwald, REGIONAL DEVELOPMENT: Lindberg,
TRADE: Galtung, Green.

Balassa, Bela, ECONOMIC DEVELOPMENT AND INTEGRATION,
    Washington, D.C., CED Publications, 1965.
    Analyzes the role of exports in economic growth
    and the adaptation of the customs union theory
    to the requirements of the developing countries;
    reviews the problems of economic policy that
    emerge in the less developed countries from the
    attempts to establish customs unions or similar
    trade arrangements; deals with the role that
    big scale economies can play in the process of
    economic integration. (BPA)

Balassa, Bela, THE THEORY OF ECONOMIC INTEGRATION,
    Homewood, Illinois, Richard D. Irwin, Inc.,
    1961.

Council of the Americas, THE ANDEAN PACT: Defini-
    tion, Design and Analysis, New York, Council of
    the Americas, November 1973.

Ghat, Dharam P., CURRENT PROBLEMS OF ECONOMIC INTE-
    GRATION: State Trading and Regional Economic
    Integration Among Developing Countries, New
    York, United Nations, 1973.

Hansen, Roger D., CENTRAL AMERICA: Regional Inte-
    gration and Economic Development, Washington,
    D.C., National Planning Association, 1967.

International Economic Studies Institute, RAW
    MATERIALS AND FOREIGN POLICY, Washington, D.C.,
    International Economic Studies Institute,
    1976. Eschewing extremes in both diagnosis and
    prescription, the producers of this very sub-
    stantial volume provide expert discussions of
    past and present difficulties, and show in some
    detail how serious problems can be kept from
    becoming alarming if they are not neglected
    now. National and international action, the
    specific problems of a number of materials, and
    the policy organization of the U.S. government
    are all dealt with. (FA)

Kahnert, F.; Richards, P.; Stoutjesdijk, E.; and Thomopoulos, P., ECONOMIC INTEGRATION AMONG DEVELOPING COUNTRIES, Paris, Development Centre of the Organization for Economic Co-Operation and Development, 1969.

Krause, Walter and Mathis, F. John, LATIN AMERICA AND ECONOMIC INTEGRATION: Regional Planning for Development, Iowa City, Iowa, University of Iowa Press, 1970.

LOMÉ CONVENTION, The Courier, No. 37, May-June 1976. Contains copies of the agreement and other official documents and presentations when the Lomé Convention was set up. (Ed)

Machlup, Fritz, ed., ECONOMIC INTEGRATION: Worldwide, Regional, Sectoral Proceedings of the Fourth Congress of the International Economic Association, held at Budapest, Hungary, New York, Halsted Press, 1977. A collection of papers (many from socialist countries) that examines types of economic integration, worldwide vs. regional integration, measuring integration's degree or process, industrial policy, migration, and integration of labor markets, international capital movements and integration of capital markets, monetary and fiscal integration, socio-political and institutional aspects of integration, integration in developing areas, and integration through market forces and planning. (BPA)

Machlup, Fritz, A HISTORY OF THOUGHT ON ECONOMIC INTEGRATION, New York, Columbia University Press, 1977. The relatively recent use of "integration" as a word of power in international relations permits one of the deans of American economics to perform extraordinary acrobatics in this entertaining and valuable volume. Detective work on first use is followed by a brilliantly compact and lucid exposition of the essentials of international economics. Then come an annotated bibliography and biographical dictionary which are a bit idiosyncratic in the choice of entries--but who has a better right? One wishes more attention could have been given to how the word passed into policy in the 1940s as something between "cooperation" and "unification." (FA)

Milenky, Edward S., "From Integration to Developmental Nationalism: The Andean Group 1965-1971," Inter-American Economic Affairs, Vol. 25, No. 3, Winter 1971, pp. 77-91.

Milenky, Edward S., THE POLITICS OF REGIONAL ORGANIZATION IN LATIN AMERICA, THE LATIN AMERICAN FREE TRADE ASSOCIATION, New York, Praeger, 1973.

Morawetz, David, THE ANDEAN GROUP: A Case Study in Economic Integration Among Developing Countries, Cambridge, Massachusetts, MIT Press, 1974. A concise study, oriented to readers versed in economics. The author concludes that ANCOM, although no panacea, is potentially beneficial, and that the comparative extent of any such benefits depends on the alternative arrangements one postulates. (FA)

Muritano, Nino, A LATIN AMERICAN ECONOMIC COMMUNITY, Notre Dame, Indiana, University of Notre Dame Press, 1970. An informative and competent account covering the history, status and contributions of the various hemispheric integration movements, regional and subregional. Useful tables and basic documents are included. (FA)

McClelland, Donald, THE CENTRAL AMERICAN COMMON MARKET, New York, Praeger, 1972. Updates and rounds out the numerous writings already devoted to economic integration in Central America. (FA)

Rivkin, Arnold, AFRICA AND THE EUROPEAN COMMON MARKET: A Perspective, Denver, Colorado, University of Denver, 1964.

Switzer, Kenneth A., "The Andean Group: A Reappraisal," Inter-American Economic Affairs, Vol. 26, No. 4, Spring 1973.

Urquidi, Victor L., FREE TRADE AND ECONOMIC INTEGRATION IN LATIN AMERICA, TOWARD A COMMON MARKET, Berkeley and Los Angeles, University of California Press, 1962.

Wionczek, Miguel S., ed., LATIN AMERICAN ECONOMIC INTEGRATION, EXPERIENCES AND PROSPECTS, New York, Praeger, 1966.

Yudelman, Montague and Howard, Frederic, AGRICUL-
TURAL DEVELOPMENT AND ECONOMIC INTEGRATION IN
LATIN AMERICA, Inter-American Development Bank,
April 1969.

Education

X-REF: CHILE: Silvert, CHINA: Ayres, Seybolt,
COLOMBIA: Jallade, EMPLOYMENT: Ilo, Sorkin, INCOME
DISTRIBUTION PRINCIPLES: Chiswick, ISRAEL: Glober-
son, NEW INTERNATIONAL ECONOMIC ORDER: Unesco,
PUERTO RICO: Maldonado.

Anderson, Arnold C., ed., EDUCATION AND ECONOMIC
DEVELOPMENT, Chicago, Aldine Publishing Co.,
1971.

Beeby, C. E., THE QUALITY OF EDUCATION IN DEVELOPING
COUNTRIES, Cambridge, Massachusetts, Harvard
University Press, 1966.

Becker, G., HUMAN CAPITAL, New York, Columbia, 1975.

Bhagwati, J., "Education, Class Structure and Income
Equality," World Development, Vol. 1, No. 5,
May 1973.

Blaug, Mark, "Approaches to Educational Planning,"
Economic Journal, June 1967.

Blaug, Mark, EDUCATION AND THE EMPLOYMENT PROBLEM IN
DEVELOPING COUNTRIES, Geneva, International
Labour Office, 1974.

Coombs, P. H., with Ahmed, M., ATTACKING RURAL
POVERTY: How Nonformal Education Can Help,
prepared for the World Bank by the International
Council on Educational Development, Baltimore
and London, the Johns Hopkins University Press,
1974.

Curle, Adam, EDUCATIONAL STRATEGY FOR DEVELOPING
SOCIETIES: A Study of Educational and Social
Factors in Relation to Economic Growth, second
edition, New York, Barnes and Noble/Harper and
Row, 1970.

Damachi, Ukandi, and Diejomoah, Victor P., eds.,
HUMAN RESOURCES AND AFRICAN DEVELOPMENT. The
essays are divided into four main topics:
employment generation, formal education, nonformal education, and the brain drain. (BPA)

EDUCATIONAL ENROLLMENT, UNESCO, World Survey of
Education, V, Educational Policy, Legislation,
and Administration, Paris, 1971.

Edwards, E. O. and Todaro, M. P., "Educational
Demand and Supply in the Context of Growing
Unemployment in Less Developed Countries,"
World Development, Vol. 1, No. 3-4, March-April
1973.

Fields, G., "Higher Education and Income Distribution in a Less Developed Country," (Kenya),
Oxford Economic Papers, Vol. 27, No. 2, July
1975.

Gallman, Robert E., "Human Capital in the First 80
Years of the Republic: How Much Did America
Owe the Rest of the World?" American Economic
Review, Vol. 67, No. 1, February 1977.

Hansen, W. Lee, ed., EDUCATION, INCOME AND HUMAN
CAPITAL, New York, Columbia University Press,
1972.

Harbison, Frederick H. and Myers, C. A., EDUCATION,
MANPOWER AND ECONOMIC GROWTH, New York,
McGraw-Hill, 1964.

Harbison, Frederick H., HUMAN RESOURCES AS THE
WEALTH OF NATIONS, New York, London, and
Toronto, Oxford University Press, 1973.

Huq, Muhammed S., EDUCATION, MANPOWER, AND DEVELOP-
MENT IN SOUTH AND SOUTHEAST ASIA, New York,
Praeger, 1975. Analyzes the major challenges
to education in the Third World and reviews
major studies on the development of human
capital through education in the U.S., USSR,
and Japan. Offers a critique of the educational
structure in India, Pakistan, Bangladesh,
Indonesia, Malaysia, and the Philippines. (BPA)

International Council for Educational Development, EDUCATION IN THE NATION'S SERVICE: Experiments in Higher Education for Development, Final Report, New York, International Council for Educational Development, 1975.

Piper, Don C. and Cole, Taylor, eds., POST-PRIMARY EDUCATION AND POLITICAL AND ECONOMIC DEVELOPMENT, Durham, North Carolina, Duke University Press, 1964.

Psacharopoulos, George, "Schooling, Experience and Earnings: The Case of an LDC," Journal of Development Economics, Vol. 4, No. 1, March 1977, pp. 39-48.

Ramati, Yohanan, ed., ECONOMIC GROWTH IN DEVELOPING COUNTRIES--MATERIAL AND HUMAN RESOURCES: Proceedings of the Seventh Rehovot Conference, Praeger Special Studies in International Economics and Development, New York, Praeger in cooperation with the Continuation Committee of the Rehovot Conference, 1975. Collection of 49 papers presented in September 1973. The papers are grouped into five sections following the structure of the conference. Part I includes papers setting the framework to analyze natural and human resources as factors in development and problems of planning and the quality of life. Part II includes papers on resources, technology, and income distribution. Part III deals with external constraints on development. Part IV examines planning and implementation. Part V contains the very brief closing addresses by Simon Kuznets and Abba Eban. No index. (JEL)

Ritzen, J. J. M., EDUCATION, ECONOMIC GROWTH AND INCOME DISTRIBUTION, Amsterdam and New York, North-Holland, 1977.

Schultz, T. W., "Investing in Poor People: An Economist's View," American Economic Review, Vol. LV, No. 2, May 1965.

Selowsky, Marcelo, A NOTE ON PRESCHOOL-AGE INVESTMENT IN HUMAN CAPITAL IN DEVELOPING COUNTRIES, World Bank Reprint Series, Number 32, 1976.

Simmons, John, RETENTION OF COGNITIVE SKILLS ACQUIRED
    IN PRIMARY SCHOOL, World Bank Series, No. 35
    reprinted from Comparative Education Review,
    Vol. 20, February 1976.

World Bank, EDUCATION, Sector Working Paper,
    December 1974.

Zymelman, Manuel, TEACHING INDUSTRIAL SKILLS IN
    DEVELOPING COUNTRIES, an overview of the
    Economic Evaluation of Vocational Training
    Programs, World Bank, 1976.

Employment and Labor

X-REF: AFRICA: Ammann, Brownwood, Frank, Kraus,
Liedholm, Sandbrook, AGRARIAN REFORM: Sinha,
Sternberg, AGRICULTURAL DEVELOPMENT: Clayton, Ger-
ken, Shaw, BOLIVIA: Lora, BRAZIL: Ilo, CHINA:
Howe, Karcher, COLOMBIA: Berry, Ilo, CUBA: Mesa,
Ritter, EDUCATION: Blaug, Edwards, EGYPT: Abed,
Hansen, Mabro, ETHIOPIA: Blaug, Ilo, GHANA: Steel,
HUNGER, NUTRITION, HEALTH: Poleman, IMPORT SUBSTI-
TUTION: Bruton, INCOME DISTRIBUTION PRINCIPLES:
Webb, INDIA: Ilo, IRAN: Ilo, ISRAEL: Globerson,
IVORY COAST: Ilo, JAPAN: Okochi, Taira, Yakabe,
KENYA: Ilo, MEXICO: Ruiz, MULTINATIONAL CORPORA-
TIONS: Hellinger, Ilo, NIGERIA: Calloway, Frank,
Smock, PHILIPPINES: Rogers, POPULATION: Sweezy,
PUERTO RICO: Holbik, Reynolds, Ribera, RURAL DEVEL-
OPMENT: Saxena, SMALL BUSINESS: Ho, World, SRI
LANKA: Ilo, SUDAN: Ilo, TANZANIA: Friedland, TECH-
NOLOGY: Baer, Bottomley, Timmer, TRADE: Lydall,
URBAN DEVELOPMENT: Ilo, VENEZUELA: Hassan,
ZIMBABWE: Ilo.

Acharya, Shankar N., FISCAL/FINANCIAL INTERVENTION,
    FACTOR PRICES AND FACTOR PROPORTIONS: A Review
    of Issues, International Bank for Reconstruc-
    tion and Development, Staff Working Paper No.
    183, August 1974.

Alba, Victor, POLITICS AND THE LABOR MOVEMENT IN
    LATIN AMERICA, Stanford, California, Stanford
    Press, 1968.

Bairoch, Paul, URBAN UNEMPLOYMENT IN DEVELOPING COUNTRIES: The Nature of the Problem and Proposals for Its Solution, International Labor Office, Geneva, 1976. The pace of urbanisation in the developing countries is now so rapid that the size of the total urban population considerably exceeds that of the active population engaged in manufacturing. This is quite unlike the situation that existed in the countries of continental Europe during the early stages of their own development: in fact, in the developing countries urbanisation is a forerunner of industrialisation and growth rather than their consequence. The result is the extremely high unemployment rates that characterised the towns of the Third World during the 1960s. What are the causes underlying this state of affairs, and what measures may be put forward as a remedy? These are the two major questions that this study attempts to answer. (BPA)

Barnett, Vincent M., IMPLEMENTATION OF POLICIES FOR FULLER EMPLOYMENT IN LESS DEVELOPED COUNTRIES, Williams College Center for Development Economics, Research Memorandum #55, 1973.

Bass, James, UNEMPLOYMENT IN LATIN AMERICA, Report to the Inter-American Development Bank, Washington, D.C., 1978.

Berry, Albert, "Open Unemployment as a Social Problem in Urban Colombia: Myth and Reality," Economic Development and Cultural Change, Vol. 23, No. 2, 1975, pp. 276-291.

Betancourt, Roger, and Clague, Christopher, "Multiple Shifts and the Employment Problem in Developing Countries," International Labour Review, Vol. 114, No. 2, 1976.

Bhagwat, A., "Main Features of the Employment Problem in Developing Countries," Indian Economic Journal, Vol. 19, No. 4-5, April-June 1972.

Brownwood, David O., TRADE UNIONS IN AFRICA, K.I.A. Occasional Papers, No. 2, Kenya Institute of Administration, Lower Kabete, Kenya, November 1969.

43

Bruton, Henry J., "Economic Development and Labor
    Use: A Review," World Development, 1973; also
    published in Edwards, Edgar O., EMPLOYMENT IN
    DEVELOPING NATIONS, Columbia University Press,
    1974, pp. 49-82.

Bruton, Henry J., "Unemployment Problems and Policies
    in Less Developed Countries," The American
    Economic Review, Vol. 68, No. 2, May 1978.

Cairncross, Alec and Puri, Mohinder, eds., EMPLOY-
    MENT, INCOME DISTRIBUTION AND DEVELOPMENT
    STRATEGY: Problems of the Developing Countries.
    Essays in Honour of H. W. Singer, New York,
    Holmes & Meier, 1976. A collection of 17 essays,
    only one previously published, examining the
    economic and social problems confronting the
    developing countries. (JEL)

Chakraborty, A. K., "The Causes of Educated Unemploy-
    ment in India," Economic Affairs, Vol. 20, No.
    7, July 1975.

Cohn, Edwin J., and Eriksson, John R., EMPLOYMENT AND
    INCOME DISTRIBUTION OBJECTIVES FOR A.I.D. PRO-
    GRAMS AND POLICIES, Policy Background Paper,
    Washington, D.C., Agency for International
    Development, October 1972.

Costa, E., "Maximising Employment in Labour-intensive
    Development Programmes," International Labour
    Review, Vol. 108, No. 5, November 1973.

Davies, David G., AN ESSAY ON EMPLOYMENT CONCEPTS:
    The Definition of Labor Force in Terms of
    Socialization, New York, Southeast Asia Advis-
    ory Group, Asia Society, Seadag Papers on Prob-
    lems of Development in Southeast Asia, #73-8,
    1973.

Davis, Stanley M., and Goodman, Louis Wolf, WORKERS
    AND MANAGERS IN LATIN AMERICA, Lexington,
    Massachusetts and London, D.C. Heath and
    Company, 1972.

Denti, E., "Africa's Labour Force, 1960-80," Inter-
    national Labour Review, Vol. 104, No. 3,
    September 1971.

Durand, John D., THE LABOR FORCE IN ECONOMIC
DEVELOPMENT, Princeton, New Jersey, Princeton
University Press, 1975.

Edwards, Edgar O., EMPLOYMENT IN DEVELOPING NATIONS:
Report on a Ford Foundation Study, New York and
London, Columbia University Press, 1974.
Collection of 20 previously unpublished papers
selected from among the papers prepared for
three international seminars in 1973 on employment problems in developing nations. The papers
approach the employment problem from the points
of view of policy, technology, rural development,
international issues, and education. Four
papers dealing with country experiences are
included. (JEL)

Edwards, Edgar O., "Work Effort, Investible Surplus
and the Inferiority of Competition," Southern
Economic Journal, Vol. 38, No. 1-2, 1971,
pp. 193-205.

Emmerij, L., "Research Priorities of the World Employment Programme," International Labour Review,
Vol. 105, No. 5, May 1972.

Eriksson, John Rudolph, WAGE CHANGE AND EMPLOYMENT
GROWTH IN LATIN AMERICAN INDUSTRY, Williams
College Center for Development Economics,
Research Memorandum #36, 1970.

Fei, J. C. H. and Ranis, G., "A Model of Growth and
Employment in the Open Dualistic Economy: The
Cases of Korea and Taiwan," Journal of Develop-
ment Studies, Vol. 11, No. 2, January 1975.

Fine, S. M., "The Employment Effects of Import Duties
and Export Subsidies in the Developing Countries," ILO, Fiscal Measures for Employment
Promotion in Developing Countries, pp. 233-267.

Frank, Charles R. Jr., URBAN UNEMPLOYMENT AND ECO-
NOMIC GROWTH IN AFRICA, Center Paper #120,
New Haven, Connecticut, Yale University,
Economic Growth Center, 1968.

Galenson, Walter, ed., ESSAYS ON EMPLOYMENT, Geneva,
International Labour Office, 1971.

Galenson, Walter, ed., LABOR IN DEVELOPING ECONOMIES, Los Angeles and Berkeley, University of California Press, 1962.

Gerken, Egbert, LAND PRODUCTIVITY AND THE EMPLOY-MENT PROBLEM OF RURAL AREAS, Discussion Paper No. 176, New Haven, Connecticut, Yale University, Economic Growth Center, March 1973.

Gupta, J. R., "The Growth of Unemployment with Particular Reference to Unemployment in India (1951-66)," Economic Affairs, Vol. 16, No. 12, December 1971.

Gupta, R. D., WAGE FLEXIBILITY AND FULL EMPLOYMENT, Delhi, India, Vikas Publications, 1971.

Gutkind, Peter C. W.; Carstens, Peter; and Lux, Andre, eds., MANPOWER AND UNEMPLOYMENT RESEARCH IN AFRICA: A Newsletter, Montreal, Quebec, Canada, McGill University, various issues.

Gutkind, Peter C. W., UNEMPLOYMENT IN AFRICA, Bibliography Series, Montreal, Quebec, Canada, Centre for Developing-Area Studies, McGill University, December 1972.

Hawkins, Carroll, TWO DEMOCRATIC LABOR LEADERS IN CONFLICT, Lexington, Massachusetts, Lexington Books, D. C. Heath and Company, 1973.

Herve, Michel E. A., "Employment and Industrializa-tion in Developing Countries," Quarterly Journal of Economics, Vol. LXXX, No. 1, pp. 88-107.

Holland, Joe, THE ILO WORLD EMPLOYMENT CONFERENCE, Draft, September 7, 1976; the author is a Staff Associate at the Center of Concern, Washington, D.C. (BPA)

Hunter, Guy, EMPLOYMENT POLICY IN TROPICAL AFRICA, Madison, University of Wisconsin, Land Tenure Center, LTC Reprint No. 90, 1972.

International Business Machines (United Kingdom) and
Overseas Development Institute, INDUSTRY EMPLOY-
MENT AND THE DEVELOPING WORLD: The Contribution
of Private Foreign Business to the Employment
Objectives of Developing Countries, report of a
seminar jointly sponsored by IBM and ODI in
Oxford, November 20-22, 1974, London Overseas
Development Institute, 1975.

ILO, EDUCATION AND THE EMPLOYMENT PROBLEM IN
DEVELOPING COUNTRIES, Geneva, 1973. Analyzes
the problems of defining employment and unemployment, the costs and economic value of
education, and various traditional and radical
solutions to the problems of education and
employment. (BPA)

ILO, EMPLOYMENT, GROWTH AND BASIC NEEDS: A One-
World Problem: Report of the Director-General
of the International Labour Office, Tripartite
World Conference on Employment, Income Distribution and Social Progress and the International
Division of Labour, Geneva, 1976. Divided into
three parts. Part one looks at the global
aspects of employment, income distribution and
poverty and outlines the approach of a "basic
needs" strategy for developing countries to
overcome these problems. Part two reviews
strategies that have been taken by developing
countries, European Socialist countries, and
industrialized market economy countries. Part
three looks at international efforts on issues
such as adjustment assistance, international
migration, international technology transfer,
and multinational enterprises, all issues that
affect the international division of labor.
(JEL)

ILO, EMPLOYMENT IN AFRICA: Some Critical Issues,
Geneva, Switzerland, International Labor Office,
1973.

ILO, EMPLOYMENT POLICY IN THE SECOND DEVELOPMENT
DECADE: A United Nations Family Approach,
Washington, D.C., I.L.O., 1973.

ILO, LABOR FORCE PARTICIPATION IN LOW-INCOME COUN-
TRIES, Geneva, 1978. Case studies from Latin
America, the Caribbean, Africa, southeast Asia,
and Europe. (BPA)

ILO, LABOR FORCE PROJECTIONS, 1965-1985; separate
volumes for Asia, Africa, Latin America, Europe,
Northern America, Oceania and USSR, Geneva.

ILO, MINIMUM WAGE FIXING AND ECONOMIC DEVELOPMENT,
Geneva, 1968. This is the first published survey of the problems caused by minimum wage fixing in developing countries and its relationship
to economic development. The book discusses
the effects of wage decisions on costs, prices,
productivity, employment, and economic growth.
(BPA)

ILO, Ninth Conference of American States members of
the International Labor Organization, Caracas,
April, May 1970, remuneration and conditions
of work in relation to economic development,
including plant-level welfare facilities and the
workers' standard of living, fourth item on the
agenda, Geneva, International Labor Office,
1970, Report IV.

ILO, TIME FOR TRANSITION: A Mid-term Review of
Progress in Attaining Employment and Income Dis-
tribution Objectives of the Second United
Nations Development Decade, Washington, D.C.,
I.L.O., 1975.

ILO, TRADE AND EMPLOYMENT, Geneva, ILO, 1977.

ILO, WAGES AND WORKING CONDITIONS IN MULTINATIONAL
ENTERPRISES, Geneva, 1976.

ILO, THE WORLD EMPLOYMENT PROGRAM, Washington, D.C.,
I.L.O., 1971.

ILO, WORLD EMPLOYMENT PROGRAM: Population and
Development, Geneva, 1978. This book is a
progress report on ILO research work in the
areas of labor, employment, and income distribution. It analyzes the relationships among
these three components of the population field,
and in addition contributes to an ongoing ILO
program of research and technical cooperation
in the area of population and development. (Ed)

Jolly, Richard (ed.), THIRD WORLD EMPLOYMENT, PROB-
LEMS AND STRATEGY: Selected Readings, Harmondsworth, England, Penguin Education, 1973.

Karcher, Martin, "Unemployment and Underemployment
    in the People's Republic of China," reprinted
    from China Report, Vol. 11, September-December
    1975.

Kritz, Ernesto and Ramos, Joseph, "The Measurement of
    Urban Underemployment: A Report on Three
    Experimental Surveys," International Labour
    Review, Vol. 113, No. 1, 1976.

Krueger, Anne O., "Alternative Trade Strategies and
    Employment in LDCs," The American Economic
    Review, Vol. 68, No. 2, May 1978.

Kuzmin, S. A., "An Integrated Approach to Develop-
    ment and Employment," International Labour
    Review, Vol. 115, No. 3, 1977.

Kuz'min, S. A., THE DEVELOPING COUNTRIES: Employ-
    ment and Capital Investment, White Plains,
    New York, International Arts and Sciences Press,
    Inc., 1969.

Lewis, W. A., "Summary: The Causes of Unemployment
    in Less Developed Countries and Some Research
    Topics," International Labour Review, Vol. 101,
    No. 5, May 1970.

Lydall, H. F., TRADE AND EMPLOYMENT, Geneva Inter-
    national Labour Office, 1975. The main purpose
    of this study is to estimate the likely effects
    on employment of an increase in exports of 12
    selected products from developing to developed
    countries. This study highlights the very
    great contribution that trade liberalisation
    can make to the expansion of employment in
    developing countries. (BPA)

Mayer, Jean, "Space, Employment and Development:
    Some Thoughts on the Regional Dimension of
    Employment Policy," International Labour
    Review, 1977.

McDiarmid, Orville John, UNSKILLED LABOR FOR DEVELOP-
    MENT: Its Economic Cost, World Bank, 1977.

Mehta, M. M., EMPLOYMENT ASPECTS OF INDUSTRIALIZA-
    TION (with special reference to Asia and the
    Far East), Working Paper #1, Bangkok, Thailand,
    U.N. Asian Institute for Economic Development
    and Planning, 1972.

Morawetz, D., "Employment Implications of Industriali-
    sation in Developing Countries: A Survey,"
    Economic Journal, September 1974. This paper
    surveys the post-1966 literature on the employ-
    ment implications of industrialization in devel-
    oping countries. (JEL)

Mouly, J., and Costa, E., EMPLOYMENT POLICIES IN
    DEVELOPING COUNTRIES: A Comparative Analysis,
    edited by P. Lamartine Yates, for the Inter-
    national Paper Office, London, published on
    behalf of the ILO by George Allen and Unwin,
    1974.

Ndegwa, Philip and Powelson, J. P., eds., EMPLOYMENT
    IN AFRICA: Some Critical Issues," Geneva,
    International Labor Office, 1974. A volume of
    essays originally published in International
    Labour Review, with an introduction by the
    editors. (Ed)

Oberai, A. S., "Migration, Unemployment and the Urban
    Labour Market: A Case Study of the Sudan,"
    International Labour Review, Vol. 115, No. 2,
    1977.

Pack, H., "The Employment-Output Trade-off in LDC's:
    A Microeconomic Approach," Oxford Economic
    Papers, Vol. 26, No. 3, November 1974,
    pp. 388-404. This paper analyzes the possibili-
    ties for substituting labor for equipment in
    the production process. The data are firm
    level observations in a number of less developed
    and semi-developed countries. (JEL)

Poblete, Moises, and Burnett, Ben G., THE RISE OF
    THE LATIN AMERICAN LABOR MOVEMENT, New York,
    Bookman Associates, 1960.

Ramos, R. Joseph, LABOR AND DEVELOPMENT IN LATIN
    AMERICA, New York, Columbia University Press,
    1970. The overall aim of this study is to
    analyze the role of the labor force in Latin
    American development since the Second World War.
    The author inquires into the nature of the vari-
    ous shifts in the composition of the labor
    force and explains employment cannot be fully
    understood without analyzing related qualita-
    tive movements. (BPA)

Ranis, Gustav, "Employment, Equity and Growth:
Lessons from the Philippine Employment Mission,"
The International Labour Review, Vol. 110,
No. 1, July 1974, pp. 17-27.

Ranis, Gustav, INDUSTRIAL SECTOR LABOR ABSORPTION,
Center Paper #193, New Haven, Connecticut,
Yale University Economic Growth Center, 1973.

Ranis, Gustav, "Industrial Sector Labor Absorption,"
World Bank Reprint #6 from Economic Development
and Cultural Change, Vol. 21, No. 3, April 1973.

Reynolds, Lloyd G., ECONOMIC DEVELOPMENT WITH SURPLUS
LABOUR: Some Complications, Center Paper #133,
New Haven, Connecticut, Yale University Economic
Growth Center, 1969.

Sahoo, B., "Approach to the Problem of Unemployment
in India," Economic Affairs, Vol. 15, No. 6-8,
August 1970.

Seers, D., "New Approaches Suggested by the Colombia
Employment Programme," International Labour
Review, Vol. 102, No. 4, October 1970.

Sen, Amartya Kumar, EMPLOYMENT, TECHNOLOGY AND
DEVELOPMENT, a study prepared for the International Labor Office within the framework of
the World Employment Program, Oxford, Clarendon
Press, 1975.

Sinfield, Adrian, THE LONG-TERM UNEMPLOYED, Paris,
Organization for Economic Co-operation and
Development, 1968.

Sorkin, Alan, EDUCATION, UNEMPLOYMENT AND ECONOMIC
GROWTH, Baltimore, Maryland, Johns Hopkins
University, 1974. This study investigates
some of the more fundamental relationships
between schooling, employment, and the level of
economic activity. Discussing the concepts
used to measure labor force status, the author
compares these with labor force participation
rates and jobless rates of various segments of
the population such as women, blacks, and
teenagers. (BPA)

Stewart, Frances, ed., EMPLOYMENT, INCOME DISTRIBU-
TION AND DEVELOPMENT, London, Frank Cass, 1975.

Stewart, F. and Streeten, P., CONFLICTS BETWEEN OUT-
PUT AND EMPLOYMENT OBJECTIVES IN DEVELOPING
COUNTRIES, Oxford, Queen Elizabeth House, July
1971. Discusses conditions for conflict
between output and employment targets, and
reasons for giving independent weight to employment in developing countries. These include
implications for income distribution, the view
that lack of work opportunities is an evil, and
political reasons. Conflict between employment
and output gives rise to complex questions,
involving rates of time preference for both output and employment, once the interaction between
current and future levels of output and employment is considered. In the absence of a particular kind of technical progress the path which
maximizes the rate of growth of output is also
likely to maximize the rate of growth of
employment. (JEL)

Stiglitz, J. G., "Alternative Theories of Wage
Determination and Unemployment in LDC's: The
Labor Turnover Model, Quarterly Journal of
Economics, Vol. 88, No. 2, May 1974, pp. 194-
227. This paper analyzes the simultaneous
determination of the urban and rural wage rate
and the level of urban unemployment, and rural
and urban output and employment. (JEL)

Sturmthal, Adolph, WORKERS' COUNCILS, Cambridge,
Massachusetts, Harvard University Press, 1964.

Sundrum, R. M., DEVELOPMENT STRATEGY WITH REFERENCE
TO EMPLOYMENT, DPS #6, Development Program Study
Group, International Bank for Reconstruction
and Development, June 1970.

Thiesenhusen, William C., LATIN AMERICA'S EMPLOYMENT
PROBLEM, Madison, University of Wisconsin,
Land Tenure Center No. 70, 1971.

Thorbecke, Erik, and Sengupta, Jati K., A CONSISTENCY
FRAMEWORK FOR EMPLOYMENT OUTPUT AND INCOME
DISTRIBUTION PROJECTIONS APPLIED TO COLOMBIA,
Development Research Center of the International
Bank for Reconstruction and Development, 1972.

Turner, H. A., WAGE TRENDS, WAGE POLICIES, AND
    COLLECTIVE BARGAINING: The Problems of Under-
    developed Countries, Cambridge, University of
    Cambridge, Department of Applied Economics,
    Occasional Papers No. 6, 1965.

Turnham, David with assistance by Jaeger, Ingelies,
    THE EMPLOYMENT PROBLEM IN LESS DEVELOPED
    COUNTRIES: A Review of Evidence, Paris,
    Development Centre of the Organization for
    Economic Co-operation and Development, 1971.

Tyler, W. G., LABOR ABSORPTION WITH IMPORT SUBSTI-
    TUTING INDUSTRIALIZATION: An Examination of
    Elasticities of Substitution in the Brazilian
    Manufacturing Sector, Kiel Discussion Papers
    #24, Institute of World Economics, October 1972.

Uppal, J. S., DISGUISED UNEMPLOYMENT IN AN UNDERDE-
    VELOPED ECONOMY: Its Nature and Measurement,
    New York, Asia Publishing House, 1973. An
    investigation of the theory and measurement of
    disguised unemployment. Discusses various
    causes of this phenomenon, looks at the excess
    aggregate labor cause in detail, examines some
    models of a dual economy, surveys attempts to
    measure disguised unemployment, presents land/
    output ratios, and applies this technique to
    Punjab (India) agriculture. (JEL)

Vanck, Jaroslav, THE GENERAL THEORY OF LABOR-MANAGED
    MARKET ECONOMICS, Ithaca, New York, Cornell
    University Press, 1970.

World Employment Conference, DECLARATION OF PRINCI-
    PLES AND PROGRAMME OF ACTION ADOPTED BY THE
    TRIPARTITE WORLD CONFERENCE ON EMPLOYMENT,
    INCOME DISTRIBUTION, AND SOCIAL PROGRESS AND
    THE INTERNATIONAL DIVISION OF LABOUR, Geneva,
    4-17 June 1976.

Energy

X-REF: AFRICA: Emembolu, ALGERIA: Schliphake,
ARGENTINA: Solberg, CHINA: Hardy, INDONESIA: Carl-
son, IRAN: Fesharaki, JAPAN: Japan, MIDDLE EAST:
Stone, NEW INTERNATIONAL ECONOMIC ORDER: Al-Khalef,
VENEZUELA: Petras, Salazar, Taylor, Tugwell, Val-
lenilla.

Adelman, M. A., THE WORLD PETROLEUM MARKET, Baltimore, Maryland, Johns Hopkins University Press (for Resources for the Future), 1972. Years of work have borne fruit at a very propitious time. Professor Adelman of MIT, one of the leading academic experts on the oil industry, has long examined the intricacies of prices, costs, taxes and the structure of the market. His conclusions are not those of the American oil industry and at key points they challenge the widely held view that there is an energy crisis. (FA)

Akins, James E., "The Oil Crisis: This Time the Wolf is Here," Foreign Affairs, Vol. 51, No. 3, April 1973.

Al-Otaiba, H. E. Mana Saeed, "Energy, Affluence, and Poverty," The Journal of Energy and Development, Vol. 1, No. 2, Spring 1976.

Amuzegar, Jahangir, "The Oil Story: Facts, Fiction, and Fair Play," Foreign Affairs, Vol. 51, No. 4, July 1973.

Blitzer, C.; Meeraus, A.; and Stoutjesdijk, A., "A Dynamic Model of OPEC Trade and Production," Journal of Development Economics, Vol. 2, No. 4, December 1975.

Darmstadter, Joel, with Teitelbaum, Perry D. and Palach, Jaroslav G., ENERGY IN THE WORLD ECONOMY: A Statistical Review of Trends in Output, Trade, and Consumption Since 1925, Baltimore, Maryland, Johns Hopkins Press (for Resources for the Future), 1972. An impressive collection of statistics plus an interpretive essay by a senior research associate of Resources for the Future. (FA)

de Janosi, P. E. and Grayson, L. E., "Patterns of Energy Consumption and Economic Growth and Structure," Journal of Development Studies, Vol. 8, No. 2, January 1972.

El Mallakh, Ragaei and McGuire, Carl, eds., ENERGY AND DEVELOPMENT, Boulder, Colorado, International Research Center for Energy and Development, 1974.

El Mallakh, Ragaei and McGuire, Carl, U.S. AND WORLD
    ENERGY RESOURCES: Prospects and Priorities,
    Boulder, Colorado, International Research Cen-
    ter for Energy and Economic Development, 1977.

Emembolu, G. E. and Pannu, S. S., "Africa: Oil and
    Development," Africa Today, Vol. 22, No. 4,
    Fall 1975, pp. 39-47.

Enders, Thomas O., "OPEC and the Industrial Coun-
    tries: The Next Ten Years," Foreign Affairs,
    Vol. 53, No. 4, July 1975.

Faramnfarmaian, Khodadad; Gutowski, Armin; Okita,
    Saburo; Roosa, Robert V.; and Wilson, Carroll
    L., "How Can the World Afford OPEC Oil?" Foreign
    Affairs, Vol. 53, No. 2, January 1975.

Fischer, D.; Gately D.; and Kyle, J. F., "The Pros-
    pects for OPEC: A Critical Survey of Models of
    the World Oil Market," Journal of Development
    Economics, Vol. 2, No. 4, December 1975.

Ghadar, Fariborz, THE EVOLUTION OF OPEC STRATEGY,
    Lexington, Massachusetts, Lexington Books, 1977.

Kalymon, B. A., "Economic Incentives in OPEC Oil
    Pricing Policy," Journal of Development
    Economics, Vol. 2, No. 4, December 1975.

Lambertini, Adrian, "Energy Problems of the non-OPEC
    Developing Countries, 1974-80," Finance and
    Development, Vol. 13, No. 3, September 1976.

Levy, Walter J., "World Oil Cooperation or Inter-
    national Chaos," Foreign Affairs, Vol. 52,
    No. 4, July 1974.

Mikdashi, Zuhayr, "Energy and Minerals: Some
    Developmental Issues," The Journal of Energy
    and Development, Vol. 1, No. 2, Spring 1976.

Pollack, Gerald A., "The Economic Consequences of
    the Energy Crisis," Foreign Affairs, Vol. 52,
    No. 3, April 1974.

Powelson, John P., "The Oil Price Increase: Impacts
    on Industrialized and Less-Developed Countries,"
    Journal of Energy and Development, Vol. III,
    No. 1, Autumn 1977.

Robichek, E. Walter, "The Payments Impact of the Oil
    Crisis: The Case of Latin America," Finance
    and Development, Vol. 11, No. 4, December 1974.

Rouhani, Fuad, A HISTORY OF O.P.E.C., New York,
    Praeger, 1971. The establishment, structure
    and functions of the Organizations of Petroleum
    Exporting Countries--up to its finest hour, the
    highly successful negotiations with the major
    oil companies in 1971. (FA)

Vernon, Raymond, ed., THE OIL CRISIS, New York,
    Norton, 1976.

Williams, Maurice J., "The Aid Programs of the OPEC
    Countries," Foreign Affairs, Vol. 54, No. 2,
    January 1976.

Entrepreneurship and Management

X-REF: COLOMBIA: Lipman, INDIA: Broehl, Nafziger,
JAPAN: Hirchmeier, MEXICO: Derossi.

Bell, Peter F., "A Quantitative Study of Entrepre-
    neurship and Its Determinants in Asia," Cana-
    dian Journal of Economics, Vol. II, No. 2,
    1969, pp. 288-298.

Brown, R. H., "The Achievement Norm and Economic
    Growth: The Case of Elizabethan England,"
    Rev. Soc. Economics, Vol. 27, No. 2, September
    1969, pp. 181-201. While virtually all theor-
    ists agree that the existence of a body of inno-
    vative businessmen is indispensable to economic
    growth, they differ as to how innovators came
    into existence in the first place. One explana-
    tory factor frequently overlooked may be a
    generalized "achievement norm"--that is, mani-
    fest values throughout a society which
    encourage or enforce such behavioral character-
    istics as means-end rationality, independent
    judgment, risk-taking, and perseverance. The
    present study examines evidence from the family
    relations, child socialization, and formal edu-
    cation of Elizabethan England, as well as from
    cosmological, psychological, and moral litera-
    ture of this period, to determine whether an
    achievement norm existed and had a causal rela-
    tion to Elizabethan economic growth. Similar

evidence is taken from Medieval England to provide a time control. (JEL)

Kilby, Peter, ENTERPRENEURSHIP AND ECONOMIC DEVELOPMENT, New York, The Free Press, 1971.

Leibenstein, Harvey, "Entrepreneurship and Development," American Economic Review, Vol. LVIII, No. 2, May 1968.

Marris, Peter and Somerset, Anthony, THE AFRICAN ENTREPRENEUR: A Study of Entrepreneurship and Development in Kenya, New York, African Publishing, 1972.

McClelland, David C., THE ACHIEVING SOCIETY, Princeton, New Jersey, D. Van Nostrand Company, Inc., 1961. The classic work in which "need for achievement" is developed. (Ed)

McClelland, David C. and Winter, David G., MOTIVATING ECONOMIC ACHIEVEMENT, with Winter, Sara K.; and Danzig, Elliott R.; Nadkarni, Manohar S.; Pahaney, Aziz; and Pareek, Udai, New York, The Free Press; London, Collier-Macmillan, 1969. The study presents an economic development model incorporating the authors' theory and discusses at length the conceptual and technical problems of testing the model. The empirical content of the study reports on the success of a number of experimental training programs conducted in India and elsewhere. Index. (JEL)

Nafziger, E. Wayne, "Entrepreneurship, Social Mobility, and Income Redistribution in South India," The American Economic Review, Vol. 67, No. 1, February 1977.

Vernon, Raymond, MANAGER IN THE INTERNATIONAL ECONOMY, New Jersey, Prentice-Hall, Inc., 1968.

Finance

X-REF: INDONESIA: Gautam, LATIN AMERICA: Griffin, MALAYSIA: Drake, MEXICO: Bennett, Brothers, FISCAL: Bird.

Adler, J. H. and Kuznets, P. W., eds., CAPITAL MOVE-
   MENTS AND ECONOMIC DEVELOPMENT, New York, St.
   Martin's Press; London, Macmillan, 1967.

Basch, Antonin, FINANCING ECONOMIC DEVELOPMENT, New
   York, The Macmillan Company; London, Collier-
   Macmillan Limited, 1964.

Bhatt, V. V. and Meerman, J., "Resource Mobilization
   in Developing Countries: Financial Institutions and Policies," World Development, Vol. 6,
   No. 1, January 1978.

Boskey, Shirley, PROBLEMS AND PRACTICES OF DEVELOP-
   MENT BANKS, Baltimore, The Johns Hopkins Press,
   1959.

Cairncross, (Sir) Alec, INFLATION, GROWTH AND INTER-
   NATIONAL FINANCE, Albany, State University of
   New York Press, 1975. Seven papers and addresses, several previously published, intended for
   lay audiences, on inflation, economic growth,
   and international economics. Discusses in particular: the forces governing the rate of
   technical change, economic growth in Britain;
   the causes of and remedies for inflation; the
   case for and against floating exchange rates;
   and the long-term controls of international
   capital movements. Also includes the author's
   presidential address to the British Association for the Advancement of Science, where the
   contribution that science could make to the
   solution of Britain's economic problems is discussed. (JEL)

Desai, V., "Role of Banks in Economic Growth,"
   Economic Affairs, Vol. 21, No. 6, June 1976.

Diamond, William, DEVELOPMENT BANKS, Baltimore,
   Maryland, The Johns Hopkins Press, 1957.

Friedman, Irving S., and Costanzo, G. A., THE EMERG-
   ING ROLE OF PRIVATE BANKS IN THE DEVELOPING
   WORLD, New York, New York, Citicorp, 1977.

Goldsmith, Raymond W., FINANCIAL STRUCTURE AND
   DEVELOPMENT, New Haven, Connecticut and London,
   Yale University Press, 1969.

Gray, Olive S., RESOURCE FLOWS TO LESS-DEVELOPED
COUNTRIES: Financial Terms and Their Constraints, New York, Frederick A. Praeger, 1969.

Gurley, John G. and Shaw, Edward S., MONEY IN A
THEORY OF FINANCE, Washington, D.C., The Brookings Institution, 1964. A theory of the manner
in which financial instruments and financial
institutions develop. (Ed)

Leff, N. H., "Rates of Return to Capital, Domestic
Savings, and Investment in the Developing
Countries," Kyklos, Vol. 28, No. 4, 1975,
pp. 827-851. For analytical and for policy purposes, it would be helpful to know whether the
economy-wide rate of return to reproducible
capital is in general relatively high or relatively low in developing countries. This paper
surveys the available theoretical and empirical
materials on both sides of this question. The
paper also discusses the implications for government project selection and for domestic
savings and investment. (JEL)

McKinnon, Ronald I., MONEY AND CAPITAL IN ECONOMIC
DEVELOPMENT, Washington, D.C., The Brookings
Institution, 1973.

Mikesell, Raymond F. and Zinser, J. E., "The Nature
of the Savings Function in Developing Countries," Journal of Economic Literature, March
1973.

Newlyn, W. T., THE FINANCING OF ECONOMIC DEVELOPMENT,
with contributions and collaboration from U.
Avramides et al., Oxford, Oxford University
Press; Clarendon Press, 1977. An inquiry into
ways the "potential national surplus (of developing countries) can be maximized" and channeled
into "capacity-creating" expenditures and also
into the role that foreign finance can play in
this process. The first half of the study considers the major policy issues of intermedia-
tion and credit creation, government finance,
and foreign finance; and then integrates them
into a macro-model for fifteen developing
countries. The second half examines the financing of economic development in three South Asian
countries (India, Malaysia, and Thailand), in
Ghana (1960-69), and in Nigeria (1950-71); also
presents case studies of "Company Savings in

Kenya's Manufacturing Sector" and the mining
industry in Zambia. Bibliography; author index;
subject index. (JEL)

Nurkse, Ragner, PROBLEMS OF CAPITAL FORMATION IN
UNDERDEVELOPED COUNTRIES AND PATTERNS OF TRADE
AND DEVELOPMENT, New York, Oxford University
Press, 1967.

Prest, A. R., PUBLIC FINANCE IN UNDERDEVELOPED
COUNTRIES, second edition, New York, Wiley,
1972.

Sametz, Arnold W., editor, FINANCIAL DEVELOPMENT AND
ECONOMIC GROWTH, New York, New York University
Press, 1972.

Shaw, Edward S., FINANCIAL DEEPENING IN ECONOMIC DE-
VELOPMENT, Economic Development Series, New
York, Oxford University Press, 1973. A book on
the role which financial markets can play in the
economic development process. The emphasis is
on financial deepening, i.e., the "accumulation
of non-financial wealth." The author discusses
the importance of financial deepening, the
wealth and debt-intermediation views on money,
finance, and capital accumulation, financial
regression and reform, coordination of fiscal
and financial strategies, financial deepening in
open economies, and instability in lagging
economies. Index. (JEL)

Tanzi, V., "Fiscal Policy, Keynesian Economics and
the Mobilization of Savings in Developing
Countries," World Development, Vol. 4, Nos.
10/11, October-November 1976, pp. 907-917. This
paper argues that the uncritical transplanting
of the basic Keynesian framework--which was
developed for other situations and other
institutions--to the developing countries has
provided support and/or justification for
policies that may have retarded the development
of these countries. It is argued that the
model implicit in those policies has been too
aggregative, too simple, politically naive, and
too oblivious to important interrelationships
among macro variables. It is concluded that
classical economics can still provide a useful
framework for determining desirable policies in
developing countries. (JEL)

Tun Wai, U, FINANCIAL INTERMEDIARIES AND NATIONAL
    SAVINGS IN DEVELOPING COUNTRIES, Praeger
    Special Studies in International Economics and
    Development, New York, Praeger, 1972. The book
    deals with the evolution of net national sav-
    ings in developing countries, financial inter-
    mediation, the relevance of existing theories
    of savings for developing countries, some
    econometric approaches to financial intermedia-
    tion and national savings, and attempts to
    build an integrated theory of savings. (JEL)

Tun Wai, U, ROLE OF FINANCIAL MARKETS IN DEVELOP-
    MENT, Finafrica Bulletin, Cassa di Risparmio
    delle Provincie Lombarde, 1976.

Villanueva, Delano P., "A Survey of the Financial
    System and the Saving-Investment Process in
    Korea and the Philippines," Finance and Develop-
    ment, Vol. 8, No. 2, June 1971.

Wilson, Frank A., "The Role of Commercial Banks in
    Financing Farmers: Some Reflections on the
    Situation in Zambia," Agricultural Administra-
    tion, Vol. 1, 1974, pp. 245-257.

World Bank, DEVELOPMENT FINANCE COMPANIES, Sector
    Policy Paper, April 1976.

Fiscal and Monetary Policy and Inflation

X-REF: ASIA: Chandavarkar, BRAZIL: Kahil, Silveira,
CENTRAL AMERICA: Best, CHILE: Lioi, Nowak, COLOMBIA:
Bird, Gillis, INDIA: Panandikar, Roy, KOREA: Bank,
LATIN AMERICA: Geithman, MEXICO: Griffiths,
PHILIPPINES: Baldwin.

Acharya, Shankar N., "Fiscal Financial Intervention,
    Factor Prices and Factor Proportions: A Review
    of Issues," Bangladesh Development Studies,
    No. 3, October 1975.

Ahluwalia, Montek S., TAXES, SUBSIDIES, AND EMPLOY-
    MENT, World Bank Reprint Series, No. 7,
    Washington, D.C., International Bank for
    Reconstruction and Development, 1973.

Afxentiou, P. C., "Inflation and Economic Develop-
    ment: A General Evaluation," South African
    Journal of Economics, Vol. 39, No. 2, June 1971,
    pp. 130-148. This article examines the his-
    torical and theoretical influences that render
    support to the use of inflation as a means of
    economic development, those structural charac-
    teristics of underdeveloped countries that make
    these countries particularly susceptible to
    inflation, and appraises inflation as a policy
    instrument. (JEL)

Aghevli, Bijan B., and Khan, Mohsin S., "Government
    Deficits and the Inflationary Process in De-
    veloping Countries," I.M.F. Staff Papers, Sep-
    tember 1978.

Baer, Werner and Kerstenetzky, Isaac, ed., INFLATION
    AND GROWTH IN LATIN AMERICA, New Haven, Connecti-
    cut, Yale University, Economic Growth Center,
    1964.

Bird, Richard and Oldman, Oliver, READINGS ON TAXA-
    TION IN DEVELOPING COUNTRIES, Baltimore, Mary-
    land, Johns Hopkins Press, 1964.

Bottomley, Anthony, "Interest Rate Determination in
    Underdeveloped Rural Areas," American Journal
    of Agricultural Economics, Vol. 57, May 1975,
    pp. 279-291.

Cameron, Rondo E., ed., BANKING AND ECONOMIC DEVELOP-
    MENT: Some Lessons of History, New York, Oxford
    University Press, 1972.

Cutt, James, TAXATION AND ECONOMIC DEVELOPMENT IN
    INDIA, New York, Praeger, 1969. India's main
    tax devices in terms of growth rate of national
    income, redistribution of wealth and stabiliza-
    tion of inflationary price increases, together
    with a study of their adequacy and with recom-
    mendations for modification. (FA)

Due, John F., INDIRECT TAXATION ON DEVELOPING
    ECONOMIES, Baltimore, Maryland, Johns Hopkins
    Press, 1970.

Emory, Robert Firestone, THE USE OF INTEREST RATE
    POLICIES AS A STIMULUS TO ECONOMIC GROWTH, Staff
    Economic Studies #65, Washington, D.C., Board of
    Governors of the Federal Reserve System, 1971.

Geithman, David T., ed., FISCAL POLICY FOR INDUSTRI-
ALIZATION AND DEVELOPMENT IN LATIN AMERICA,
Gainesville, University Presses of Florida,
1974. Collection of 19 previously unpublished
papers (and related comments) presented at the
Twenty-First Annual Latin American Conference
held in February 1971. Central theme of the
conference was the analysis and evaluation of
the interaction among fiscal problems, fiscal
tools, and fiscal systems in the industrializing economies of Latin America. (JEL)

Heller, Peter S., "A Model of Fiscal Behavior in
Developing Countries: Aid, Investment, and
Taxation," The American Economic Review, Vol.
LXV, No. 3, June 1975.

Hinrichs, Harley H., A GENERAL THEORY OF TAX STRUC-
TURE CHANGE DURING ECONOMIC DEVELOPMENT,
Cambridge, Massachusetts, The Law School of
Harvard University, 1966.

Hirsch, Fred and Goldthorpe, John H., THE POLITICAL
ECONOMY OF INFLATION, Cambridge, Massachusetts,
Harvard University Press, 1978. In this volume,
a group of distinguished historians, political
scientists, economists, and sociologists
examines the persistence and spread of the
inflationary virus since the last world war.
Their findings indicate that inflation is as
much a political as an economic phenomenon, and
that, while economic forces are important, the
politics and structure of a society are equally
decisive. (BPA)

ILO, FISCAL MEASURES FOR EMPLOYMENT PROMOTION IN
DEVELOPING COUNTRIES, Geneva, International
Labour Office, 1973.

Joint Tax Program, OAS/IDB/ECLA, PROBLEMS OF TAX
ADMINISTRATION IN LATIN AMERICA, Baltimore,
Maryland, Johns Hopkins Press, 1971. A general
survey of the fiscal conditions prevailing in
Latin America...an authoritative analysis of
the theory and practice of tax administration
in those countries. The noninitiated as well
as the student and the specialist can read it
with much profit. (BPA)

Jud, Gustav Donald, INFLATION AND THE USE OF INDEXING IN DEVELOPING COUNTRIES, New York, Praeger, 1978. Analyzes the standard theoretical arguments for indexation, and employs case studies (Brazil, Chile, Colombia, Mexico) to illuminate the operation and impact of indexation when applied to the domestic economy. Highlights different approaches to indexation and the application of indexing to wages, taxes, capital funds, etc. Investigates on-going and potential global uses of indexing as a means for stabilizing export earnings and for exchange rate management in a world of floating currencies. Assesses indexation as a policy device to reduce or combat inflation, and to eliminate price distortions and relation inequities. (BPA)

Kaldor, Nicholas, "Will Underdeveloped Countries Learn to Tax?" Foreign Affairs, January 1963, pp. 410-419.

Krause, Lawrence B. and Salant, Walter S., eds., WORLDWIDE INFLATION: Theory and Recent Experience, Washington, D.C., The Brookings Institution, 1977.

Krzyzaniak, Marian and Oxmucur, Suleyman, THE DISTRIBUTION OF INCOME AND THE SHORT-TERM BURDEN OF TAXES IN TURKEY, 1968, Houston, Texas, Rice University Paper No. 28, Fall 1972.

Organization for Economic Cooperation and Development, INTEREST RATES 1960-74, in OECD Financial Statistics, Paris, 1976.

Panandikar, D. H. Pai, INTEREST RATES AND FLOW OF FUNDS, A CASE STUDY: India, India, Macmillan, 1973.

Pazos, Felipe, "Chronic Inflation in Latin America," Challenge, Vol. 20, No. 2, May/June 1977, p. 48.

Pazos, Felipe, MEDIDAS PARA DETENER LA INFLACION CRONICA EN AMERICA LATINA, Centro de Estudios Monetarios Latinoamericanos, Mexico, 1969.

Pinto, Anibal, INFLACION: Raices Estructurales, Ensayos, No. 3, Fondo De Cultura Economica, Mexico, 1973.

Randall, L., "Inflation and Economic Development in Latin America: Some New Evidence," Journal of Development Studies, Vol. 9, No. 2, January 1973.

Schweizerische Bankgesellschaft, AN INTERNATIONAL SURVEY OF INTEREST RATES: Patterns and Differentials, Zurich, Switzerland, Union Bank of Switzerland, 1970.

Sommerfeld, Raynard M., TAX REFORM AND THE ALLIANCE FOR PROGRESS, Austin and London, The University of Texas Press, 1966.

Tanzi, Vito, "Inflation, Real Tax Revenue, and the Care for Inflationary Finance: Theory with an Application to Argentina," I.M.F. Staff Papers, September 1978.

Tun Wai, U, THE RELATION BETWEEN INFLATION AND ECONOMIC DEVELOPMENT: A Statistical Inductive Study, reprinted from International Monetary Fund Staff Papers, Washington, D.C., October 1959.

Tun Wai, U, A REVISIT TO INTEREST RATES OUTSIDE THE MONEY MARKETS OF UNDERDEVELOPED COUNTRIES, No. 122, Banca Nazionale del Lavoro Quarterly Review, September 1977.

Tun Wai, U, TAXATION PROBLEMS AND POLICIES OF UNDERDEVELOPED COUNTRIES, Lecture presented at Institute for International Development, Staff Papers, International Monetary Fund, Washington, D.C., November 1962.

Vogel, R. C., "The Dynamics of Inflation in Latin America, 1950-1969," American Economic Review, Vol. 64, No. 1, March 1974, pp. 102-114. To investigate the impact of monetary factors on inflation, this article extends Harberger's Chilean model to 16 Latin American countries for the period 1950-1969. Pooled regressions, together with individual time-series and cross-section regressions, reveal that countries with widely varying inflationary experiences exhibit strikingly homogeneous behavior in their responses to money supply changes. The impact of money supply changes on prices is significant, rapid, and proportionate. The principal implication for the monetarist-structuralist contro-

versy is that differences among countries in
rates of inflation can be explained largely by
differences in money supply behavior and without recourse to structural variables. (JEL)

Wachter, Susan M., LATIN AMERICAN INFLATION: The
Structuralist-monetarist Debate, Lexington,
Massachusetts and Toronto, Heath, Lexington
Books, 1976. Discusses the structuralist-
monetarist debate concerning Latin America's
apparently chronic inflation with emphasis on
the causes given by these theories as well as
their implications concerning the relationship
between growth and inflation. The principal
objective is to develop an adequate statement of
the structuralist position, especially with
regard to the role of agricultural difficulties.
The secondary objective is to test both theories
using data from Chile, Argentina, Brazil, and
Mexico and analyze the policy implications.(JEL)

Wang, T. N., ed., TAXATION AND DEVELOPMENT, New
York, Praeger, 1976. Studies the relationship
between taxation and economic development, with
special attention to the impact of specific tax
measures in developing countries. Four selected taxes are examined: the property tax, the
export tax, and the relatively new value-added
tax and pollution tax. (BPA)

Zolotas, Xenophon, INTERNATIONAL MONETARY ISSUES AND
DEVELOPMENT POLICIES, Athens, Greece, Bank of
Greece Printing Works, 1977.

Foreign Aid

X-REF: AFRICA: Streeten, HUNGER, NUTRITION, HEALTH:
Srivasta, NIGERIA: Hawbaker, PAKISTAN: Brecher,
TAIWAN: Jacoby, THAILAND: Caldwell.

Abbott, G. C., "Two Concepts of Foreign Aid," World
Development, Vol. 1, No. 9, September 1973.

Asher, Robert E., DEVELOPMENT ASSISTANCE IN THE
SEVENTIES: Alternatives for the United States,
Washington, D.C., Brookings Institution, 1970.
One of the best-informed and balanced books on
aid. Wasting no words, it deals with all the
central issues of policy, weighs the evidence of

experience and shows the implications of alternative choices. The author reaches concrete and
well-reasoned conclusions on the wisdom of continuing aid, making it more multilateral, doing
more about trade and a variety of related
matters. (FA)

Asher, Robert E., GRANTS, LOANS, AND LOCAL CURREN-
    CIES: Their Role in Foreign Aid, Washington,
    D.C., The Brookings Institution, 1961.

Bartke, Wolfgang, CHINA'S ECONOMIC AID, New York,
    Holmes & Meier (for the Institute of Asian
    Affairs, Hamburg), 1975. A monograph which
    lists all of China's foreign aid projects and
    briefly analyzes their impact. Most favored
    projects: textile mills, medical groups. Most
    favored recipients: Pakistan, Tanzania.
    General effectiveness: high. (FA)

Bhagwati, Jagdish and Eckaus, Richard S., eds.,
    FOREIGN AID, Baltimore, Maryland, Penguin, 1970.

Bhattacharya, D., "Foreign Aid and Economic Develop-
    ment," Economic Affairs, Vol. 18, No. 1-2,
    Annual Number 1973.

Boserup, Ester and Sachs, Ignacy, eds., FOREIGN AID
    TO NEWLY INDEPENDENT COUNTRIES, The Hague,
    Mouton, 1971; New York, Humanities Press, 1972.

Carter, James Richard, THE NET COST OF SOVIET FOREIGN
    AID, New York, Praeger Special Studies in Inter-
    national Economics and Development, 1971.
    Professor Carter has made an important contri-
    bution to the literature on both foreign aid and
    Soviet foreign economic relations in his
    analysis of the net cost of Soviet foreign aid
    over the 1955-68 period. . . .The author has
    gone beyond the task of estimating direct bene-
    fits and costs of Soviet foreign assistance to
    a consideration of the indirect benefits aris-
    ing from the expansion of Soviet trade which
    can be attributed to the Soviet aid program and
    to the probable gains from such trade to the
    Soviet economy. (BPA)

Central Intelligence Agency, COMMUNIST AID TO THE
    LESS DEVELOPED COUNTRIES OF THE FREE WORLD,
    1976, published for the use of U.S. Government
    officials, August 1977.

Chenery, Hollis B., and Carter, Nicholas G., "Foreign Assistance and Development Performance, 1960-1970," The American Economic Review, Vol. LXIII, No. 2, May 1973.

Clark, Paul G., AMERICAN AID FOR DEVELOPMENT, New York, Praeger (for the Council on Foreign Relations), 1972. Contrary to widespread impressions, many poor countries made marked economic progress in the 1960s. They and others could make good use of increased foreign aid to grow further in the 1970s. These well-reasoned conclusions by the head of the Center of Development Economics at Williams College (and a former AID official) lead to concrete recommendations for the reshaping of American aid policies. (FA)

Committee on Economic Development, ASSISTING DEVELOPMENT IN LOW-INCOME COUNTRIES, Washington, D.C., 1969. Offers a rationale for public support of the U.S. economic assistance program and recommends a far-ranging set of priorities for U.S. Government policy. Proposes better ways by which the developed nations can speed the growth of low-income countries through the application of public and private resource. (BPA)

Dacy, D. C., "Foreign Aid, Government Consumption, Saving and Growth in Less Developed Countries," Economic Journal, Vol. 85, No. 339, September 1975, pp. 548-561. Static models of growth and development indicate that aid always improves the rate of growth if domestic saving does not fall by the amount of aid. Using a simple dynamic model it is demonstrable that aid also can help to produce a lower long-term growth rate than would occur in a no-aid situation. (JEL)

Esman, Milton J., and Cheever, Daniel S., THE COMMON AID EFFORT, Columbus, Ohio, Ohio State University Press, 1967.

Frank, Charles R.; Bhagwati, Jagdish N.; Shaw, Robert D'A.; and Malmgren, Harald B., ASSISTING DEVELOPING COUNTRIES: Problems of Debts, Burden-Sharing, Jobs, and Trade, New York, Washington, and London, Praeger Publishing, 1972.

Goulet, Denis, and Hudson, Michael, THE MYTH OF AID:
The Hidden Agenda of the Development Reports,
prepared by the Center for the Study of Development and Social Change, New York, International Documentation on the Contemporary
Church, North America-Orbis Books, 1971. A
critique of recent development reports resulting from the first "Development Decade." The
author feels that "major recommendations...are
mere palliatives to underdevelopment and that
"this faulty vision constitutes, with excep-
tions to be noted below, a rationalization for
the rich world's desire to domesticate the
development of the Third World." No index.
(JEL)

Gray, Olive S., RESOURCE FLOWS TO LESS-DEVELOPED
COUNTRIES: Financial Terms and Their Constraints, New York, Praeger, 1969. How much a
developing country gets out of aid depends on
the forms in which resources are transferred
(grants, hard and soft loans, etc.) and the
conditions attached by the countries exporting
the capital. This effort to provide quantitative measures is comprehensive, thoughtful and
technical. (FA)

Hawkins, E. K., THE PRINCIPLES OF DEVELOPMENT AID,
Baltimore, Maryland, Penguin, 1970.

Holzman, F. D., "The Real Economic Costs of Granting
Foreign Aid," Journal of Development Studies,
Vol. 7, No. 3, April 1971.

Horowitz Proposal, A PLAN FOR FINANCING ECONOMIC
DEVELOPMENT OF THE DEVELOPING COUNTRIES, May
1969.

Horvath, Janos, CHINESE TECHNOLOGY TRANSFER TO THE
THIRD WORLD, A Grants Economy Analysis, New
York, Praeger, 1976. A comprehensive analysis
of China's economic assistance programs, 1950-
72 in terms of resources sacrificed, identifica-
tion of objectives, and measurable achievements. Includes an analysis of China's aid
balance-sheet within the Communist bloc nations;
places the various analytic measurements on a
comparable scale and estimates the measure of
achievements per unit of grant.(BPA)

Little, I. M. D. and Clifford, J. M., INTERNATIONAL
AID: A Discussion of the Flow of Public Re-
sources from Rich to Poor, Chicago, Aldine
Publishing Company, 1965.

Loehr, William; Price, David; and Raichur, Satish, A
COMPARISON OF U.S. AND MULTILATERAL AID RE-
CIPIENTS IN LATIN AMERICA, 1957-1971, Inter-
national Studies Series, Vol 4, Beverly Hills,
California, Sage Publications, 1976.

Loutfi, Martha F., THE NET COST OF JAPANESE FOREIGN
AID, New York, Praeger, 1973. Japan is now
second only to the United States as a source of
capital outflow to the developing areas. But
only the U.S. and Italy have such low ratios of
aid to production. The author estimates the
real cost of this aid to be about 60 percent
of face value, with an additional cost of the
political embarrassment provided by the seeming
gain in the Japanese balance of payments with
the recipient. (FA)

Mickelwait, Donald R.; Sweet, Charles F.; and Morss,
Elliott R., NEW DIRECTIONS IN DEVELOPMENT: A
Study of U.S. Aid, Boulder, Colorado, Westview
Press, July-December 1978. In 1973 Congress
legislated a fundamental change in U.S. foreign
aid policy; rather than providing general
assistance to developing nations, the U.S.
Agency for International Development (AID)
would focus on helping the rural poor in those
nations. The authors describe the bureaucratic
and administrative problems that confronted
Development Alternatives in this job, giving
particular attention to the administrative and
bureaucratic barriers within AID itself. They
conclude with a set of recommendations for
reform that are essential if the agency is to
attain its "New Directions" objectives. (BPA)

OECD, DEVELOPMENT CO-OPERATION, REVIEW, Annual report
by the Chairman of the Committee, Efforts and
Policies of the members of the Development
Assistance Committee.

OECD, GEOGRAPHICAL DISTRIBUTION OF FINANCIAL FLOWS
TO DEVELOPING COUNTRIES, Data on Disbursements
1969 to 1975, October 1977.

OAS, Department of Economic Affairs, EXTERNAL FINANC-
ING FOR LATIN AMERICAN DEVELOPMENT, Baltimore,
Maryland, Johns Hopkins Press, 1971. A study
of the flow of aid between the U.S. and Latin
America from 1961 to 1968 demonstrates that the
volume of external financing, both governmental
and private, never reached anticipated levels
and has in fact declined in recent years. In
addition, the terms and conditions of development financing have been more strict than presumed and have in the last two years become
increasingly tough. (Ed)

Owens, Edgar and Shaw, Robert, DEVELOPMENT RECON-
SIDERED: Bridging the Gap Between Government
and People, Lexington, Massachusetts, Lexington
Books, 1972. Based "more on recent historical
evidence than on theory," the book "sets forth
a new strategy of development--a strategy in
which participation by all the people is both
the means and the end to development itself."
It is also an examination of why and where foreign aid has failed, and it calls for a new
foreign aid policy where funds are to benefit
"the great mass of labor" rather than a small
number of capital intensive projects. Index.
(JEL)

Pearson, Lester B., Chairman, PARTNERS IN DEVELOP-
MENT: Report of the Commission on Interna-
tional Development, New York, Washington and
London, Praeger Publishers, 1969.

Tendler, Judith, INSIDE FOREIGN AID, Baltimore,
Maryland, Johns Hopkins University Press, 1975.
The author shows convincingly how the conditions in which aid is given produce aims, attitudes and results quite different from those
intended. The relations of giver and receiver,
perceptions of what is scarce and what abundant, and the methods of calculating costs and
benefits are all shown to be distorted by
organization, bureaucracy, fiscal and legislative deadlines and the flow of informed and
uninformed criticisms. (FA)

Williams, Maurice J., "The Aid Programs of the OPEC
Countries," Foreign Affairs, Vol. 54, No. 2,
January 1976, pp. 308-324.

71

Williams, Maurice J., DEVELOPMENT CO-OPERATION:
Efforts and Policies of the Members of the
Development Assistance Committee, Paris,
Organization of Economic Co-operation and
Development, November 1975.

Foreign Investment

X-REF: CHILE: Baklanoff, Lau, JAPAN: Henderson,
LATIN AMERICA: Behrman, HUNGER, NUTRITION, HEALTH:
Population, Fao.

Alejandro, Carlos F. Diaz, DIRECT FOREIGN INVESTMENT
IN LATIN AMERICA, Center Paper #150, New Haven,
Connecticut, Economic Growth Center, Yale
University, 1970.

Baklanoff, Eric N., EXPROPRIATION OF U.S. INVEST-
MENTS IN CUBA, MEXICO, AND CHILE, New York,
Praeger, 1975. A brief but useful account of
the philosophies and events relating to an
important area of political and economic conflict. The author advocates "an official
investment policy of prudential disengagement."
(FA)

Basch, Antonin and Kybal, Milic, with collaboration
of Sanchez-Masi, Luis, CAPITAL MARKETS IN LATIN
AMERICA: A General Survey, Praeger Special
Studies in International Economics and Development, 1970. Contending that Latin American
economic development depends essentially on the
region's own efforts to generate an increased
volume of domestic savings for investment, the
authors of this study ask: What is the best
way to organize the financial institutions and
capital markets of Latin America? (BPA)

Behrman, Jack N., DECISION CRITERIA FOR FOREIGN
DIRECT INVESTMENT IN LATIN AMERICA, New York,
Council of the Americas, 1974.

Bergsten, C. Fred, "Coming Investment Wars?" Foreign
Affairs, Vol. 53, No. 1, October 1974.

Dell, Sidney, THE INTER-AMERICAN DEVELOPMENT BANK:
A Study in Development Financing, New York,
Washington, and London, Praeger Publishers,
1972.

Killick, T., "The Benefits of Foreign Direct Investment and Its Alternatives: An Empirical Exploration," <u>Journal</u> of <u>Development</u> <u>Studies</u>, Vol. 9, No. 2, January 1973.

Lall, S., "Less-Developed Countries and Private Foreign Direct Investment: A Review Article," <u>World</u> <u>Affairs</u>, Vol. 2, Nos. 4 and 5, April-May 1974.

Mikesell, Raymond F., ed., U.S. PRIVATE AND GOVERNMENT INVESTMENT ABROAD, Eugene, University of Oregon Books, 1962.

Reuber, Grant L., PRIVATE FOREIGN INVESTMENT IN DEVELOPMENT, Oxford, Oxford University Press, 1973.

Stamp, M., "Has Foreign Capital Still a Role to Play in Development?" <u>World</u> <u>Development</u>, Vol. 2, No. 2, February 1974.

Swansbrough, Robert H., THE EMBATTLED COLOSSUS: Economic Nationalism and United States Investors in Latin America, Latin American Monographs--Second Series, No. 16, Gainesville, The University Presses of Florida for the Center for Latin American Studies, University of Florida, 1976. The emergence of economic nationalism in the industrialized Western countries and its background in Latin America, illustrating the difficulty of grafting American-style private enterprise on a society where political astuteness, not entrepreneurial ability, is the key to social mobility. Costs and advantages of foreign investment are evaluated, first by the Latins and then by the Americans. The role of private enterprise in the U.S. foreign assistance program is examined, a role that continued to be emphasized even as the investment climate in Latin America became more and more inhospitable. (BPA)

Winkler, Max, INVESTMENTS OF UNITED STATES CAPITAL IN LATIN AMERICA, Kennikat Press, Spring 1978. The book examines Latin America's international commercial and financial life from 1913 to the beginning of the great depression of 1929. (BPA)

Growth Theory

Abramovitz, Moses, and David, Paul A., "Reinterpret-
ing Economic Growth: Parables and Realities,"
The American Economic Review, Vol. LXIII, No.
2, May 1973.

Britto, Ronald, "Some Recent Developments in the
Theory of Economic Growth: An Interpretation,"
Journal of Economic Literature, December 1973.

Burmeister, Edwin and Dobell, A. Rodney, MATHE-
MATICAL THEORIES OF ECONOMIC GROWTH, Foreword
by Robert M. Solow, Macmillan Series in Economics, New York, Macmillan, 1970. A graduate
level text comprehensively covering the issues
of growth in one-sector and two-sector models
including the problem of technological change
and money; principally uses phase diagrams
associated with differential equation systems.
The subsequent three chapters discuss various
multi-sector growth models with alternative
techniques, and neoclassical multisector models
without joint production, utilizing the theory
of non-negative matrices as the main analytical
tool. The problems of efficiency and optimality
of economic growth are discussed in the succeeding two chapters covering several versions
of turnpike theorems and utilizing the techniques of variational methods. (JEL)

Denison, Edward F., assisted by Poullier, Jean-
Pierre, WHY GROWTH RATES DIFFER, Washington,
D.C., The Brookings Institution, 1967.

Domar, Evsey D., ESSAYS IN THE THEORY OF ECONOMIC
GROWTH, New York, Oxford University Press,
1957.

Dorfman, Robert; Samuelson, Paul; and Solow, Robert,
LINEAR PROGRAMMING AND ECONOMIC ANALYSIS, New
York, McGraw-Hill, 1958.

Findlay, Ronald, "Implications of Growth Theory for
Trade and Development," The American Economic
Review, Vol. LXV, No. 2, May 1975.

Hahn, F. H., ed., READINGS IN THE THEORY OF GROWTH,
New York, St. Martin's Press, 1971. This
volume contains a selection of twenty important

contributions to the modern theory of economic growth. An introduction offers critical remarks on the development of the theory as represented by the contents of the book. A notable feature is that contributing authors are given the opportunity to comment on their own works in light of subsequent developments in the field. These comments appear at the end of the papers in question. No index. (JEL)

Hahn, F. H. and Matthews, R. C. O., "The Theory of Economic Growth: A Survey," Economic Journal, December 1964.

Harris, Donald J., "The Theory of Economic Growth: A Critique and Reformulation," The American Economic Review, Vol. LXV, No. 2, May 1975.

Harrod, R. F., "An Essay in Dynamic Theory," Economic Journal, Vol. 49, 1939, pp. 468-475.

Jones, Hywel G., AN INTRODUCTION TO MODERN THEORIES OF ECONOMIC GROWTH, St. Louis, McGraw-Hill Book Company, 1976.

Kelley, Allen C.; Williamson, Jeffrey C.; and Cheetham, Russell J., DUALISTIC ECONOMIC DEVELOPMENT: Theory and History, Chicago, University of Chicago Press, 1972.

Kuznets, Simon, "Modern Economic Growth: Findings and Reflections," The American Economic Review, Vol. LXIII, No. 3, June 1973.

Lipton, M., "The New Economics of Growth: A Review," World Development, Vol. 5, No. 3, March 1977.

Mehta, J. K., ECONOMICS OF GROWTH, second edition, New York, Asia Publishing House, 1970. The book was "written with the object of providing a simple and yet strictly logical treatment of the theory of fluctuations and growth of national income." (JEL)

Mishan, Edward J., THE ECONOMIC GROWTH DEBATE: An Assessment, London, George Allen and Unwin, 1977.

Nelson, Richard R., and Winter, Sidney G., "Growth
Theory from an Evolutionary Perspective: The
Differential Productivity Puzzle," The American
Economic Review, Vol. LXV, No. 2, May 1975.

Nelson, Richard R. and Winter, Sidney G., "Neoclassical vs. Evolutionary Theories of Economic
Growth: Critique and Prospectus," The Economic
Journal, Vol. 84, No. 336, December 1974,
pp. 886-905.

Phelps, Edmund, "The Golden Rule of Accumulation,"
American Economic Review, September 1961.

Samuelson, Paul, "A Catenary Turnpike Theorem Involving Consumption and the Golden Rule," American
Economic Review, June 1965.

Solow, Robert M., "A Contribution to the Theory of
Ecnomic Growth," Quarterly Journal of Economics,
February 1956.

Vanek, Jaroslav, MAXIMAL ECONOMIC GROWTH: A Geome-
tric Approach to Von Neumann's Growth Theory
and the Turnpike Theorem, Ithaca, New York,
Cornell University Press, 1968.

Wan, Henry Y., ECONOMIC GROWTH, New York, Chicago,
Atlanta, Harcourt Brace Javanovich, Inc., 1971.

History of Development

X-REF: AFRICA: Hatch, Hopkins, ARGENTINA: Randall,
BOLIVIA: Klein, Lora, BRAZIL: Baklanoff, Burns,
Conrad, Flynn, Freyre, Furtado, Randall, CHILE: de
Vylder, Hervey, Kirsch, Whitaker, Young, CHINA:
Eberhard, King, Wu, CUBA: Smith, HAITI: Lacerto,
INDUSTRIAL DEVELOPMENT: Ashton, JAMAICA: Higman,
JAPAN: Kelly, Nakayama, KENYA: Savage, KOREA: Lee,
LATIN AMERICA: Bobbs, Davis, Furtado, MALAYSIA:
Ghee, MEXICO: Atkin, Bazant, Randall, Ruiz, Toscano,
MIDDLE EAST: Goldsmith, Kedouri, MULTINATIONAL COR-
PORATIONS: Wilkins, NIGERIA: Ekundare, PERU: Kar-
sten, Randall, Werlich, POPULATION: Clark, Durand,
Habakkuk, Tilly, Trewartha, PUERTO RICO: Lopez,
TAIWAN: Gordon, TECHNOLOGY: Rosenberg, THAILAND:
Ingram.

Bairoch, Paul, THE ECONOMIC DEVELOPMENT OF THE THIRD
WORLD SINCE 1900, translated from the fourth
French edition by Cynthia Postan, Berkeley:
University of California Press, 1975. The
author covers a wide range of factors important
to development, namely population, agriculture,
extractive industry, manufacturing industry,
foreign trade, education, urbanization, the
labor force and employment, and macroeconomic
data. Particular attention is devoted to the
development of agriculture. (JEL)

Berend, Ivan T. and Ranki, Gyorgy, ECONOMIC DEVELOP-
MENT IN EAST-CENTRAL EUROPE IN THE 19th AND
20th CENTURIES, New York, Columbia University
Press, 1974.

Cameron, Rondo, ed., BANKING AND ECONOMIC DEVELOP-
MENT: Some Lessons of History, New York,
Oxford University Press, 1972. The experiences
of seven countries in the nineteenth century
analyzed in the hope of throwing light on
present problems. (FA)

Cipolla, Carlo M., BEFORE THE INDUSTRIAL REVOLUTION:
European Society and Economy, 1000-1700, London, Methuen and Co., Ltd., 1976.

Cortes-Conde, R.; Goodman, L. W.; and Stein, S. J.,
"The Economic History of Latin America," Items,
Vol. 31, Nos. 1 and 2, March/June 1977, pp.
7-10.

Falkus, Malcolm, E., ed., READINGS IN THE HISTORY OF
ECONOMIC GROWTH, Nairobi, Kenya, Oxford University Press, 1968.

Fei, John C. J. and Ranis, Gustav, ECONOMIC DEVELOP-
MENT IN HISTORICAL PERSPECTIVE, Center Paper
#135, New Haven, Connecticut, Yale University,
Economic Growth Center, 1969.

Furtado, Celso, ECONOMIC DEVELOPMENT OF LATIN
AMERICA: A Survey from Colonial Times to the
Cuban Revolution, Cambridge at the University
Press, 1970.

Gerschenkron, Alexander, ON THE CONCEPT OF CONTINUITY IN HISTORY, a reprint from Proceedings of the American Philosophical Society, Vol. 106, No. 3, June 1962, Lancaster, Pennsylvania, Lancaster Press inc.

Gould, John D., ECONOMIC GROWTH IN HISTORY: Survey and Analysis, London, Methuen, 1972.

Herring, Hubert, A HISTORY OF LATIN AMERICA FROM THE BEGINNINGS TO THE PRESENT, Second Edition, Revised, New York, Alfred A. Knopf, 1962.

Hirschman, Albert O., THE PASSIONS AND THE INTERESTS: Political Arguments for Capitalism Before Its Triumph, Princeton, New Jersey, Princeton University Press, 1977.

Holderness, B. A., PRE-INDUSTRIAL ENGLAND: Economy and Society from 1500-1750, Totowa, New Jersey, Rowman and Littlefield, 1976.

Hopkins, A. G., AN ECONOMIC HISTORY OF WEST AFRICA, New York, Columbia University Press, 1973.

Hughes, J. R. T., "What Difference Did the Beginning Make?" American Economic Review, Vol. 67, No. 1, February 1977.

Kindleberger, Charles P., ECONOMIC RESPONSE: Comparative Studies in Trade, Finance, and Growth, Cambridge, Massachusetts, Harvard University Press, 1978. The author seeks to show how economic history and economic analysis can interact and gives particular attention to the question of how history can be used in a comparative setting to test economic models for generality. His history and examples span the seventeenth to the twentieth century. (BPA)

Morawetz, David, TWENTY-FIVE YEARS OF ECONOMIC DEVELOPMENT: 1950 to 1975, Washington, D.C., World Bank, distributed by Johns Hopkins University Press, Baltimore, 1977. Broad assessment of efforts, since the early 1950's to establish targets for the economic growth of poor countries, to formulate and implement rational development plans, and to assure international cooperation. Discusses the changing objectives of development and evaluates economic growth, the reduction of poverty, and the move towards self-reliance and economic independence. (JEL)

North, Douglass C. and Thomas, Robert Paul, THE RISE OF THE WESTERN WORLD: A New Economic History, Cambridge, Cambridge University Press, 1973.

North, Douglass C., "Structure and Performance: The Task of Economic History," Journal of Economic Literature, Vol. XVI, September 1978, pp. 963-978.

Rostow, W. W., THE STAGES OF ECONOMIC GROWTH: A Non-Communist Manifesto, Cambridge, At The University, 1961.

Sen, Amartya, ed., GROWTH ECONOMICS, Harmondsworth, Penguin, 1970.

Toynbee, Arnold J., A STUDY OF HISTORY, abridgement by D. C. Somerwell, Volumes 1 and 2, New York, Dell Publishing Co., 1971.

U.S. Department of Commerce, LONG TERM ECONOMIC GROWTH 1860-1970, Washington, D.C., U.S. Government Printing Office, 1973.

Hunger, Nutrition, and Health

X-REF: AFRICA: McLoughlin, AGRICULTURAL DEVELOPMENT: Scientific, ASIA: Etienne, Shand, CHINA: Rifkin, Sidel, Un, PAKISTAN: Khan, TECHNOLOGY: Bottomley.

Amin, Galal A., FOOD SUPPLY AND ECONOMIC DEVELOPMENT, with special reference to Egypt, New York, A. M. Kelley, 1966.

Berg, Alan and Muscat, Robert J., THE NUTRITION FACTOR: Its Role in National Development, Washington, Brookings Institution, 1978. A discussion of a many-faceted problem, with strong policy recommendations. (FA)

Berg, Alan; Scrimshaw, Mevin S.; and Call, David L., NUTRITION, NATIONAL DEVELOPMENT, AND PLANNING, Cambridge, Massachusetts, MIT Press, 1973. This book contains the proceedings of the

International Conference (on Nutrition, National Development) held at MIT in October, 1971 in which world participants including economists, nutritionists, development planners and administrators, discussed nutritional problems and their effects on individuals and national development, means of alleviating those problems, and nutrition planning as part of national development programs in developing countries. (JEL)

Bryant, John, HEALTH AND THE DEVELOPING WORLD, Ithaca, New York, Cornell University Press, 1970. A physician's diagnosis of the "vast gap that exists between biomedical knowledge and our capability for bringing this knowledge within effective reach of the world's people." The author's prescriptions seem persuasive and realistic. (FA)

Chou, Marylin, et al., WORLD FOOD PROSPECTS AND AGRICULTURAL POTENTIAL, Praeger Special Studies in International Economics and Development, New York and London, Praeger, in cooperation with the Hudson Institute, 1977. This volume employs a 200-year outlook to examine various resource and institutional issues, to ascertain the problems that may hinder agricultural development, and to suggest ways to alleviate the problems. Deals with the dynamic side of agriculture and associated resource and technology availabilities and issues, treats global and developing-country institutional concerns, and examines the influence of technology on dietary changes. (JEL)

Cochrane, Willard W., THE WORLD FOOD PROBLEM: A Guardedly Optimistic View, New York, Corwell, 1969. Neither alarmist nor complacent, this agricultural economist and former government official argues that neither birth control nor miracle grains can by itself solve the food problem. That can only be done as part of general development policy for which both rich and poor nations must share responsibility. (FA)

Crosson, Pierre R., and Frederick, Kenneth, THE WORLD FOOD SITUATION: Resource and Environmental Issues in the Developing Countries and the United States, Baltimore, Maryland, Johns Hopkins University Press.

DeCastro, Josue, THE GEOPOLITICS OF HUNGER, New York and London, Monthly Review Press, 1952; 1977. Revised and updated edition of The Geography of Hunger (1952). Analyzing hunger as "the biological manifestation of underdevelopment," the author develops two themes: (1) hunger is a man-made plague, and (2) starvation causes overpopulation, not the reverse. (JEL)

Duncan, E. R., ed., DIMENSIONS OF WORLD FOOD PROBLEMS, Iowa State University Press, 1977. Discussions focus on the myriad aspects of feeding an expanding population while fossil fuel supplies are being reduced. The authors theorize that the solution to world hunger lies in a three-part effort: increasing food production in food-deficient countries, distributing the food to hungry people, and setting up a workable system of world food reserves. (BPA)

Easter, K. William and Martin, Lee R., WATER RESOURCES PROBLEMS IN DEVELOPING COUNTRIES, Economic Development Center Bulletin No. 3, Minneapolis, University of Minnesota, July 1977.

Food and Agricultural Organization, FOOD AND NUTRITION, Vol. I, No. 1, 1975, pp. 8-43.

Gish, O., "Health Planning in Developing Countries," Journal of Development Studies, Vol. 6, No. 4, July 1970.

Iowa State University, THE WORLD FOOD CONFERENCE OF 1976, June 27-July 1, 1977, Ames, Iowa State University Press, 1977.

Khanna, C. L., "A New Look at the World Food Problem," Economic Affairs, Vol. 16, No. 11, November 1971.

May, Jacques M., THE ECOLOGY OF MALNUTRITION IN EASTERN AFRICA AND FOUR COUNTRIES OF WESTERN AFRICA, New York, Hafner Publishing Company, 1970.

Mayer, Jean, "Coping with Famine," Foreign Affairs, Vol. 53, No. 1, October 1974.

Mayer, Jean, "The Dimensions of Human Hunger,"
    Scientific American, September 1976.

National Academy of Sciences, WORLD FOOD AND NUTRI-
    TION STUDY, Washington, D.C., National Academy
    of Sciences Printing and Publishing Office,
    1977. This final report of the World Food and
    Nutrition Study concludes that the worst as-
    pects of widespread hunger and malnutrition can
    be overcome within one generation. However,
    success will depend upon how effectively we
    undertake four major tasks: (1) increasing the
    supply of the right kinds of food where it is
    needed, (2) reducing poverty, (3) improving the
    stability of food supplies, and (4) decreasing
    the rate of population growth. (FA)

National Research Council, WORLD FOOD AND NUTRITION
    STUDY, Washington, D.C., National Academy of
    Sciences, 1977.

Poleman, Thomas T. and Freebairn, Donald K., Eds.,
    FOOD POPULATION AND EMPLOYMENT: The Impact of
    the Green Revolution, New York, Washington and
    London, Praeger Publishers, 1973.

Post, John D., THE LAST GREAT SUBSISTENCE CRISIS IN
    THE WESTERN WORLD, Baltimore, Maryland, Johns
    Hopkins University Press, 1977.

Reutlinger, Shlomo and Selowsky, Marcelo, MALNUTRI-
    TION AND POVERTY: Magnitude and Policy Options,
    Baltimore, Maryland, Johns Hopkins University
    Press, 1976. This study assesses the character
    and magnitude of nutritional deficiency in the
    developing countries and analyzes the cost
    effectiveness of selected policy instruments in
    reducing the deficiencies. The implications of
    projected growth in per capita calorie consump-
    tion on projected calorie deficits among
    lower-income groups are explored, followed by
    an evaluation in urban and age-specific dimen-
    sions of nutritional deficiency. Comparisons
    of food subsidies, food stamp programs, and
    direct income transfers suggest the likely need
    for programs targeted toward special groups
    among the population. (BPA)

Reutlinger, Shlomo and Selowsky, Marcelo, AN OVER-
VIEW OF: Malnutrition and Poverty: Magnitude
and Policy Options, World Bank Staff Occasional
Papers, No. 23, 1976.

Schertz, Lyle P., "World Food: Prices and the
Poor," Foreign Affairs, Vol. 52, No. 3, April
1974.

Schmitt, Bernard A., and Canterbery, Ray, PROTEIN,
CALORIES, AND DEVELOPMENT: Nutritional Variables in the Economics of Developing Countries,
Boulder, Colorado, Westview Press, 1978. Production of world food supplies is related to
more complicated socioeconomic variables than
have previously been analyzed. Besides traditional inputs of land, labor, and fertilizer,
technological capabilities and a variety of
nutritional and other human capital components
are significant independent variables in explaining agricultural production in the developing world. The integration of economic analyses with the concepts of nutritional science
offers an expanded and effective means for
analyzing the complex problems of agricultural
production in nutritionally deficient countries.
(BPA)

Sharman, A., "Nutrition and Social Planning," Journal
of Development Studies, Vol. 6, No. 4, July
1970.

Simon, Paul and Authur, THE POLITICS OF WORLD HUNGER:
Grass-Roots Politics and World Poverty, New
York, Harper's Magazine Press, 1973.

Sinha, Radha, FOOD AND POVERTY: The Political
Economy of Confrontation, New York, Holmes &
Meier, 1976. Examines the programs undertaken
in developing countries (mainly Asian) from the
viewpoint of internal and international inequalities and inequities. The book discusses
the world food problem and food productions;
employment creation; land reform; credit and
marketing problems; development assistance.
(BPA)

Srivastava, Uma K.; Heady, Earl D.; Rogers, Keith D.;
and Mayer, Leo V., FOOD AID AND INTERNATIONAL
ECONOMIC GROWTH, Ames, Iowa State University
Press, 1975. This reference quantifies the

effects of previous food aid programs on development, producer and consumer welfare, agricultural progress, and fiscal structures in recipient countries.

Talbot, Ross B., THE WORLD FOOD PROBLEM AND U.S. FOOD POLITICS AND POLICIES 1977 (A Readings Book), Ames, Iowa State University Press, 1978. This volume reviews 1977 developments, exploring the continuing causes and dimensions of the world food problem, the role of international institutions seeking to alleviate it, and policy directions adopted by the United States. (BPA)

Talbot, Ross B., THE WORLD FOOD PROBLEM AND U.S. FOOD POLITICS AND POLICIES, 1972-1976, Ames, Iowa State University Press, 1977. This collection of readings reviews the various international institutions that have recently been set up to aid in the alleviation of major world food problems. Provides an overview of the current U.S. food policy. (BPA)

Taylor, Lance; Sarris, Alexander; and Abbott, Philip C., GRAIN RESERVES, EMERGENCY RELIEF, AND FOOD AID, Washington, D.C., Overseas Development Council, 1977. Using quantitative analysis, the authors provide estimates in answer to the following policy questions: What are the costs and benefits of a grain reserve program? How large does a buffer stock need to be? How much reduction in price fluctuations could be expected? Which countries would gain and which (if any) would lose from buffer stocks? What would be the effects on producers and the effects on consumers? What would be the appropriate principle for buffer stock operation? How should the financial costs of grain reserves be shared across countries? (BPA)

United Nations, REPORT OF THE WORLD FOOD CONFERENCE, Rome, 5-6 November 1974, New York, United Nations, 1975.

U.S. Department of H.E.W., SOCIAL SECURITY PROGRAMS THROUGHOUT THE WORLD, 1973, DHEW Publication No. (SSA) 74-11801.

World Bank, HEALTH, Sector Policy Paper, March 1975.

World Food Institute of Iowa State University, PROCEEDINGS OF THE WORLD FOOD CONFERENCE OF 1976, Ames, Iowa State University, 1977. A publication detailing the proceedings of the World Food Conference held at Iowa State University. Papers focus on production, processing, distribution and utilization of food, adequate nutrition, and related world problems.

Import Substitution

X-REF: BRAZIL: Lowinger, Morley, EMPLOYMENT: Tyler, INDIA: Krueger, INDONESIA: Talmer, INDUSTRIAL DEVELOPMENT: Donges, KOREA: Suh, MEXICO: Aspa.

Alexander, Robert J., A NEW DEVELOPMENT STRATEGY, Maryknoll, New York, Orbis Books, 1976. Focusing on the demand side of the development equation, this monograph concerns itself with an economic development strategy of import substitution where industries are established to manufacture products for which a home market has already been created by imports. Analyzing the effect on development of this assured demand, and exploring the limit to which this strategy can be used, the author looks in detail at the prerequisites for the use of this method (substantial imports and protection for newly created industries) and discusses the priorities for private and public investment in this phase. (JEL)

Ayza, Juan, INTEGRACIÓN ECONÓMICA Y SUBSTITUCIÓN DE IMPORTACIONES EN AMÉRICA Latina (co-authors Gerard Fichet and Norbetto Gonzales), Mexico, Fondo de Cultura Economica, 1975.

Baer, Werner, "Import Substitution and Industrialization in Latin America: Experiences and Interpretations," Latin American Research Review, Vol. VII, No. 1, Spring 1972.

Bruton, Henry J., EMPLOYMENT, PRODUCTIVITY, AND IMPORT SUBSTITUTION, Research Memorandum #44, Williamstown, Massachusetts, Williams College Center for Development Economics, 1972.

Bruton, Henry J., EXPORT GROWTH AND IMPORT SUBSTITU-
TION, Research Memorandum #22, Williamstown,
Massachusetts, Williams College Center for
Development Economics, 1968.

Bruton, Henry J., IMPORT SUBSTITUTION AND PRODUC-
TIVITY GROWTH, Research Memorandum #13,
Williamstown, Massachusetts, Williams College
Center for Development Economics, 1967.

Bruton, Henry J., THE IMPORT SUBSTITUTION STRATEGY
OF ECONOMIC DEVELOPMENT: A Survey of Findings,
Research Memorandum #27, Williamstown, Massachusetts, Williams College Center for Development Economics, April 1969.

Bruton, Henry J., LATIN AMERICAN EXPORTS AND IMPORTS
SUBSTITUTION POLICIES, Research Memorandum #32,
Williamstown, Massachusetts, Williams College
Center for Development Economics, 1969.

Clark, Peter B., PLANNING IMPORT SUBSTITUTION, contributions to Economic Analysis, Vol. 68,
Amsterdam and London, North-Holland, 1970.
"The primary objective of this book is to intro-
duce some of the important theoretical developments of growth theory into operational terms
for use by development planners." "A secondary
objective ... is to evaluate what the impact of
import substitution will be on a typical developing economy at an early stage of industrialization." Appendix; index. (JEL)

Cukor, Gyorgy, THE ROLE OF IMPORT SUBSTITUTION AND
EXPORT DEVELOPMENT IN THE INDUSTRIALIZATION OF
DEVELOPING COUNTRIES, Budapest, Hungary, Center
for Afro-Asian Research of the Hungarian Academy
of Sciences, 1970.

Hirschman, Albert C., "The Political Economy of
Import-Substituting Industrialization in Latin
America," The Quarterly Journal of Economics,
February 1968, p. 1.

Lacroix, J. L., THE CONCEPT OF IMPORT SUBSTITUTION
IN THE THEORY OF ECONOMIC DEVELOPMENT, United
Nations, Economic and Social Council, December
1965.

Lewis, Stephen Richmond, ON A MEASURABLE MODEL
"SUCCESSFUL" IMPORT SUBSTITUTION, Research
Memorandum #7, Williamstown, Massachusetts,
Williams College Center for Development Eco-
nomics, 1967.

Maitra, P., "Import-Substitution and Changing Import
Structure in an Underdeveloped Country,"
Economic Affairs, Vol. 15, No. 4, April 1970.

Power, John Henry, IMPORT SUBSTITUTION AS AN INDUS-
TRIALIZATION STRATEGY, Research Memorandum #2,
Williamstown, Massachusetts, Williams College
Center for Development Economics, 1966.

Robock, S. H., "Industrialization Through Import-
Substitution or Export Industries: A False
Dichotomy," in Markham, Jesse William and
Papanek, Gustav, INDUSTRIAL ORGANIZATION AND
ECONOMIC DEVELOPMENT, in honor of E. S. Mason,
Boston, Massachusetts, Houghton Mifflin, 1970.

Schydlowsky, Daniel M., FROM IMPORT SUBSTITUTION TO
EXPORT PROMOTION FOR SEMI-GROWN-UP INDUSTRIES:
A POLICY PROPOSAL, Report No. 54, Cambridge,
Massachusetts, Harvard University Center for
International Affairs, Development Advisory
Service, typewritten, no date.

Sheahan, John, IMPORT SUBSTITUTION AND THE TERMS OF
TRADE WITH ASSOCIATED NOTE ON INVESTMENT CRI-
TERIA FOR IMPORT SUBSTITUTION (by Henry Bruton),
Research Memorandum #28, Williamstown, Massa-
chusetts, Williams College Center for Develop-
ment Economics, 1969.

Sheahan, John, IMPORT SUBSTITUTION AND ECONOMIC
POLICY: A Second Review, Research Memorandum
#50, Williamstown, Massachusetts, Williams Col-
lege Center for Development Economics, 1972.

Sheahan, John, TRADE AND EMPLOYMENT: INDUSTRIAL
EXPORTS COMPARED TO IMPORTS SUBSTITUTION IN
MEXICO, Research Memorandum #43, Williamstown,
Massachusetts, Williams College Center for De-
velopment Economics, 1971.

Steel, William F., and Shilling, John D., IMPORT
    LICENSING AND IMPORT SUBSTITUTION IN GHANA IN
    THE 1960s, Research Memorandum #19, Williams-
    town, Massachusetts, Williams College Center
    for Development Economics, 1968.

Syed, Hasan Ali, MANUFACTURE OF CAPITAL GOODS: Pros-
    pective Costs of Imports Substitution, Publica-
    tion #145, Lahore, Pakistan, Board of Economic
    Enquiry, 1970.

Tyler, W. G., LABOR ABSORPTION WITH IMPORT SUBSTITUT-
    ING INDUSTRIALIZATION: An Examination of
    Elasticities of Substitution in the Brazilian
    Manufacturing Sector, Kiel Discussion Papers
    #24, Kiel, West Germany, Kiel Institute of
    World Economics, October 1972.

Winston, Gordon Chester, A PRELIMINARY SURVEY OF
    IMPORT SUBSTITUTION, Research Memorandum #1,
    Williamstown, Massachusetts, Williams College
    Center for Development Economics, 1965.

Income Distribution, Principles

X-REF: AGRICULTURAL CREDIT: Abercrombie, AGRICUL-
TURAL DEVELOPMENT: Weeks, ASIA: Oshima, BRAZIL:
Fields, Fishlow, COLOMBIA: Berry, Gillis, Jallade
Thirsk, CUBA: Ritter, ECUADOR: Tokman, EDUCATION:
Bhagwati, Fields, Ritzen, EMPLOYMENT: Cairncross,
Cohn, Ilo, FISCAL MONETARY INFLATION: Krzyzaniak,
INDIA: Nafziger, Ojha, Srinivasan, INDONESIA:
Gupta, LATIN AMERICA: Foxley, Musgrove, Weisskoff,
MEXICO: Cole, Stewart, NIGERIA: Etim, Fajana,
PAKISTAN: Griffin, PERU: Van Den Berghe, Webb,
PHILIPPINES: Rodgers, POPULATION: Kogut, PUERTO
RICO: Maldonado, Weisskoff, REGIONAL DEVELOPMENT:
Mera, RURAL DEVELOPMENT: Thirsk, TECHNOLOGY: Lele,
TURKEY: Krzyzaniak, URBAN DEVELOPMENT: Ilo,
ZIMBABWE: Clarke.

Adelman, Irma and Morris, Cynthia Taft, AN ANATOMY
    OF INCOME DISTRIBUTION PATTERNS IN DEVELOPING
    NATIONS--A Summary of Findings, Economic Staff
    Working Paper No. 116, International Bank for
    Reconstruction and Development, International
    Development Association, September 1971.

Adelman, Irma and Morris, Cynthia Taft, ECONOMIC
GROWTH AND SOCIAL EQUITY IN DEVELOPING COUN-
TRIES, Stanford, California, Stanford University Press, 1973. "A quantitative investigation of the interactions among economic
growth, political participation, and the
distribution of income in noncommunist developing nations." The study is based on data
(presented in the earlier study, Society,
Politics, and Economic Development) from 74
countries which is given in the form "of 48
qualitative measures of the (countries) social,
economic, and political characteristics," and
it includes the use of discriminant analysis in
an examination of the forces tending to increase political participation and the use of
"a stepwise analysis of variance technique" in
analyzing the distribution of income. Index.
(JEL)

Adelman, I., "Growth, Income Distribution and
Equity-Oriented Development Strategies," World
Development, Vol. 3, Nos. 2 and 3, February-
March 1975. Recent findings suggest that the
initial impact of economic development on
political participation and on the relative
share of the poor in national income is to
decrease both. Even in absolute and long-run
terms, the prospects for increasing human welfare through conventional development programs
are questionable. This paper draws on these
findings together with the recent historical
experience of several developing countries to
suggest that equitable growth requires a
radical reorientation of development strategies. (JEL)

Adelman, I.; Morris, C. T.; Robinson, S., "Policies
for Equitable Growth," World Development, Vol.
4, No. 7, July 1976.

Adler, John H., "Development and Income Distribution," Finance and Development, Vol. 10, No. 3,
September 1973, pp. 2-5.

Ahluwalia, Montek S., "Income Distribution and
Development: Some Stylized Facts," American
Economic Review, Vol. 66, No. 2, May 1976.

Ahluwalia, Montek S., "Income Inequality: Some
    Dimensions of the Problem," Finance and
    Development, Vol. 11, No. 3, September 1974,
    pp. 2-8, and 41.

Ahluwalia, Montek S., "Inequality, Poverty and
    Development," Journal of Development Economics,
    Vol. 3, No. 4, December 1976.

Atkinson, A. B., and Harrison, A. J., DISTRIBUTION
    OF PERSONAL WEALTH IN BRITAIN, Cambridge,
    Cambridge University Press, 1978. The authors
    document the shares of the top wealth groups,
    how they have changed over the past 50 years,
    and analyze the underlying social and economic
    forces. (BPA)

Atkinson, A. B., THE ECONOMICS OF INEQUALITY, New
    York, Oxford University Press; Clarendon Press,
    1975. The author is concerned with the distri-
    bution of income and wealth; the explanation of
    the observed differences; and the impact of
    government resources in their redistribution.
    (JEL)

Atkinson, Anthony B., ed., THE PERSONAL DISTRIBUTION
    OF INCOMES, Boulder, Colorado, Westview Press,
    1976.

Battalio, Raymond C.; Kagel, John H.; and Reynolds,
    Morgan O., "Income Distributions in Two Experi-
    mental Economices, Journal of Political Economy,
    Vol. 85, No. 6, 1977.

Berry, A., "Changing Income Distribution Under
    Development: Colombia," Review of Income and
    Wealth, Vol. 20, No. 3, September 1974,
    pp. 289-316.

Blinder, Alan S., TOWARD AN ECONOMIC THEORY OF
    INCOME DISTRIBUTION, Cambridge, Massachusetts,
    MIT Press, 1974. In this study, Blinder devel-
    ops, tests and uses a microeconomic simulation
    model of the distribution of income and wealth
    in the United States in order to suggest some
    answers to a number of questions pertaining to
    the causes, and possible alleviation, of
    inequality. (BPA)

Chenery, Hollis, et al., REDISTRIBUTION WITH GROWTH:
Policies to Improve Income Distribution in
Developing Countries in the Context of Economic
Growth, London and New York, Oxford University
Press for the World Bank and the Institute of
Development Studies, University of Sussex,
1974. Joint study brings together policy-
makers and researchers to enumerate the problems of concentrated growth vs. income redistribution in the development process and
suggest solutions. Thirteen previously unpublished essays and an annex of six individual
country experiences (plus an overview) are
arranged in three parts. There is a general
emphasis on the importance of poverty alleviation as a major planning objective, mention-
ing that "although growth tends initially to be
concentrated in a few sectors of the economy,
with little effect on major poverty groups, a
number of countries have devised policies for
offsetting this tendency so that the benefits
of growth can be shared more equally." Bibliography; no index. (JEL)

Chiswick, B. R., "Earnings Inequality and Economic
Development," Quarterly Journal of Economics,
February Vol. 85, No. 1, February 1971, pp. 21-
39. A human capital model is used theoretic-
ally and empirically (cross-sectional international data) to examine the effects of development on earnings inequality. The analysis
predicts that inequality is positively related
to the level and inequality of training and
rates of return from training, and the rate of
growth of output. The effect of development on
these parameters is examined. (JEL)

Chiswick, Barry R., INCOME INEQUALITY: Regional
Analyses Within a Human Capital Framework,
Human Behavior and Social Institutions 4, New
York, National Bureau of Economic Research,
distributed by Columbia University Press, New
York, 1974. Part A of the book discusses the
determinants of income distribution in very
general terms for the nontechnical reader.
Part B examines the link between years of
schooling and the distribution of income for
adult males. The analysis is at two levels of
disaggregation: one within regions, the other
between regions. The author's hypothesis is
that income inequality is directly related to

the inequality of schooling and is greater the higher the rate of return from schooling. Part C presents a discussion of state differences in the level and inequality of income for all males, and for white and nonwhite males. Bibliography; index. (JEL)

Chiswick, Carmel Ullman, "On Estimating Earnings Functions for LDCs," World Bank Reprint Series #44, reprinted from the Journal of Development Economics, 3, 1976.

Cline, W. R., "Distribution and Development: A Survey of Literature," and Adelman, I. and Morris, C. Taft, "Distribution and Development: A Comment," Journal of Development Economics, Vol. 1, No. 4, February 1975.

Cline, William R., POTENTIAL EFFECTS OF INCOME REDISTRIBUTION ON ECONOMIC GROWTH: Latin American Cases, Praeger Special Studies in International Economics and Development, New York and London, Praeger, 1972. The book examines "the theoretical arguments concerning income redistribution's predicted effect on economic growth and uses simulation analysis for Latin American cases to estimate the empirical importance of each major influence proposed on a basis of theory." (JEL)

Elliott, C., "Income Distribution and Social Stratification: Some Notes on Theory and Practice," Journal of Development Studies, Vol. 8, No. 3, April 1972.

Fei, J. C.; Ranis, G.; and Kuo, S. W. Y., "Growth and the Family Distribution of Income," Quarterly Journal of Economics, February 1978. This article provides a framework for analyzing the relationship between growth and family income distribution in development. Household data for Taiwan are deployed to illustrate a technique for decomposing the overall inequality of total income patterns into the inequality and relative importance of additive factor income components. (JEL)

Foxley, Alejandro, ed., INCOME DISTRIBUTION IN LATIN AMERICA, Cambridge, New York and Melbourne, Cambridge University Press, 1976. Eleven papers, six previously published, dealing with

the distributional effects of economic growth
in the following Latin American countries:
Argentina, Brazil, Chile, Colombia, Cuba,
Mexico, Puerto Rico, Peru, and Venezuela.
(JEL)

Foxley, Alejandro and Munoz, Oscar, "Income Redistribution Economic Growth and Social Structure:
The Case of Chile," Oxford Bulletin of Economics and Statistics, Vol. 36, No. 1, 1974,
pp. 21-44.

Foxley, Alejandro, ed., LECTURAS: Distribución del
ingreso, Serie dirigida por Oscar Soberón M.,
Mexico, Fondo de Cultura Económica, 1974. A
collection of fourteen papers, all but one of
which are previously unpublished, analyzing
income distribution patterns and policies in
developing countries, particularly in Latin
America. There is a general econometric
analysis of the evidence on income distribution
in poor countries and then there are six papers
on income distribution in various countries and
regions. (JEL)

Frank, Charles R., Jr., and Webb, Richard C., eds.,
INCOME DISTRIBUTION AND GROWTH IN THE LESS-
DEVELOPED COUNTRIES, Washington, D.C., Brookings Institution, 1977. Fourteen previously
unpublished essays representing part of the
results of a project undertaken jointly by the
Brookings Institution and the Woodrow Wilson
School of Public and International Affairs at
Princeton University, dealing with the relation
between income distribution and economic growth
in the developing countries. (JEL)

Gupta, S., "The Role of the Public Sector in Reduc-
ing Regional Income Disparity in Indian Plans,"
Journal of Development Studies, Vol. 9, No. 2,
January 1973.

Horowitz, Irving, ed., EQUITY, INCOME, AND POLICY,
New York, Praeger, 1977. Compares policy making in the U.S., USSR, Scandinavia, and Third
World nations as illustrative of capitalist,
communist, social democratic, and mixed modes
of achieving equity. Policies of these systems
are discussed and the methods, costs, and
benefits of achieving equity are compared.

Concludes that equity will no longer result as an automatic consequence of economic growth. (BPA)

Jaksch, H. J., "Income Distribution as an Objective in Development Planning," De Economist, Vol. 122, No. 1, 1974, pp. 1-22. Here, we assume that the policy-maker does not know his preference function but constructs its relevant parts in a communication process with his adviser. This process converges to a (classwise) Pareto-optimal distribution vector, and under some further assumptions, any such vector may be attained in principle. (JEL)

Kravis, Irving B., "International Differences in the Distribution of Income," The Review of Economics and Statistics, Vol. XLII, No. 4, November 1960, pp. 408-416.

Lal, D., "Distribution and Development: A Review Article," World Development, Vol. 4, No. 9, September 1976.

Lampman, Robert J., "Transfer Approaches to Distribution Policy," American Economic Review, Vol. LX, No. 2, May 1970.

Laumas, G. S. and Laumas, P. S., "The Permament Income Hypothesis in an Underdeveloped Economy," Journal of Development Economics, Vol. 3, No. 3, September 1976.

Lecaillon, J. and Germidis, D., "Income Differentials and the Dynamics of Development," International Labor Review, Vol. 114, No. 1, July-August 1976, pp. 27-42.

Loehr, William and Powelson, John P., eds., ECONOMIC DEVELOPMENT, POVERTY, AND INCOME DISTRIBUTION, Westview Special Studies in Social Political, and Economic Development, Boulder, Colorado, Westview Press, 1977. Twelve previously unpublished papers by economists and sociologists on the income gap in developing countries, originally presented at a 1976 conference sponsored by the Institute of Behavioral Science at the University of Colorado, held at Estes Park, Colorado. (JEL)

Looney, Robert E., INCOME DISTRIBUTION POLICIES AND
ECONOMIC GROWTH IN SEMI-INDUSTRIALIZED COUN-
TRIES: A Comparative Study of Iran, Mexico,
Brazil, and South Korea, Praeger Special Studies
in International Economics and Development, New
York, Praeger, 1975. Mexico, Iran, Brazil, and
South Korea are examined to determine whether
increasing income disparities can be prevented
while high rates of economic growth are sustained. These countries, excluding South Korea
have emphasized production for the domestic
market, supporting this policy with tariffs,
exchange controls, overvalued exchange rates,
subsidized credit, and low taxes. South Korea
emphasized production for the world market,
with few external controls. Both strategies resulted in high rates of growth. In Mexico,
Brazil, and Iran there was increased inequality
in the distribution of income; in South Korea
income distribution remained fairly stable. The
author examines the implications of these findings. Bibliography; no index. (JEL)

Mellor, John W., "Food Price Policy and Income Distribution in Low-Income Countries," Economic
Development and Cultural Change, Vol. 27, No.
1, October 1978.

Metcalf, Charles E., AN ECONOMETRIC MODEL OF THE
INCOME DISTRIBUTION, a volume in the Institute
for Research on Poverty Monograph Series, New
York, Academic Press, 1972.

Millar, Jayne C., FOCUSING ON GLOBAL POVERTY AND
DEVELOPMENT; a resource book for educators,
Washington, D.C., Overseas Development Council,
1974.

Myrdal, G., "Growth and Social Justice," World
Development, Vol. 1, Nos. 3-4, April 1973, pp.
119-120. A short article in which the traditional conflict between growth and equality of
income distribution is questioned, particularly
in the context of developing countries. The
devotion of resources to "consumption--i.e.
non-productive-investment," contrary to conventional theory, is not necessarily inimical to
growth; it may rather be the key to faster
growth. (JEL)

Okun, Arthur M., EQUALITY AND EFFICIENCY: The Big
    Tradeoff, Washington, D.C., Brookings Institu-
    tion, 1975. The book examines the scope of
    economic policies designed to reduce inequality
    without impairing efficiency. It focuses on
    national institutions and problems, reflecting
    the values, judgments, and experience of the
    author. The role of the market in promoting
    efficiency is emphasized. The author outlines
    the arguments in favor of market capitalism,
    comparing the merits of this system with those
    obtainable under socialism. He argues that
    efficiency and equality can be increased if
    inequalities of opportunity are removed, citing
    examples of racial and sexual discrimination.
    Index. (JEL)

Oshima, Harry T., "The International Comparison of
    Size Distribution of Family Incomes with Spe-
    cial Reference to Asia," The Review of Eco-
    nomics and Statistics, Vol. XLIV, No. 4,
    November 1962, pp. 439-445.

Paglin, M., "The Measurement and Trend of Inequality:
    A Basic Revision," American Economic Review,
    Vol. LXV, No. 4, September 1975. Takes into
    account age structure as a factor in income
    distribution. (Ed)

Pasinetti, Luigi L., GROWTH AND INCOME DISTRIBUTION:
    Essays in Economic Theory, London, Cambridge
    University Press, 1974.

Paukert, Felix, "Income Distribution at Different
    Levels of Development: A Survey of Evidence,"
    The International Labour Review, Vol. 108, Nos.
    2-3, August/September 1973, pp. 97-126.

Pryor, Frederic L., THE ORIGINS OF THE ECONOMY: A
    Comparative Study of Distribution in Primitive
    and Peasant Economies, New York, Academic
    Press, 1977. The author carries out a cross-
    cultural comparison of distribution in sixty
    primitive and peasant societies. He employs
    the analytical techniques of economics to
    explore systematically a large number of hypo-
    theses drawn from anthropology, economics,
    history, and sociology. (BPA)

Robinson, Sherman, "A Note on the U Hypothesis
    Relating Income Inequality and Economic Devel-
    opment," The American Economic Review, Vol. 66,
    No. 3, June 1976.

Robinson, Sherman, "Toward an Adequate Long-Run
    Model of Income Distribution and Economic
    Development," American Economic Review, Vol.
    66, No. 2, May 1976.

Sahota, Gian Singh, "Theories of Personal Income
    Distribution: A Survey," Journal of Economic
    Literature, Vol. XVI, March 1978, pp. 1-55.

Schultz, T. Paul, "Long-Term Changes in Personal
    Income Distribution: Theoretical Approaches,
    Evidence and Explanations," American Economic
    Review, Vol. LXII, No. 2, May 1972.

Shourie, Arun, GROWTH, POVERTY AND INEQUALITIES,
    World Bank Reprint Series, #5, reprinted from
    Foreign Affairs, January 1973.

Singer, H. W., "Dualism Revisited: A New Approach
    to the Problems of the Dual Society in Develop-
    ing Countries," Journal of Development Studies,
    Vol. 7, No. 1, October 1970.

Stoikov, Vladimir, "How Misleading are Income Dis-
    tributions?" The Journal on Research on Income
    and Wealth, Vol. 21, No. 2, June 1975, pp. 239-
    250.

Tinbergen, Jan, INCOME DISTRIBUTION: Analysis and
    Policies, Amsterdam and Oxford, North-Holland;
    New York, American Elsevier, 1975.

United Nations, INCOME DISTRIBUTION IN LATIN
    AMERICA, New York, United Nations, 1971.

Vaitsos, Constantine V., INTERCOUNTRY INCOME DISTRI-
    BUTION AND TRANSNATIONAL ENTERPRISES, London,
    Clarendon Press, distributed by Oxford Univer-
    sity Press, New York, 1974.

Van Ginneken, Wouter, RURAL AND URBAN INCOME INEQUAL-
    ITIES IN INDONESIA, MEXICO, PAKISTAN, TANZANIA
    AND TUNISIA, A WEP Study, Geneva, International
    Labour Office, 1976. Provides a general descrip-
    tion of the five countries and examines income
    inequalities in each: country-wide inequality,

inequality in urban areas and rural areas, and inequality between areas. (JEL)

Ward, R. J., "Aspects of the Income Inequality Problem in the Less Developed Country," Economic Internazionale, Vol. 25, No. 1, February 1972. The degree of inequality in LDC's may not exceed that which existed in developed countries in comparable stages of development, but structural rigidities in less developed countries offer more serious obstacles. (JEL)

Webb, Richard and Frank, Charles Jr., INCOME DISTRIBUTION IN LESS DEVELOPED COUNTRIES: Policy Alternatives and Design, Princeton University-Brookings Institution,May 1975.

Webb, Richard C., WAGE POLICIES AND INCOME DISTRIBUTION IN DEVELOPING COUNTRIES (with the assistance of Carl Dahlman and Louka, Papaefotratiou), Princeton, New Jersey, 1974 (prepared for the Princeton-Brookings Income Distribution Study).

Wiles, Peter, DISTRIBUTION OF INCOME: EAST AND WEST, from the lectures of Professor Dr. F. De Vries, Oxford, North-Holland Publishing Co., 1974.

Income Distribution Statistics and Measurement

Bentzel, Ragnar, "The Social Significance of Income Distribution Statistics," Review of Income and Wealth, Vol. 16, No. 3, September 1970, pp. 253-264.

Champernowne, D. G., "A Comparison of Measures of Inequality of Income Distribution," Economic Journal, Vol. 84, No. 336, December 1974, pp. 787-816. The paper discusses the results of an investigation of the comparative performance of six general indexes of inequality and two indexes of special aspects of inequality when tried out on over a hundred theoretical income distributions. (JEL)

Cowell, F. A., MEASURING INEQUALITY: Techniques for
the Social Sciences, New York, Wiley, Halsted
Press, 1977. Discusses theoretical and practical problems involved in the techniques of
inequality measurement. Specification of an
individual social unit (persons), description
of particular personal attributes (incomes),
and method of representation and/or aggregation
of the allocation of "income" among the "persons" in a given population are indicated as
the essential ingredients of a "Principle of
Inequality Measurement" and are discussed in
the test. Assumes basic knowledge of algebra.
Mathematical appendix. Index. (JEL)

Dahiya, L. N., "Some Evidence of Economic Inequalities in India," Economic Affairs, Vol. 16, No.
6, June 1971.

Dich, Jorgen S., "On the Possibility of Measuring
the Distribution of Personal Income," The
Review of Income and Wealth, Vol. 16, No. 3,
September 1970, pp. 265-272.

Jain, Shail, SIZE DISTRIBUTION OF INCOME: A Compilation of Data, Washington, D.C., A World
Bank Publication, 1975. A comprehensive set of
data on income distributions in many countries;
compilation of studies done by World Bank and
others; percentile distributions, gini coefficients, and other measures. (Ed)

Kuznets, Simon, "Quantitative Aspects of the Economic Growth of Nations," Economic Development
and Cultural Change, Vol. XI, No. 2, Part II,
January 1963.

Morgan, James, "The Anatomy of Income Distribution,"
The Review of Economics and Statistics, Vol.
XLIV, No. 3, August 1962, pp. 270-283.

Paukert, F., "Income Distribution at Different
Levels of Development: A Survey of Evidence,"
International Labour Review, Vol. 108, Nos. 2-
3, August-September 1973.

Pyatt, Graham, "On the Interpretation and Disaggre-
gation of Gini Coefficients," reprinted from
The Economic Journal, World Bank Reprint Series,
No. 38, June 1976.

Pyatt, Graham, "On International Comparisons of
    Inequality," The American Economic Review, Vol.
    67, No. 1, February 1977, pp. 71-75.

Roberti, Paolo, "Income Distribution: A Time-Series
    and a Cross-Sectional Study," The Economic
    Journal, Vol. 84, No. 335, September 1974, pp.
    629-638.

Soligo, Ronald and Land, James W., MODELS OF DEVEL-
    OPMENT INCORPORATING DISTRIBUTION ASPECTS,
    Paper No. 22, Houston, Texas, Rice University,
    Program of Development Studies, 1972.

United Nations Economic and Social Council, A DRAFT
    COMPLEMENTARY SYSTEM OF STATISTICS ON THE DIS-
    TRIBUTION OF INCOME AND WEALTH, New York,
    United Nations, 1969.

Indicators

Banks, A., and Textor, R., A CROSS-POLITY SURVEY,
    Cambridge, Massachusetts, Harvard University
    Press, 1963.

Baster, Nancy, MEASURING DEVELOPMENT: The Role and
    Adequacy of Development Indicators, London,
    Frank Cass, 1972.

Berle, A. A. Jr., "What GNP Doesn't Tell Us," Satur-
    day Review, August 31, 1968.

Blades, Derek W., NON-MONETARY (SUBSISTENCE) ACTIV-
    ITIES IN THE NATIONAL ACCOUNTS OF DEVELOPING
    COUNTRIES, OECD Publishing Center, July 1975.

ILO, HOUSEHOLD INCOME AND EXPENDITURE STATISTICS,
    1960-1972, Vol. I: Africa, Asia, Latin America
    (covering 45 countries); Vol. II: Northern
    America, Europe and USSR, Oceania (covering 32
    countries), Geneva.

Kendrick, John W., THE HISTORICAL DEVELOPMENT OF
    NATIONAL-INCOME ACCOUNTS, reprinted from The
    History of Political Economy, Vol. 2, No. 2,
    Fall 1970.

Kravis, Irving B.; Heston, Alan; and Summers, Robert, INTERNATIONAL COMPARISONS OF REAL PRODUCT AND PURCHASING POWER, Baltimore, Maryland, Johns Hopkins (for the World Bank), 1978. This second installment of a major U.N. World Bank survey digs deeply into the real value of production and income in 165 countries during the 1970s. Valuable in itself, it is a cautionary tale for those who confuse exchange rates with purchasing power. (FA)

Kravis, Irving B.; Kenessey, Zoltan; Heston, Alan; and Summers, Robert, A SYSTEM OF INTERNATIONAL COMPARISONS OF GROSS PRODUCT AND PURCHASING POWER, Baltimore, Maryland, Johns Hopkins University Press, 1978. A companion to the preceding volume. (Ed)

Kuznets, Simon, ECONOMIC GROWTH OF NATIONS: Total Output and Production Structure, Cambridge, Massachusetts, Harvard University Press, 1971. A volume on the long-term economic growth of nations. The author reviews and summarizes in seven chapters the long-term trends in the growth of aggregate output and changes in the production structure in a number of major developed countries. (JEL)

Kuznets, Simon, MODERN ECONOMIC GROWTH: Rate, Structure and Spread, New Haven, Connecticut, Yale University Press, 1966.

Organization for Economic Cooperation and Development, "Social Indicators," in OECD Observer, No. 64, June 1973, pp. 36-7.

Pyatt, Graham, and Roe, Alan, SOCIAL ACCOUNTING FOR DEVELOPMENT PLANNING, New York, Cambridge University Press, 1977. This book develops a system of national accounts which is designed to capture a complete statistical picture of the questions of growth and inequality. The system is applied to Sri Lanka and shown to be practical using the data available in developing countries. (BPA)

Russett, B., et al., WORLD HANDBOOK OF POLITICAL AND SOCIAL INDICATORS, New Haven, Connecticut, Yale University Press, 1964.

Sheldon, Eleanor and Moore, Wilbert E., INDICATORS
    OF SOCIAL CHANGE: Concepts and Measurement,
    New York, Russell Sage Foundation, 1968.

UNESCO, THE USE OF SOCIO-ECONOMIC INDICATORS IN
    DEVELOPMENT PLANNING, New York, 1976. This
    volume considers such indicators as: popula-
    tion; health and nutrition; housing and envi-
    ronment; education and culture; employment,
    working conditions, and social security; social
    welfare; income, consumption, and wealth. (BPA)

UNESCO, INDICATORS OF SOCIAL AND ECONOMIC CHANGE AND
    THEIR APPLICATIONS, New York, 1977. In April,
    1976, the first meeting of experts specifically
    dealing with indicators of social and economic
    change was held and one of the papers presented
    there on "Human needs, human rights and the
    theories of development" now constitutes the
    first part of this publication. Part two of
    this report cites case studies with an applica-
    tion of territorial indicators as an input in
    the development planning process. (BPA)

U.N., TOWARDS A SYSTEM OF SOCIAL AND DEMOGRAPHIC
    STATISTICS, New York, U.N., 1975. Technical
    report on a system of social and demographic
    statistics to cover: world and regional popu-
    lation; density and urbanization; consumption;
    natural resources and environment; families,
    social class, income, leisure; social security
    and welfare series; education; health; public
    order and safety. (BPA)

United Nations Research Institute for Social Devel-
    opment, CONTENTS AND MEASUREMENT OF SOCIO-ECO-
    NOMIC DEVELOPMENT, Geneva, 1970, (Report No.
    70.10).

World Bank, WORLD ECONOMIC AND SOCIAL INDICATORS,
    May-June 1977, Report No. 700/77/04.

Industrial Development

X-REF: CHILE: Kirsch, CHINA: Andors, Sigundson,
EAST AFRICA: Pearson, EGYPT: Abed, Barbour,
BRAZIL: Baer, Tyler, EMPLOYMENT: Mehta, Morowetz,
IRAQ: Jalal, PUERTO RICO: Holbik.

Adler, John H., INTERNATIONAL DEVELOPMENT 1968: Accomplishments and Apprehensions, Dobbs Ferry, New York, Oceana Publications, Inc., 1969.

Ashton, T. S., THE INDUSTRIAL REVOLUTION 1760-1830, London, New York, and Toronto, Oxford University Press, 1948.

Baranson, Jack, INDUSTRIAL TECHNOLOGIES FOR DEVELOPING ECONOMIES, New York, Praeger, 1969.

Carnoy, Martin, INDUSTRIALIZATION IN A LATIN AMERICAN COMMON MARKET, Washington, Brookings Institution, 1972. Research institutions in ten Latin American countries and the United States have combined efforts to devise a method of showing where industries can be most economically located (and how to estimate the cost of locating them elsewhere). The method is then tried out on six industries. (FA)

Chenery, Hollis B., THE INTERNATIONAL DIVISION OF LABOR: THE CASE OF INDUSTRY, World Bank Reprint Series, Number 11, 1976.

Collier, David, "Industrialization and Authoritarianism in Latin America," Items, Vol. 31/32, No. 4/1, March 1978, New York.

Cukor, Gyorgy, STRATEGIES FOR INDUSTRIALIZATION IN DEVELOPING COUNTRIES, New York, St. Martin's Press, 1974. Translation from the Hungarian of a 1971 study. After describing the interrelation between the development of agriculture, industrial development, and economic growth, the author analyzes three problems of strategy: size of plant, choice of technology, and import substitution and export promotion. The role of government and planning, past and future industrial growth in developing countries, the experience of industrialization in the European socialist countries are then particularly discussed. (JEL)

Donges, J. B., "A Comparative Survey of Industrialization Policies in Fifteen Semi-Industrial Countries," Weltwirtsch. Arch., Vol. 112, No. 4, 1976, pp. 626-659. The survey is based on the policy-making experience of Brazil, Colombia, Egypt, Hong Kong, India, Israel, Korea (South), Malaysia, Mexico, Pakistan, Singapore,

103

Spain, Taiwan, Turkey, and Yugoslavia. It is
shown that import substitution policies played
a prominent role even beyond the early phases
of industrialization, with the exception of
Hong Kong, Malaysia, and Singapore. (JEL)

Hensley, R. J., "Industrial Organization and Economic Development," Econ. Int., Vol. 28, Nos.
3-4, August-November 1975, pp. 356-377. This
paper explores some of the possible ways in
which isolation and analysis of certain key
economic structure, economic behavior, and
economic performance variables might be used
more effectively to extend development theory
and policy. This would seem to apply to the
various blends of planning and markets that
characterize most of the less developed economies. (JEL)

Markham, J. W., and Papanek, G. F., INDUSTRIAL OR-
GANIZATION AND ECONOMIC DEVELOPMENT, Boston,
Massachusetts, Houghton Mifflin Co., 1970.

Needham, Douglas, ECONOMIC ANALYSIS AND INDUSTRIAL
STRUCTURE, New York, London and Toronto, Holt,
Rinehart and Winston, Inc., 1969.

Niho, Y., "The Role of Capital Accumulation in the
Industrialization of a Labor Surplus Economy:
A Formulation of the Fei-Ranis Model," Journal
of Development Economics, Vol. 3, No. 2, July
1976.

Resnick, Stephen A., THE DECLINE OF RURAL INDUSTRY
UNDER EXPORT EXPANSION: A Comparison Among
Burma, Philippines, and Thailand, 1870-1938,
Center Paper #147, New Haven, Connecticut, Yale
University, Economic Growth Center, 1970.

Stepanek, Joseph E., NEW PERSPECTIVES: Industrial
Development in the Third World, Austria, Institute of Research in Education and Development,
1972.

Sutcliffe, R. B., INDUSTRY AND UNDERDEVELOPMENT,
READINGS, Reading, Massachusetts, Addison-
Wesley Publishing, 1971.

Teubal, M., "Heavy and Light Industry in Economic Development," American Economic Review, Vol. 63, No. 4, September 1973, pp. 588-596. The paper analyzes some resource allocation implications of factor accumulation and country size in the context of a three sector (agriculture, heavy industry, light industry), two factor (capital, labor) neoclassical model with agriculture subject to decreasing returns. Conditions are given for light industry or heavy industry to be optimal initial stages of industrialization. The analysis is carried out in the context of an open, small economy model of international trade. Elementary calculus and diagrams are used in the proofs. (JEL)

Van Roy, E., "The 'Industrial Organization' of a Pre-Industrial Economy, and Some Development Implications," Journal of Development Studies, Vol. 7, No. 1, October 1970.

World Bank, INDUSTRY, Sector Working Paper, April 1972.

International Economics

Baldwin, Robert E., NONTARIFF DISTORTIONS OF INTERNATIONAL TRADE, Washington, D.C., The Brookings Institution, 1970.

Balogh, T. and Balacs, P., "Fact and Fancy in International Economic Relations," World Development, Vol. 1, Nos. 3-4, March-April 1973.

Bergsten, C. Fred and Krause, Lawrence B., Eds., WORLD POLITICS AND INTERNATIONAL ECONOMICS, Washington, D.C., The Brookings Institution, 1975.

Bhagwati, Jagdish N., and Krueger, Anne O., "Exchange Control, Liberalization, and Economic Development," The American Economic Review, Vol. LXIII, No. 2, May 1973.

Chenery, Hollis B., "Restructuring the World Economy," Foreign Affairs, Vol. 53, January 1975.

Cline, William R., INTERNATIONAL MONETARY REFORM AND
THE DEVELOPING COUNTRIES, Washington, D.C., the
Brookings Institution, 1976. Remarkably comprehensive for its length, this analysis tells
LDCs they have more to gain from flexible rates
than they thought and less from "the link" than
they hoped. (FA)

Diaz-Alejandro, Carlos F., "International Markets
for LDCs--The Old and The New," The American
Economic Review, Vol. 68, No. 2, May 1978.

di Marco, Luis Eugenio, ed., INTERNATIONAL ECONOMICS
AND DEVELOPMENT: Essays in Honor of Raul
Prebisch, New York, Academic Press, 1972. A
Collection of 23 original essays, written by
economists from many parts of the world, in
honor of Raul Prebisch. (JEL)

Fleming, J. Marcus, ESSAYS IN INTERNATIONAL ECONOM-
ICS, Cambridge, Massachusetts, Harvard University Press, 1971. The Deputy Director of
Research of the International Monetary Fund,
who was formerly a British civil servant, has
written many first-rate articles linking economic theory and practice. Those in this
volume deal largely with import restrictions,
liquidity and exchange rates. (FA)

Holsen, John A. and Waelbroeck, Jean L., "The Less
Developed Countries and the International Monetary Mechanism," American Economic Review, Vol.
66, No. 2, May 1976.

Johnson, Harry G., INTERNATIONAL TRADE AND ECONOMIC
GROWTH: Studies in Pure Theory, London, George
Allen & Unwin Ltd., 1958.

Kindleberger, Charles P., FOREIGN TRADE AND THE
NATIONAL ECONOMY, New Haven, Connecticut, and
London, Yale University Press, 1962.

Manickavasagam, J., "International Trade and Less
Developed Countries," Economic Affairs, Vol.
19, No. 4, April 1974.

McCulloch, Rachel, and Pinera, Jose, "Trade as Aid:
The Political Economy of Tariff Preferences for
Developing Countries," The American Economic
Review, Vol. 67, No. 5, December 1977.

Meier, Gerald M., EMPLOYMENT, TRADE, AND DEVELOP-
MENT: A Problem in International Policy Analysis, International Economics Series, No. 4,
Leiden, Sijthoff for Institut Universitaire de
Hautes Etudes Internationales, Geneva, 1977.
Extension of three lectures delivered at the
Institut Universitaire de Hautes Etudes Internationales in Geneva in 1974. Lecture one is a
study of the problem of absorption of surplus
labor in LDC's, and lecture two comments on the
potential of alleviating this unemployment
problem via implementation of policies of
North-South economic cooperation. The final
selection analyzes the policy issues of employment and development. (JEL)

Meier, Gerald M., THE INTERNATIONAL ECONOMICS OF
DEVELOPMENT: Theory and Policy, New York,
Evanston and London, Harper and Row, Publishers,
1968.

Meier, Gerald M., PROBLEMS OF COOPERATION FOR DEVEL-
OPMENT, New York, London and Toronto, Oxford
University Press, 1974.

Meier, Gerald M., PROBLEMS OF TRADE POLICY, New
York, Oxford University Press, 1973.

Surr, John V., "The Committee of Twenty," Finance
and Development, Vol. 11, No. 2, June 1974.

United Nations, THE FUTURE OF THE WORLD ECONOMY,
New York, United Nations, 1976.

U.S. Government Printing Office, INTERNATIONAL ECO-
NOMIC REPORT OF THE PRESIDENT, Washington,
D.C., U.S. Government Printing Office, trans-
mitted to the Congress each year.

Viner, Jacob, STUDIES IN THE THEORY OF INTERNATIONAL
TRADE, New York and London, Harper and Brothers,
Publishers, 1937.

Issues

Bauer, P. T., DISSENT ON DEVELOPMENT: Studies and
Debates in Development Economics, Cambridge,
Massachusetts, Harvard University Press, 1972.
A collection of previously published articles,

essays, and book reviews, dealing with various
theoretical and empirical issues in economic
development. Part One ("Ideology and Experience") examines general problems of concept,
method, analysis, historical experience and
policy in economic development, such as the
vicious circle of poverty, the widening gap,
central planning, foreign aid, Marxism, etc.
Part Two ("Case Studies") features five of the
author's studies on developing countries, particularly Nigeria and India. Part Three ("Review Articles") brings book reviews on well
known books. Index. (JEL)

Club of Rome: Meadows, Donella H.; Meadows, Dennis
L.; Randers, Jorgen; and Behrens, William W.,
THE LIMITS TO GROWTH: A Report for the Club of
Rome's Project on the Predicament of Mankind,
Washington, D.C., Potomac Associates Book,
Signet Book, 1972.

Cole, H. S. D., et al., eds., MODELS OF DOOM: A
Critique of the Limits to Growth, New York,
Universe Books, 1973. A multidisciplinary team
at the University of Sussex finds the Club of
Rome's report "not good enough"--to put it
mildly. To close critical analyses of data,
models and methods ("Malthus in, Malthus out")
are added some interesting essays relating the
new approach to economic theory, environmen-
talism, technocracy, the history of population
predictions and other relevant matters. A
spirited response by the authors of the original report makes the volume a major contribution to the continuing debate. (FA)

Haq, Mahbub ul, "The Limits to Growth: A Critique,"
Finance and Development, Vol. 9, No. 4, December 1972.

Havens, Eugene, METHODOLOGICAL ISSUES IN THE STUDY
OF DEVELOPMENT, LTC Reprint No. 100, Madison,
University of Wisconsin, Land Tenure Center,
1972.

Hirschman, Albert O., THE STRATEGY OF ECONOMIC
DEVELOPMENT, New Haven, Connecticut, Yale University Press, 1959.

Meadows, Dennis L., ed., ALTERNATIVES TO GROWTH--I: A Search for Sustainable Futures, Cambridge, Ballinger, 1978. The propagators of The Limits to Growth should be applauded for trying to work out ways for society to live in a stable state. The discussions in this collection range from global food and energy systems to backyard microfarms. There is good material on decentralization, fairly standard stuff on planning, and some interesting efforts to deal with equity and the market. (FA)

Meadows, Donella H., et al., THE LIMITS TO GROWTH, New York, Universe Books, 1972. The Club of Rome's little doomsday book. The controversy about it will enter a second stage when the data underlying its dramatic conclusions are released, and a third stage when global generalizations are brought closer to the levels of regions and nations. (FA)

Mesavoric, Mihaljo, and Pestel, Edward, MANKIND AT THE TURNING POINT: The Second Report To The Club of Rome, New York, Dutton/Reader's Digest Press, 1974. The quest for an alternative to the deadly endings traced in Limits to Growth has produced a more sophisticated computer model. While stressing global interdependence, this one deals separately with regions and permits the testing of a variety of assumptions. The results reported here still point to danger, but make a case for "differentiated growth," international cooperation, and coordinated action across a wide front. (FA)

Millikan, Max F., and Rostow, W. W., A PROPOSAL: Key to an Effective Foreign Policy, New York, Harper Brothers, 1957.

Psilos, Diomedes D.; Halevi, Nadev; Kawano, Shigeto; and Mitani, Katsumi, ECONOMIC DEVELOPMENT ISSUES: Greece, Israel, Taiwan, Thailand, Washington, D.C., CED, 1968. Four economists seek to identify the key factors that have stimulated or inhibited growth in selected countries. (BPA)

Stern, N. H., "Professor Bauer on Development: A Review Article," Journal of Development Economics, Vol. 1, No. 3, December 1974.

Ward, Richard J., DEVELOPMENT ISSUES FOR THE 1970's,
    Foreword by William S. Gaud, New York, Dun-
    ellen, 1973. An assessment of "key issues and
    problems which emerged from the Decade of
    Development and which will continue to absorb
    the attention of students of development in the
    present decade." The book is divided into
    three parts: "Food and Human Welfare," "De-
    velopment Problems for This Decade," and
    "Planning Programs and Strategies." The
    chapters specifically discuss such issues as
    labor absorption in agriculture, means of
    population control, the burden of debt service,
    the role of foreign aid, big-push development,
    etc. Index. (JEL)

Militarism

X-REF: BRAZIL: Stepan, ECUADOR: Fitch, VENEZUELA:
Burggraaff.

Benoit, Emile, DEFENSE AND ECONOMIC GROWTH IN DE-
    VELOPING COUNTRIES: Studies in International
    Development and Economics, Lexington, Massachu-
    setts, Heath; Lexington Books, 1973. A study
    of the effects of national defense budgets on
    growth in developing countries exclusively.
    The author uses multiple regression analysis on
    1950-65 data for 44 countries. Results are
    checked through partial regression analysis.
    The findings suggest that the size of defense
    spending relative to GDP is positively, rather
    than inversely, correlated to the rate of
    growth of the economy. No index. (JEL)

Fidel, Kenneth, MILITARISM IN DEVELOPING COUNTRIES,
    New Brunswick, New Jersey, Transaction Books,
    1975.

Johnson, John J., THE MILITARY AND SOCIETY IN LATIN
    AMERICA, Stanford, California, Stanford Univer-
    sity Press, 1974.

Lieuwen, Edwin, ARMS AND POLITICS IN LATIN AMERICA,
    New York, Praeger, Inc., 1960.

Lowenthal, Abraham F., ed., ARMIES AND POLITICS IN
    LATIN AMERICA, New York, Holmes and Meier,
    1976. Military involvement in politics is now

seen as a many-faceted phenomenon, far more
complicated than earlier simplistic analyses
indicated. These 12 essays explore the subtle-
ties, and stress the relationship of the
"military institutions themselves to the social
context in which they operate," and the nature
and extent of the institutionalization of the
civilian political process. (FA)

Schmitter, Philippe C., ed., MILITARY RULE IN LATIN
AMERICA: Function, Consequences, and Perspectives, Beverly Hills, California, Sage Publications, 1973. Five lengthy essays explore the
changing functions and characteristics of military rule, the consequences of these tendencies, and future prospects for arms control and
praetorian governments. (FA)

Simon, Sheldon W., THE MILITARY AND SECURITY IN THE
THIRD WORLD: Domestic and International Impacts, Boulder, Colorado: Westview Press,
1978. This book explores two of the most
important dimensions of the military as an
institution in Third World politics: its role
in domestic power structures and internal
development, and its impact on the formation
and execution of the security aspects of foreign policy. These internal and external
orientations are compared here across selected
Third World countries in Asia, Africa, and
Latin America. (BPA)

Solaun, Mauricio and Quinn, Michael A., SINNERS AND
HERETICS: The Politics of Military Intervention in Latin America, Urbana, Illinois: University of Illinois Press, 1973. The Latin
American coup d'etat in the period 1943 to 1967
is dissected through intricate analysis of 30
examples, in an effort to define a framework
and isolate the core of the process. The inquiry brings in the relevant social and cultural characteristics. (FA)

Miscellaneous

Adelman, I. and Morris, C. T., "Analysis-of-Variance
Techniques for the Study of Economic Develop-
ment," Journal of Development Studies, Vol. 8,
No. 1, October 1971.

Adelman, Irma, "Development Economics--A Reassessment of Goals," American Economic Review, Vol.
LXV, No. 2, May 1975.

Adelman, I., "On the State of Development Economics,"
Journal of Development Economics, Vol. 1, No.
1, June 1974.

Adelman, Irma and Morris, Cynthia Taft, SOCIETY,
POLITICS AND ECONOMIC DEVELOPMENT: A Quantitative Approach, Baltimore, Johns Hopkins Press,
1967.

Adler, John H., ABSORPTIVE CAPACITY: The Concept
and Its Determinants, Brookings Staff Paper,
Washington, D.C., The Brookings Institution,
June 1965.

Alatas, Syed Hussein, INTELLECTUALS IN DEVELOPING
SOCIETIES, London, Frank Cass, 1977. The
author examines the role of the intellectuals
in various developing societies, and, finding
serious shortcomings in their performance,
analyses the sources and causes of this inade-
quacy. (BPA)

Alexander, Robert J., A NEW DEVELOPMENT STRATEGY,
Maryknoll, New York, Orbis Books, 1976.

Alpert, Paul, PARTNERSHIP OF CONFRONTATION? Poor
Lands and Rich, New York, Free Press, 1973.
Argues that the central political and economic
conflict in the world has shifted from a conflict of ideologies between East and West
toward one between the richly developed countries of the North and the poorer nations of
the South. The author, Chief of Training
Programs in the Field of Technical Assistance
of the United Nations Institute for Training
and Research, analyzes the internal problems of
development and considers the questions of why
and how the developed countries should contribute to the economic growth of the South.
Index. (JEL)

Basch, Antonin, A PRAGMATIC APPROACH TO ECONOMIC
DEVELOPMENT, New York, Vantage, 1970. A non-
theoretical approach to development issues
based largely on the author's own experiences
in Asia and Latin America. The book's assumption is that outside forces cannot provide all

of the conditions necessary for growth; too
much emphasis has been placed on the role of
foreign aid and foreign capital. Index. (JEL)

Birnberg, Thomas B. and Resnick, Stephen A., COLONI-
AL DEVELOPMENT: An Econometric Study, New
Haven, Connecticut, Yale University Press,
1975.

Boserup, Ester, WOMAN'S ROLE IN ECONOMIC DEVELOP-
MENT, New York, St. Martin's Press, 1970.
Investigates the changes in the traditional
division of labor between the sexes; contends
the changes were initiated by the development
process and conditioned by the socio-cultural
milieu of the area in transition. This study
reflects the experience of some 34 countries in
Africa, the Mid-East, South and East Asia, and
Latin America. The patterns of these changes
and their impact in development are examined.
(JEL)

Boulding, Kenneth E., "The Puzzle of the North-South
Differential," Southern Humanities Review, Vol.
10, No. 2, Spring 1976. Delivered at Auburn
University, as one of the Franklin Lectures in
the Sciences and Humanities. (Ed)

Chenery, Hollis and Syrquin, Moises, PATTERNS OF
DEVELOPMENT, 1950-1970, assisted by Hazel
Elkington, New York, Oxford University Press
for World Bank, 1975. Examines "principal
changes in economic structure that normally
accompany economic growth," focusing on "resource mobilization and allocation, particularly those aspects needed to sustain further
growth." These aspects are treated in a uniform econometric framework "to provide a
consistent description of a number of inter-
related types of structural change and also to
identify systematic differences in development
patterns among countries that are following
different development strategies." Bibliography; index. (JEL)

Chenery, Hollis B., "The Structuralist Approach to
Development Policy," American Economic Review,
Vol. LXV, No. 2, May 1975.

Child, Sarah, POVERTY AND AFFLUENCE: An Introduction to the International Relations of Rich and Poor Economies, New York, Schocken Books, 1970. Describes the structure of the western industrialized, communist, and underdeveloped countries and outlines their historical development in the first nine chapters. The last six chapters discuss the major problems of the world economy and consider approaches to solutions. Addressed to layman. Index. (JEL)

Culbertson, John V., ECONOMIC DEVELOPMENT: An Ecological Approach, New York, Alfred A. Knopf, 1971. Descriptive exposition of the determinants of the standard of living and the "relation of population growth and environmental destruction" to this standard. A chapter in the book surveys and examines inter alia Rostow's important theory of economic development. Index. (JEL)

DaGregori, Thomas R. and Pi-Sunyer, Oriol, ECONOMIC DEVELOPMENT: The Cultural Context, New York, Wiley, 1969.

Davis, Lance E. and North, Douglass C., INSTITUTIONAL CHANGE AND AMERICAN ECONOMIC GROWTH, New York, Cambridge University Press, 1972.

Day, Richard H., and Singh, Inderjit, ECONOMIC DEVELOPMENT AS AN ADAPTIVE PROCESS, New York, Cambridge University Press, 1977. A recursive programming model is developed as an approximation to adaptive theory and used to simulate recent Punjab agricultural development and to project its future course to 1980. Thus a detailed quantitative chronicle of input utilization, capital-labor substitution, technological change, growing productivity and structural change in the seasonal and aggregate demand for labor is generated.

deVries, Barend A., "The Plight of Small Countries," Finance and Development, Vol. 10, No. 3, September 1973, pp. 6-8, 634.

Dunn, Edgar S., Jr., ECONOMIC AND SOCIAL DEVELOPMENT: A Process of Social Learning, Baltimore, Maryland, Johns Hopkins Press for Resources for the Future, Inc., 1971. An economist's analysis of "human problem solving seen as a process

of social learning." The author reviews the
principal characteristics of the modern syn-
thetic theory of evolution while establishing
"the sense in which it functions as a learning
system"; he then attempts to identify the
peculiarities of social evolution and development, hoping to reach an understanding of the
components of social learning. (JEL)

Farmanfarmaian, Khodadad, ed., THE SOCIAL SCIENCES
    AND PROBLEMS ON DEVELOPMENT: Papers Presented
    at an International Conference in Persepolis,
    Iraq, June 1-4, 1974, Princeton Studies on the
    Near East, Princeton, New Jersey: Princeton
    University Program in Near Eastern Studies,
    1976. Seventeen conference papers. The first
    eight papers consider general aspects of devel-
    opment including social, historical, economic,
    and political development. The remaining
    papers deal with development in Iran including
    the transfer of technology, the role of in-
    formation, land reform, migration, medical
    change, the effect on the urban family and a
    macroeconomic projection for Iran. No index.
    (JEL)

Field, Mark G., ed., SOCIAL CONSEQUENCES OF MODERNI-
    ZATION IN COMMUNIST COUNTRIES, Baltimore,
    Maryland, Johns Hopkins, 1976. "Guided or
    directed or managed modernization" is different
    from the non-communist brand. But how differ-
    ent? And what happens in the process to the
    party that directs the modernization? These
    papers have some careful and some stimulating
    answers to suggest. (FA)

Geiger, Theodore, THE CONFLICTED RELATIONSHIP: The
    West and the Transformation of Asia, Africa,
    and Latin America, for Council of Foreign
    Relations, by McGraw-Hill, 1967.

Goulet, Denis, THE CRUEL CHOICE: A New Concept in
    the Theory of Development, Center for the Study
    of Development and Social Change, Cambridge,
    Massachusetts, New York, Atheneum, 1971. This
    work is intended to probe moral dilemmas faced
    by economic and social development. Its cen-
    tral concern is that philosophical conceptions
    about the "good life" and the "good society"
    should be of more profound importance in
    assessing alternative paths to development than

115

economic, political, or technological questions. The theoretical analysis is based on two concepts: "vulnerability" and "existence rationality." Index. (JEL)

Haberler, Gottfried, ECONOMIC GROWTH AND STABILITY: An Analysis of Economic Change and Policies, Los Angeles, California, Nash Publishing, 1974.

Helleiner, G. K., ed., A WORLD DIVIDED: The Less Developed Countries in the International Economy, New York, Cambridge University Press, 1976. Distinguished international economists and policymakers consider the practical alternatives open to the less developed countries in relations with the rich nations. (BPA)

Horowitz, Irving L., THREE WORLDS OF DEVELOPMENT: The Theory and Practice of International Stratification, New York, Oxford University Press, 1972.

Horvat, B., "The Relation Between Rate of Growth and Level of Development," Journal of Development Studies, Vol. 10, No. 3-4, April-July 1974.

Hoyle, B. S., ed., TRANSPORT AND DEVELOPMENT IN THE LESS DEVELOPED COUNTRIES, New York, Harper and Row, 1973.

Janossy, Ferenc, THE END OF THE ECONOMIC MIRACLE: Appearance and Reality in Economic Development, White Plains, New York, International Arts and Sciences Press, Inc., 1971. Dr. Janossy seeks to demonstrate that all postwar "miracles" lasted only until the actual level of production reached the position that would have been obtained had there been no war. He draws the conclusion that the trend of economic development arches over any distortion with surprising constancy. (BPA)

Kalecki, Michal, ESSAYS ON DEVELOPING ECONOMIES, Introduction by Joan Robinson, Highlands, New Jersey, Humanities Press, 1976. A collection of eleven essays (mostly written in the 1960's). All essays were previously published, but not always in English and were not heretofore easily available. They cover three areas: (1) economic problems of underdeveloped non-Socialist economies, (2) financing economic develop-

116

ment; (3) case studies of specific problems in Israel, Cuba, Bolivia, and the Third World. Index. (JEL)

Kamarck, Andrew M., THE TROPICS AND ECONOMIC DEVELOPMENT: A Provocative Inquiry into the Poverty of Nations, Baltimore, Maryland and London, The Johns Hopkins University Press for the World Bank, 1976. This study focuses on the role of climate in economic development. Outlines the major characteristics of the tropical climates and examines their adverse effects on agriculture and economic development. (JEL)

Kahn, Herman, WORLD ECONOMIC DEVELOPMENT, Boulder, Colorado, Westview Press, 1979. Starting from the premise that both population and production growth will slow because of natural forces, Kahn and his colleagues criticize the current conventional wisdom. Do not stop growth, they argue. If the hungry are to be fed, the third world must industrialize; advanced or at least appropriate technology must be employed. (BPA)

Kristensen, Thorkil, DEVELOPMENT IN RICH AND POOR COUNTRIES: A General Theory with Statistical Analyses, Praeger Special Studies in International Economics and Development, New York, Praeger, 1974. Provides a first step towards a more comprehensive approach to development, namely that an understanding of the development process requires the study of the economic, social, political, and cultural aspects of development. The accumulation of knowledge is viewed as a dominant force in development, therefore, knowledge is treated as a separate factor of production. (JEL)

Lecomber, Richard, ECONOMIC GROWTH VERSUS THE ENVIRONMENT, New York, Wiley, Halsted Press, 1975. Attempts to explain the group of controversies related to the arrangement of national policy priorities between GNP growth and environmental quality. Surveys the pro- and antigrowth literature. Discusses the inadequacies of GNP as an index of welfare and examines two attempts to construct a more satisfactory measure. Appendix, bibliography; no index. (JEL)

Lewis, W. Arthur, "A Review of Economic Development,"
American Economic Review, Vol. LV, No. 2, May
1965.

Maddison, Angus, ECONOMIC PROGRESS AND POLICY IN
DEVELOPING COUNTRIES, New York, Norton, 1971.
(FA) Taking the knell-ringers firmly in hand,
a leading student of economic growth shows that
there has been not only economic improvement in
the poor countries but a better understanding
of their problems and how to deal with them.
He assesses the relative contribution of development policy and foreign aid to growth and
sets out recommendations for doing better in
the future. (FA)

Maitra, P., "Concept of Economic Development--Re-Ex-
amined," Economic Affairs, Vol. 17, No. 1-2,
January-February 1972.

Meier, Gerald M., PROBLEMS OF COOPERATION FOR DE-
VELOPMENT, New York, Oxford University Press,
1974.

Moyer, Reed, and Hollander, Stanley C., eds., MAR-
KETS AND MARKETING IN DEVELOPING COUNTRIES,
Homewood, Illinois, Richard D. Irwin Inc.,
1968.

Nash, Manning, ESSAYS ON ECONOMIC DEVELOPMENT AND
CULTURAL CHANGE IN HONOR OF BERT F. HOSELITZ,
Economic Development and Cultural Change,Vol.
25, Supplement, Chicago, Illinois, University
of Chicago, 1977.

Owens, Edgar, and Shaw, Robert, DEVELOPMENT RECON-
SIDERED, Lexington, Massachusetts, Lexington
Books, D. C. Heath and Co., 1974.

Pincus, J. A., editor, RESHAPING THE WORLD ECONOMY:
Rich and Poor Countries, Englewood Cliffs, New
Jersey, Prentice-Hall, 1968.

Powelson, John P., INSTITUTIONS OF ECONOMIC GROWTH:
A Theory of Conflict Management in Developing
Countries, Princeton, New Jersey, Princeton
University Press, 1972. Author develops a
general theory of institution-building for
economic growth using some developing countries
in Latin America as his foundation for expound-
ing its mechanism. The book is in two parts:

Part I introduces and summarizes a theory of
institutions which is discussed in detail in
two key chapters as a microeconomic theory and
a macroeconomic theory of institution building;
Part II dwells on the implications of the
theory and outlines its potential contribution
to the theory of economic growth. Appendix;
index.(JEL)

Prachowny, Martin F., SMALL OPEN ECONOMIES, Lexington, Massachusetts, Lexington Books, 1975.

Ranis, Gustav, ed., THE GAP BETWEEN RICH AND POOR
NATIONS: Proceedings of a Conference held by
the International Economic Association at Bled,
Yugoslavia, International Economic Association
Publication, London, Macmillan; New York, St.
Martin's, 1972. Part I ("The Size and Consequences of the Gap"), Part II ("International
Flows and their Effects on the Gap") has papers
on foreign aid, overseas investment, trade
policies, the technology gap, the multinational
firm, and the brain drain, Part III ("The Outlook"), Sir Arthur Lewis sums up the objectives
and prognostications for the future. (JEL)

Resnick, Stephen A., "State of Development Economics," American Economic Review, Vol. LXV,
No. 2, May 1975.

Reynolds, Lloyd G., THE CONTENT OF DEVELOPMENT
ECONOMICS, Center Paper #136, New Haven, Con-
necticut, Yale University, Economic Growth
Center, 1969.

Reynolds, Lloyd G., IMAGE AND REALITY IN ECONOMIC
DEVELOPMENT, New Haven, Yale University Press,
Yale University Economic Growth Center Series,
1977. Outlines the current perceptions of the
economics of development, defining the core of
the field as the author sees it. Part one sets
out the theoretical concepts of development,
including discussion of agriculture; a model of
a closed economy; and growth, trade, and technological and capital transfer in an open
economy. (JEL)

Reynolds, Lloyd G., THE THREE WORLDS OF ECONOMICS,
New Haven, Connecticut, Yale University Press,
1971.

Rimmer, Douglas, MACROMANCY: The Ideology of "Development Economics," London, Institute of Economic Affairs, 1973.

Robinson, Ronald, ed., DEVELOPING THE THIRD WORLD: The Experience of the Nineteen-Sixties, Cambridge Commonwealth Series, New York, Cambridge University Press, 1971. Contains selections from the annual meetings of the Cambridge Conferences on Development attended by general administrators and technical specialists from all parts of the world. The 23 chapters are papers of two kinds: 1) individual statements of an issue, written from a technical point of view to indicate topics for discussion; and 2) extracts from the "Argument" of the conference written by the editor, who was also chairman of the Conference. The chapters focus on a general perspective, industrialization, rural development, the role of government, and aid. Index. (JEL)

Saunders, Robert J. and Warford, Jeremy J., EQUITY WITH RESPONSIBILITY IN VILLAGE WATER SUPPLY, an overview of Village Water Supply: Economics and Policy in the Developing World, World Bank, Baltimore, Maryland, Johns Hopkins University Press, 1976.

Scott, George M., ACCOUNTING AND DEVELOPING NATIONS, International Business Series, No. 9, studies in accounting, Seattle, University of Washington, International Accounting Studies Institute and the Graduate School of Business Administration, 1970. Focuses on enterprise accounting as an aid to economic development. Deals with: the status, environment and information-gathering process of accounting in developing nations; some accounting experiences of advanced nations; and a framework termed "economic evaluation accounting" for suggested use in developing nations. No index. (JEL)

Seers, D. and Joy, L., eds., DEVELOPMENT IN A DIVIDED WORLD, Middlesex, England, Penguin, 1971.

Seers, Dudley, "Why Visiting Economists Fail," Journal of Political Economy, Vol. LXX, No. 4, August 1962.

Singer, Hans W. and Ansari, Javed A., RICH AND POOR
COUNTRIES, Studies in Economics, No. 12, Baltimore, Maryland and London, Johns Hopkins
University Press, 1977. Part one describes the
structure of international economy and the
nature of development process. Part two discusses the importance of the international
trade sector to development in the poorer
countries and reviews the trade policies of the
rich and poor countries. Part three deals with
the role of aid in the development process; and
part four is concerned with international
factor movement. (JEL)

Singer, H. W., THE STRATEGY OF INTERNATIONAL DEVEL-
OPMENT: ESSAYS IN THE ECONOMICS OF BACKWARD-
NESS, edited by Sir Alec Cairncross and Mohinder Puri, White Plains, New York, International Arts and Sciences Press, 1975. After
two decades of productive activity at the
United Nations, Mr. Singer continues to concern
himself with development problems at the University of Sussex, England. In these papers he
deals with a dozen or more central and difficult issues. (FA)

Stewart, I. G., ed., ECONOMIC DEVELOPMENT AND STRUC-
TURAL CHANGE, Edinburgh, Scotland, Edinburgh
University Press; Chicago, Aldine, 1969. Contains eleven papers from a spring 1968 conference at the University of Edinburgh. Contributors are H. Myint on trade, education, and
development, A. I. MacBean on trade and development planning; P. Ady on commodity agreements; R. M. Stern on financing foreign aid; W.
T. Newlyn on monetary policy; T. D. Williams on
Malawi; W. B. Reddaway on Ghana; J. B. K.
Hunter on Kenya; A. R. Prest on the finances of
small countries; S. Hymer and S. Resnick on
public and private interplay; and D. Wall on
the second UNCTAD conference. Index. (JEL)

Streeten, Paul, THE FRONTIERS OF DEVELOPMENT STUDIES,
New York, John Wiley & Sons, 1972. A collection of mostly previously published (but all to
some degree revised) essays on issues in the
theory and practice of economic development.
The papers included deal with development
theories, the use of economic models, problems
in the planning of growth, the role of international trade, investment, and aid, problems

in the world transfer of technology, the relationship between the lesser and more developed countries, etc. Index. (JEL)

Tinker, Irene, and Bramsen, Michele Bo, WOMEN AND WORLD DEVELOPMENT, Washington, D.C., Overseas Development Council. A collection of various papers on women and development, presented at the World Conference of International Women's Year in Mexico City, 1975. The final appendix provides a detailed analysis of the conference. (Ed)

Wall, David, ed., CHICAGO ESSAYS IN ECONOMIC DEVELOPMENT, Chicago, University of Chicago Press, 1972. Fifteen reprinted essays by six eminent University of Chicago economists. They are arranged around three focal points; "General · Features of developing economies," "Domestic policy" (in developing countries), and "Trade and aid." As one would expect there is a judicious mixture of theory and empirical consideration in each of the selected essays. Index. (JEL)

Wallman, Sandra, ed., PERCEPTIONS OF DEVELOPMENT, New York, Cambridge University Press, 1977. Dealing directly with the perceptions of non-expert, ordinary people, this volume will be of interest to those with a professional or academic interest in development problems. (BPA)

Ward, Barbara, et al., eds., THE WIDENING GAP: Development in the 1970's, New York, Columbia University Press, 1971. Out of a mountain of paper generated for a major conference, the editors have fashioned a readable book in which a number of authorities are permitted to delineate the major issues and often their conflicting views on what should be done. (FA)

Wilkinson, Richard G., POVERTY AND PROGRESS: An Ecological Perspective on Economic Development, introduction by Kenneth E. Boulding, New York, Praeger, 1973. Draws from anthropology, sociology, history, and economics to set forth "a new foundation of explicitly empirical theories of development." Argues that ecological disequilibrium is the spur to economic development. This approach contends that industrialization was forced upon societies by the increasing scarcity of all land-based resources for and thus "comes out of poverty, not out of plenty." Topics include a presentation of ecological model, cultural evolution, ecological equilibrium, disequilibrium, structure of development, English industrial revolution, innovation, the American experience, and explanations of underdevelopment. Index. (JEL)

World Bank, ENVIRONMENTAL, HEALTH AND HUMAN ECOLOGICAL CONSIDERATIONS IN ECONOMIC DEVELOPMENT PROJECTS, May 1974.

World Bank, INTEGRATING WOMEN INTO DEVELOPMENT, Washington, D.C., World Bank, August 1975.

World Bank, TRANSPORTATION, Sector Working Paper, January 1972.

World Bank, WORLD DEVELOPMENT REPORT, 1978, a World Bank Publication Summary, Washington, D.C., 1978.

Modernization

X-REF: ASIA: Evers, JAPAN: Marsh, POLITICAL DEVELOPMENT: Tachau.

Barringer, Herbert; Blanksten, George; and Mack, Rayment, eds., SOCIAL CHANGE IN DEVELOPING AREAS, Cambridge, Massachusetts, Schenkman, 1965.

Biesanz, John and Mavis, MODERN SOCIETY: An Introduction to Social Science, Englewood Cliffs, New Jersey, Prentice-Hall, Inc., 1968.

Brode, John, THE PROCESS OF MODERNIZATION: An Annotated Bibliography on the Socio-Cultural Aspects of Development, Cambridge, Massachusetts, Harvard University Press, 1969.

DeSouza, Anthony R. and Porter, Philip W., THE UNDERDEVELOPMENT AND MODERNIZATION OF THE THIRD WORLD, Washington, D.C., Association of American Geographers, Commission on College Geography, 1974.

123

Deutsch, Karl W., "Social Mobilization and Political Development," The American Political Science Review, Vol. LV, No. 3, September 1961, pp. 493-514.

Eaton, Joseph W., ed., INSTITUTION BUILDING AND DEVELOPMENT: From Concepts to Application, Beverly Hills, Sage Publications with cooperation of the Inter-University Research Program in Institution Building, 1972. A collection of ten original essays plus an introduction by the editor on the elements of, methodological issues in, strategies for, and guidelines to institution building and administrative change within the context of economic development. The essays provide a theoretical approach to conceptual issues in institution building as well as a guideline for field application of institution building and change. (JEL)

Erasmus, Charles J., MAN TAKES CONTROL: Cultural Development and American Aid, Minneapolis, Minnesota, University of Minnesota Press, 1961.

Etzioni, Amitai and Etzioni, Eva, ed., SOCIAL CHANGE: Sources Patterns and Consequences, New York and London, Basic Books, Inc., 1964. An excellent set of readings selected from among the "great books" on social change. (Ed)

Inkeles, Alex and Smith, David H., BECOMING MODERN: Individual Change in Six Developing Countries, Cambridge, Massachusetts, Harvard University Press, 1974. A study of characteristics of "modern individuals" and the development of a measure for "over-all modernity." (Ed)

Kahl, Joseph A., THE MEASUREMENT OF MODERNISM: A Study of Values in Brazil and Mexico, Austin, Texas, University of Texas Press, published for the Institute of Latin American Studies, 1968.

Lerner, Daniel, THE PASSING OF TRADITIONAL SOCIETY: Modernizing the Middle East, London, The Free Press of Glencoe, Collier-Macmillan Limited, 1958.

Masannet, George S., ed., THE DYNAMICS OF MODERNIZATION AND SOCIAL CHANGE: A Reader, Pacific Palisades, California, Goodyear Publishing Co., 1973.

Murray, Charles A., A BEHAVIORAL STUDY OF RURAL
    MODERNIZATION: Social and Economic Change in
    Thai Villages, New York, Praeger, 1977. Pre-
    senting an original causal model capable of
    measuring native response to rural development
    projects, this behavioral study demonstrates
    that acceptance and success of Thai moderniza-
    tion programs depends primarily on the economic
    environment in each village. Government at-
    tempts at modernization have emphasized the
    short-term developmental approach by promoting
    entrepreneurs projects at the expense of civil
    programs. Murray shows that, traditional
    values aside, Thai peasants will readily accept
    these innovative civic projects when some
    margin for loss exists. (BPA)

Smelser, Neil J., ed., SOCIAL STRUCTURE AND MOBILITY
    IN ECONOMIC DEVELOPMENT, Chicago, Aldine Pub-
    lishing, 1971.

Multinational Corporations

X-REF: CHILE: Moran, COLOMBIA: Lombard, CUBA:
Gordon, INCOME DISTRIBUTION, PRINCIPLES: Vaitsos,
IVORY COAST: Masini, JAPAN: Young, MALAYSIA: Lim,
MEXICO: Wright, MIDDLE EAST: Kapoor, PERU: Good-
sell, Pinelo, TECHNOLOGY: Thomas, Un, UGANDA:
Gerschenberg, ZAMBIA: Bostock, Sklar.

Agmon, Tamir and Kindleberger, Charles P., eds.,
    MULTINATIONALS FROM SMALL COUNTRIES, Cambridge,
    Massachusetts and London, MIT Press, 1977.
    Seven papers and related comments presented at
    conference sponsored by the Center for Interna-
    tional Studies and the Sloan School of Manage-
    ment held at the Massachusetts Institute of
    Technology on January 8-9, 1976. (OECD)

Angel, Juvenal L., compiler, DIRECTORY OF AMERICAN
    FIRMS OPERATING IN FOREIGN COUNTRIES, 3 vol-
    umes, New York, Uniworld Business Publications,
    1978.

Ball, George W., ed., GLOBAL COMPANIES: The Political Economy of World Business, Englewood Cliffs, New Jersey, Prentice-Hall, (for the American Assembly), 1975. The American Assembly's volume includes a critical statement by a co-author of Global Reseach. (BPA)

Baranson, Jack, TECHNOLOGY AND THE MULTINATIONALS, Lexington, Massachusetts, Lexington Books, 1978. Sixteen case studies provide solid content for this study of why and how American companies transfer technology to foreign enterprises they do not control. For a number of quite different reasons, their interest in doing this is increasing, according to the experienced author who has looked at the aircraft and automotive industries, computers, consumer electronics and chemical engineering. (FA)

Barnet, Richard J. and Müller, Ronald E., GLOBAL REACH: The Power of the Multinational Corporations, New York, Simon and Schuster, 1974. Straw men have become scarecrows. Extravagant claims about the global outlook and benevolent effects of multinational corporations are easily and readably refuted in this book. But by piling on indictments, the authors do little justice to some hard problems. Some of their own good points are smothered by lengthy statements of the negative conventional wisdom that sweepingly condemns business in America and investment in developing countries. (FA)

Behrman, Jack N., CONFLICTING CONSTRAINTS ON THE MULTINATIONAL ENTERPRISE: Potential for Resolution, New York, Council of the Americas and Fund for Multinational Management Education, 1974.

Behrman, Jack N., DECISION CRITERIA FOR FOREIGN DIRECT INVESTMENT IN LATIN AMERICA, New York, Council of the Americas, 1974.

Behrman, Jack N., et al., INTERNATIONAL BUSINESS-GOVERNMENT COMMUNICATIONS: U.S. STRUCTURES, ACTORS, AND ISSUES, Lexington, Massachusetts, Lexington Books, 1975. In a report prepared for the State Department, three American business school professors look at relations between American business and foreign governments, U.S. embassies and Washington departments. (FA)

Bergsten, C. Fred, Horst, Thomas and Moran, Theodore
    H., AMERICAN MULTINATIONALS AND AMERICAN INTER-
    ESTS, Washington, D.C., The Brookings Institu-
    tion, 1978. Agnostic and eclectic are words
    for this valuable and remarkably comprehensive
    study. The first applies to the analysis,
    which rejects generalizations about foreign
    investment and registers doubt about its net
    effect on the American economy. The policy
    prescriptions are eclectic. A number of mea-
    sures are aimed at governmental neutrality
    toward most investment. But taxes and O.P.I.C.
    are to be used to push U.S. companies out of
    the ownership of foreign raw materials and into
    selling their services on contract. Develop-
    ment of the poorest countries is to be helped
    but other foreign subsidies to American invest-
    ment are to be resisted. Transactions with
    communist countries are to be licensed. The
    authors have done original research on a number
    of points and have especially good chapters on
    taxes and the relation of foreign investment to
    domestic market positions and profits. Much
    familiar ground is surveyed at length and some
    of that space ought to have been given over by
    a fuller discussion of proposals, made in the
    last 30 pages, for U.S. leadership in interna-
    tional agreements and a case-by-case system of
    U.S. supervision that could lead to the banning
    of some investment. (FA)

Bernstein, Marvin D., ed., FOREIGN INVESTMENT IN
    LATIN AMERICA: Cases and Attitudes, Fredonia,
    State University of New York at Fredonia,
    Alfred A. Knopf, 1966.

Cohen, Benjamin I., MULTINATIONAL FIRMS AND ASIAN
    EXPORTS, New Haven, Connecticut, Yale Univer-
    sity Press, 1975. Comparing a limited number
    of foreign manufacturing companies with local
    firms in South Korea, Taiwan and Singapore,
    Cohen finds less difference in performance than
    might have been expected. (FA)

Council of the Americas, CONFLICTING CONSTRAINTS ON
    THE MULTINATIONAL ENTERPRISE: POTENTIAL FOR
    RESOLUTION, New York, Council of the Americas,
    1974. Examines effect of U.S. government
    incentives and constraints on corporate deci-
    sions, conflicts between U.S. regulations and

host country policies, and pressures for international controls. (BPA)

Council of the Americas, COMMUNICATING THE SOCIO-
ECONOMIC IMPACT OF MULTINATIONAL CORPORATIONS
IN DEVELOPING COUNTRIES, New York, Council of
the Americas, 1976. Discusses how multinational companies can effectively communicate impact
of their operations on social and economic
development of host countries. (BPA)

Council of the Americas, DECISION CRITERIA FOR FOR-
EIGN DIRECT INVESTMENT IN LATIN AMERICA, New
York, Council of the Americas, 1974. Explains
how structure of multinational corporations and
environment in which they operate affect their
decision-making process. Discusses impact of
MNC decisions on host countries, and response
of host governments in regulating foreign
investment and licenses. (BPA)

Council of the Americas, THE MULTINATIONAL CORPORA-
TIONS IN LATIN AMERICA, New York, Council of
the Americas, 1975. This publication describes
the actual economic effects that investments
made by multinational corporations (MNCs) have
had on the well-being of Brazil and Mexico.
(BPA)

Cox, Robert W., "Labor and the Multinationals,"
Foreign Affairs, Vol. 54, No. 2, January 1976.

Cronje, Suzanne; Ling, Margaret; and Cronje, Gillian,
THE LONRHO CONNECTION: A MULTINATIONAL AND ITS
POLITICS IN AFRICA, Encino, California, Bell-
wether Books, 1977. Despite Lonrho's massive
holdings in white-ruled southern Africa, its
London-based chief, Tiny Rowland, has extended
Lonrho's operations in black Africa and often
deeply into black politics. This saga of
Lonrho's wheeling and dealing simultaneously
north and south of the Zambezi is recounted in
a deadpan style that underplays the message the
book conveys--that of charlatanism on a fabu-
lous scale. (FA)

Deo, S., "The Multinational Corporations and the
Developing Countries," Economic Affairs, Vol.
20, No. 8, August 1975.

Drucker, Peter F., "Multinationals and Developing Countries: Myths and Realities," Foreign Affairs, Vol. 53, No. 1, October 1974.

Dunning, J. H., "Multinational Enterprises and Trade Flows of Less Developed Countries," World Development, Vol. 2, No. 2, February 1974.

Dunning, John H., ed., THE MULTINATIONAL ENTERPRISE, New York, Praeger, 1971. Dunning, a leading British academic authority on investment, has brought together a good team for an integrated study. (BPA)

Eells, Richard, GLOBAL CORPORATIONS: The Emerging System of World Economic Power, New York, Interbook, 1972. A veteran student of corporations, Professor Eells of Columbia tackles the popular new model. The strength of his book is in raising broad political, social and even philosophical issues; its weakness is that he does not get very deeply into them. (FA)

Forsyth, D. J. C. and Solomon, R. F., "Choice of Technology and Nationality of Ownership in Manufacturing in a Developing Country," Oxford Economic Papers, Vol. 29, No. 2, July 1977, pp. 258-282 Multinational corporations are widely believed to install "inappropriate," excessively capital-intensive technologies in less-developed countries. It is argued that the simple multinational corporation/local firm dichotomy often used in examining this hypothesis is misleading, as firms owned by resident expatriates are also likely to display distinctive patterns of technology choice. Multigroup discriminant analysis and ranking procedures are applied to data drawn from a questionnaire survey of manufacturers in Ghana. Nationality of ownership is found to be an important determinant of factor proportions, skill profiles, and wage rates. (JEL)

Gershenberg, Irving, "Multinationals and Development: Commercial Banking in Uganda," Africa Today, Vol. 20, No. 4, 1973, pp. 19-27.

Gilpin, Robert, U.S. POWER AND THE MULTINATIONAL CORPORATION: The Political Economy of Foreign Direct Investment, New York, Basic Books, 1975. A political scientist weighs the costs and

benefits of private foreign investment for the
United States and other countries, using a neo-
mercantilist scale (and perhaps not even "neo").
He recommends selective controls and taxation
to carry out a trade-dominated rather than an
investment-dominated strategy for the United
States. One does not have to agree with him to
believe that the clarity of the argument, the
fair statement of contrary views, and the com-
prehensiveness of the approach make this one of
the best additions for some time to the literature of the multinationals. (FA)

Gunter, Hans, ed., TRANSNATIONAL INDUSTRIAL RELA-
TIONS: The Impact of Multi-national Corporations and Economic Regionalism on Industrial
Relations, New York, St. Martin's Press, 1972.
Will the multinational corporation someday face
the multinational labor union? The most interesting papers in this volume deal with aspects
of that question; in a field where good data
are sparse, some have a good bit of documentary
value. (FA)

Haendel, Dan, FOREIGN INVESTMENTS AND THE MANAGEMENT
OF POLITICAL RISK, Boulder, Colorado, Westview
Press, 1979. After discussing various aspects
of the relationships between multinational corporations and host countries, the author considers the definitional and conceptual issues
of political risk. He examines techniques and
information sources of companies for political
forecasting. (BPA)

Helleiner, Gerald K., "Manufactured Exports from
Less Developed Countries and Multinational
Firms," Economic Journal, March 1973.

Helleiner, Gerald K., "The Role of Multinational
Corporations in the Less Developed Countries'
Trade in Technology," World Development, Vol.
3, No. 4, April 1975.

Helleiner, Gerald K., "Transnational Enterprises in
the Manufacturing Sector of the Less Developed
Countries," World Development, Vol. 3, No. 9,
September 1975.

Hellinger, Douglas A. and Hellinger, Stephen H.,
UNEMPLOYMENT AND THE MULTINATIONALS: A Strategy for Technological Change in Latin America,
Port Washington, New York and London, National
University Publications, Kennikat Press, 1976.
Concentrates on "the technological adaptations
required to significantly reduce the high
levels of joblessness that exist today in Latin
America and the role of the multinational
corporation (MNC) in this endeavor." After
examining the labor-absorbing potential of
various sectors and labor-intensive technological possibilities, productivity and the appro-
priation of technologies are discussed. (JEL)

Hildebrand, George H., "Problems and Policies Affecting Labor's Interests in MNCs," American Economic Review, Vol. LXIV, No. 2, May 1974.

Hirschman, Albert O., HOW TO DIVEST IN LATIN AMERICA,
AND WHY, ESSAYS IN INTERNATIONAL FINANCE,
Princeton, New Jersey, Princeton University,
1969. An intriguing proposal for a negotiated
withdrawal of MNCs from Latin America. (Ed)

Hone, A., "Multinationals at Bay? A Review Article,"
World Affairs, Vol. 2, Nos. 4 & 5, April-May
1974.

Hufbauer, G. C., "Multinational Corporations and the
International Adjustment Process," American
Economic Review, Vol. LXIV, No. 2, May 1974.

Hymer, Stephen, "The Efficiency (Contradictions) of
Multinational Corporations," American Economic
Review, Vol. LX, No. 2, May 1970.

Hymer, Stephen, H., THE INTERNATIONAL OPERATIONS OF
NATIONAL FIRMS: A Study of Direct Foreign
Investment, Cambridge, Massachusetts, MIT
Press, 1976. Best known for his stimulating
and sometimes radical essays on international
business, the late Stephen Hymer wrote a
doctoral dissertation at MIT in 1960 which was
highly influential in exploding the idea that
direct investment can largely be explained by
capital movements. After a long "underground"
existence it is now published, with an attractive introduction by Hymer's teacher Charles
Kindleberger, who did his part in spreading its
influence. (FA)

Hymer, Stephen and Rowthorn, Robert, MULTINATIONAL
CORPORATIONS AND INTERNATIONAL OLIGOPOLY: The
Non-American Challenge, Center Paper #149, New
Haven, Connecticut, Yale University, Economic
Growth Center, 1970.

Ingram, George M., EXPROPRIATION OF U.S. PROPERTY IN
SOUTH AMERICA: Nationalization of Oil and
Copper Companies in Peru, Bolivia, and Chile,
New York, Praeger, 1974.

ILO, THE IMPACT OF MULTINATIONAL ENTERPRISES ON
EMPLOYMENT AND TRAINING, Geneva, 1976. An
analysis of the multinational impact on employment, technology transfer and training in
industrialized and developing countries. (BPA)

ILO, INTERNATIONAL PRINCIPLES AND GUIDELINES ON
SOCIAL POLICY FOR MULTINATIONAL ENTERPRISES,
Geneva, 1976. Investigates the usefulness and
feasibility of establishing international
standards for multinational activities falling
within ILO's competence. Examines current
international labor standards and the possible
areas of proposed standards for multinational
activities. (BPA)

ILO, MULTINATIONAL ENTERPRISES AND SOCIAL POLICY,
Geneva, 1973. A general survey of the nature
and significance of multinational enterprises,
their impact on manpower, the working and
living conditions they provide, how industrial
relations operate in a multinational framework,
and the role of ILO international standards and
social principles. Includes the Report of the
ILO Meeting on the Relationship between Multinational Corporations and Social Policy (1972).
(BPA)

ILO, WAGES AND WORKING CONDITIONS IN MULTINATIONAL
ENTERPRISES, Geneva, 1976. Compares wage levels, fringe benefits and conditions of employment of foreign-owned corporations with locally-
owned firms in selected developed and developr
ing countries. (BPA)

ILO, WAGES AND WORKING CONDITIONS IN MULTINATIONAL
ENTERPRISES, Geneva, 1976. Comparisons are
made between remuneration, hours of work,
holidays and retirement benefits provided for

locally recruited personnel by the bulk of
foreign and locally owned firms. (BPA)

Irish, Donald P., ed., MULTINATIONAL CORPORATIONS IN
   LATIN AMERICA: Private Rights--Public Responsibilities. Athens, Ohio, Ohio University
   Center for International Studies, Edited proceedings of five symposia, Associated Colleges
   of the Twin Cities, papers in International
   Studies, Latin America Series No. 2, 1978.

Joshi, B., "Multinational Corporations and the Less
   Developed Countries," Indian Economic Journal,
   Vol. 20, No. 2, October-December 1972.

Kapoor, A. and Grub, Phillip D., eds., THE MULTI-
   NATIONAL ENTERPRISE IN TRANSITION, Princeton,
   New Jersey, Darwin Press, 1972. Ranging widely,
   the authors have put together an excellent comprehensive collection, recommended for those
   who would like to survey the field. (FA)

Kapoor, Ashok, PLANNING FOR INTERNATIONAL BUSINESS
   NEGOTIATION, Cambridge, Ballinger, 1975.
   Kapoor analyzes negotiations between investors
   and host governments in four case studies.
   (BPA)

Knickerbocker, Frederick T., OLIGOPOLISTIC REACTION
   AND MULTINATIONAL ENTERPRISE, Cambridge, Massachusetts, Harvard University Press, 1978.
   After World War II the leading U.S. firms in
   one industry after the next marched overseas
   country by country to set up plants in a remarkably similar sequence. Some of those who
   observed this surge abroad saw it as further
   evidence of interdependent decision making.
   This book uses facts and figures drawn from the
   data bank of the Harvard Multinational Enterprise Study to test whether the claims for
   follow-the-leader behavior were grounded in
   fact. It does so by exploring the post-World
   War II foreign investment patterns of U.S.
   manufacturing enterprises. (BPA)

Lauterbach, Albert, ENTERPRISE IN LATIN AMERICA:
   Business Attitudes in a Developing Economy,
   Ithaca, New York, Cornell University Press,
   1966.

Ledogar, Robert J., U.S. FOOD AND DRUG MULTINA-
    TIONALS IN LATIN AMERICA: Hungry for Profits,
    New York, IDOC, North America, 1975.

Lim, David, "Do Foreign Companies Pay Higher Wages
    Than Their Local Counterparts in Malaysian
    Manufacturing," Journal of Development Eco-
    nomics, Vol. 4, No. 1, March 1977.

Madden, Carl, H., ed., THE CASE FOR THE MULTINA-
    TIONAL CORPORATION, New York, Praeger, 1976.
    Papers presented at 1975 National Conference on
    Multinational Corporations for Corporate
    Leaders.

Manser, W. A. P., THE FINANCIAL ROLE OF MULTINA-
    TIONAL ENTERPRISES, New York, Halsted Press,
    1973. Manser, an English business economist
    writing for the International Chamber of Com-
    merce, presents data in what is essentially a
    systematic and well-ordered argument that in
    financial matters the multinational firms do
    more good than harm. (BPA)

McCann, Thomas P., AN AMERICAN COMPANY: The Tragedy
    of United Fruit, New York, Crown, 1976. The
    history of the legendary Frutera, with emphasis
    on the disasters that followed its acquisition
    by the Eli Black interests, is recounted by a
    former Vice President for Public Relations of
    the trouble-plagued two-billion dollar enter-
    prise. The manner of telling is lively, inti-
    mate and candid. (FA)

Morley, Samuel A. and Smith, Gordon W., "The Choice
    of Technology: Multinational Firms in Brazil,"
    Economic Development and Cultural Change, Vol.
    25, No. 2, January 1977. Finds that MNCs in
    Brazil do use significantly more labor inten-
    sive techniques than in the United States;
    reason is primarily smaller scale, rather than
    lower labor costs. (Ed)

Negandhi, Anant R., ORGANIZATION THEORY IN AN OPEN
    SYSTEM: A Study of Transferring Advanced Man-
    agement Practices to Developing Nations. The
    book reports the findings of an empirical study
    of 126 industrial firms located in seven coun-
    tries: The United States, Argentina, Brazil,
    India, the Philippines, Uruguay, and Taiwan.

134

The analysis of the organizational practices
and effectiveness of those industrial firms.
(BPA)

Negandhi, Anant R., and Prasad, S. Benjamin, THE
FRIGHTENING ANGELS: A Study of U.S. Multi-
nationals in Developing Nations, Kent, Ohio:
Kent State University Press, 1975. Compares
management practices in Argentina, Brazil,
Uruguay, India, and the Philippines and finds
U.S. subsidiaries coming off rather better than
local firms. (BPA)

Nieckels, Lars, TRANSFER PRICING IN MULTINATIONAL
FIRMS: A Heuristic Programming Approach and a
Case Study, New York, Halsted Press, 1976.
Approaches the problem of transfer pricing by
formulating a mathematical model of a multinational firm, which is in turn analyzed by an
algorithm. (BPA)

Nye, Joseph S. Jr., "Multinational Corporations in
World Politics," Foreign Affairs, Vol. 53, No.
1, October 1974.

Osborn, T. Noel; Garnier, G.; Aries, F.; and Lecon,
R., "Who Makes the Decisions?" Mexican-Ameri-
can Review, January 1978. The authors questioned a large sample of MNC's in Mexico to discover that the range of decisions made by Mexican subsidiaries (rather than foreign parent
companies) is wider than is often supposed.
(Ed)

Parry, T. G., MULTINATIONAL MANUFACTURING ENTERPRIS-
ES AND IMPERFECT COMPETITION, Occasional Papers,
No. 1, Kensington, N.S.W., Australia, University of New South Wales, Center for Applied
Economic Research, 1977. Analyzes the effects
of international direct investment when multinational enterprises are based on responses to
and within market imperfections, arguing that
this is the case in Australian manufacturing
operations. Discusses the effects of multinational enterprise interaction with the host
nation on the structure and performance of
industries in which the nultinational enterprise operates. Uses Australian data for 1973.
(JEL)

135

Phatak, Arvind V., MANAGING MULTINATIONAL CORPORA-
TIONS, New York, Praeger, 1974. Chiefly about
management problems. (BPA)

Pinelo, Adalberto, J., THE MULTINATIONAL CORPORATION
AS A FORCE IN LATIN AMERICAN POLITICS: A Case
Study of the International Petroleum Company in
Peru, New York, Praeger, 1973.

Robbins, Sidney M. and Stobaugh, MONEY IN THE MULTI-
NATIONAL ENTERPRISE: A Study of Financial
Policy, New York, Basic Books, 1973. Stobaugh
and Robbins' book (from the Harvard Multinational Enterprise series) is a model of clarity
and condensation and a major contribution to
our understanding of how international business
works. Their report shows patterns, differences and changes which confirm the impression
that business management is an experimental
science. (BPA)

Rolfe, Sidney E. and Samm, Walter, THE MULTINATIONAL
CORPORATION IN THE WORLD ECONOMY: Direct Investment in Perspective, New York, Praeger (for
the Atlantic Institute, the Committee for
Atlantic Economic Cooperation and the Atlantic
Council of the United States), 1970. Useful
papers, economic and legal, presented to a conference better described by the subtitle than
the title of the book. Special emphasis on
foreign investment in the United States. (FA)

Sampson, Anthony, THE SOVEREIGN STATE OF ITT, New
York, Stein and Day, Publishers, 1973.

Sauvant, Karl P. and Lavepour, Farid G., eds., CON-
TROLLING MULTINATIONAL ENTERPRISES: Problems,
Strategies, Counterstrategies, Boulder, Colorado, Westview Press, 1976. Illustrates the
main strategies and the specific tactics imposed for the control of MNCs, the natural tendency of MNCs to resist controlling mechanisms,
and the whole range of difficulties associated
with controlling actions. (BPA)

Sethi, S. Prakash and Holton, Richard H. MANAGEMENT
OF THE MULTINATIONALS: Policies, Operations,
and Research, New York: Free Press, 1974. A
rather wide-ranging collection. (BPA)

Stephenson, Hugh, THE COMING CLASH: The Impact of
    Multinational Corporations on National States,
    New York, Saturday Review Press, 1972. Stephen-
    son, a British editor, covers some familiar
    ground but has much good material. (BPA)

Streeten, P., "Policies Towards Multinationals,"
    World Development, Vol. 3, No. 6, June 1975.

Swansbrough, Robert H., "The American Investor's
    View of Latin American Economic Nationalism,"
    InterAmerican Economic Affairs, Vol. 26, No. 3,
    1972.

Torneden, Roger L., FOREIGN DISINVESTMENT BY U.S.
    MULTINATIONAL CORPORATIONS: With Eight Case
    Studies, New York, Praeger, 1975. At a time
    when many American businesses are thinking how
    best to get as much of their assets as possible
    out of tight foreign spots, this book is a good
    bit more interesting than many studies of why
    multinational corporations invest. Many of the
    cases examined by the author, a businessman,
    suggest that scientific and systematic methods
    of management are scarcer than personalistic,
    ill-considered and not very well-informed
    actions. (FA)

Tugendhat, Christopher, THE MULTINATIONALS, New
    York, Random House, 1972. It seems suitable
    that the MP for the Cities of London and West-
    minster should write about the newest complex
    of government-business relations. Lucidly, as
    befits a former financial journalist, he dis-
    cusses the activities of the big international
    companies and makes moderate proposals for
    national and international measures that will
    strengthen the hands of governments in dealing
    with them. (FA)

Turner, Louis, MULTINATIONAL COMPANIES AND THE THIRD
    WORLD, New York, Hill and Wang, 1973. This
    young English economist's lively discussion of
    a wide range of issues is well-informed and
    usually very balanced. (BPA)

United Nations, THE ACQUISITION OF TECHNOLOGY FROM
    MULTINATIONAL CORPORATIONS BY DEVELOPING COUN-
    TRIES, New York, United Nations, 1974. Ex-
    amines role of multinationals in supplying
    technology to developing countries, choice of

appropriate technologies, alternative sources of proprietary technology, and relevant national technical and economic policies.

United Nations, THE IMPACT OF MULTINATIONAL CORPORATION ON DEVELOPMENT AND ON INTERNATIONAL RELATIONS, New York, United Nations, 1974. Analysis of the role of multinationals in development and international relations, with recommendations for international machinery and action. Examines ownership and control of economic sectors, balance of payments, technology, labor, consumer protection, competition, transfer pricing, taxation, and information disclosures. (BPA)

United Nations, MULTINATIONAL CORPORATIONS IN WORLD DEVELOPMENT, New York, United Nations, 1973. Basic data on the size, distribution, structure, and ownership of multinationals. Impact of multinationals on developing countries and on international monetary and trade policies is analyzed. Includes 43 tables. (BPA)

U.S., Department of Commerce, THE MULTINATIONAL CORPORATION STUDIES IN U.S. FOREIGN INVESTMENT, U.S., Department of Commerce, prepared by the Office of International Investment, Volume 1, March 1972.

U.S., Department of Commerce, REVISED DATA SERIES ON U.S. DIRECT INVESTMENT ABROAD, 1966-1974, Bureau of Economic Analysis, 1976.

Vaitsos, Constantino V., INTERCOUNTRY INCOME DISTRIBUTION AND TRANSNATIONAL ENTERPRISES, London, Clarendon Press, distributed by Oxford University Press, New York, 1974.

Vaupel, James W. and Curhan, Joan P., THE MAKING OF MULTINATIONAL ENTERPRISE, Cambridge, Massachusetts, Harvard University Press, 1978.

Vernon, Raymond, "Competition Policy Toward Multinational Corporations," American Economic Review, Vol. LXIV, No. 2, May 1974.

Vernon, Raymond, ed., HOW LATIN AMERICA VIEWS THE U.S. INVESTOR, New York, Praeger, 1966.

Vernon, Raymond, SOVEREIGNTY AT BAY: THE MULTI-
    NATIONAL SPREAD OF U.S. ENTERPRISES, New York,
    Basic Books, 1971. This book is the principal
    product of a major research effort at Harvard.
    Focusing mainly on American-controlled multina-
    tional enterprises, Professor Vernon deals com-
    prehensively with their character, their impact
    on the world economy and national political and
    economic reactions to them. Finally the need
    and prospects for increased international
    supervision are sensitively, and somewhat
    cautiously, explored. A major work. (FA)

Vernon, Raymond, STORM OVER THE MULTINATIONALS: The
    Real Issues, Cambridge, Massachusetts, Harvard
    University Press, 1977. Deals with the nature
    and consequences of the multinational enter-
    prises. Discusses such questions as: are
    multinational enterprises and nation-states
    incompatible in goals and outlook? Should
    their economic (and political) behavior differ
    in developing countries as compared to advanced
    industrial states? Argues that the threat of
    conflict between the goals of the multinational
    enterprises and the nation-state seems to be
    growing and that such differences have usually
    been manageable in the industrialized countries,
    while the problem is more complicated in the
    case of developing countries. Concludes that
    "(one) necessary condition for constructive
    action is to sort out those problems only par-
    tially related to the multinational enterprise
    and to recognize that they cannot be dealt with
    effectively by any program targeted at the
    multinational enterprise alone." (JEL)

Weigel, Dale R., "Multinational Approaches to Multi-
    national Corporations," Finance and Development,
    Vol. 11, No. 3, September 1974, pp. 27-29, and
    42.

Wells, Louis T., Jr., THE PRODUCT LIFE CYCLE AND
    INTERNATIONAL TRADE, Boston, Massachusetts,
    Harvard University, Graduate School of Business
    Administration, Division of Research, 1972.
    Louis Wells' collection brings together most of
    the basic works concerning one of the principal
    contributions to new thought made by the Har-
    vard Business School's project. (FA)

Widstrand, Carl, ed., MULTINATIONAL FIRMS IN AFRICA,
    Uppsala, Scandinavian Institute of African
    Studies, 1975; New York, Africana Publishing
    Company, 1976. A superior collection--best on
    concrete data about multinational corporate
    penetration of Africa (including individual
    studies of Ethiopia, Kenya, Tanzania, and
    Nigeria). Proposals for African achievement of
    independence and control over those firms are
    vague and repetitive--the confusion of the
    economists about how to overcome dependency
    seems to parallel that of the host countries.
    (FA)

Wilkins, Mira, THE EMERGENCE OF MULTINATIONAL ENTER-
    PRISE: American Business Abroad from the
    Colonial Era to 1914, Cambridge, Massachusetts,
    Harvard University Press, 1970. A major work
    that does much to explain as well as describe
    the growth of direct foreign investment by
    Americans up to 1914. A prodigious amount of
    material is well organized, interestingly pre-
    sented and made to respond to questions prompt-
    ed by modern studies of international business.
    (FA)

Wilkins, Mira, THE MATURING OF MULTINATIONAL ENTER-
    PRISE: American Business Abroad from 1914 to
    1970, Cambridge, Massachusetts, Harvard Uni-
    versity Press, 1974. Exceptionally rich
    material on the foreign investment activities
    of major U.S. firms provides the basis for a
    history, model and the analysis of a number of
    interesting problems. Miss Wilkins does not
    try to construct new statistical estimates but
    builds effectively on her earlier volume con-
    cerning the history of U.S. foreign investment
    before World War I.   (FA)

Wilson, J. S. G. and Scheffer, C. F., eds., MULTI-
    NATIONAL ENTERPRISES: Financial and Monetary
    Aspects, Leiden: Sijthoff, 1974. A large
    European and British contribution. (BPA)

New International Economic Order

X-REF: AFRICA: Okwuosa, JAPAN: Ced, LATIN AMERICA:
Grunwald, MISCELLANEOUS: ul Haq, POPULATION:
Finkle, TRADE: Helleiner.

140

Adler-Karlsson, G., THE POLITICAL ECONOMY OF EAST-WEST SOUTH CO-OPERATION, New York, Springer-Verlag, 1976. What can developing countries learn from developed capitalist and socialist countries? From the former, something about efficiency, international cooperation and freedom; from the latter, more about how to provide employment, essentials and relative equality with limited resources, and maybe how to bargain effectively with multinationals. In arguing his case, the Swedish social democratic author has many provocative things to say about many subjects. (FA)

Al-Khalaf, Nazar, "OPEC Members and the New International Economic Order," The Journal of Energy and Development, Vol. 2, No. 2, Spring 1977, pp. 239-251.

Alvarez, Francisco Casanova, NEW HORIZONS FOR THE THIRD WORLD, Washington, D.C., Public Affairs Press, 1976. Presents the factors leading to approval of the Charter of Economic Rights and Duties of States by the United Nations General Assembly on 12 December 1974. Shows that the charter, with the main objective of overcoming "the injustice prevailing in economic relations between nations and (elimination of) the dependence of Third World countries on industrial nations," owes its origin and adoption to President Luis Echeverria of Mexico. Argues that developing nations remain essentially colonized and dependent entities of the industrialized world. Concludes that the future world will "be less unjust and less ridden with anxiety, more secure and better able to care for its own if we respect the principles of the charter." (JEL)

Amuzegar, Jahangir, "The North-South Dialogue: From Conflict to Compromise," Foreign Affairs, Vol. 54, No. 3, April 1976, pp. 547-562.

Bauer, P. T., and Yamey, B. S., "Against the New Economic Order," Commentary, April 1977, pp. 25-32.

Behrman, Jack N., TOWARD A NEW INTERNATIONAL ECONOMIC ORDER, PARIS, The Atlantic Institute for International Affairs, 1974.

Bhagwati, Jagdish N., THE NEW INTERNATIONAL ECONOMIC
ORDER: The North-South Debate, Cambridge,
Massachusetts, MIT Press, 1977.

Dolman, Antony J. and Ettinger, Jan van, PARTNERS IN
TOMORROW, Strategies for a New International
Order, New York, E. P. Dutton, 1978.

Gosovic, Branislav, UNCTAD: North-South Encounter,
New York, Carnegie Endowment for International
Peace, 1968.

Green, R. H. and Singer, H. W., "Toward a Rational
and Equitable New International Economic Order:
A Case for Negotiated Structural Changes,"
World Development, Vol. 3, No. 6, June 1975.

Hudson, Michael, GLOBAL FRACTURE: The New International Economic Order, New York, Harper,
1977. An Alliance of Europe and the Third
World; statism replacing the market interna-
tionally with socialism resulting at home; a
contraction of American income as the U.S.
loses the ability to appropriate the output of
the rest of the world. The case for these
provocative prospects is based on some good and
some poor arguments. The faults that many
readers will find with Mr. Hudson's interpretation of the past and present should not blind
them to the need to think seriously about a
number of the possibilities he suggests for the
future. (FA)

Kamrany, Nake, ed., THE NEW ECONOMICS OF THE LESS
DEVELOPED COUNTRIES: Changing Perceptions in
the North-South Dialogue, Boulder, Colorado,
Westview Press, 1978. The contributors to
this volume explore--with supporting theoretical frameworks and empirical evidence--the
new perceptions concerning the development of
the poor countries, providing treatments of
North-South bargaining, commodity power, indexation, the theory of power and the international distribution of rights and resources,
and the effectiveness of international organizations as vehicles for conflict resolution.
The authors discuss the position and prospects
of the non-oil-producing, less developed countries, focusing on measurements of the quality
of life in these countries, growth and income

distribution policies, and the effectiveness of public expenditures to enhance social welfare.

Leontief, Wassily, et al., THE FUTURE OF THE WORLD ECONOMY: A United Nations Study, New York, Oxford University Press, 1977. Investigates the interrelationships between future world economic growth and availability of natural resources, pollution, and the impact of environmental policies. Includes a set of alternative projections of the demographic, economic, and environmental states of the world in the years 1980, 1990, and 2000 with a comparison with the world economy of 1970. Constructs a multiregional input-output economic model of the world economy. Investigates some of the main problems of economic growth and development in the world as a whole, with special accent on problems encountered by the developing countries. (JEL)

Lewis, W. Arthur, THE EVOLUTION OF THE INTERNATIONAL ECONOMIC ORDER, The Elliot Janeway Lectures on Historical Economics in Honor of Joseph Schumpeter, 1977, Princeton, New Jersey, Princeton University Press, 1978. Discusses the evolution and changing nature of the international economic order, emphasizing various elements of the relationship between the developing and the developed countries irksome to LDC's, including: division of world trade into exporters of primary products and exporters of manufactures, adverse factoral terms of trade for LDC's; dependence of LDC's on developed countries for finance; and LDC dependence on advanced nations for their "engine of growth." (JEL)

Mendlovitz, Saul H., ON THE CREATION OF A JUST WORLD ORDER: Preferred Worlds for the 1990's, New York, Macmillan Publishing Co., 1975.

Montbrial, Thierry de, "For a New World Economic Order," Foreign Affairs, Vol. 54, No. 1, October 1975.

Moss, Alfred G. and Winton, Harry N., A NEW INTERNATIONAL ECONOMIC ORDER: SELECTED DOCUMENTS, 1945-1975, New York, UNITAR/Published in cooperation with Unipub, 1976. Compilation of the principal declarations, programs of action, and other texts produced by international meetings

within and outside the UN relevant to the
General Assembly's "Declaration on the Establishment of a New Economic Order." Includes
texts, in chronological order, concerning
industrial development, transfer of technology,
international trade, the role of women, and
food and population policies in developing
countries. (BPA)

Pugwash Newsletter, from Report of Working Group 3,
     "The Evolving International System and Its
     Implications for the Development and Security
     of the Developing Countries," Continuing Com-
     mittee of the Pugwash Conferences on Science
     and World Affairs, London, Vol. 13, No. 3,
     January, 1976.

Sauvant, Karl P. and Hasenpflug, Hajo, eds., THE NEW
     INTERNATIONAL ECONOMIC ORDER: Confrontation or
     Cooperation Between North and South? Boulder,
     Colorado, Westview Press, 1977. A well-put-
     together combination of documents and public
     statements with specially prepared commentar-
     ies, mostly by young American and German schol-
     ars, makes a comprehensive and thoughtful
     review of major issues. (FA)

Schacter, Oscar, SHARING THE WORLD'S RESOURCES, New
     York, Columbia University Press, 1977. Oscar
     Schacter seeks to apply historical, legal, and
     moral criteria to the problem of justice in
     international distribution of at least those
     things that are perceived as not firmly distri-
     buted--e.g., the resources of the ocean. (BPA)

Schmidt, Helmut, "The Struggle for the World Prod-
     uct," Foreign Affairs, Vol. 52, No. 3, April
     1974.

Singh, Jyoti Shankar, A NEW INTERNATIONAL ECONOMIC
     ORDER: Toward a Fair Redistribution of the
     World's Resources, Praeger Special Studies in
     International Economics and Development, New
     York, Praeger, 1977. Discusses the issues and
     actions by international bodies involved in the
     post-World War II transition from the old
     economic international order to the new. Mat-
     ters dealing with hunger, population, technolo-
     gy, and the role of selected countries are
     emphasized as is the work yet to be done.
     (JEL)

Tinbergen, Jan, Coordinator, RIO: Reshaping the International Order: A Report to the Club of Rome, New York, Dutton, 1978. Unlike the two earlier reports to the Club of Rome, this one emphasizes development, distribution and improved welfare that will require a good deal of economic growth. An uneven document, it can sometimes be quoted against itself; the tone is, in turn, hortatory, pragmatic, defiant and sweet. Different readers will detect different biases in the discussion of many familiar issues. These defects of committee work, however, should not obscure the need to consider carefully the "proposals for action" of Professor Tinbergen's group, which are stated more carefully than some others--and are therefore more challenging. (FA)

ul Haq, Mahbub, THE POVERTY CURTAIN: Choices for the Third World, New York, Columbia University Press, 1976. A gifted Pakistani official of the World Bank has produced one of the best books on the New International Economic Order. Growth, aid, the environment, bargaining power and development strategies are all treated with sophistication combined with vigorous advocacy of new approaches. Three passages describing the evolution of the author's thinking are exceptionally good. (FA)

UNESCO, "Aid to Education and the New International Order," Prospects, Vol. VI, No. 4, 1976. This issue of UNESCO's quarterly review of education contains a dossier on the new international economic order as it relates to educational aid. Topics covered include: cooperation among developing countries; aid to the least developed nations; the use of "experts"; and APEID as an example of regional co-operation. (BPA)

UNESCO, "Towards a New International Economic and Social Order," International Social Science Journal, Vol. 28, No. 4, 1976. Fifteen international authors discuss the relevance of such subjects as natural disasters, multinational corporations, citizen mobility and employment problems to the new international order. (BPA)

United Nations, DECLARATION ON THE ESTABLISHMENT OF
A NEW INTERNATIONAL ECONOMIC ORDER, Resolutions
of the General Assembly at its Sixth Special
Session, 9 April-2 May 1974.

U.S. Joint Economic Committee, "Issues at the Summit: North-South Dialogue," testimony by Anne
O. Krueger, April 22, 1977.

U.S. Joint Economic Committee, "North-South Issues
at the Summit," statement by John P. Lewis
before the Joint Economic Committee, Friday,
April 22, 1977.

Planning

X-REF: AFRICA: Seidman, Simmons, AGRICULTURAL DE-
VELOPMENT: Cochrane, ASIA: Ghosh, BANGLADESH:
Islam, BRAZIL: Sahoter, CHILE: Cleaves, Zammit,
CHINA: Berger, Perkins, COLOMBIA: Catanese,
Colombia, Sloan, CUBA: Mesa, INCOME DISTRIBUTION,
PRINCIPLES: Jaksch, IMPORT SUBSTITUTION: Clark,
INDIA: Baghwati, Bhattacharya, Das Gadgil, Ghosh,
Mishra, Repetto, Shenoy, INDICATORS: Pyatt, Unesco,
IRAN: Baldwin, KOREA: Cohen, Kim, NIGERIA: Dean,
PAKISTAN: Islam, Lewis, MacEwan, POPULATION:
Todaro, SAUDI ARABIA: Cleron, Crane, United, Wells,
SMALL BUSINESS: Hart, SRI LANKA: Sirisena, TURKEY:
Fry, World.

Alexander, Robert Jackson, A NEW DEVELOPMENT STRATE-
GY, Mary Knoll, New York, Orbis Books, 1976.

Aharoni, Yair, MARKETS, PLANNING AND DEVELOPMENT:
The Private and Public Sectors in Economic Development, Cambridge, Ballinger, 1977. It was
a good idea to pursue the subject of the subtitle and Professor Aharoni of Tel Aviv is particularly good on publicly owned enterprises.
However, too many subjects are treated in a
textbook-like way. (FA)

Balassa, Bela, POLICY REFORM IN DEVELOPING COUNTRIES,
New York, Pergamon Press, 1977. Brings to-
gether eight essays the author wrote between
March 1974 and October 1976 as a policy advisor
to the governments of Mexico, Venezuela, Chile,
Egypt, Portugal, Korea and the Junta of the
Andean Common Market. Addresses questions of

146

policy reform in developing countries, including foreign trade and industrial policy in Mexico and Portugal; tariff reform in Chile; and development strategy for Venezuela, Egypt, and Korea. Index. (JEL)

Bhagwati, Jagdish and Eckaus, Richard S., eds., DEVELOPMENT AND PLANNING (ESSAYS IN HONOR OF PAUL ROSENSTEIN-RODAN), Cambridge, Massachusetts, MIT Press, 1973.

Bicanci, R., PROBLEMS OF PLANNING: East and West, The Hague and Paris, Mouton Publishers, 1971.

Birmingham, Walter B. and Ford, A. G., eds., PLANNING AND GROWTH IN RICH AND POOR COUNTRIES, New York, Praeger, 1966.

Blitzner, Charles R.; Clark, P.; and Taylor, L.; eds., ECONOMY-WIDE MODELS AND DEVELOPMENT PLANNING, London, Oxford University Press, 1975.

Bornstien, Morris, ed., ECONOMIC PLANNING, EAST AND WEST, Cambridge, Massachusetts, Lippincott, Ballinger, 1975. Eight revised essays given at a 1974 conference organized by the Comparative Economics Program at the University of Michigan. Academic specialists and government planners compare the theory and practice of planning in eastern Eugopean centrally-administered economies and western market-oriented economies; comments accompany most essays. (JEL)

Bryce, Murray D., INDUSTRIAL DEVELOPMENT: A Guide for Accelerating Economic Growth, New York, Toronto, and London, McGraw-Hill Book Company, 1960.

Bryce, Murray D., POLICIES AND METHODS FOR INDUSTRIAL DEVELOPMENT, New York, London, Sydney, and Toronto, McGraw-Hill Book Company, Inc., 1965.

Cairncross, Alex, ESSAYS IN ECONOMIC MANAGEMENT, Albany, New York, Suny Press, 1972.

Chenery, Hollis B. and Clark, Paul G., INTERINDUSTRY ECONOMICS, New York, John Wiley & Sons, Inc., 1965.

Chenery, Hollis B., "The Structuralist Approach to
Development Policy," The American Economic
Review, Vol. LXV, No. 2, May 1975.

Chenery, Hollis B., et al., eds., STUDIES IN DEVEL-
OPMENT PLANNING, Harvard Economic Studies Vol.
136, Cambridge, Massachusetts, Harvard University Press, 1971. A collection of seventeen
essays by eighteen development scholars resulting from the Project for Quantitative Research
in Economic Development of the Center for
International Affairs at Harvard University.
Attempts to bring together the contributors'
varied backgrounds in both field work and the
use of quantitative techniques and show how
modern methods can be used in operational
development planning. (JEL)

Csikos-Nagy, Bela, SOCIALIST ECONOMIC POLICY, New
York, St. Martin's Press, 1973.

David, Wilfred, ed., PUBLIC FINANCE, PLANNING AND
ECONOMIC DEVELOPMENT, New York, St. Martin's
Press, 1973.

Diaz-Alejandro, Carlos F., "Planning the Foreign
Sector in Latin America," American Economic
Review, Vol. LX, No. 2, May 1970.

Dubin, Evan F. M., PROBLEMS OF ECONOMIC PLANNING,
New York, A. M. Kelley, 1968.

Frisch, Rogman, ECONOMIC PLANNING STUDIES, Dordrecht,
Holland; Boston, D. Reidel Publishing Co.,
1976.

Ghash, R., "The Public Sector and Economic Development," Economic Affairs, Vol. 18, No. 1-2, Annual Number 1973.

Goodwin, Chaufurd D., et al., NATIONAL ECONOMIC
PLANNING: Six Papers Presented at a Conference
in Washington, D.C., November 12, 1975, Washington, The Chamber of Commerce of the United
States, 1976. Six previously unpublished
papers dealing with "the substantive issues
raised by national economic planning." Authors
discuss the history of planning in the United
States, the present efforts, their implications, and the probable future of such planning.
(JEL)

Griffin, Keith B. and Enos, John L., PLANNING DEVEL-
OPMENT, Development Economics Series, Reading,
Massachusetts, Don Mills, 1971. Part of a
series as guidebooks on development economics,
this book is a general introductory text for
undergraduate and first year graduate students.
Deals with practical problems of planning and
economic policy in underdeveloped countries.
Consists of four parts: 1) the role of planning, 2) quantitative planning techniques, 3)
sector policies, and 4) planning in practice
with reference to Chile, Colombia, Ghana,
India, Pakistan and Turkey. Bibliography;
index. (JEL)

Hansen, Bent, LONG- AND SHORT-TERM PLANNING IN
UNDERDEVELOPED COUNTRIES, From the lectures of
Professor Dr. F. DeVries, Amsterdam, North-
Holland Publishing Company, 1972.

Heal, G. M., THE THEORY OF ECONOMIC PLANNING: Advanced Textbooks in Economics, Vol. 3, Amsterdam and London, North-Holland; New York, American Elsevier, 1973. A book on general theoretical issues of economic planning, discussing
the operational issues of planned economic
systems with "something approaching the degree
of abstraction at which traditional welfare
economics has discussed the behavior of a
competitive economy." (JEL)

International Labor Organization, PLANNING TECH-
NIQUES FOR A BETTER FUTURE, Geneva, 1976. In
the past, development planning and policies
have concentrated on the modern sector at the
expense of increased productivity and incomes
in the rural and informal urban sectors. The
authors present a detailed conceptual framework
(the social accounting matrix) for a new development strategy which includes high growth
rates and a redistribution of income and wealth
to the poorest segments of the population.
(BPA)

Judge, George G. and Takeyama, Takashi, eds.,
STUDIES IN ECONOMIC PLANNING OVER SPACE AND
TIME, Contributions to Economic Analysis No.
82, Amsterdam and London, North-Holland; New
York, American Elsevier, 1973. Selection of 35
previously unpublished papers dealing with
economic decision problems over space and time

at the regional, interregional, national, and
international levels. The book is organized
into four sections: National and International
Planning Models, Linear Planning Models over
Space and Time, Non-Linear Models over Space
and Time, and Public and Private Planning. The
scope of the book includes the application of
models to a wide range of countries "to show
the practicability and usefulness of these
models...over a spectrum of centralized-decen-
tralized allocation schemes...." Index. (JEL)

Kaldor, Nicholas, ESSAYS ON ECONOMIC POLICY, New
York, Norton, 1965.

Kanterovich, L. V., ESSAYS IN OPTIMAL PLANNING,
edited by Leon Smolinski, White Plains, New
York, International Arts and Sciences Press,
1976. Eighteen essays dealing with various
aspects of the time dimension of economic
planning including: long-run programming of
economic activity, optimization over time,
growth models, and specific difficulties and
complications arising in dynamic optimal planning. No index. (JEL)

Kaynor, Richard S. and Schultz, Konrad F., INDUS-
TRIAL DEVELOPMENT: A Practical Handbook for
Planning and Implementing Development Programs,
Praeger Special Studies in International Economics and Development, New York, Praeger,
1973. The authors, drawing on years of experience as private consultants in economic development in countries around the world, present design criteria for industrial development
programs and detailed information on such
topics as finance and investment, industrial
advisory services and technology transfer,
industrial location, ways in which industrial
development opportunities can be encouraged and
expanded by government, and an organization
plan for the industrial development corporation. (JEL)

Kendrick, David A., PROGRAMMING INVESTMENT IN THE
PROCESS INDUSTRIES: An Approach to Sectoral
Planning, Cambridge, Massachusetts, MIT Press,
1968.

Kennessey, Zoltan, THE PROCESS OF ECONOMIC PLANNING, New York, Columbia University Press, 1978. An introductory textbook designed around eight major topics involved in planning in the market-oriented economy: (1) the possibilities and limitations of planning; (2) institutional aspects; (3) aims, strategies, and policies of development planning; (4) the elaboration of development plans; (5) scientific and quantitative evidence; (6) techniques of planning; (7) plan implementation; and (8) planning and politics in the United States. Index. (JEL)

Khachatnrov, T. S., ed., METHODS OF LONG-TERM PLANNING AND FORECASTING, New York, Halsted Press, 1976.

Killick, T., "The Possibilities of Development Planning," Oxford Economic Papers, Vol. 41, No. 4, October 1974, pp. 477-491. The paper argues that development planning in practice has achieved few of the benefits that its advocates expected from it. Most reasons that have been given for this poor performance do not get to the source of the problem, which is the naivety of the implicit model of governmental decision-making incorporated in the literature. More realistic views of politics and decision-making pose the questions whether development planning is feasible at all and, even if feasible, whether it could be an efficient instrument of economic policy. Suggestions are made on what could be rescued from the debris. (JEL)

Lerner, Abba and Ben-Shahar, Haim, THE ECONOMICS OF EFFICIENCY AND GROWTH: Lessons from Israel and the West Bank, Cambridge, Massachusetts, Lippincott, Ballinger, 1975. Using Israel as the specific example, the authors discuss macroeconomic policy objectives. Attention is given to Israel's experience in economic planning, the role of the government in economic activity, and the economic effects of the 1973 war. Also reviews economic development in the West Bank and Gaza Strip. The book presents a critical review of Israel's achievements and failures, arguing that the "splendid picture of economic growth was not a result" of Israel's economic policy and showing that the government has failed to make the best use of the market mechanism to promote economic efficiency and faster economic growth. Index. (JEL)

Lewis, W. Arthur, DEVELOPMENT PLANNING: The Essentials of Economic Policy, New York, Harper & Row, 1966.

Liggins, David, NATIONAL ECONOMIC PLANNING IN FRANCE, Lexington, Massachusetts, Lexington Press, 1975. The selection of France as the subject of a study of an advanced industrialized economy has given the author an opportunity to provide a presentation of the techniques of economic planning. The main emphasis of the book is on quantitative tools and techniques to be used in projecting economic patterns. (BPA)

Maddison, Angus, ECONOMIC PROGRESS AND POLICY IN DEVELOPING COUNTRIES, New York, W. W. Norton & Company, Inc., 1970.

Mason, Edward S., ECONOMIC PLANNING IN UNDERDEVELOPED AREAS: Government and Business, New York City, Fordham University Press, 1958.

Meade, J. E., THE THEORY OF INDICATIVE PLANNING, New York, Humanities Press, 1970. Three lectures given by the author (at the University of Manchester) setting out the method of treating uncertainty used in the Arrow-Debreu analysis. Comments on specific practical problems arising from the application of this use of uncertainty to planning in a developed, industrialized, free enterprise. No index. (JEL)

Nutter, G. Warren, CENTRAL ECONOMIC PLANNING: The Visible Hand, Domestic Affairs Study No. 41, Washington, D.C., American Enterprise Institute for Public Policy Research, 1976. An adversely critical essay discussing the major issues raised by the landmark introduction in Congress of legislation to institute central economic planning. Reviews the historical emergence of central planning and the Soviet and French experiences, as well as various aspects of the Western trend toward bigger government. No index. (JEL)

Organizacion de los Estados Americanos, ESTADO DE LA
PLANIFICACION EN AMERICA LATINA, Organization
of American States, Washington, D.C., 1969.

Papanek, Gustav, F., ed., DEVELOPMENT POLICY:
Theory and Practice, Cambridge, Massachusetts,
Harvard University Press, 1968. Eleven well-
documented essays by 13 authors highlighting
problems of theorists and practitioners of
development economics in Pakistan, Liberia,
Argentina and Colombia. Topics covered include:
1) planning, macroeconomic models and development strategy, 2) stabilization and short-term
policies, 3) fiscal policy, 4) agricultural
development, and 5) education, manpower, labor
and wages. Index. (JEL)

Ponsioen, J. A., "Reflections on the Scientific
Character of Planning, Illustrated in the
Fields of Education and Health," World Develop-
ment, Vol. 2, No. 2, February 1974.

Portes, Richard D., "Decentralized Planning Procedures and Centrally Planned Economies," American Economic Review, Vol. LXI, No. 2, May 1971.

Ranis, Gustav, ed., GOVERNMENT AND ECONOMIC DEVELOP-
MENT, New Haven, Connecticut, Yale University
Economic Growth Center, 1971. A collection of
papers, early versions of which were originally
presented at a 1968 Economic Growth Center Conference on "The Role of Government in Economic
Development." Fourteen articles (grouped into
5 sections) on the development of different
countries are given, each with separate commentaries. (JEL)

Ranis, Gustav, RELATIVE PRICES IN PLANNING FOR
ECONOMIC DEVELOPMENT, Center Discussion Paper
No. 90, New Haven, Connecticut, Yale Univer-
sity, Economic Growth Center, 1970.

Robbins, Lionel C., POLITICAL ECONOMY, PAST AND
PRESENT: A Review of Leading Theories of
Economic Policy, New York, Columbia University
Press, 1976.

Rosenstein-Rodan, Paul, DEVELOPMENT AND PLANNING:
Essays in Honour of Paul Rosenstein-Rodan,
edited by Jagdish N. Bhagwati and Richard S.
Eckaus, Cambridge, Massachusetts, MIT Press,

1973. A Festschrift collection of 18 previously unpublished essays on various aspects of economic development and growth. There are two articles on the evolution of development economics. Five essays are on various planning and policy aspects of economic development. Four other papers are on regional development and income distribution. Three articles are on various international economics aspects of the development process. Finally, there is a paper on cost-benefit analysis, two papers on labor productivity, and one on value theory. Index. (JEL)

Sellekaerts, Willy, ed., ECONOMIC DEVELOPMENT AND PLANNING: Essays in Honour of Jan Tinbergen, White Plains, New York, International Arts and Sciences Press, 1974. Collection of ten previously unpublished essays by leading North American and European economists focusing upon international trade, economic development and planning, econometrics, and economic theory. Also included is a previously published essay by Bent Hansen appraising Tinbergen's contributions to economics. Bibliography of Jan Tingergen; index. (JEL)

Spulber, Nicolas and Horowitz, Ira, QUANTITATIVE ECONOMIC POLICY AND PLANNING: Theory and Models of Economic Control, New York, W. W. Norton & Company, 1976.

Swerdlow, Irving, THE PUBLIC ADMINISTRATION OF ECONOMIC DEVELOPMENT, Praeger Special Studies in International Economics and Development, New York, Praeger, 1975. The thesis is that government administrators are an important element in expediting or slowing down the pace of economic planning requires public administrators to understand the planning process. The main determinants of growth are discussed, showing the role of government in improving income distribution. There is considerable discussion of planning operations, administration of economic policies, and processes of administration. No index. (JEL)

Tinbergen, Jan, CENTRAL PLANNING, New Haven, Connecticut, Yale University Press, 1964.

Tinbergen, Jan, THE DESIGN OF DEVELOPMENT, Baltimore, Maryland, The Johns Hopkins Press, 1958.

Tinbergen, Jan, DEVELOPMENT PLANNING, translated
from the Dutch by N. D. Smith, New York &
Toronto, McGraw-Hill Book Company, 1967.

Tinbergen, Jan, ECONOMIC POLICY, Amsterdam, North-
Holland Publishing Co., 1967.

Todaro, Michael P., DEVELOPMENT PLANNING: Models
and Methods, series of undergraduate teaching
works in economics, Vol. V, New York, Oxford
University Press, 1971. This book is an introduction to development planning, with emphasis
on plan formulation rather than implementation.
Requiring no mathematical background beyond
elementary algebra, the book deals with the
role of development planning, the basic framework of static and dynamic input-output analysis the relationship of input-output analysis
and central economic planning, and generalized
development planning through the use of aggregate and main-sector models. No index. (JEL)

Walinsky, Louis J., THE PLANNING AND EXECUTION OF
ECONOMIC DEVELOPMENT: A Nontechnical Guide for
Policy Makers and Administrators, New York,
Toronto, & London, McGraw-Hill Book Company,
Inc., 1963.

Waterston, Albert, DEVELOPMENT PLANNING: Lessons of
Experience, Baltimore, Maryland, The Johns
Hopkins Press, 1965.

World Bank Operations, SECTORAL PROGRAMS AND POLI-
CIES, Baltimore, Maryland, The Johns Hopkins
University Press, 1972.

Political Development

X-REF: AFRICA: Scarritt, ARGENTINA: Ciria,
BOLIVIA: Klein, BRAZIL: Leal, Schmitter, Stepan,
CARIBBEAN: Ameringer, CHILE: Burnett, Caviedes,
Cleaves, Drake, Sigmund, Valenzuela, GUATEMALA:
Silvert, INTERNATIONAL ECONOMICS: Bergsten, LATIN
AMERICA: Blachman, Chalmers, Gordon, Wynia, MALAY-
SIA: Musolf, MEXICO: Gonzales, Johnson, Mabry,
Reyna, von Sauer, PERU: Astiz, Hilliker, PUERTO

RICO: Maldonado, TURKEY: Cohn, Ray, URUGUAY: Weinstein, VENEZUELA: Kolb, Levine, Martz, Powell.

Alexander, Robert J., LATIN AMERICAN POLITICAL PAR-
    TIES, New York, Praeger, 1973. A broad de-
    scription by a prolific Latin Americanist,
    covering both historical and contemporary
    phenomena of all the important political party
    structures in the region. (FA)

Almond, Gabriel A., and Coleman, James S., ed., THE
    POLITICS OF THE DEVELOPING AREAS, Princeton,
    New Jersey, Princeton University Press, 1960.

Clark, Robert P., Jr., DEVELOPMENT AND INSTABILITY:
    Political Change in the Non-Western World, New
    York, Dryden (Holt, Rinehart, and Winston),
    1974.

Deutsch, Karl W., "Social Mobilization and Political
    Development," American Political Science Re-
    view, September 1961.

Fagen, Richard R. and Cornelius, Wayne A., Jr., eds.,
    POLITICAL POWER IN LATIN AMERICA: Seven Con-
    frontations, Englewood Cliffs, New Jersey, Pren-
    tice-Hall, 1970. The technique adopted here is
    interesting and difficult, making heavy demands
    upon the editors' fairness and balance. Seven
    recent power confrontations--in Chile, Venezue-
    la, Argentina, Brazil, Mexico, Cuba and the
    Dominican Republic--are illuminated by extensive
    excerpts from variegated accounts and studies,
    many by observers and scholars in Latin America.
    (FA)

Finkle, Jason L., and Gable, Richard W., eds.,
    POLITICAL DEVELOPMENT AND SOCIAL CHANGE, second
    edition, New York, Wiley, 1971. A comprehen-
    sive reader with articles by well-known authors
    (Ed)

Gamer, Robert E., THE DEVELOPING NATIONS: A Com-
    parative Perspective, Boston, Allyn and Bacon,
    1976.

Heeger, Gerald A., THE POLITICS OF UNDERDEVELOPMENT,
    New York, St. Martin's Press, 1974.

Harris, Louis K. and Alba, Victor, THE POLITICAL CULTURE AND BEHAVIOR OF LATIN AMERICA, Kent, Ohio, Kent State University Press, 1974.

Holt, Robert T., and Turner, John E., THE POLITICAL BASIS OF ECONOMIC DEVELOPMENT: An Exploration in Comparative Political Analysis, Princeton, New Jersey, D. Van Nostrand Company, Inc., 1966.

Huntington, Samuel P., NO EASY CHOICE: Political Participation in Developing Countries, Cambridge, Massachusetts, Harvard University Press, 1976.

Huntington, Samuel, POLITICAL ORDER IN CHANGING SOCIETIES, New Haven, Connecticut, Yale University Press, 1969. A classical work on political development, in which the concepts of civil and praetorian societies are introduced. Also contains a review of data on the relationship between violence and growth. While this relationship is positive, the author attributes greater violence to the process of growth and not to poverty. (Ed)

Jaguaribe, Helio, POLITICAL DEVELOPMENT: A General Theory and a Latin American Case Study, New York, Harper and Row, 1973. A brilliant Brazilian political scientist presents "a general study of the political and the overall development of societies, particularly those of the Latin American countries...from a broad political, anthropological, economic, and historico-sociological perspective, with an emphasis on a global and systemic approach." The work concludes with analysis of the basic Latin American future alternatives of dependency or autonomy vis-a-vis the U.S. Vast in scale, yet intricate as a fine tapestry, this remarkable volume deserves wide recognition. (FA)

Jalan, Bimal, ESSAYS IN DEVELOPMENT POLICY, Delhi, S. G. Wasani for Macmillan of India, 1975. A common theme of the 11 essays (some previously published) is the explicit reference to political philosophies involved in the choices of means and objectives of development and social change. (JEL)

Johnson, John J., POLITICAL CHANGE IN LATIN AMERICA, THE EMERGENCE OF THE MIDDLE SECTORS, Stanford, California, Stanford University Press, 1958.

Jorrin, Miguel, and Martz, John D., LATIN-AMERICAN POLITICAL THOUGHT AND IDEOLOGY, Chapel Hill, University of North Carolina Press, 1970. A useful examination into the theoretical and philosophical basis of political thought in Latin America, through analysis of the writings and themes of the region's foremost thinkers. (FA)

Kathari, Rajul, ed., STATE AND NATION BUILDING: A Third World Perspective, Bombay, India, Allied Publishers Private, Ltd., for Centre of Developing Studies, Delhi, 1976.

Leys, Colin ed., POLITICS AND CHANGE IN DEVELOPING COUNTRIES: Studies in the Theory and Practice of Development, Institute of Development Studies at the University of Sussex, New York, Cambridge University Press, 1969. Brings together in nine papers by as many authors some of the recent work on the theoretical and empirical study of the subject. The essence of the problem is the close interdependence of social, economic, and political factors and therefore a need for an inter-disciplinary approach. Papers are presented under the following headings: I. Development as Problem for Research; II. Perspectives on Political Development; III. Working Papers on Political Development. (JEL)

Lipset, Seymour Martin, "University Students and Politics in Underdeveloped Countries," Reprint No. 255, Berkeley, California, University of California, Institute of Industrial Relations and Institute of International Studies.

Mansbach, Richard W., Yale H. Ferguson, and Donald E. Lampert, THE WEB OF WORLD POLITICS: NON-STATE ACTORS IN THE GLOBAL SYSTEM, Englewood Cliffs, New Jersey: Prentice-Hall, 1976. Mansbach and others cover the activities of a wider range of "nonstate" entities (such as terrorist groups, labor organizations, individual newspapers). Uses substantial and sometimes new data to support interpretations. (BPA)

Palmer, Monte, and Stern, Larry, eds., POLITICAL
    DEVELOPMENT IN CHANGING SOCIETIES: An Analysis
    of Modernization, Lexington, Massachusetts,
    Heath Lexington Books, 1971.

Petras, James, POLITICS AND SOCIAL STRUCTURE IN
    LATIN AMERICA, New York, Monthly Review Press,
    1970. Essays directed to sociology, politics
    and U.S.-Latin American relations. The author
    takes his firm stance on the Left, and tends to
    overestimate economic motivations and causa-
    tions. (FA)

Russett, Bruce M., ed., ECONOMIC THEORIES OF INTER-
    NATIONAL POLITICS, Chicago, Markham Publishing
    Company, 1968.

Sigmund, Paul E., ed., MODELS OF POLITICAL CHANGE IN
    LATIN AMERICA, New York, Praeger, 1970. An
    interesting technique: excerpts from source
    materials, linked by short commentaries, to
    illuminate recent political developments in
    nine nations selected as models of revolution-
    ary, military and constitutional democratic
    change. (FA)

Tachau, Frank, THE DEVELOPING NATIONS: What Path to
    Modernization? New York, Dodd Mead, 1972. A
    book of readings. (Ed)

Tullis, F. Lamond, POLITICS AND SOCIAL CHANGE IN
    THIRD WORLD COUNTRIES, New York, Wiley, 1973.

Uphoff, Norman Thomas, and Ilchman, Warren F., THE
    POLITICAL ECONOMY OF CHANGE, London, University
    of California Press, Ltd.; Los Angeles, Univer-
    sity of California Press, 1969. Develops a
    model of political economy intended as an
    analytical tool for dealing with developing na-
    tions' problems of production and allocation of
    political resources. Uses many of the tools
    and assumptions of conventional economic analy-
    sis but unlike the economist who analyzes only
    goods and services, the authors propose that
    the new political economy must also be concerned
    with existing and future allocation of status
    authority. (JEL)

Uphoff, Norman, and Ilchman, Warren, eds., THE
POLITICAL ECONOMY OF DEVELOPMENT: THEORETICAL
AND EMPIRICAL CONTRIBUTIONS, Berkeley, Cali-
fornia, University of California Press, 1972.

van Niekerk, A. E., POPULISM AND POLITICAL DEVELOP-
MENT IN LATIN AMERICA, Rotterdam: Rotterdam
University Press, 1974. Latin American popul-
ism--its specific functions and aims--is analyzed against the background of the populist
phase in the historical development of the
advanced countries and the populist variations,
called "mobilization systems," now current in
Afro-Asian countries. (FA)

Welch, Claude E., Jr., ed., POLITICAL MODERNIZATION:
A Reader in Comparative Political Change,
Belmont, California, Duxbury Press, Wadsworth
Publishing Co., 1971.

Population

X-REF: AFRICA: de Walle, Hance, Organ, ASIA: Eti-
enne, Wriggins, BRAZIL: Daly, CHILE: Fox, CHINA:
Orleans, COSTA RICA: Waisanen, HUNGER, NUTRITION,
HEALTH: Poleman, INDIA: Frandia, Mandlebaum,
JAMAICA: Walsh, KENYA: Cole, LATIN AMERICA: Smith,
MIDDLE EAST: Cooper, NIGERIA: Hill, Morgan, PERU:
Fox, PHILIPPINES: Rodgers, Ruprecht, TAIWAN: Muel-
ler, VENEZUELA: Edmonston.

Baldwin, George B., "Population Policy in Developed
Countries," Finance and Development, Vol. 10,
No. 4, December 1973.

Berelson, Bernard (ed.), POPULATION POLICY IN DE-
VELOPED COUNTRIES, New York, McGraw-Hill, 1974.
Twenty-four studies of countries where "population is not an issue of really high priority,"
the desire for stability is widespread, and
political aims sometimes lead to "pronatalist"
policies. (FA)

Bowen, Ian, "Nature's Feast Today," Finance and
Development, Vol. 10, Vol. 4, December 1973.

Birdsall, Nancy, "Analytical Approaches to the Relationship of Population Growth and Development," Population and Development Review, Vol. 3, Nos. 1 and 2, March/June 1977.

Blomquist, A. G., "Foreign Aid, Population Growth, and the Gains from Birth Control," Journal of Development Studies, Vol. 8, No. 1, October 1971.

Cassen, R. H., "Population and Development: A Survey," World Development, Vol. 4, No. 10-11, October-November 1976.

Chaplin, David, ed., POPULATION POLICIES AND GROWTH IN LATIN AMERICA, Lexington, Massachusetts, Toronto, London, Lexington Books, D. C. Heath and Company, 1971.

Clark, Colin, POPULATION GROWTH AND LAND USE, New York, Macmillan, St. Martin's Press, 1968. Contains a very useful chapter (No. 4) on the history of world population growth. (Ed)

Coale, Ansley J., ed., ECONOMIC FACTORS IN POPULATION GROWTH, New York, Halsted Press, 1976. Examines the consequences of an optimum population in light of an optimum population change. Considers the problem of fertility as an exercise in economic choice, and discusses the ramifications of population and employment, labor transfer, migration, food supplies, and education. (BPA)

Cuca, Roberto and Pierce, Catherine S., EXPERIMENTS IN FAMILY PLANNING: Lessons from the Developing World, Washington, D.C., World Bank Research Publication, 1978.

Demeny, Paul, "The Populations of the Underdeveloped Countries," Scientific American, September 1974, pp. 149-159.

Denton, F. T. and Spencer, B. G., POPULATION AND THE ECONOMY, Lexington, Massachusetts, Lexington Books, 1975. Interaction of economic and demographic phenomena makes this study important for all concerned with the medium and long-term development of the economy and the population. Hence this book, containing a series of macro-models developed to meet that need, is of interest to planners.

de Walle, Etienne Van, "Trends and Prospects of Population in Tropical Africa," The Annals, Vol. 432, 1977.

Durand, John J., "Historical Estimates of World Populations," Population and Development Review, Vol. 3, No. 3, September, 1977, pp. 253-296. Contains useful data on world populations at different eras and by regions; also bibliography. (Ed)

FAO, POPULATION, FOOD SUPPLY AND AGRICULTURAL DEVELOPMENT, Rome, 1975. Studies food production resources, problems, institutions, services in relation to population: dimensions and causes of hunger and malnutrition; demand for food; food problem of the future; possibilities for increasing production. (BPA)

Finkle, Jason L., and Crane, Barbara B., "The Politics of Bucharest: Population, Development, and the New International Order," Population and Development Review, Vol. 1, No. 1, September 1975.

Habakkuk, H. J., POPULATION GROWTH AND ECONOMIC DEVELOPMENT SINCE 1750, New York: Humanities Press, 1971. Contains four Arthur Pool Memorial Lectures delivered at the University of Leicester (England) in 1968: 1) "Pre-Industrial Population Change," 2) "The Demographic Revolution," 3) "The Decline in Fertility," and 4) "Western Population Patterns and the Underdeveloped Areas." (JEL)

Hawkins, E. K., "A Family View of Population Questions," Finance and Development, Vol. 10, No. 4, December 1973.

Hazledine, T. and Moreland, R. S., "Population and Economic Growth--A World Cross-Section Study," Review of Economic Statistics, Vol. 59, No. 3, August 1977, pp. 253-263. The paper uses cross-section data on 82 countries in four regions to specify the links between economic and demographic variables, and, in particular, to assess the empirical relevance of the neo-

Malthusian low-level equilibrium trap hypothesis and the limits to growth debate. (JEL)

IDRC (Canada), POPULATION POLICY AND NATIONAL DEVELOPMENT, IDRC, 1972. Summarizes possible approaches to the population problem--economic, social, and legal. (BPA)

Johl, S. C., "Process of Growth in a Dualistic Economy: The Interaction of Population Growth and Technological Development in Agriculture," Indian Economic Journal, Vol. 20, No. 2, October-December 1972.

Keeley, Michael, C., ed., POPULATION, PUBLIC POLICY, AND ECONOMIC DEVELOPMENT, New York, Praeger, 1976. Uses economic-demographic modeling and simulation analyses as well as mathematical analytic techniques and the microeconomics of individual decision making. Reveals the importance of accounting for demographic variables in development planning. (BPA)

Keesing, D. B., "Population and Industrial Development," American Economic Review, Vol. LVIII, No. 3, Part 1, June 1968.

Kelley, Allen C., "The Role of Population in Models of Economic Growth," American Economic Review, Vol. LXIV, No. 2, May 1974.

King, Timothy, ed., POPULATION POLICIES AND ECONOMIC DEVELOPMENT, for the World Bank, Baltimore, Maryland, Johns Hopkins, 1974.

Kogut, E. L. and Langoni, C. G., "Population Growth, Income Distribution, and Economic Development," International Labour Review, Vol. III, No. 4, April 1975.

Kuznets, Simon, POPULATION, CAPITAL, AND GROWTH: Selected Essays, New York, Norton, 1973. Clear but never simple answers to basic questions. The Nobel Prize winner more often stresses the limits rather than the extent of our knowledge. (FA)

MacDonald, Maurice and Mueller, Eva, "The Measurement of Income in Fertility Surveys in Developing Countries," Studies in Family Planning Vol. 6, No. 1, January 1975, pp. 22-28.

163

McNamara, Robert S., ACCELERATING POPULATION STABI-
    LIZATION THROUGH SOCIAL AND ECONOMIC PROGRESS,
    Overseas Development Council Development Paper
    No. 24, August 1977.

Mehta, B. C., "Population Explosion and Public
    Policy," Economic Affairs, Vol. 16, No. 12,
    December 1971.

Morgan, Robert W., "Niveaux de fécondité et évolu-
    tion de la fecondite," CROISSANCE DÉMOGRAPHIQUE
    ET ÉVOLUTION SOCIOÉCONOMIQUE EN AFRIQUE DE
    L'QUEST, Paris, Gustave Harcourt, 1973.

Morgan, Robert W., "A Population Dynamics Survey in
    Lagos Nigeria," Social Science and Medical
    Journal, Vol. 7, 1973.

Mueller, Eva, "The Impact of Demographic Factors on
    Economic Development in Taiwan," POPULATION AND
    DEVELOPMENT REVIEW, Vol. 2, Nos. 1 & 2, March
    and June 1977.

National Academy of Sciences, Office of the Foreign
    Secretary, RAPID POPULATION GROWTH: Conse-
    quences and Policy Implications, prepared by a
    study committee of the Office of the Foreign
    Secretary, National Academy of Sciences with
    the support of the Agency for International
    Development, Baltimore, published for the
    National Academy of Sciences by the Johns
    Hopkins Press, 1971.

Pitchford, J. D., POPULATION IN ECONOMIC GROWTH, New
    York, American Elsevier Publishing Company,
    1974. Mathematical theorems and models of
    population growth; optimal population with
    respect to scale returns, trade, resources, and
    age-structure, population in an optimal growth
    structure. (Ed)

Population Reference Bureau, WORLD POPULATION GROWTH
    AND RESPONSE: 1965-1975 A Decade of Global
    Action, Washington, D.C., 1976.

Powelson, John P., "Population Growth and Unemploy-
    ment in Africa (with special reference to
    Kenya)" Cultures et Developpement, Vol. VII,
    No. 1, 1975.

Razin, A., and Ben-Zion, U., "An Intergenerational Model of Population Growth," *American* *Economic* *Review*, Vol. 65, No. 5, December 1975.

Ridker, Ronald G., ed., POPULATION AND DEVELOPMENT: The Search for Selective Interventions, Baltimore, Johns Hopkins University Press, 1976. The specialists who contributed to this volume investigate probable socio-economic determinants of fertility that might be amenable to selective interventions or policy manipulation. They combine the effects upon fertility of income distribution, education, nutrition, and health, mortality, residential location, the direct cost and value of children, the employment and status of women, and the prevalence of mass media and modern consumer goods. In addition to presenting their findings, they recommend various ways in which these determinants can be used to stimulate the desire for smaller families. Providing valuable insights into contemporary population problems, it is hoped that this book will provide an incentive for further research. (BPA)

Ridker, Ronald G., "Resource and Amenity Implications of Population Changes," *American* *Economic* *Review*, Vol. LXIV, No. 2, May 1974.

Samuelson, P. A., "The Optimum Growth Rate for Population: Agreement and Evaluation," *Inter-* *national* *Economic* *Review*, June 1976. High population growth in a model with consumption at different ages of life tends to lower lifetime consumption because of need to widen capital; but, in a model with consumption at different ages, it tends to raise lifetime consumption because of more workers per retiree. There may therefore be an optimal rate of population growth. These counterforces may balance at a minimum rather than maximum growth rate. The present analysis shows that, once land's scarcity is recognized and realistic properties of production are assumed at low and high capital/labor ratios, it becomes doubtful that strong growth could be optimal. Life-cycle considerations, at best, bias optimal growth paths toward higher population growth, *ceteris* *paribus*. (JEL)

Sanchez-Albornoz, Nicolas, THE POPULATION OF LATIN
AMERICA: A History, Berkeley, University of
California Press, 1974. This volume is useful
and welcome: a complete demographic history,
including migration, race mixtures, immigration
and urbanization, from pre-Columbian times to
the present, with a forward projection to the
year 2000. The treatment achieves an unusual
combination of scholarship, readability, and
wide historical and human awareness. (FA)

Sankaran, Sundaram, "Population and the World Bank,"
Finance and Development, Vol. 10, No. 4,
December 1973.

Scientific American, THE HUMAN POPULATION, New York,
September 1974. The entire issue of Scientific
American is devoted to articles on the world
population issue.

Simon, Julian L., THE ECONOMICS OF POPULATION GROWTH,
Princeton, New Jersey, Princeton University
Press, 1977. Comparison with stationary and
very fast rates of population growth shows moderate population growth to have long-run positive effects on the standard of living. Since
each person constitutes a burden in the short
run, whether population growth is judged good
or bad depends on the importance the short run
is accorded relative to the long run. (BPA)

Singh, Jyoti Shankar, ed., WORLD POPULATION POLI-
CIES, New York, Praeger, 1978. This volume
provides detailed information on developments
in major geographic regions and points out
similarities and differences among regional
approaches. It includes the World Population
Plan of Action and Recommendations from the
World Population Conference (Bucharest, 1974);
subsequent regional consultation results;
inter-regional consultation results; reports on
monitoring population policies and trends.
International Population Assistance; resource
allocation priorities; and an overview of
developments since Bucharest. (BPA)

Spengler, Joseph, POPULATION CHANGE, MODERNIZATION,
AND WELFARE, Englewood Cliffs, New Jersey,
Prentice-Hall, 1974. A remarkable condensation

of data and analysis by one of the seniors in the field comes to fairly familiar conclusions. (FA)

Spengler, Joseph J., "The Population Problem: Yesterday, Today, Tomorrow," The Southern Economic Journal, Vol. XXVII, No. 3, 1961.

Stamper, Maxwell B., POPULATION AND PLANNING IN DEVELOPING NATIONS: A Review of Sixty Development Plans for the 1970's, New York, The Population Council, 1977.

Stryker, J. D., "Population Density, Agricultural Technique, and Land Utilization in a Village Economy," American Economic Review, Vol. 66, No. 3, June 1976.

State, Department of, "United Nations World Population Conference," Bucharest, August 19-30, 1974, reprint from The Department of State Bulletin, Washington, D.C., Department of State, 1974.

Sweezy, Alan, and Owens, Aaron, "The Impact of Population Growth on Employment," American Economic Review, Vol. LXIV, No. 2, May 1974.

Teitelbaum, Michael S., "Population and Development: Is a Consensus Possible?" Foreign Affairs, Vol. 52, No. 4, July 1974.

Tilly, Charles, HISTORICAL STUDIES OF CHANGING FERTILITY, Princeton, New Jersey: Princeton University Press, 1978. The nine papers in this volume examine the historical experience of particular populations in Western Europe and North America in a search for the processes that change fertility patterns. The authors stress the effects on fertility of changing mortality. Several theoretical discussions emphasize the importance both of the turnover in adult positions due to mortality and of the highly variable life expectancy of children. The empirical analyses consistently reveal strong associations between levels of fertility and mortality. On the other hand, some essays question whether variations in opportunities to marry acted as quite the regulator that Malthus and many after him have thought. In both pre-industrial and industrial populations, fertility regulation within marriage emerges as the primary mechanism by which adjustment occurred. (BPA)

Todaro, Michael P., "Development Policy and Population Growth: A Framework for Planners," Population and Development Review, Vol. 3, Nos. 1 & 2, March and June 1977, pp. 23-43.

Trewartha, Glenn T., A GEOGRAPHY OF POPULATION: World Patterns, New York, Wiley, 1969. Population numbers and their distributions over the earth's land surface are traced from prehistoric times to the beginning of the modern era. Emphasis is upon how the map of world population changed through several millenniums. Then, the focus shifts to the last three centuries, or the period since about 1650. A third section involves the contemporary scene. (BPA)

United Nations, CONCISE REPORT ON THE WORLD POPULATION SITUATION IN 1970-1975 AND ITS LONG-RANGE IMPLICATIONS, New York, United Nations, 1974. Information on population size and growth, birth and death rates, international migration, aage structure, school enrollment, labor, urbanization, population dynamics and structure. United Nations long-range projections. (BPA)

United Nations, THE DETERMINANTS AND CONSEQUENCES OF POPULATION TRENDS: New Summary of Findings on Interaction of Demographic, Economic, and Social Factors, Volume I, New York, United Nations, 1973. Important analytic inventory of existing knowledge and hypotheses concerning the factors affecting population trends and the influence of these trends upon economic and social conditions. Synthesizes the findings of major research on population change through review of relevant literature in demography, economics, sociology, geography, history, and related fields. (BPA)

UNFPA, INVENTORY OF POPULATION PROJECTS IN DEVELOPING COUNTRIES AROUND THE WORLD 1973/74, UNFPA, 1975. The donor agencies--an overview; country programs; regional, interregional, global programs; source materials--published sources, where to write for additional information. (BPA)

United Nations, REPORT OF THE UNITED NATIONS WORLD
    POPULATION CONFERENCE, 1974, New York, United
    Nations, 1975. Conference plan of action and
    recommendations for: rural development, study
    of socio-economic factors in demographic change,
    promotion of the status of women, improvement
    of world food program, equitable distribution
    of world resources. (BPA)

United Nations, WORLD POPULATION PLAN OF ACTION,
    World Population Conference, Bucharest, Romania,
    19-30 August, 1974, New York, United Nations,
    1974.

U.S. Department of Commerce, Bureau of Census, WORLD
    POPULATION 1977: Recent Demographic Estimates
    for the Countries and Regions of the World,
    Washington, D.C., 1978. The findings show that
    the "population explosion" may be slowing down,
    but slightly. (Ed)

Watson, Walter B., FAMILY PLANNING IN THE DEVELOPING
    WORLD: A Review of Programs, New York, The
    Population Council, 1977. A Population Council
    fact book.

World Bank, ATLAS: Population, Per Capita Product,
    and Growth Rates, published annually by the
    World Bank.

World Bank, POPULATION PLANNING, Sector Working
    Paper, Washington, D.C., World Bank, 1972.

Young, Louise B., ed., POPULATION IN PERSPECTIVE,
    New York, Oxford University Press, 1968. The
    factors which influence fertility are complex
    and interrelated. The people of India, for
    instance, want more children than the people of
    France, and they want them for different rea-
    sons. Methods of family planning which are
    acceptable to Germans or Scandinavians may not
    be acceptable to the Puerto Ricans for aesthetic
    or religious reasons. An understanding of
    these differences, a sensitivity to the beliefs
    and aspirations of all the world's peoples will
    help to achieve a wise population policy.
    Oversimplification, on the other hand, is
    likely to do more harm than good. (BPA)

Poverty

X-REF: INDIA: Dandekar, ISRAEL: Greenberg, AGRI-
CULTURAL DEVELOPMENT: Gittinger, FINANCE: Leff.

Balogh, Thomas, THE ECONOMICS OF POVERTY, second
edition, White Plains, New York, International
Arts and Sciences Press, Inc., 1974.

Beckerman, Wilfred, "Are the Poor Always With Us?"
New Statesman, September 10, 1976, pp. 334-336.

Beckford, George L., PERSISTENT POVERTY, New York,
Oxford University Press, 1972. "The persistence of underdevelopment in plantation economies derives basically from the nature of the
plantation system itself." The case for this
conclusion is well argued in this interesting
book, by a Jamaican economist who succeeds in
his aim "to present a genuinely Third World
perspective" on some old but still contemporary
institutions. (FA)

Eames, Edwin, and Goode, Judith Granich, URBAN POV-
ERTY IN A CROSS-CULTURAL CONTEXT, New York, The
Free Press (Macmillan), 1973.

Elliott, Charles, PATTERNS OF POVERTY IN THE THIRD
WORLD: A Study of Social and Economic Stratification, assisted by Francoise deMorster,
Praeger Special Studies in International Economics and Development, New York, Praeger, in
cooperation with the World Council of Churches,
1975. The author examined 13 countries, 10 in
Africa and 3 in Asia, selected on the basis of
relative availability of data, rather than as
representative of the Third World as a whole.
The book is concerned with the causes of poverty within a country, in particular the influence of socioeconomic status, intragroup competition (which determines which individuals
within a group have control over resources),
and intergroup competition (showing how resources are divided between groups with differ-
ing interests). Index. (JEL)

Goodwin, Leonard, DO THE POOR WANT TO WORK? A
Social-Psychological Study of Work Orientations,
Washington, D.C., The Brookings Institutions,
1972.

Myrdal, Gunnar, THE CHALLENGE OF WORLD POVERTY: A
World Anti-Poverty Program in Outline, Foreword
by Francis O. Wilcox, New York, Pantheon, 1970.
Besides a brief summary of his Asian drama, the
book contains Myrdal's major policy recommendations for the problems facing the Third World--
especially with reference to agriculture, population, education, "social indiscipline,"
trade, and aid. Concludes with a discussion of
the "politics of development." No index.
(JEL)

Pechman, Joseph A., and Timpane, P. Michael, ed.,
WORK INCENTIVES AND INCOME GUARANTEES: The New
Jersey Negative Income Tax Experiment, Wash-
ington, D.C., The Brookings Institute, 1975.

Papanek, Gustav F., "The Poor of Jakarta," Economic
Development and Cultural Change.

Simpson, David, "The Dimensions of World Poverty,"
Scientific American, Vol. 219, No. 5, November
1968, pp. 27-35.

Stamp, Elizabeth, GROWING OUT OF POVERTY, Oxford,
England, Oxford University Press, 1977.

World Bank, THE ASSAULT ON WORLD POVERTY: Problems
of Rural Development, Education and Health,
Baltimore and London: Johns Hopkins University
Press for World Bank, 1975. The collection of
five sector policy papers analyzes the causes
of poverty, the ways it can be alleviated, and
the role of the World Bank in reducing the
incidence of poverty. The first paper on rural
development analyzes how rural poverty is
reflected in poor nutrition, inadequate shelter, and poor health standards. The paper on
agricultural credit discusses aspects of productivity, suggesting that the credit flow to
small farmers is inadequate. The next paper
shows that land reform is consistent with the
objectives of increased agricultural production, more equitable distribution of income,
and expanded employment. The paper on education suggests that educational systems in
developing countries are inequitable, favoring
city dwellers, and do not necessarily serve
economic and social development. The final
paper on health shows that programs need to be

redesigned to serve the poor more effectively
and to increase productivity. (JEL)

Project Analysis

Adler, Hans A., SECTOR AND PROJECT PLANNING IN
TRANSPORTATION, World Bank Staff Occasional
Papers Number Four, Washington, D.C., International Bank for Reconstruction and Development, 1967.

Anderson, L. G., and Settle, R. F., BENEFIT-COST
ANALYSIS: A Practical Guide, Lexington, Massachusetts, Lexington Books, 1977. A two-pronged
analysis that provides a basic understanding of
the theoretical foundations of benefit-cost
analysis and a demonstration of its application to realistic situations. (BPA)

Baker, Bruce N., and Eris, Rene L., AN INTRODUCTION
TO PERT-CPM, Homewood, Illinois, Richard D.
Irwin, Inc., 1964.

Balassa, Bela, "The Income Distribution Parameter
in Project Appraisal," World Bank Reprint
series No. 41, reprinted from Economic Progress,
Private Values, and Public Policy, Amsterdam,
North-Holland, 1977.

Congress, THE ANALYSIS AND EVALUATION OF PUBLIC
EXPENDITURES: The PPB System, A Compendium of
Papers submitted to the Subcommittee on Economy
in Government of the Joint Economic Committee,
Congress of the U.S., Washington D.C., U.S.
Government Printing Office, 1969.

Dorfman, Robert, ed., MEASURING BENEFITS OF GOVERN-
MENT INVESTMENTS, Washington, D.C., The Brookings Institution, 1965.

Enke, Stephen, ed., DEFENSE MANAGEMENT, New Jersey,
Prentice-Hall, Inc., 1967.

FitzGerald, Edmund V. K., PUBLIC SECTOR INVESTMENT
PLANNING FOR DEVELOPING COUNTRIES, London,
Macmillan, New York; Holmes & Meier, 1978.
Textbook on social cost-benefit analysis and
public investment planning for developing
countries. Restricts the treatment of the

172

social dimensions of public sector project analysis to assessment of project impact on national objectives, such as income redistribution and autonomous industrialization. (JEL)

Gittinger, J. Price, ECONOMIC ANALYSIS OF AGRICULTURAL PROJECTS, Baltimore, Maryland, The Johns Hopkins University Press, 1972.

Grant, Eugene L., and Ireson, W. Grant, PRINCIPLES OF ENGINEERING ECONOMY, New York, The Ronald Press Company, 1960.

Hagen, Everett E., HANDBOOK FOR INDUSTRY STUDIES, Glencoe, Illinois, The Free Press, 1958.

Harberger, Arnold C., PROJECT EVALUATION: Collected Papers, Markham Economics Series, Chicago, Illinois, Markham, 1973. A collection of twelve essays on project appraisal, cost-benefit analysis, and similar issues in development planning written by the author during the last few years. Specifically, the papers deal with such topics, as techniques of project appraisal, a survey of the cost-benefit analysis literature, discount rates, social opportunity cost measurement, rate of return to capital estimation, social opportunity cost of labor measurement, marginal cost pricing and social investment criteria, cost-benefit analysis as applied to transportation projects, an example of cost-benefit analysis applied to an irrigation dam with Lucio G. Reca and Juan A. Zapata, and issues concerning capital assistance to developing nations. Index. (JEL)

King, John A., Jr., ECONOMIC DEVELOPMENT PROJECTS AND THEIR APPRAISAL: Cases and Principles from the Experience of the World Bank, Baltimore, Maryland, The Johns Hopkins Press, 1967.

Lal, Deepak, METHODS OF PROJECT ANALYSIS: A Review, Baltimore and London, The Johns Hopkins University Press, 1974.

Lal, Deepak, METHODS OF PROJECT ANALYSIS: A Review, World Bank Staff Occasional Papers, No. 16, Baltimore, Maryland, The Johns Hopkins University Press, 1974. A comparison and critical evaluation of "various alternative project selection procedures which have been put forward, particularly for application in less developed countries." The author proceeds by analyzing cost-benefit analysis in the light of foreign trade, factor markets, income distribution and employment, and balance of payments distortions. (JEL)

Little, Ian M. D., and Mirrlees, James A., MANUAL OF INDUSTRIAL PROJECT ANALYSIS IN DEVELOPING COUNTRIES, Vol. II: SOCIAL COST BENEFIT ANALYSIS, Paris, Development Centre of the Organization for Economic Co-operation and Development, 1969. "Aimed first to convince its readers that, especially for industrial projects, social cost-benefit analysis is both important and possible (Part I); and, secondly, to teach them how it can best be done (Part II)." The techniques considered apply particularly to developing countries, where the price machanism is not a reliable guide for policy and data are scarce. Useful as a manual. (JEL)

Little, I. M. D., and Mirrlees, James A., PROJECT APPRAISAL AND PLANNING FOR DEVELOPING COUNTRIES, New York, Basic Books, 1974. In this work, the shadow wage is more explicitly dependent on income distribution, and several additions of material are noted--a lengthier discussion of the organization of project planning and evaluation and of its relationship to sectoral and macroeconomic planning, more concern with agricultural and infrastructural projects, more work with the measurement of production benefits of non-traded goods and services, more treatment of income distribution, a more detailed application of "the principles to private investment, particularly private overseas investment." (JEL)

Little, I. M. D., and Scott, M. FG., USING SHADOW PRICES, New York, Holmes and Meier, 1976. Seven papers showing the relevance of shadow pricing to economic policy questions other than project appraisal; uses the Little-Mirrlees approach to shadow pricing. Includes two case studies, one a cost-benefit analysis of the Trinidad Hilton and the other on low-income housing in Kenya, bringing out the importance of prices as a determinant of social profitability. The remaining papers examine the social profitability of foreign and domestic

174

timber firms in Ghana; shadow wages in Mauritius, illustrating one way of estimating income weights; the problems of appraising private investment projects; estimating the accounting rate of interest using a dynamic model of the entire economy; and problems in implementing accounting prices. Index. (JEL)

Mansfield, Edwin, ed., MANAGERIAL ECONOMICS AND OPERATIONS RESEARCH: A nonmathematical Introduction, New York, W. W. Norton and Company, Inc., 1966.

Misham, E. J., COST-BENEFIT ANALYSIS, New York, Praeger, 1976. The author uses case studies to explain economic concepts and their uses and limitations which are relevant to cost-benefit analysis. The book includes a section on program evaluation that confronts some of the issues which frequently arise in estimating the benefits of public projects. (BPA)

Muthoo, M. K., "Planned Growth and the Rate of Discount for Project Appraisal in Developing Countries with Special Reference to India," Economic Affairs, Vol. 15, Nos. 1-2, January-February 1970.

OECD, MANUAL OF INDUSTRIAL PROJECT ANALYSIS: In Developing Countries, Volume 1: METHODOLOGY AND CASE STUDIES, Paris, Development Centre of the Organisation for Economic Co-operation and Development, 1968.

Papandreou, Andreas and Zohar, Uri, PROJECT SELECTION FOR NATIONAL PLANS, Praeger Special Studies in International Economics and Development, New York, Praeger, in cooperation with York University, Toronto, Canada, 1974. Study concerned with the formulation and evaluation of economic development projects and programs which carries out evaluation under the assumption of "an articulated complete social ranking of alternative states of the world...." (JEL)

Reutlinger, Shlomo, TECHNIQUES FOR PROJECT APPRAISAL UNDER UNCERTAINTY, World Bank Staff Occasional Papers No. 10, Baltimore, Maryland, Johns Hopkins Press for the International Bank for Reconstruction and Development, 1970. "This paper recommends that the best available judg-

ments about the various factors underlying the
cost and benefit estimates of the (investment)
project be recorded in terms of probability
distributions and that these distributions be
aggregated in a mathematically correct manner
to yield a probability distribution of the rate
of return or net present worth, of the project."
(JEL)

Rondinelli, Dennis A., ed., PLANNING DEVELOPMENT
PROJECTS, Community Development Series, Vol.
35, Stroudsburg, Pennsylvania, Dowden, Hutchinson and Ross, 1977. Fifteen previously published papers and case studies. The primary
theme is that social, political, and cultural
considerations must be integrated into the
economic and technical rationality of project
planning, implementation, and management in
developing countries. (JEL)

Sassone, Peter G., and Schaffer, William A., COST-
BENEFIT ANALYSIS: A Handbook, New York, Academic Press, 1978. This book is addressed to
practicing cost-benefit analysts, to government
officials who commission, oversee, and use
cost-benefit studies, to citizens who wish to
understand the workings of an analysis that may
recommend turning their favorite trout stream
into a lake, and to students in such courses as
environmental economics, engineering economics,
applied microeconomics, applied welfare economics, public sector decision making, and, of
course, cost-benefit analysis. The material is
accessible to readers with little or no formal
training in economics. (BPA)

Schneider, Hartnut, NATIONAL OBJECTIVES AND PROJECT
APPRAISAL IN DEVELOPING COUNTRIES, OECD Publication Center, June 1975.

Schwartz, Hugh and Berney, Richard, eds., SOCIAL AND
ECONOMIC DIMENSIONS OF PROJECT EVALUATION,
Washington, D.C., Inter-American Development
Bank, 1977.

Solomon, Morris J., ANALYSIS OF PROJECTS FOR ECONOMIC
GROWTH: An Operational System for Their Formu-
lation, Evaluation, and Implementation, Praeger
Special Studies in International Economics and
Development, New York, Praeger, 1970. Contains
a format for drawing up and executing projects,

as suggested by the title, in developing countries. Discusses project selection, market analysis, financing, timing, and similar aspects associated with any one project. Includes a case study of a proposed chemical project based on the author's experience in establishing such a plant in an undisclosed Middle East country. (JEL)

Squire, Lyn and van der Tak, Herman C., ECONOMIC ANALYSIS OF PROJECTS, A World Bank Research Publication, Baltimore, The Johns Hopkins University Press for the World Bank, 1975. Contains a nontechnical review of the basic notions of cost-benefit analysis, an explanation of the nature and derivation of shadow prices, and a review of various approximate methods for estimating shadow prices in practice. (JEL)

United Nations, MANUAL ON ECONOMIC DEVELOPMENT PROJECTS, New York, United Nations, 1958.

United Nations, GUIDE TO PRACTICAL PROJECT APPRAISAL: Social Benefit-Cost Analysis in Developing Countries, New York, United Nations Industrial Development Organization, 1978.

van Delft, Ad, and Nijkamp, Peter, MULTI-CRITERIA ANALYSIS AND REGIONAL DECISION-MAKING, Studies in Applied Regional Science, Vol. 8, Leiden, Martinus Nijhoff Social Sciences Division, 1977. Focuses on the use of operational methods for multi-criteria decision-making regarding evaluation of planning projects. Traditional unidimensional (single criterion) objective evaluation techniques, such as cost-benefit and cost-effectiveness analyses, and shadow project approach are reviewed along with multi-criteria evaluation methods, such as trade-off analyses, goals-achievement method, expected-value method, correspondence analysis, permutation method, discrepancy analysis, and concordance analyses. Study then focuses on concordance analysis, which selects an optimum plan out of a series of competing alternatives on the basis of simultaneously existing multiple objectives. (JEL)

X-REF: ASIA: Morgan, PROJECT ANALYSIS: van Delft,
TRADE: Ghai.

Barkin, David and King, Timothy, REGIONAL ECONOMIC
    DEVELOPMENT: The River Basin Approach in
    Mexico, New York, Cambridge University Press,
    1970.   Evaluates the strategy of using river
    basin projects as the core of regional develop-
    ment policies from both economic and political
    angles.   (BPA)

Bendavid, Avrom, REGIONAL ECONOMIC ANALYSIS FOR
    PRACTITIONERS: An Introduction to Common
    Descriptive Methods (Revised Edition), New   ·
    York, Praeger, 1974.   Covers the most widely
    useful methods of regional economic analysis,
    such as regional accounting, flow studies,
    economic base analysis, input-output analysis,
    and employment-shift analysis methods oriented
    to the availability of limited resources in
    developing countries.   (BPA)

Bendavid-Val, Avrom and Waller, Peter P., eds.,
    ACTION ORIENTED APPROACHES TO REGIONAL DEVELOP-
    MENT PLANNING, New York, Praeger, 1975.   Sug-
    gests alternatives to conventional "comprehen-
    sive" regional planning for developing regions.
    Includes studies of Zambia, Thailand, and Ethi-
    opia.   Shows techniques used to minimize time
    lag between start of planning and implementa-
    tion by focusing on central issues, while main-
    taining an overall coordinated approach to
    development.   (BPA)

Boudeville, J-R., PROBLEMS OF REGIONAL ECONOMIC
    PLANNING, Edinburgh, Scotland, Edinburgh Uni-
    versity Press, 1966.

El Mallakh, Ragaei, ECONOMIC DEVELOPMENT AND RE-
    GIONAL COOPERATION: Kuwait, Chicago, Univer-
    sity of Chicago Press, 1970.

Gillie, F. B., BASIC THINKING IN REGIONAL PLANNING,
    The Hague and Paris, Mouton Publishers, 1971.

Hirsch, Werner Z. and Sonenblum, Sidney, SELECTING
    REGIONAL INFORMATION FOR GOVERNMENT PLANNING
    AND DECISION MAKING, New York, Praeger, 1970.

Isard, Walter and Cumberland, John H., REGIONAL ECO-
NOMIC PLANNING: Techniques of Analysis for
Less Developed Countries, Paris, The European
Productivity Agency of the Organisation for
European Economic Co-operation, 1960.

Lindberg, Leon N. and Scheingold, Stuart A., eds.,
REGIONAL INTEGRATION/Theory and Research,
Washington, D.C., Center for International
Affairs, 1971. The ten critical essays in this
work represent the variety of theories and
approaches of the chief contributors in the
field of regional integration, the study of
non-coercive integration among nations. Focusing on research strategies and techniques, the
authors probe new directions for added insights
into the integrative process--problems of
nation-building, integration of planned economies, and consequences of regional consolida-
tion. (BPA)

Mera, Koichi, INCOME DISTRIBUTION AND REGIONAL
DEVELOPMENT, Tokyo, Japan, University of Tokyo
Press, 1976. Relates income distribution to
main body of economics in context of regional
development. (BPA)

Rural Development

X-REF: AFRICA: Lele, ASIA: Asian, BOLIVIA:
McEwen, CHILE: Loveman, CHINA: Sigurdson, COLOMBIA:
Berry, EAST AFRICA: Chambers, Institute, ETHIOPIA:
Tecle, KENYA: Kenya, MEXICO: Beals, Puebla,
NIGERIA: Federal, Olatunbosun, Smock, PAKISTAN:
Khan, PERU: Whyte, PHILIPPINES: Resnick, POVERTY:
World, SOUTH AFRICA: Palmer, TANZANIA: Cunningham,
Finucane, Macpherson, Mwapachu, Odia, Omari, TECH-
NOLOGY: Bottomley.

Adams, Dale W., "Mobilizing Household Savings
Through Rural Financial Markets," Economic
Development and Cultural Change, Vol. 26, No.
3, April 1978, pp. 547-560.

Amey, Alan, URBAN-RURAL RELATIONS IN TANZANIA:
Methodology Issues and Preliminary Results,
Development Studies Discussion Paper, Univer-
sity of East Anglia, December 1976.

Apthorpe, R., "African Rural Development Planning
and the Conceptions of the Human Factor,"
Journal of Development Studies, Vol. 6, No. 4,
July 1970.

Bardhan, P. K., "On the Minimum Level of Living and
the Rural Poor," Indian Economic Review, Vol.
V, No. 1, April 1970.

Bolnick, B. R., COMPARATIVE HARAMBEE: History and
Theory of Voluntary Collective Behavior, Uni-
versity of Nairobi, Institute for Development
Studies, Discussion Paper No. 198, April 1974.

Don, Yehuda, "Industrialization in Advanced Rural
Communities: The Israeli Kibbutz," Land Tenure
Center No. 112, Madison, Wisconsin, January
1977.

Fry, James, "Rural-Urban Terms of Trade, 1960-73: A
Note," in African Social Research, No. 19, June
1975, pp. 730-738.

Hewes, Laurence I., RURAL DEVELOPMENT: World Frontiers, Iowa State University Press, 1974.
Explored in this text are the capacity of the
environment to bear increased pressures of
intensified agriculture and human capacity to
increase agricultural output within environmental limitations. Topics include the Green
Revolution, advancing technology, the politics
of poverty, the role of energy, rural and urban
planning, and international development
assistance. (BPA)

Jedlicka, Allen D., ORGANIZATION FOR RURAL DEVELOP-
MENT: Risk Taking and Appropriate Technology,
New York, Praeger, 1977. Jedlicka suggests that
extension services and extension agents supply
the best impetus for successful technology
transfer through democratically organized small
groups. He points out, however, that most
developing nations underutilize their extension
services . (BPA)

Loomis, Charles P. and Beegle, J. Allan, A STRATEGY
FOR RURAL CHANGE, New York, Schenkman Publish-
ing Co., Halsted Press Division, John Wiley and
Sons, Inc., 1975.

North Central Regional Center for Rural Development,
RURAL DEVELOPMENT: Research Priorities, Iowa
State University Press, 1973. Emphasis is on
aid to nonfarm rural areas and the pursuit of
various avenues of research to help rural communities deal with social and economic inequities resulting from rapid urban expansion.(BPA)

Saxena, P. S. and Dubey, R. M., "Rural Unemployment:
A Direct Approach," Economic Affairs, Vol. 18,
No. 6, June 1973.

Thirsk, Wayne, RURAL CREDIT AND INCOME DISTRIBUTION
IN COLOMBIA, Houston, Texas, Rice University,
Program of Development Studies, Summer 1974.

Whitby, M. C.; Tansey, A. W.; Robins, D. L. J.; and
Willis, K. G., RURAL RESOURCE DEVELOPMENT, New
York, Harper and Row, 1974.

Wilson, Frank A. and Amann, Victor F., eds., FINANC-
ING RURAL DEVELOPMENT: Proceedings of the
Eastern Africa Agricultural Economics Society
Conference, Kampala, Uganda, Eastern Africa
Agricultural Economics Society and The Makerere
Institute of Social Research, 1975.

World Bank, RURAL DEVELOPMENT, Sector Policy Paper,
February 1975.

World Bank, RURAL ELECTRIFICATION, A World Bank
Paper, October 1975.

World Bank, VILLAGE WATER SUPPLY, A World Bank
Paper, March 1976.

Yudelman, Montague, "Integrated Rural Development
Projects: The Bank's Experience," Finance and
Development, Vol. 14, No. 1, March 1977.

Rural-Urban Migration

X-REF: AGRARIAN REFORM: Shaw, BRAZIL: Yap,
COLOMBIA: Flinn, MEXICO: Cornelium, Toscano, PERU:
Smith, TANZANIA: Amey.

Berry, R. Albert and Soligo, Ronald, RURAL-URBAN
    MIGRATION, AGRICULTURAL OUTPUT, AND THE SUPPLY
    PRICE OF LABOUR IN A LABOUR-SURPLUS ECONOMY,
    Center Paper #118, New Haven, Connecticut, Yale
    University, Economic Growth Center, 1968.

Brown, Alan A., and Neunberger, Egon, INTERNAL
    MIGRATION: A Comparative Perspective, New
    York, Academic Press, 1977.

Connell, John, et al., MIGRATION FROM RURAL AREAS:
    The Evidence from Village Studies: A Study
    Prepared for the International Labor Office,
    within the framework of the World Employment
    Programme, Institute of Development Studies,
    Village Studies Programme, Delhi, New York,
    London and Melbourne, Oxford University Press,
    1976. Analysis of migration patterns from
    villages in the Third World. Considers char-
    acteristics of villages with highest migration
    rates, of the migrants themselves, and the
    impact on the village. Based on data from
    previous village studies plus data from 40
    Indian village studies for the 1950's and early
    1960's. Concludes that "intra-rural inequality
    is at once the main cause, and a serious conse-
    quence, of rural emigration," and that movement
    of the rural poor to the urban sector in search
    of high incomes does not aid in reducing both
    rural-urban and intra-rural income inequality.
    Statistical tables on migration, remittances,
    education, and occupation. (JEL)

Fields, G. S., "Rural-Urban Migration, Urban Unem-
    ployment and Under-Employment, and Job-Search
    Activity in LCDs," Journal of Development
    Economics, Vol. 2, No. 2, June 1975.

Guade, J. and Peek, P., "The Economic Effects of
    Rural-Urban Migration," International Labour
    Review, Vol. 114, No. 3, November-December
    1976.

Harris, J. R. and Todaro, M. P., "Migration, Unem-
    ployment and Development: A Two-Sector Analy-
    sis," American Economic Review, Vol. LX, No. 1,
    March 1970, pp. 126-142. A follow-up and
    further elaboration of the classic Todaro
    model. (Ed)

182

Mazumdar, Dipak, "The Rural-Urban Wage Gap, Migration, and the Shadow Wage," World Bank Reprint Series, No. 42, reprinted from Oxford Economic Papers, (November 1976).

Mazumdar, Dipak, "The Urban Informal Sector," World Development, Vol. 4, No. 8, 1976, pp. 655-679.

Moots, Baron L., "Migration, Community of Origin, and Status Attainment: A Comparison of Two Metropolitan Communities in Developing Societies," Social Forces, Vol. 54, June 4, 1976, pp. 816-832.

Oberai, A. S., "Migration, Unemployment and the Urban Labour Market: A Case Study of the Sudan," International Labour Review, Vol. 115, No. 2, 1977.

Roussel, L., "Measuring Rural-Urban Drift in Developing Countries: A Suggested Method," International Labour Review, Vol. 101, No. 3, March 1970.

Sadove, Robert, "Urban Needs of Developing Countries," Finance and Development, Vol. 10, No. 2, June 1973.

Sethuraman, S. V., "The Urban Informal Sector: Concept, Measurement and Policy," International Labour Review, 1976.

Todaro, Michael P., INTERNAL MIGRATION IN DEVELOPING COUNTRIES: A Review of Theory, Evidence, Methodology and Research Priorities, Geneva, ILO, 1976. In this study the author points to the need to recognize the central importance of internal migration and to integrate the two-way relationship between migration and population distribution, on the one hand, and economic variables, on the other, into a more comprehensive analytical framework designed to improve development policy; and to understand both the causes and consequences of internal migration for rural and urban economic and social development. To this end he examines the literature on migration models and the role of internal migration; identifies what has been empirically tested and where; explores the strengths and limitations of various methodological approaches to estimating the parameters of micro and

macro econometric functions, and suggests the
most promising avenues for further investigation; and, building on these foundations,
identifies the major priority questions in
migration research which still remain to be
answered, and suggests appropriate methodological approaches for dealing with them.
(BPA)

Todaro, Michael P., "A Model of Labor Migration and
Urban Unemployment in Less Developed Countries," American Economic Review, Vol. LIX, No.
1, March 1969, pp. 138-148. This article is
the first presentation of what has become the
classic model of rural-urban migration. (Ed)

Todaro, Michael P., "Urban Job Expansion, Induced
Migration and Rising Unemployment: A Formulation and Simplified Empirical Test for LDCs,"
Journal of Development Economics, Vol. 3, No.
3, September 1976.

Warriner, D., "Problems of Rural-Urban Migration:
Some Suggestions for Investigation," International Labour Review, Vol. 101, No. 5, May
1970.

Yap, Lorene Y. L., "The Attraction of Cities: A
Review of the Migration Literature," Journal of
Development Economics, Vol. 4, 1977, pp. 239-
264.

Sea: Resources and Controversy

Amacher, Ryan C. and Sweeney, Richard James, eds.,
THE LAW OF THE SEA: U.S. Interests and Alternatives, Washington, American Enterprise
Institute, 1976. Papers of a U.N. 1974 conference and summary of debate in U.S. (FA)

Bell, Frederick W., FOOD FROM THE SEA: The Economics and Politics of Ocean Fisheries, Boulder,
Colorado, Westview Press, 1977. In this book,
an exploration of the factors at work in determining the past, present, and future of the
sea as an important source of protein, Frederick
Bell provides an analysis of the current use of
living marine resources and the prospects for
and obstacles to obtaining maximum utilization.

184

He covers such topics as the current exploitation levels of fishery stocks, fishery management and the new world order of extended fishery jurisdiction, the conflict between pollution and fishery resources, the potential for fish farming, the plight of the individual fishing firm, and alternative uses of fish resources (e.g., for recreational activities), and includes a critique of the role of the government in coming to grips with fishery problems. Economic and biological principles are integrated to provide a comprehensive analysis of how economic and political forces interact to determine how effectively the countries of the world, especially the United States, are dealing with fishery problems. (BPA)

Buzan, Barry, SEABED POLITICS, New York, Praeger, 1976. Few topics have received as much recent attention as the preparation and proceedings of the apparently paralyzed Third United Nations Conference on the Law of the Sea. Buzan's study concludes in winter 1974-75 and places the political and legal issues in a wider historical context. (FA)

Charney, Jonathan I., LAW OF THE SEA: Breaking the Deadlock, Foreign Affairs, Vol. 55, No. 3, April 1977, p. 598.

Larson, David L., ed., MAJOR ISSUES OF THE LAW OF THE SEA, Durham, New Hampshire, University of New Hampshire, 1976.

Swing, John Temple, "Who Will Own the Oceans?" Foreign Affairs, Vol. 54, No. 3, April 1976.

Varon, Bension, "Slow Sailing at Law of the Sea," Finance and Development, Vol. 12, No. 1, March 1975.

Small Business

Asian Productivity Organization, Selected reference material on small industry development, published March, 1970, the secretariat, Asian Productivity Organization, Aoyama Dai-ichi Man-

185

sions, 4-14, Akasaka 8-Chome, Minato-ku, Tokyo 107, Japan.

AID, Proceedings of the conference and seminar on techniques and methodologies for stimulating small-scale labor intensive industries in developing countries, edited by Donald E. Lodge and Key Ellen Auchiello, Industrial Development Division, Engineering Experiment Station, Georgia Institute of Technology, September 1975.

Asociacion Latinoamericana de Instituciones Financieras de Desarrollo; La Pequeña y Mediana Industria en Espana y los Paises Andinos, Instituto de Credito Oficial de Espana, Madrid, Spain, September 1975.

Child, Frank C. and Kempe, Mary E., eds., SMALL SCALE ENTERPRISE, Occasional Paper No. 6, 1973.

Chuta, Enyinna and Liedholm, Carl, THE ROLE OF SMALL SCALE INDUSTRY IN EMPLOYMENT GENERATION AND RURAL DEVELOPMENT: Initial Research Results from Sierra Leone, African Rural Employment Paper No. 11, East Lansing, Michigan State University, 1975.

Harper, Malcolm H., A PROTOTYPE EXPERIMENT TO TEST THE POSSIBILITY OF A COST EFFECTIVE EXTENSION SERVICE FOR SMALL SCALE GENERAL RETAILERS, Nairobi, Kenya, University of Nairobi, Institute for Development Studies Discussion Paper No. 193, January 1974.

Harper, Malcolm, CONSULTANCY FOR SMALL BUSINESSES: The Concept Training the Consultants, London, Intermediate Technology Publishing, Ltd., 1976.

Hart, K., "Small Scale Entrepreneurs in Ghana and Development Planning," Journal of Development Studies, Vol. t, No. 4, July 1970.

Ho, Yhi-Min and Huddle, Donald L., THE CONTRIBUTION OF TRADITIONAL AND SMALL SCALE CULTURE GOODS IN INTERNATIONAL TRADE AND IN EMPLOYMENT, Program of Development Studies Paper #35, Houston, Texas, Rice University.

ILO, SMALL ENTERPRISE DEVELOPMENT: Policies and
    Programs, Geneva, 1978. This book examines the
    development of the small enterprise--policies,
    supporting structures, action programs, and
    strategies. (BPA)

Kochav, David; Bohlin, Holger; DiTullio, Kathleen;
    Roostal, Ilmar; and Wahl, Nurit, FINANCING THE
    DEVELOPMENT OF SMALL SCALE INDUSTRIES, Inter-
    national Bank for Reconstruction and Develop-
    ment, International Development Association, &
    Swedish International Development Authority,
    Bank Staff Working Paper No. 191, November
    1974.

Koo, Hagen, "Small Entrepreneurship in a Developing
    Society: Rural Patterns of Labor Absorption
    and Social Mobility," Social African Forces,
    Vol. 54, No. 4, June 1976, pp. 775-787.

Liedholm, Carl and Chuta, Enyinna, THE ECONOMICS OF
    RURAL AND URBAN SMALL-SCALE INDUSTRIES IN
    SIERRA LEONE, African Rural Economy Paper No.
    14, 1976.

Liedholm, Carl, RESEARCH ON EMPLOYMENT IN THE RURAL
    NONFARM SECTOR IN AFRICA, East Lansing, Michi-
    gan State University, African Rural Employment
    Paper No. 5, 1973.

Mikkelsen, Britha, SKILL FORMATION AND RURAL INDUS-
    TRIAL DEVELOPMENT, Institute for Development
    Studies, December 1974.

NCAER, STUDY OF SELECTED SMALL INDUSTRIAL UNITS, New
    Delhi, National Council of Applied Economic
    Research, 1972.

Sanzo, Richard, RATIO ANALYSIS FOR SMALL BUSINESS,
    Small Business Management Series No. 20, 1970.

UNIDO, SMALL-SCALE INDUSTRIES IN ARAB COUNTRIES OF
    THE MIDDLE EAST, Report of the Expert Group
    meeting held in Beirut, Lebanon, 11-15 November
    1968 and selected papers presented to the meet-
    ing, New York, United Nations, 1970.

OECD, PROBLEMS AND POLICIES RELATING TO SMALL AND
    MEDIUM-SIZED BUSINESSES, Analytic report drawn
    up by the industry committee of OECD, Washing-
    ton, D.C., OECD, 1971.

World Bank, RURAL ENTERPRISE AND NONFARM EMPLOYMENT,
A World Bank Paper, January 1978.

Sociology and Anthropology

X-REF: LATIN AMERICA: Holjer, MEXICO: Diaz,
AFRICA: DeGregori, Uchendu, AGRICULTURAL DEVELOP-
MENT: Clayton.

Banfield, Edward C., THE MORAL BASIS OF A BACKWARD
SOCIETY, New York, Free Press (Macmillan),
1958. Develops the well-known concept of
"amoral familism." (Ed)

Barringer, Herbert R.; Blanksten, George I.; and
Mack, Raymond W., eds., SOCIAL CHANGE IN DEVEL-
OPING AREAS, A Reinterpretation of Evolutionary
Theory, Cambridge, Massachusetts, Schenkman
Publishing Company, 1965.

Bauer, Raymond A., ed., SOCIAL INDICATORS, Cambridge
and London, Massachusetts Institute of Technology, 1966.

Becker, Howard, and Boskoff, Alvin, MODERN SOCIOLOGI-
CAL THEORY, New York, Holt, Rinehart, and Winston, 1966. A book of readings, more on sociology per se, but with some emphasis on social
change. (Ed)

Bennis, Warrin G.; Benne, Kenneth D.; and Chin,
Robert, eds., THE PLANNING OF CHANGE: Readings
in the Applied Behavioral Sciences, New York,
Chicago, and London, Holt, Rinehart and
Winston, 1964.

Black, Max, ed., THE SOCIAL THEORIES OF TALCOTT PAR-
SONS: A Critical Examination, Englewood Cliffs,
New Jersey, Prentice-Hall, Inc., 1961. A very
good explication of Parsons' social theories for
those who do not have time to read all of Parsons themselves, or who wish to review the major
critiques of Parsons. (Ed)

Blase, Melvin G., INSTITUTION BUILDING: A Source
Book, Washington, D.C., Agency for International Development, U.S. Department of State,
1973.

Braibanti, Ralph, and Spengler, Joseph J., eds.,
TRADITION, VALUES, AND SOCIO-ECONOMIC DEVELOP-
MENT, Durham, North Carolina, Duke University
Press, 1961.

Durkheim, Emile, THE DIVISION OF LABOR IN SOCIETY,
TRANSLATED BY George Simpson, New York, The
Free Press, 1933. A classic. (Ed)

Etzioni, Amitai and Eva, eds., SOCIAL CHANGE:
Sources, Patterns, and Consequences, New York
and London, Basic Books, Inc., Publishers,
1964. A book of readings; it is perhaps the
best summary of what sociology and anthropology
had to offer (up to 1964) for social change.
(Ed)

Goldthorpe, J. E. THE SOCIOLOGY OF THE THIRD WORLD:
Disparity and Involvement, New York, Cambridge
University Press, 1975. A text devoted to the
developing countries, studying the disparity
between rich and poor nations, both within and
without. Pulls together the different strands
of the social sciences to develop a sociological view. (BPA)

HEW, TOWARD A SOCIAL REPORT, Washington, D.C., U.S.
Department of Health, Education and Welfare,
1969.

Hirschman, Albert O., EXIT, VOICE, AND LOYALTY:
Responses to Decline in Firms, Organization,
and States, Cambridge, Massachusetts, Harvard
University Press, 1970. The author argues that
we "vote" in different ways to determine social
choices; switching a loyalty from one social
unit to another is (like not buying a product)
or way of "voting." (Ed)

Hoselitz, Bert F., SOCIOLOGICAL ASPECTS OF ECONOMIC
DEVELOPMENT, Glencoe, Illinois, Free Press,
1960.

Hunt, Chester L., SOCIAL ASPECTS OF ECONOMIC DEVELOP-
MENT, New York, London, Toronto, and Sydney,
McGraw-Hill Book Company, 1966.

Kunkel, John H., SOCIETY AND ECONOMIC GROWTH: A Behavioral Perspective of Social Change, New York, Oxford University Press, 1970. The author declares that "the knowledge and application of behavioral principles makes the success of a development program possible, while ignorance guarantees its failure unless there is a generous portion of luck." This theme is developed throughout the text as social, cultural, and psychological components of industrialization are described in detail. (JEL)

MacRae, Duncan Jr., THE SOCIAL FUNCTION OF SOCIAL SCIENCE, New Haven, Connecticut and London, Yale University Press, 1976.

McGranahan, D. V.; Richard-Proust, C.; Sovani, N. V.; and Subramian, M., CONTENTS AND MEASUREMENT OF SOCIOECONOMIC DEVELOPMENT, New York, Washington, and London, Praeger Publishers, 1972.

Mead, Margaret, ed., CULTURAL PATTERNS AND TECHNICAL CHANGE: A Manual prepared by the World Federation for Mental Health, New York, The New American Library, 1955.

Merton, Robert K., SOCIAL THEORY AND SOCIAL STRUCTURE, New York, The Free Press, 1957.

Mitchell, William, SOCIOLOGICAL ANALYSIS AND POLITICS: The Theories of Talcott Parsons, Englewood Cliffs, New Jersey, Prentice-Hall, Inc., 1967.

Moore, Barrington, SOCIAL ORIGINS OF DICTATORSHIP AND DEMOCRACY: Lord and Peasant in the Making of the Modern World, Boston, Massachusetts, Beacon Press, 1966.

Ness, Gayl D., ed., THE SOCIOLOGY OF ECONOMIC DEVELOPMENT: A Reader, New York, Harper and Row, 1970. Contains 33 selections, reprinted from various sources, concerned with the measurement of development, economic development theories, the rate of population growth, the "politics of development," and the "bureaucratic aspects of development." Introductory essays by the editor preface each topic. (JEL)

Seiler, John A., SYSTEMS ANALYSIS IN ORGANIZATIONAL
BEHAVIOR, Homewood, Illinois, Richard D. Irwin,
Inc. and The Dorsey Press, 1967.

Sigmund, Paul E., ed., THE IDEOLOGIES OF THE DE-
VELOPING COUNTRIES, New York, Washington, and
London, Frederick A. Praeger, Publishers, 1967.

Smelser, Neil J., READINGS ON ECONOMIC SOCIOLOGY,
Englewood Cliffs, New Jersey, Prentice-Hall,
Inc., 1965.

Smelser, Neil J. and Lipset, Seymour Martin, ed.,
SOCIAL STRUCTURE AND MOBILITY IN ECONOMIC
DEVELOPMENT, Chicago, Aldine Publishing Com-
pany, 1966.

Weber, Max, THE PROTESTANT ETHIC AND THE SPIRIT OF
CAPITALISM, translated by Talcott Parsons, New
York, Charles Scribner's Sons, 1958. A classic.
(Ed)

Technology

X-REF: BRAZIL: Knight, CHINA: Rawski, Ridley,
Sigmundson, ECUADOR: Tokman, EMPLOYMENT LABOR:
Achary, Pack, Sen, JAPAN: Ozawa, LATIN AMERICA:
Thebaud, MEXICO: Watanabe, MULTINATIONAL CORPORA-
TIONS: Forsyth, Helleiner, Hellinger, Morley, Un,
PUERTO RICO: Strassman, THAILAND: Inukai.

Allal, M., and Edmonds, G. A., (with A. S. Brella),
MANUAL ON THE PLANNING OF LABOUR-INTENSIVE ROAD
CONSTRUCTION, Geneva, International Labor
Office, 1977. The belief that labour-intensive
construction methods are economically the most
efficient for many roads in developing coun-
tries has been vindicated by studies carried
out by the International Labour Office in the
Philippines and in Thailand and by the World
Bank, in India and Indonesia. (BPA)

Arrow, K. J.; Chenery, H. B.; Minhas, B. S.; and
Solow, R. M., "Capital-Labor Substitution and
Economic Efficiency," in The Review of Eco-
nomics and Statistics, Vol. XLIII, No. 3,
August 1961.

Baer, Werner, "Technology, Employment and Development: Empirical Findings," World Development, Vol. 4, No. 2, 1976.

Baraneb, William, and Ranis, Gustav, eds., SCIENCE, TECHNOLOGY, AND ECONOMIC DEVELOPMENT, New York, Praeger, 1978. This study assesses the symbiotic relationship between science and technology and its effect on economic development. Employing both historical and comparative perspectives, the essays trace the impact of science and technology on Britain, Germany, Brazil, the United States, Ghana, and Japan. (BPA)

Baranson, J., INDUSTRIAL TECHNOLOGIES FOR DEVELOPING ECONOMIES, New York, Praeger, 1969.

Bass, L. W., "The Transfer of Commercial Systems to Developing Countries," World Development, Vol. 2, Nos. 4-5, April-May 1974. "Technology transfer" is an over-simplification of the complex of managerial skills needed in a new commercial system for the success of an innovative enterprise in a developing country. In addition to manufacturing expertise there must be provided, to ensure long-lasting viability, enlightened general management, aggressive marketing programs, and more effective financial controls, all of which are subject to greater cultural barriers than the technology itself. These requirements should be recognized by local entrepreneurs and financiers, government planners, foreign suppliers of know-how, and international development agencies. This paper defines the types of improved skills which are needed. (JEL)

Batra, R. N., "Technological Change in the Soviet Collective Farm," American Economic Review, Vol. LXIV, No. 4, September 1974.

Beach, Nancy, "Research Priorities on Technology Transfer to Developing Countries," Survey of Selected Studies and Research on Technology, Vol. 2, Evanston, Illinois, Northwestern University, 1974.

Berry, R. A., "Factor Proportions and Urban Employment in Developing Countries," International Labour Review, Vol. 109, No. 3, March 1974.

Bhatt, V. V., ON THE TECHNOLOGY POLICY AND ITS INSTITUTIONAL FRAME, World Bank Reprint Series: Number 29, from World Development 3, September 1975.

Binswanger, Hans P., Ruttan, Vernon W., et al., INDUCED INNOVATION: Technology, Institutions, and Development. This study expands the concept of induced innovation to include both institutional and technical change, integrating several different approaches to the analysis of the rate and direction of change into one investment framework. The model is tested against historical data from both developing and developed nations, and the implications for development policy are explored in full. (BPA)

Bhalla, A. S., ed., TECHNOLOGY AND EMPLOYMENT IN INDUSTRY: A Case Study Approach, Geneva, ILO, 1976. Contrary to what has often been assumed, appropriate technology choice in industry is not a myth and substitution possibilities do exist in both primary and secondary operations. This is demonstrated in these eight case studies, preceded by a penetrating review of some of the conceptual and measurement issues relevant to the problems of technological choice. (BPA)

Bottomley, Anthony, FACTOR PRICING AND ECONOMIC GROWTH IN UNDERDEVELOPED RURAL AREAS, London, Crosby Lockwood, 1971. A study of the ways in which traditional marginal factor pricing must be reinterpreted within the context of underdeveloped rural areas. Such reinterpretations include emphasis on the relationship between marginally higher wages and marginally higher output at subsistence levels where wage increases directly improve nutrition and thus, physical strength of labor supply. Also, the case of hidden unemployment is interpreted as part of an institutional framework obligating the owners of land and capital to provide labor employment. (JEL)

Bruton, H. J., "Productivity Growth in Latin America," American Economic Review, Vol. LVII, No. 5, 1967.

193

Bulfin, Robert, and Greenwell, Richard, THE APPLICA-
TION OF TECHNOLOGY IN DEVELOPING COUNTRIES,
Tucson, University of Arizona, 1977.

Bulfin, Robert and Weaver, Harry, APPROPRIATE TECH-
NOLOGY FOR NATURAL RESOURCES DEVELOPMENT: An
Overview, annotated bibliography, and a guide
to sources of information, Tucson, University
of Arizona, 1977.

Cooper, C., "Science, Technology and Production in
the Underdeveloped Countries: An Introduction," Journal of Development Studies, Vol. 9,
No. 1, October 1972.

Costa, Emile; Ciha, Sunil; Hussain, M. Ibrahim;
Thuy, N. I. B.; and Farden, Aime, GUIDELINES
FOR THE ORGANIZATION OF SPECIAL LABOR-INTENSIVE
WORKS PROGRAMS, Geneva, ILO, 1977. This document provides planners, administrators, engi-
neers and technicians responsible for preparing
and implementing labor-intensive works programs
at the national and provincial levels with
guidelines which are based on past experience
in developing countries. It deals with the
preparation of such comprehensive programs in
harmony with economic development programs;
organizational and institutional aspects;
financing problems; technical problems in
project selection and choice of technologies;
workers' recruitment; conditions of work; and
socio-economic evaluation. (BPA)

Council of the Americas, TECHNOLOGY TRANSFER AND THE
DEVELOPING NATIONS, New York, Council of the
Americas, 1974. Explores some of the key
issues in technology transfer: relative value
of various transfer processes; ownership;
costs, and quality of technology; payment
schemes; and the role of governments. (BPA)

Council of the Americas, TECHNOLOGY TRANSFER AND
DEVELOPMENT: An Historical and Geographical
Perspective, New York, Council of the Americas,
1974. An introductory workbook that summarizes
current knowledge on the subject of technology
transfer, studies corporate responses and limitations along with the developing or host country's point of view. Contains case studies.
(BPA)

194

Cubas, Jose de, TECHNOLOGY TRANSFER AND THE DEVELOP-
ING NATIONS, New York, Fund for Multinational
Management Education in cooperation with Coun-
cil of the Americas, 1974.

Daniels, M. R., "Differences in Efficiency Among
Industries in Developing Countries," American
Economic Review, Vol. LIX, No. 1, March 1969.

Dasgupta, Ajit K., ECONOMIC FREEDOM, TECHNOLOGY AND
PLANNING FOR GROWTH, New Delhi, India, Associated Publishing House; distributed in the U.S.
and Canada by International Scholarly Book
Services, 1973. Development study contending
"it is...impossible to increase the rate of
economic growth by increasing rate of domestic
saving" and "that only by resorting to factors
which are exogenous to the (nation's) economic
system can an acceleration of the economic
growth process be obtained." Technological
development is identified as an exogenous
factor sufficient to initiate the development
process in a nearly closed economy. Index.
(JEL)

Davis, Harlan L., "Appropriate Technology: An
Explanation and Interpretation of its Role in
Latin America," Inter-American Economic Af-
fairs, Vol. 32, No. 1, Summer 1978.

Eckaus, Richard S., APPROPRIATE TECHNOLOGIES FOR
DEVELOPING COUNTRIES, prepared for the Panel on
Appropriate Technologies for Developing Coun-
tries, Washington, D.C., National Academy of
Sciences, 1977.

Felix, D., "Technological Dualism in Late Industrializers: On Theory, History and Policy,"
Journal of Economic History, Vol. 34, No. 1,
March 1974. Analysts of "inappropriate" technological borrowing by industrializing LDC's
disagree on trends in flexibility and factor
biases of the process technology available to
borrowers. The debate has disregarded two
other trends: rising economies of scale and
the shift of product differentiation over the
past century from workshop to mass production.
An alternative analysis and supporting data are
offered in which K/L intensity derives from
scale; capital constraints relate to massing
rather than K/L intensity, and product dif-

195

ferentiation converts from stimulant to local innovation in 19th century late industrializers to drag in 20th century LDC's. Implications for industrial strategies are drawn. (JEL)

Fortner, Robert S., "Strategies for Self-Immolation: The Third World and the Transfer of Advanced Technologies," Inter-American Economic Affairs, Vol. 31, No. 1, Summer 1977.

Gaude, J., "Capital-Labour Substitution Possibilities: A Review of Empirical Evidence," chapter 2 of: Bhalla, A. S., and Sen, Amartya, TECHNOLOGY AND EMPLOYMENT IN INDUSTRY: A Case Study Approach, Geneva, International Labour Office, 1975.

Goulet, Denis, THE UNCERTAIN PROMISE: Value Conflicts in Technology Transfer, New York, IDOC, 1977.

Hawrylyshyn, Oil, "Capital-Intensive Biases in Devel-oping Country Technology Choice," Journal of Development Economics, September 1978.

Hetzler, Stanley A., APPLIED MEASURES FOR PROMOTING TECHNOLOGICAL GROWTH, International Library of Sociology, Boston, Massachusetts, Routledge and Kegan Paul, 1973. Addresses the developmental problems facing technologically retarded societies. The treatment is based on the thesis that social change is the consequence of a forerunning technological change. Solutions to the problems are offered, and the author deals, in detail, with the areas of industrial development, agricultural development, the raising of finance, and the methods for organizing and installing the national planning facilities required for development programming. (BPA)

Hughes, J. R. T., "American Economic Growth: Imported or Indigenous? What Difference Did the Beginning Make?" The American Economic Review, Vol. 67, No. 1, February 1977, pp. 15-20.

ILO, AUTOMATION IN DEVELOPING COUNTRIES, Round-Table
Discussion on the Introduction of Automation
and Advanced Technology in Developing Countries, Geneva, 1-3 July 1970, Geneva, International Labour Office, 1974.

ILO, GUIDELINES FOR THE ORGANIZATION OF SPECIAL
LABOR-INTENSIVE WORKS PROGRAMS, Geneva, ILO,
1977.

ILO, MEN OR MACHINES: A Study of Labor-Capital Substitution in Road Construction in the Philippines. This study investigates the technical
and economic feasibility of labor-intensive
road construction techniques in the Philippines.
(BPA)

ILO, TECHNOLOGY AND EMPLOYMENT IN INDUSTRY, Geneva,
1975. This collection of case studies is
concerned with identifying and analyzing alternative production techniques and examining
their implications for policy making. The case
studies examine the choice of techniques for
can-making in Kenya, Tanzania, and Thailand;
second-hand jute processing machinery in Kenya;
sugar processing techniques in India; cement
block manufacture in Kenya; capacity of the
engineering industry in Colombia; technological
choice in metalworking, with special reference
to Mexico; and productivity and employment in
copper and aluminum industries of the USA,
Zambia, Zaire, and Chile. (BPA)

Johnson, Harry G., TECHNOLOGY AND ECONOMIC INTERDE-
PENDENCE, New York, St. Martin (for the Trade
Policy Research Centre, London), 1976. Insisting persuasively on the economic character of
technology, Professor Johnson deals some hard
knocks to widely held views about economic
growth, multinational corporations, the environment, the brain drain, and science policy.
One of his best books. (FA)

Lele, Uma J. and Mellor, John W., TECHNOLOGICAL
CHANGE AND DISTRIBUTIVE BIAS IN A DUAL ECONOMY,
World Bank Occasional Paper No. 43, October
1972.

Marsden, K., "Progressive Technologies for Developing Countries," International Labour Review,
Vol. 101, No. 5, May 1970.

197

Mason, R. Hal, THE TRANSFER OF TECHNOLOGY AND THE
FACTOR PROPORTIONS PROBLEM: The Philippines
and Mexico, New York, United Nations Institute
for Training and Research Reports, No. 10,
1971.

Mingo, J. J., "Capital Economic Equilibrium: Pur-
pose, Analytic Techniques, Collective Choice,"
American Economic Review, Vol. LXIV, No. 3,
June 1974.

Montgomery, John D., TECHNOLOGY AND CIVIC LIFE:
Making and Implementing Development Decisions,
MIT Studies in Comparative Politics, Cambridge,
Massachusetts, MIT Press, 1974. The Third
World development experience is looked upon
from the point of view of the effects of technological improvements and modernization on the
people, whose welfare was the original, yet
forgotten, goal in an introduction and six
chapters (aspirants to modernization, technology as modernization, modernizing behavior,
agents of change, systems of change, decisions),
the author reviews the Third World experience
during the past 25 years, analyzing technology,
organization, and administrative systems and
their interaction with civic life in what
constitutes a new approach in development
studies. Index. (JEL)

Nader, Clair and Zahlan, A. B., eds., SCIENCE AND
TECHNOLOGY IN DEVELOPING COUNTRIES, New York,
Cambridge University Press, 1969. Application
of advanced scientific and technological methods to the development problems of the Middle
East is discussed by a group of specialists,
primarily American and Arab. The book contains, inter alia, a wealth of information on
the place of science in Middle East Universities. (Proceedings of a conference held at the
American University, Beirut, in 1967.) (FA)

Nau, Henry R., TECHNOLOGY TRANSFER AND U.S. FOREIGN
POLICY, New York, Praeger, 1976.

Nelson, Richard R., "Less Developed Countries--Tech-
nology Transfer and Adaptation: The Role of
the Indigenous Science Community," Economic
Development and Cultural Change, October 1974.

Nelson, Richard R.; Peck, Merton J.; and Kalacheck, Edward D., TECHNOLOGY, ECONOMIC GROWTH, AND PUBLIC POLICY, Washington, D.C., The Brookings Institution, 1967.

Nordhaus, William D., INVENTION, GROWTH AND WELFARE: A Theoretical Treatment of Technological Change, Cambridge, Massachusetts, MIT Press, 1969.

OECD, CHOICE AND ADAPTATION OF TECHNOLOGY IN DEVEL-OPING COUNTRIES, An Overview of Major Policy Issues, Development Centre of the Organisation for Economic Co-operation and Development, Paris, 1974.

O'Herlihy, C. St. J., "Capital/Labour Substitution and the Developing Countries: A Problem of Measurement," Bulletin of Oxford Institute on Economics and Statistics, Vol. 34, 1972, pp. 269-280.

Pickett, J.; Forsyth, D. J.; and McBain, N. S.; "The Choice of Technology, Economic Efficiency and Employment in Developing Countries," World Development, Vol. 2, No. 3, March 1974.

Poats, Rutherford M., TECHNOLOGY FOR DEVELOPING NATIONS: New Directions for U.S. Technical Assistance, Washington, D.C., The Brookings Institution, 1972.

Rosenberg, Nathan, "American Technology: Imported or Indigenous?" American Economic Review, Vol. 67, No. 1, February 1977.

Rosenberg, N., "Economic Development and the Transfer of Technology: Some Historical Perspectives," Technology and Culture, October 1970.

Rosenblatt, Samuel A., ed., TECHNOLOGY AND ECONOMIC DEVELOPMENT: A Realistic Perspective, Boulder, Colorado, Westview Press, 1979. The authors focus on the technological choices that confront both less developed countries and multinational corporations in establishing new industrial enterprises. They also discuss the necessity to calculate appropriate relative factor pric-es, establish realistic exchange rates, and pro-vide adequate protection of proprietary tech-

nology. The book considers relevant U.S.
policy. (BPA)

Rymes, Thomas K., ON CONCEPTS OF CAPITAL AND TECH-
NICAL CHANGE, New York, Cambridge University
Press, 1972.

Schumacher, E. F., SMALL IS BEAUTIFUL: Economics as
if People Mattered, New York, Harper and Row,
1974. That economics can serve human values
should be no news, but the variations on the
theme in this volume make attractive reading.
Size, resources, environment, religion, property and socialism are all drawn in. Not every-
one will agree with the author's early-1960s
argument for preserving the coal industry (he
was adviser to the British Coal Board) or his
case for protecting agriculture as a way of
life, but he was a pioneer in recommending
labor-intensive technologies for developing
countries. (FA)

Singer, Hans, TECHNOLOGIES FOR BASIC NEEDS, Geneva,
ILO, 1977. This study suggests new criteria
for establishing socially oriented technology
policies in developing economies and demonstrates how technology can be related to the
fundamental objectives of satisfying basic
human needs. (BPA)

Solo, Robert A. and Rogers, Everett M., eds., INDUC-
ING TECHNOLOGICAL CHANGE FOR ECONOMIC GROWTH
AND DEVELOPMENT, Lansing, Michigan State University Press, 1972. An experienced aid
administrator, Poats sees a "renaissance in
technical assistance" and suggests how it ought
to be organized to make more use of U.S. non-
governmental talents. The second volume contains some very interesting papers on the
diffusion of technology in a variety of circumstances. (FA)

Stewart, F., "Choice of Technique in Developing
Countries," Journal of Development Studies,
Vol. 9, No. 1, October 1972.

Stewart, F., "Technology and Employment in LDCs,"
World Development, Vol. 2, No. 3, March 1974.
The paper examines the relationship between employment and technology in LDC's. Employment
problems are analyzed as deriving largely from

a dualistic form of development, with modern capital-intensive and high-productivity technology in one sector and traditional, low-productivity technology in the other. The inappropriate nature of modern technology is defined and analyzed. Its appropriate characteristics include scale, skill, resource requirements, and capital intensity in relation to resource availability. Possible sources of appropriate technology include old technology from developed countries, improved traditional LDC technology, and adapted modern technology. (JEL)

Stewart, Frances, TECHNOLOGY AND UNDERDEVELOPMENT, Boulder, Colorado, Westview Press, 1977.

Street, J. H., "The Technological Frontier in Latin America: Creativity and Productivity," Journal of Economic Issues, Vol. 10, No. 3, September 1976, pp. 538-558. The characteristics of frontier penetration as defined by C. E. Ayres are applied to the Latin American region, with special attention to structural changes induced by technological innovation. Current dependency theory is shown to neglect the potential for increasing domestic technical creativity and thus enhancing productivity in critical sectors. Examples of success in agriculture are noted. (JEL)

Thebaud, Schiller, STATISTICS ON SCIENCE AND TECHNOLOGY IN LATIN AMERICA: Experience with UNESCO Pilot Projects 1972-1974, Paris, France, The UNESCO Press, Statistical Reports and Studies, 1976.

Thomas, 'd. Babatunde, ed., IMPORTING TECHNOLOGY INTO AFRICA, New York, Praeger, 1976. Provides the specific parameters for multinational corporations interested in transferring technology to African states, such as the level and trend in scientific technological manpower development, the state of industrial science, and the learning potential of the labor force. (BPA)

Timmer, C. Peter, et al., THE CHOICE OF TECHNOLOGY
    IN DEVELOPING COUNTRIES: Some cautionary
    tales, Harvard Studies in International Affairs,
    No. 32, Cambridge, Massachusetts, Center for
    International Affairs, Harvard University,
    1975. Argues that the use of less capital-
    intensive methods of production than those used
    in advanced countries could be one solution to
    the problems of unemployment in developing
    countries. (JEL)

Uchendu, Victor C., "The Impact of Changing Agri-
    cultural Technology on African Land Tenure,"
    Journal of Developing Areas, Vol. 4, July 1970,
    pp. 477-485.

United Nations, THE ACQUISITION OF TECHNOLOGY FROM
    MULTINATIONAL CORPORATIONS BY DEVELOPING COUN-
    TRIES, New York, Department of Economic and
    Social Affairs, The United Nations, 1974.

UNCTAD, "An International Code of Conduct on Trans-
    fer of Technology: Report by the Secretariat,"
    TD/B/C.6/Ac.I/2/Supp.I/Rev. I, 1975.

UNCTAD, "Major Issues Arising from the Transfer of
    Technology to Developing Countries: A Study by
    the UNCTAD Secretariat," TD/B/AC.II/IO/Rev. 2,
    1975.

U.S. Department of Commerce, "Technology and Econom-
    ics in International Development: Report of a
    Seminar," Washington, D.C., Agency for Inter-
    national Development, May 1972.

Vaitsos, Constantino, "Patents Revisited: Their
    Function in Developing Countries," Journal of
    Developing Studies, Vol. 9, 1972. Vaitsos is
    one of the leading exponents of a "Third World"
    point of view on the terms under which technolo-
    gy should be transferred from more developed
    countries. (Ed)

Vaitsos, Constantino, "Transfer of Resources and
    Preservation of Monopoly Rents," Economic De-
    velopment Report #168, Cambridge, Massachu-
    setts, Harvard University, Center of Inter-
    national Affairs, 1970. (See preceding annota-
    tion.)

Wells, Louis T., Jr., "Economic Man and Engineering
    Man: Choice of Technology in a Low Wage Coun-
    try," Public Policy, Vol. 21, No. 3, 1973.

White, Lawrence J., "The Evidence on Appropriate
    Factor Proportions for Manufacturing in Less
    Developed Countries: A Survey," Economic De-
    velopment and Cultural Change, Vol. 27, No. 1,
    October 1978.

                    Terms of Trade

X-REF: AGRICULTURAL DEVELOPMENT: Mitra, INDIA:
Appleyard, RURAL DEVELOPMENT: Fry.

Bairoch, Paul, "The Terms of Trade," Chapter 6 in
    THE ECONOMIC DEVELOPMENT OF THE THIRD WORLD
    SINCE 1900, Berkeley, University of California
    Press, 1975. Reviews the argument that the
    terms of trade are moving against LDCs and con-
    cludes that it is based on statistical misin-
    terpretation; contains a review of the
    literature. (Ed)

Batra, R., "Economic Expansion and the Terms of
    Trade Under Conditions of Variable Factor
    Supplies," Indian Economic Journal, Vol. 18,
    No. 1, July-September 1970.

Eddie, Scott McNeil, TERMS OF TRADE CHANGE AND IN-
    COME TRANSFER FROM AGRICULTURE IN A PROGRAM OF
    INDUSTRIAL IMPORT SUBSTITUTION, New York, Wil-
    liams College, Center for Development Eco-
    nomics, 1970, Research Memorandum #35.

Ellsworth, P. T., "The Terms of Trade Between Pri-
    mary Producing and Industrial Countries,"
    Inter-American Economic Affairs, Vol. I, No. 1,
    Summer 1956. An answer to the Prebisch argu-
    ment (see Prebisch, below). (Ed)

Lewis, W. Arthur, "World Production, Prices and
    Trade, 1870 Thru 1960," Manchester School of
    Economic and Social Studies, Vol. 20, May 1952,
    pp. 105-138.

Mathur, A. B., "India's Terms of Trade with U.S.A., 1951-52 to 1968-69," Indian Economic Journal, Vol. 21, No. 2, October-December 1973.

Powelson, John P., "The Strange Persistence of the 'Terms of Trade'," Inter-American Economic Affairs, Vol. 30, No. 4, Spring 1977.

Powelson, John P., "The Terms of Trade Again," Inter-American Economic Affairs, Vol. 23, No. 4, Spring 1970.

Prebisch, Raul, "The Economic Development of Latin America and Its Principal Problems," United Nations Economic Bulletin for Latin America, February 1962. This is the classic essay that first presented the case that the terms of trade had moved secularly against less developed countries from 1876 to 1947. Originally published (unattributed) as a U.N. document in 1950. (Ed)

Textbooks

Agarwala, A. N. and Singh, S. P., eds., THE ECONOMICS OF UNDERDEVELOPMENT, New York, Oxford University Press, 1963.

Baldwin, Robert E., ECONOMIC DEVELOPMENT AND GROWTH, second edition, Introduction to Economics Series, New York, John Wiley & Sons, Inc., 1972. This short text seeks to provide "an analysis of economic development that in terms of breadth and sophistication lies between the usual elementary and advanced approaches to the development topic." It is organized around three themes, i.e., what the nature of the growth problem is, what the main theories of growth and development are, and what the main policy issues facing less developed countries are. Index. (JEL)

Bauer, P. T. and Yamey, B. S., THE ECONOMICS OF UNDERDEVELOPED COUNTRIES, New York, Cambridge University Press, 1957.

Bhagwati, Jagdish, THE ECONOMICS OF UNDERDEVELOPED COUNTRIES, New York, McGraw-Hill, 1971.

Bairoch, Paul, THE ECONOMIC DEVELOPMENT OF THE THIRD WORLD SINCE 1900, translated by Cynthia Postan, Berkeley and Los Angeles, University of California Press, 1975. An excellent set of essays by a noted French economist covering population, extractive industry, manufacturing, foreign trade, terms of trade, education, urbanization, labor, and macroeconomic data. (Ed)

Bruton, Henry J., PRINCIPLES OF DEVELOPMENT ECONOMICS, Englewood Cliffs, New Jersey, Prentice-Hall, 1965.

Committee on Economics Teaching Material for Asian Universities, THE ECONOMICS OF DEVELOPMENT, Economic Theory and Practice in the Asian Setting, Vol. 4, New York, Wiley, Halsted Press, 1976. A collection of supplementary readings designed to accompany a standard introductory textbook in economic development. They provide empirical studies and results from the development experience of various Asian countries, illustrating the main concepts in the study of economic development, such as: poverty and inequality, dimensions of growth, agriculture and development, capital accumulation, foreign trade, education, projections and development planning, and an overview of the Asian economic scene. No index. (JEL)

Dunn, Edgar S., Jr., ECONOMIC AND SOCIAL DEVELOPMENT, Baltimore, Johns Hopkins Press, 1970.

Elkan, Walter, AN INTRODUCTION TO DEVELOPMENT ECONOMICS, Harmondsworth, England, Penguin Books, 1973.

Galbraith, John Kenneth, ECONOMIC DEVELOPMENT, Cambridge, Massachusetts, Harvard University Press, 1964.

Garzouzi, Eva, ECONOMIC GROWTH AND DEVELOPMENT: The Less Developed Countries, New York, Vantage Press, 1972. Essays to consolidate into one

readable text the whole of the economics of
growth and development. Part I discusses the
meaning and theories of economic development,
outlines historical patterns of development,
and summarizes the impact of capital, agriculture, industry, monetary and fiscal policies,
international trade, and foreign aid on economic growth. Part II presents comparative
analyses of developing regions. Index. (JEL)

Gianaris, Nicholas V., ECONOMIC DEVELOPMENT: Thought
and Problems, North Quincy, Massachusetts,
Christopher Publishing House, 1978. Part one
examines the process of development, the historical perspective, mathematical models, and
modern theories of development; part two considers domestic problems of development, specifically land and other natural resources, human
resources (particularly the role of education),
capital formation and technological change, the
allocation of resources, and the role of government and planning; part three discusses the
international aspects of development (foreign
trade, aid, investment, and multinationals) and
current issues such as environmental problems,
the status of women, income inequalities, and
discrimination. (JEL)

Gill, Richard T., ECONOMIC DEVELOPMENT: Past and
Present, third edition, Foundations of Modern
Economics, Englewood Cliffs, New Jersey,
Prentice-Hall, 1973. Third edition of an
introductory textbook with revisions of the
discussions. More graphical treatment is given
many economic concepts than in earlier editions
and all concepts are defined. Contains a list
of further readings on development. Index.
(JEL)

Hagen, Everett E., THE ECONOMICS OF DEVELOPMENT, revised edition, The Irwin Series in Economics,
Homewood, Illinois, Irwin; London; Irwin-Dorsey
International; Georgetown, Ontario; Irwin-
Dorsey Ltd., 1975. Revised edition with two
new chapters added, one dealing with the earth's
stock of minerals and economic growth, and the
other on the relationships between economic
growth and the distribution of income. Chapters on population and economic planning have
been extensively revised, with the former
focusing on the relationship of food supply to

continued world growth. Additional changes
include: reorganization of the discussion of
growth theories; a considerably augmented
discussion of entrepreneurship; and a reorganization of the chapters on import substitution versus export expansion and external
finance. (JEL)

Higgins, Benjamin, ECONOMIC DEVELOPMENT: Principles, Problems, and Policies, New York, Harper
and Row, 1973.

Kindleberger, Charles P. and Herrick, Bruce, ECO-
NOMIC DEVELOPMENT, third edition, Economics
Handbook Series, New York; London; Paris and
Tokyo, McGraw-Hill, 1958, 1965, 1977. Textbook
that "survey(s) the present panorama of international poverty, the applications to it of
economic analysis, and the policies for improvement that the analysis implies." This edition,
which has been completely rewritten and updated, includes new chapters on: population,
urbanization, collective international action,
employment, income distribution, and the
theories of economic development. (JEL)

Meier, Gerald M., ed., LEADING ISSUES IN ECONOMIC
DEVELOPMENT, third edition, New York, Oxford
University Press, 1964, 1970, 1976. This edition with an introductory note by the editor
emphasizes the interrelatedness of the readings
selected on each issue, with the leading issues
now coalescing in a central theme: "policies
which are designed to eradicate poverty, reduce
inequality, and deal with problems of employment." Replaces the earlier readings selections so as to reflect the central theme and
adds several new chapters. Also includes new
selections "to raise the level of theoretical
analysis and provide more empirical relationships." More than 100 selections, reprinted
from various sources, discuss the history of
development, various theories of development,
industrialization, agriculture, trade, human
resources, and planning. (JEL) The editor has
written essays that link the various topics into an integrated whole, thus making this a high-
level, very readable textbook. (Ed)

Morgan, Theodore, ECONOMIC DEVELOPMENT: Concept and
Strategy, New York, Harper & Row, 1975. Textbook in economic development with emphasis on
policy, its appropriate definition, its targets, and its improvement of application.
Diverts focus from GNP and average income
growth rates and into issues such as income
distribution, nutrition, disease, climate, and
population increases and their effects on
development. Surveys existing theoretical
literature. Discusses development planning and
the importance of the statistical foundation of
decision-making, and planning techniques such
as cost-benefit analysis. Index. (JEL)

Myint, Hla U., THE ECONOMICS OF THE DEVELOPING COUN-
TRIES, London, Hutchinson, 1973.

Neher, Philip A., ECONOMIC GROWTH AND DEVELOPMENT:
A Mathematical Introduction, New York, John
Wiley & Sons, 1971. A college textbook in
intermediate macroeconomic theory, mathematical
economics, and economic growth and development.
The author presents the growth of two basic
single-sector models: a neoclassical model of
an advanced economy, and a dynamic model of a
primitive economy. Index. (JEL)

Papanek, Gustav F.; Schydlowski, Daniel M.; and
Stern, Joseph J., DECISION MAKING FOR ECONOMIC
DEVELOPMENT: Text and Cases, Boston, Massachusetts, Houghton Mifflin, 1971. This textbook
uses the case study method to analyze development problems based on first-hand experiences
in Pakistan, Colombia, and Peru. The 13 cases,
which are simplified for classroom work, deal
with issues of: 1) investment decisions,
2) policies for the external sector, 3) short-
term fiscal and monetary policy, or 4) long-
term problems of macroeconomic planning. No
index. (JEL)

Salvatore, Dominick and Dowling, Edward T., SCHAUM'S
OUTLINE OF THEORY AND PROBLEMS OF DEVELOPMENT
ECONOMICS, Schaum's Outline Series, New York,
McGraw-Hill, 1977. Presents the theoretical
and practical core of development economics,
intended as a supplement to all current development textbooks. Each chapter includes a statement of theory and principles, illustrated with
examples; a set of multiple-choice review ques-

tions with answers; and a set of theoretical, numerical, and practical problems with step-by-step solutions. (JEL)

Szentes, Tamas, THE POLITICAL ECONOMY OF UNDERDE-VELOPMENT, third edition, translated by I. Veges, translation revised by A. Gardiner, Budapest, Hungarian Academy of Sciences, Aka-demiai Kiado, 1976. Third edition of a marxist analysis of the causes, substance, and the laws of motion of underdevelopment. The text, documentation, and illustrating material in this edition remains unchanged. A new chapter on neo-classical investment patterns, the policies of the multinational corporations, and the crisis phenomena in the international economy is included in the appendix. No index. (JEL)

Thirlwall, A. P., GROWTH AND DEVELOPMENT: With Spe-cial Reference to Developing Economies, second edition, London, Macmillan; New York, Wiley, Halsted Press, 1977. Textbook. Following an introduction, the material is divided into five parts: factors of production, obstacles to development; planning and resource allocation; financing development; and the international aspects of development. (JEL)

Todaro, Michael P., ECONOMIC DEVELOPMENT IN THE THIRD WORLD: An Introduction to Problems and Policies in a Global Perspective, London and New York, Longman, 1977. Undergraduate text for students from various disciplines; emphasis is on a problem- and policy-oriented approach. In four parts: Part one discusses the nature of underdevelopment and its various manifesta-tions in the Third World, and parts two and three focus on major development problems and policies, both domestic (growth, income distri-bution, population, unemployment, education, and migration) and international (trade, balance of payments, and foreign investment). The last part reviews the possibilities and prospects for Third World development. Chap-ters supplemented with review concepts and questions. (JEL)

Ward, Richard J., THE CHALLENGE OF DEVELOPMENT, Chicago, Aldine Publishing Co., 1971. A com-pendium of readings for student use, within a six-point framework: methodology, strategy and decision-making criteria in development; manpower needs and projections; the intrinsic value of land, including its agricultural potential in relation to development plans; practical problems of promoting the industrial sector; the development of infrastructure power, transportation and communications; and possible solutions to social problems created by modern growth trends. (BPA)

Wilber, Charles K., ed., THE POLITICAL ECONOMY OF DEVELOPMENT AND UNDERDEVELOPMENT, New York, Random House, 1973. Thirty-three predominantly reprinted readings, which are designed "to be used with a standard textbook in advanced undergraduate and beginning graduate courses." Emphasis in approach and content is on political economy in the sense of attempting to "incorporate such noneconomic influences as social structures, political systems, and cultural values as well as such factors as technological change and the distribution of income and wealth." (JEL)

Theory of Development

Adelman, Irma, THEORIES OF ECONOMIC GROWTH AND DE-VELOPMENT, Stanford, California, Stanford University Press, 1961.

Adelman, Irma and Thorbecke, Erik, eds., THE THEORY AND DESIGN OF ECONOMIC DEVELOPMENT, Baltimore, Maryland, Johns Hopkins Press, 1969. Presents a collection of papers designed to help bridge the gap between the theoretical and practical approaches to development problems and to explore the most promising avenues for future research. Analyzes the relation between the agricultural sectors of a developing economy and points out possibilities for closer interaction between the theoretical and empirical approaches to development planning. (JEL)

Amin, Aamir, ACCUMULATION ON A WORLD SCALE: A Critique of the Theory of Underdevelopment, 2 volumes, translated by Brian Pearce, New York, Monthly Review Press, 1974. An English translation of the 1971 French second edition. It is a critique of current economic theory (marginalism) and an attempt to extend Marxist analysis to deal explicitly with "underdeveloped" countries. A basic thesis of the book is that all countries are integrated into a worldwide system of commercial and financial relations, but that current economic theory is inapplicable for the analysis of these relations. Bibliography; no index. (JEL)

Brenner, Y. S., THEORIES OF ECONOMIC DEVELOPMENT AND GROWTH, New York and Washington, Frederick A. Praeger, 1966.

Brookfield, H., INTERDEPENDENT DEVELOPMENT, Pittsburgh, Pennsylvania, University of Pittsburgh Press, 1975.

Chenery, Hollis and Syrquin, Moises, PATTERNS OF DEVELOPMENT, 1950-1970, Washington, D.C., World Bank, 1975.

Currie, Lauchlin, Ph.D., ACCELERATING DEVELOPMENT, THE NECESSITY AND THE MEANS, New York, London, Sydney, Toronto, McGraw-Hill Book Company, 1966.

Currie, Laughlin B., OBSTACLES TO DEVELOPMENT, East Lansing, Michigan State University Press, 1967.

Fei, John C. H. and Ranis, Gustav, DEVELOPMENT OF THE LABOR SURPLUS ECONOMY: Theory and Policy, New Haven, Connecticut, Yale University Press, 1964.

Galbraith, John Kenneth, ECONOMIC DEVELOPMENT, Cambridge, Massachusetts, Harvard University Press, 1964.

Gerschenkron, Alexander, ECONOMIC BACKWARDNESS IN HISTORICAL PERSPECTIVE: A Book of Essays, Cambridge, Massachusetts, Belknap Press of Harvard University Press, 1962.

Hagen, Everett, E., ON THE THEORY OF SOCIAL CHANGE: How Economic Growth Begins, A Study from the Center for International Studies, Massachusetts Institute of Technology, Homewood, Illinois, The Dorsey Press, Inc., 1967.

Hirschman, Albert O., THE STRATEGY OF ECONOMIC DE-
    VELOPMENT, New Haven, Connecticut, Yale Univer-
    'sity Press, 1958.

Johnson, Harry G., MONEY, TRADE AND ECONOMIC GROWTH:
    Survey Lectures in Economic Theory, Harvard
    University Press, Cambridge, Massachusetts,
    1962.

Kelley, Allen C., et al., DUALISTIC ECONOMIC DEVEL-
    OPMENT: Theory and History, Chicago, Illinois,
    University of Chicago Press, 1972.

Kristensen, Thoukil, DEVELOPMENT IN RICH AND POOR
    COUNTRIES: A General Theory with Statistical
    Analyses, New York, Praeger, 1974. The Danish
    economist and politician, who formerly headed
    the OECD, here takes the first step in con-
    structing a general theory of development, good
    for all sorts of countries. He counts on
    others to add to this interesting start, which
    stresses the importance of knowledge, and thus,
    because its dissemination is now more rapid, is
    optimistic. (FA)

Kuz'min, S. A., THE DEVELOPING COUNTRIES: Employ-
    ment and Capital Investment, Mowcow, "Mysl"
    Publishing House 1965; New York, International
    Arts and Sciences Press, 1969. English lan-
    guage edition of a Soviet treatment of the
    problems of underdeveloped countries. Uses
    statistical tests on official data from less
    developed countries to criticize the theories
    of Chenery, Ranis, Leibenstein, and Sen.
    Concludes that such countries should invest in
    small-scale industry. No Index. (JEL)

Leibenstein, H., "Allocative Efficiency Versus X-
    Efficiency," American Economic Review, June
    1966.

Lewis, W. Arthur, "A Review of Economic Develop-
    ment," American Economic Review, May 1965.

Lewis, W. Arthur, THE THEORY OF ECONOMIC GROWTH,
    Homewood, Illinois, Richard D. Irwin, 1955.

Morgan, Theodore and Betz, George W., eds., ECONOMIC
    DEVELOPMENT: Readings in Theory and Practice,
    Belmont, California, Wadsworth, 1970. Contains
    44 complete or excerpted articles by 45 writers.

Grouped as follows: Central problems of economic growth (8 selections); Growth theories
(9); Land and the peasants (4); International
trade and economic growth (4); Education and
growth (2); Unemployment (1); and Development
policy (16). No index. (JEL)

Myint, H., ECONOMIC THEORY AND THE UNDERDEVELOPED
COUNTRIES, New York, Oxford University Press,
1971. Selected papers by a Burmese economist
who has long been one of the most balanced
thinkers about development. The analysis is
"middle level" between pure theory and empirical study. (FA)

Powelson, John P., INSTITUTIONS OF ECONOMIC GROWTH:
A Theory of Conflict Management in Developing
Countries, Princeton, New Jersey, Princeton
University Press, 1972.

Ranis, Gustav and Fei, John C. H., "A Theory of Economic Development," The American Economic
Review, Vol. LI, No. 4, September 1961.

Rostow, W. W., THE STAGES OF ECONOMIC GROWTH: A
Non-Communist Manifesto, second edition, New
York, Cambridge University Press, 1971. The
second edition of the well-known work. Changes
are in the preface and in an appendix in which
the author adduces evidence, in large part
derived from what he terms Kuznets' earlier
approach, to answer some of his critics.
Rostow concludes, after lengthy consideration
and in spite of the attacks of many critics,
that the stages of growth approach remains "a
useful tool in viewing the past as well as the
present" developments. Index. (JEL)

Sadhu, A. N., "Labour Surplus Models of Economic
Growth--A Critical Appraisal," Indian Economic
Journal.

Schumpeter, Joseph A., THE THEORY OF ECONOMIC DEVEL-
OPMENT: An Inquiry into Profits, Capital,
Credit, Interest, and the Business Cycle,
translated by Redvers Opie, Cambridge, Massachusetts, Harvard University Press, 1936. This
is the classic work, originally written in Ger-
man in 1911, in which Schumpeter introduced his
distinctions among entrepreneur, capitalist, and
manager, showing how their interactions pro-

moted development in a way that also explains
the business cycle. (Ed)

Siebert, Horst, REGIONAL ECONOMIC GROWTH: Theory
and Policy, Scranton, Pennsylvania, International Textbook Company, 1969.

Ward, Richard J., ed., THE CHALLENGE OF DEVELOPMENT:
Theory and Practice, Chicago, Aldine Publishing
Co., 1971.

Whyte, William F., and Williams, Lawrence K., TOWARD
AN INTEGRATED THEORY OF DEVELOPMENT: Economic
and Noneconomic Variables in Rural Development,
Ithaca, New York, Cornell University, 1968.

Zachariah, K. C., and Gholl, Joseph E., "Toward the
Year 2000," Finance and Development, Vol. 10,
No. 4, December 1973.

Zarembka, Paul, TOWARD A THEORY OF ECONOMIC DEVELOP-
MENT, Mathematical Economics Texts, No. 9, San
Francisco, California, Holden-Day, under the
auspices of the Institute of International
Studies, University of California at Berkeley,
1972. Focuses on "general and partial equilibrium problems," and stresses the importance of
"transformation from agriculture to industry"
during economic Development. Part I examines
the theory of surplus labor. Part II studies
the structure of a closed economy with the help
of a dual economy model. Part III introduces
the external sector and explores the relationship of trade with development. The final part
examines the theoretical and empirical aspects
of the agricultural sector. (JEL)

Trade and Exchange

X-REF: BRAZIL: Donges, CHILE: Behrman, CHINA:
Hsiao, COLOMBIA: Diaz, ECUADOR: Gibson, EMPLOYMENT
LABOR: Fine, Lydall, HAITI: Morrison, INDIA:
Bhagwati, JAPAN: Kershner, Ozaki, LATIN AMERICA:
Bell, MULTINATIONAL CORPORATIONS: Dunning, PAKIS-
TAN: Islam, PERU: Roemer, PHILIPPINES: Baldwin,
SMALL BUSINESS: Ho, TURKEY: Krueger, UGANDA:
Parson.

Anjaria, S. J., "Nontariff Issues in the MTN,"
Finance and Development, Vol. 13, No. 2, June
1976.

Balassa, Bela and Associates, THE STRUCTURE OF PRO-
TECTION IN DEVELOPING COUNTRIES, Baltimore and
London, The Johns Hopkins University Press,
1971.

Balassa, Bela and Associates, STUDIES IN TRADE
LIBERALIZATION, Baltimore, Maryland, Johns
Hopkins Press, 1967.

Balassa, Bela, TRADE LIBERALIZATION AMONG INDUSTRIAL
COUNTRIES, New York, McGraw-Hill, 1967.

Balassa, Bela, TRADE POLICIES IN DEVELOPING COUN-
TRIES, World Bank Reprint Series, No. 1, from
The American Economic Review, Washington, D.C.,
International Bank for Reconstruction and De-
velopment, 1971.

Baldwin, Robert E., NONTARIFF DISTORTIONS OF INTER-
NATIONAL TRADE, Washington, D.C., Brookings
Institution, 1970. The best book yet on nontariff barriers and related practices that
interfere with international trade, such as
subsidies and taxes. Strong on economic analysis, this study by a Wisconsin professor with
governmental experience is also valuable for
its descriptive material and suggestions about
the kinds of international agreements that
would improve matters. (FA)

Bell, Harry H., TARIFF PROFILES IN LATIN AMERICA:
Implications for Pricing Structures and Eco-
nomic Integration, New York, Washington,
London, Praeger Publishers, 1971.

Bhagwati, Avinash, and Onitsuka, Yusuke, "Export-
Import Responses to Devaluation: Experience of
the Non-Industrial Countries in the 1960's, in
International Monetary Fund," Staff Papers,
Vol. 21, 1974, pp. 414-462.

CED, NONTARIFF DISTORTIONS OF TRADE, New York, CED
Publications, 1969. Examines the complex
problem of dealing with nontariff distortions
of trade arising from governmental measures
that create special barriers to imports and
incentives to exports. Statement was developed

jointly with CED counterpart organizations in
Europe, Japan, and Australia. (BPA)

CED, TRADE POLICY TOWARD LOW-INCOME COUNTRIES, New
York, CED Publications, 1967. Presents 12 recommendations concerning trade policies of the
high-income countries toward the low-income
countries. It includes specific proposals to
help increase the export earnings of the
world's developing regions. Statement was
developed jointly with CED counterpart organizations in Europe and Japan. (BPA)

Cohen, Benjamin I., THE USE OF EFFECTIVE TARIFFS,
Center Paper #160, Economic Growth Center, New
Haven, Connecticut, Yale University, 1970.

Corden, W. M., THE THEORY OF PROTECTION, Oxford,
Clarendon Press, 1971.

de Vries, Margaret G., EXCHANGE DEPRECIATION IN DE-
VELOPING COUNTRIES, Staff Papers, Vol. XV, No.
3, Washington, D.C., International Monetary
Fund, 1968.

de Vries, Margaret G., MULTIPLE EXCHANGE RATES: Ex-
pectations and Experiences, July 1965 issue of
Staff Papers, Washington, D.C., International
Monetary Fund Staff, 1965.

Diebold, William Jr., "U.S. Trade Policy: The New
Political Dimensions," Foreign Affairs, Vol.
52, No. 3, April 1974.

Fine, S. M., "The Employment Effects of Import
Duties and Export Subsidies in the Developing
Countries," ILO, FISCAL MEASURES FOR EMPLOYMENT
PROMOTION IN DEVELOPING COUNTRIES, Geneva, pp.
233-267.

Galtung, Johan, "The Lomé Convention and Neo-Capi-
talism," in The African Review, Vol. 6, No. 1,
1976, pp. 33.

Ghai, Dharam P., STATE TRADING AND REGIONAL ECONOMIC
INTEGRATION AMONG DEVELOPING COUNTRIES, New
York, United Nations, 1973, (United Nations
Conference on Trade and Development, Current
Problems of Economic Integration, United Na-
tions publications sales No. E.73.II.d.17;
United Nations document TB/B/436).

Gosovic, Branislav, UNCTAD: Conflict and Compromise, Leyden, Sijthoff, 1972. An exceptionally thorough analysis of the work of UNCTAD up to 1970, stressing substantive issues, the development of the organization and the resolution of conflicts among the members. Very much on the side of the less-developed nations, the Jugoslav author (Ph.D. Berkeley) is a little saddened by the "taming" of UNCTAD, which he believes has accomplished much. (FA)

Green, Reginald Herbold, "The Lomé Convention: Updated Dependence or Departure Toward Collective Self-Reliance?" in The African Review, Vol. 6, No. 1, 1976, pp. 43-54.

Hansen, Bent and Nashashibi, Karim, FOREIGN TRADE REGIMES AND ECONOMIC DEVELOPMENT: Egypt, New York, Columbia University Press, 1975.

Helleiner, G. K., WORLD MARKET IMPERFECTIONS AND THE DEVELOPING COUNTRIES, Occasional Paper No. 11, NIEO Series, Washington, D.C., ODC, 1978. This paper addresses a fundamental theme that permeates the various proposals for NIEO reforms: Do imperfections in the international markets systematically operate to the disadvantage of developing countries? The author discusses the limitations of international markets in the achievement of efficiency and equity objectives. He assesses the two major world market imperfections--restrictions on the international mobility of labor and differences in access to market information--as well as imperfections in developing-country export and import markets, including restrictive trade practices, and imperfections in technology and capital markets. (BPA)

Hemphill, William L., THE EFFECT OF FOREIGN EXCHANGE RECEIPTS ON IMPORTS OF LESS DEVELOPED COUNTRIES, International Monetary Fund, Staff Papers Volume 21, 1974.

IMF Survey, ISSUE ON TRADE, July 4, 1977. Outlining European trade arrangements; regional arrangements among LDCs, East-West trade, Tokyo round developments, and the integrated program for commodities. (Ed)

Islam, Nurul, EXPORT POLICY IN PAKISTAN, Center Paper
    #137, Economic Growth Center, New Haven, Con-
    necticut, Yale University, 1969.

Johnson, Harry G., ed., TRADE STRATEGY FOR RICH AND
    POOR NATIONS, Toronto, Canada, University of
    Toronto Press, 1971.

Kahn, Mohsins, IMPORT AND EXPORT DEMAND IN DEVELOP-
    ING COUNTRIES, I.M.F. Staff Papers, Volume 21,
    1974.

Kravis, I. B., "External Demand and Internal Supply
    Factors in LDC Export Performance," Banca
    Nazionale del Lavoro-Quarterly Review, June
    1970, Vol. 23, No. 93. The failure of the less
    developed countries (LDCs) to share fully in
    the unprecedented expansion of world trade has
    most frequently been ascribed to unfavorable
    external demand conditions rather than to inter-
    nal conditions that militate against exports.
    The evidence however indicates the absence of a
    general dependence of export performances of
    individual LDCs on the behavior of the world
    markets for their traditional products. The
    evidence also supports the empirical generaliza-
    tion that the lines of causation generally run
    from domestic growth to export success. Support
    is found for the further hypothesis that an open
    or outward oriented development strategy leads
    not only to higher exports but to faster growth.
    (JEL)

Linder, Staffan Burenstam, TRADE AND TRADE POLICY FOR
    DEVELOPMENT, New York, Frederic A. Praeger,
    1967.

Lydall, H. F., TRADE AND EMPLOYMENT: A Study of the
    Effects of Trade Expansion on Employment in
    Developing and Developed Countries, Geneva,
    International Labour Office, 1975.

Maizels, Alfred, et al., EXPORTS AND ECONOMIC GROWTH
    OF DEVELOPING COUNTRIES, New York, Cambridge
    University Press, 1969. A major study of past
    and projected exports of sterling area countries
    and their relation to growth. Commodity pros-
    pects, the supply positions of individual coun-
    tries, and policy issues for both the industri-
    alized and the less developed countries are
    examined. (FA)

218

Mayer, Helmut W., THE ANATOMY OF OFFICIAL EXCHANGE-
RATE INTERVENTION SYSTEMS, Princeton, New
Jersey, Princeton University, 1974.

Metzger, Stanley D., LOWERING NONTARIFF BARRIERS:
U.S. Law, Practice, and Negotiating Objectives,
Washington, Brookings Institution, 1974. While
giving special attention to the difficulties of
negotiation and suggesting some possible forms
of international agreement, this study provides
an authoritative examination of American practice in such matters as government procurement,
anti-dumping, duties, quotas, subsidies and
other aids to business. The author, a leading
expert on trade law, was formerly chairman of
the Tariff Commission. (FA)

Michaely, Michael, FOREIGN TRADE REGIMES AND ECO-
NOMIC DEVELOPMENT: Israel, New York, Columbia
University Press, 1975.

Morrison, Thomas K., MANUFACTURED EXPORTS FROM
DEVELOPING COUNTRIES, New York, Praeger, 1975.
Investigates the effect of import restrictions
of developed countries and the efforts of developing countries to promote exports. Examines the future prospects and determinants of
success in exporting manufactures from developing nations, and demonstrates that the level of
development market size, endowment of natural
resources, and export promotion are key factors
determining performance. (BPA)

Morton, Kathryn and Tulloch, Peter, TRADE AND DEVEL-
OPING COUNTRIES, New York and Toronto, Wiley,
Halsted Press, 1977. Examines the role of
international trade in the development process
and discusses the arguments for and against
trade focusing on the debate between "outward-
looking" and "inward-looking" strategies;
discusses the roles of the international or-
ganizations--GATT, UNCTAD, and others, and
those of national governments and foreign
investors--in international trade. Discusses
some of the moves made towards greater economic
and trade cooperation among developing countries. Concludes that external trade is strategic, but not the key to economic development
and that the emphasis placed in development
strategies on trade will depend on the resource-
base and the economic characteristics of the

219

country concerned. Contains data for 1960-75.
(JEL)

Murray, Tracy, TRADE PREFERENCES FOR DEVELOPING
COUNTRIES, New York, Halsted Press, 1977. Discusses the conceptual origins of trade preferences for development, the political problems
in negotiating change in the rules governing
international trade, and the economic impact
that trade preferences would have on developing
country exports. Also examines the operation
and effects of the preference system that was
introduced to the European Economic Community.
(BPA)

Rahman, A. H. M. Mahfuzur, EXPORTS OF MANUFACTURES
FROM DEVELOPING COUNTRIES: A Study in Comparative Advantage, Rotterdam, Rotterdam University
Press, 1973. An economist from Bangladesh here
carries through a series of well-focused
studies which support the view that developing
countries do best in selling manufactured goods
in rich countries if they concentrate on labor-
intensive production and diversify their
markets. (FA)

Ramaswami, V. K., TRADE AND DEVELOPMENT, edited by
Jagdish Bhagwati, Harry G. Johnson, and T. N.
Srinivasan, Cambridge, Massachusetts, MIT
Press, 1972. Essays dealing with the choice of
optimal trade intervention policies when the
workings of the competitive system are distorted by imperfections, or when the government
for some reason cannot adopt the "first-best"
policies indicated by pure economic theory.
(BPA)

Myint, Hla, PROTECTION AND ECONOMIC DEVELOPMENT,
Economic Research Project, Economics Papers #6
and 7, Department of Economics, Statistics and
Commerce, University of Rangoon, 1961.

Small, Albert H., THE AMERICAN MARKET FOR MANU-
FACTURING EXPORTS FROM THE DEVELOPING COUN-
TRIES, New York, Praeger, 1972.

Streeten, Paul, ed., TRADE STRATEGIES FOR DEVELOP-
MENT: Papers of the Ninth Cambridge Conference
on Development Problems, September 1972, Cambridge University Overseas Studies Committee,
New York, Wiley, 1973. Topics considered in-

clude: outward-looking vs. inward-looking
strategies, the impact of the developed countries, regional integration of the developing
countries, the impact of like action by developed countries, trade and technology, domestic
farm policies and trade in agricultural goods,
trade negotiations for manufactured goods,
multinational enterprises, and some general information concerning international trade (given
in an Overseas Development Administration staff
paper which served as a background document to
the conference). (JEL)

Theberge, James D., ed., ECONOMICS OF TRADE AND
DEVELOPMENT, New York, London, and Toronto,
John Wiley and Sons, Inc., 1968.

United Nations, TOWARDS A NEW TRADE POLICY FOR
DEVELOPMENT, Report by the Secretary-General of
the United Nations Conference on Trade and Development, New York, United Nations, 1964.

Walter, Ingo, "Nontariff Barriers and the Export
Performance of Developing Economies," The
American Economic Review, Vol. LXI, No. 2, May
1971.

Walter, Ingo, "United States Non-Tariff Measures and
Trade Preferences for Latin America," Inter-
American Economic Affairs, Vol. 23, No. 4,
Spring 1970.

Wilkinson, Joe R., LATIN AMERICA AND THE EUROPEAN
ECONOMIC COMMUNITY: An Appraisal, Denver,
Colorado, University of Denver, 1965.

Wilson, P. R. D., EXPORT INSTABILITY AND ECONOMIC
DEVELOPMENT--A SURVEY, Part 2: The Empirical
Work, Warwick Economic Research Papers, Coven-
try, University of Warwick, Department of
Economics, May 1977.

Urban Development

X-REF: AFRICA: Gugler, BRAZIL: Ilo, CHINA: Howe,
COLOMBIA: Whiteford, GUATEMALA: Roberts, INDONESIA:
Ilo, LATIN AMERICA: Field, MEXICO: Fox, PERU:
Collier, Fox, PHILIPPINES: Wheelock.

Alberti, Giorgio, THE BREAKDOWN OF PROVINCIAL URBAN
    POWER STRUCTURE AND THE RISE OF PEASANT MOVE-
    MENTS, LTC Reprint No. 103, Madison, University
    of Wisconsin, Land Tenure Center, 1972.

Amey, Alan, URBAN-RURAL RELATIONS IN TANZANIA:
    Methodology Issues and Preliminary Results,
    Development Studies Discussion Paper, Univer-
    sity of East Anglia, December 1976.

Barnes, Sandra T., "Political Transition in Urban
    Africa," The Annals, Vol. 432, July 1977, pp.
    26-41.

Beier, G., et al., "The Task Ahead for the Cities of
    the Developing Countries," World Development,
    Vol. 4, No. 5, May 1976.

Bernstein, Beverly, A SURVEY OF EUROPEAN PROGRAMMES:
    Education for Urbanisation in Developing Coun-
    tries, International Urbanisation Survey Report
    to the Ford Foundation, New York, 1972.

Beyer, Glenn H., ed., THE URBAN EXPLOSION IN LATIN
    AMERICA: A Continent in Process of Moderniza-
    tion, Ithaca, New York, Cornell University
    Press, 1967.

Bryant, C., "Comparative Urbanization and Political
    Change (Review Article)," Journal of Develop-
    ment Studies, Vol. 7, No. 1, October 1970.

Cebula, R. J., "The City as a Source of Regional
    Economic Disparity in Latin America: A Com-
    ment," Review of Social Economy, Vol. 31, No.
    1, April 1973. Walter's study in the Review of
    Social Economy, April 1973, regards the city in
    Latin America as exploiting the rural area.
    Walter maintains that as the rural area gener-
    ates and exports resources to the urban area,
    the urban area fails to generate a significant
    return flow of income and commodities. This
    position may be incompatible with conventional
    analysis of interdependent economics, however.
    The citations Walter invokes to support his
    position seem inadequate. In addition, his
    analysis of migration is superficial and fails
    to take account of alternative hypotheses of
    migration and divergent growth rates in develop-
    ing economies. (JEL) (See Walter, below).

Davis, Kingsley, "Asia's Cities: Problems and Options," *Population* and *Development* Review, Vol. 1, No. 1, 1975.

Dwyer, D. J., THE CITY IN THE THIRD WORLD, New York, Barnes and Noble/Harper and Row, 1974.

Eans, Edwin, and Goode, Judith Granitch, URBAN POVERTY IN A CROSS-CULTURAL CONTEXT, New York, Free Press, Macmillan, 1973.

Ekistics, THE PROBLEMS AND SCIENCE OF HUMAN SETTLEMENTS, Athens, Greece, The Athens Center of Ekistics, Vol. 42, Number 252, November 1976.

Fox, Robert W., URBAN POPULATION GROWTH TRENDS IN LATIN AMERICA, Washington, D.C., Inter-American Development Bank, 1975.

Friedmann, John and Sullivan, Flora, "The Absorption of Labor in the Urban Economy: The Case of Developing Countries," *Economic* *Development* and *Cultural* *Change*, Vol. 22, No. 3, April 1974.

Gardner, James A., URBANIZATION IN BRAZIL, International Urbanization Survey Report to the Ford Foundation, New York, 1972.

Grimes, Orville F. Jr., HOUSING WITHOUT FRILLS: An Overview of Housing for Low-Income Urban Families, Economics and Policy in the Developing World, World Bank, 1976.

ILO, THE PROMOTION OF BALANCED RURAL AND URBAN DEVELOPMENT, Geneva, ILO, 1973. Development in Africa has been characterized by an imbalance between the modern, industrial sector and the rural, traditional sector. This report considers the many problems encountered by economic and social programs designed to rectify this imbalance. Includes: rural-urban relationships; employment creation; agrarian reform and cooperatives; education. (BPA)

ILO, RURAL AND URBAN INCOME INEQUALITIES IN INDONESIA, MEXICO, PAKISTAN, TANZANIA AND TUNISIA, Geneva, ILO, 1976. An inquiry into the economic aspects of income inequality in selected developing countries, with special reference to income distribution within and between urban

and rural areas. The report discusses the
basic economies of the five countries; the
components and economic causes of urban and
rural inequalities; household expenditures;
poverty measures; and policy recommendations.
(BPA)

ILO, URBAN UNEMPLOYMENT IN DEVELOPING COUNTRIES,
Geneva, ILO, 1973. Discusses the general
causes, extent, and characteristics of urban
unemployment; the causes of urban inflation and
rural-urban drift; and the choice between urban
unemployment and rural under-employment. Suggests research requirements for a better understanding of the problem and recommends specific
measures for diminishing the rural-urban drift
and for reducing urban unemployment. (BPA)

Koenigsberger, O. H.; Bernstein, B.; Foot, M.; Rees,
J.; Roberts, M.; Tyler, M.; Wylie, J. C.,
INFRASTRUCTURE PROBLEMS OF THE CITIES OF DEVEL-
OPING COUNTRIES, International Urbanization
Survey Report to The Ford Foundation, New York,
1972.

Laurenti, Luigi and Gerhart, John, URBANIZATION IN
KENYA, an International Urbanization Survey
Report to the New York Ford Foundation, New
York, 1972.

Lipton, Michael, WHY POOR PEOPLE STAY POOR: Urban
Bias in World Development, Cambridge, Massachusetts, Harvard University Press, 1976. Examines the conflict of interest between the
urban and rural sectors of developing countries. Discusses how, why, and with what
effects the rural sector is "squeezed," both by
transfers of resources from it and by prices
that are turned against it. Surveys ideologies
of rural and urban development, including
discussions of Classical and Marginalist economies, Marxism and the rural-urban relationship,
the Soviet industrialization debate, and
"pastoral and populism" (idyllic communal
village concepts). Index. (JEL)

Little, Kenneth, URBANIZATION AS A SOCIAL PROCESS:
An Essay on Movement and Change in Contemporary
Africa, Boston, Routledge and Kegan Paul, 1974.

Mangin, William, ed., PEASANTS IN CITIES: Readings in the Anthropology of Urbanization, Boston, Massachusetts, Houghton Mifflin, 1970.

Miller, John and Gakenheimer, Ralph A., eds., LATIN AMERICAN URBAN POLICIES AND THE SOCIAL SCIENCES, Beverly Hills, California, London, England, Sage Publications, 1969.

Morse, Richard, "The Development of Urban Systems in the Americas in the Nineteenth Century," Journal of Interamerican Studies and World Affairs, Vol. 17, No. 1, February 1975.

Obudho, R. A., and El-Shakhs, Salah S., ed., AFRICAN URBAN SYSTEMS AND URBAN DEVELOPMENT: A Planning Perspective, New York, Praeger, expected 1979. African urban scholars--geographers, planners, economists, sociologists and political scientists--assess the impact of rapid urban expansion on local government, economic planning, housing, employment, apartheid, and population stabilization. Examining the modern and traditional forces shaping urbanization in each major African region, the authors distinguish the process of urbanization in Third World countries from that of developed nations and offer new development strategies suited to the social, economic, and political climate of Africa. (BPA)

OECD, DOCUMENTATION FOR URBAN MANAGEMENT: OECD Urban Management Studies, No. 1, Proceedings of a Symposium at OECD, 19-21 November, 1975, Washington, D.C., OECD, December 1977.

Portes, Alejandro and Walton, John, URBAN LATIN AMERICA: The Political Condition from Above and Below, Austin, University of Texas Press, 1976.

Robin, John P. and Terzo, Frederick C., URBANIZATION IN CHILE, International Urbanization Survey Report to The Ford Foundation, New York, 1972.

Robin, John P. and Terzo, Frederick C., URBANIZATION IN COLOMBIA, consultant: Jaime Valenzuela, International Urbanization Survey Report to the Ford Foundation, New York, 1972.

Robin, John P. and Terzo, Frederick, URBANIZATION IN
PERU, consultant: Jaime Valenzuela, Interna-
tional Urbanization Survey Report to the New
York Ford Foundation, New York, 1972.

Robin, John P. and Terzo, Frederick, URBANIZATION IN
VENEZUELA, consultant: Jaime Valenzuela,
International Urbanization Survey Report to The
New York Ford Foundation, New York, 1972.

Sabot, R. H., THE SOCIAL COSTS OF URBAN SURPLUS
LABOUR, Washington, D. C., OECD, 1977.

Smock, David R. and Smock, Audrey C., CULTURAL AND
POLITICAL ASPECTS OF RURAL TRANSFORMATION: A
Case Study of Eastern Nigeria, Praeger Special
Studies in International Economics and Development, New York and London, Praeger, 1972.
Studies "the cultural and political aspects of
social and economic development in rural Eastern Nigeria prior to the attempted secession
and the resultant civil war." Findings based
on case studies, detailed studies of land
tenure and traditions, and attitude surveys.
Contains 29 tables of data through 1966, many
of them pertinent to economic questions. (JEL)

Terzo, Frederick, URBANIZATION IN THE DEVELOPING
COUNTRIES: The Response of International
Assistance, International Urbanization Survey
Report to The Ford Foundation, New York, 1972.

Tinder, Hugh, RACE AND THE THIRD WORLD CITY, International Urbanization Survey to the Ford Foundation, New York, 1972.

United Nations, REPORT OF HABITAT: United Nations
Conference on Human Settlements, New York,
United Nations, 1976. This book, the REPORT of
the 1976 Vancouver Conference, is concerned
with the worldwide problem of human settlements, particularly with the remodelling of the
human environment to create new and more just
social balances. The REPORT defines specific
problems and recommends possible solutions on
national, regional, and international levels.
Problems receiving attention include: social,
economic, ecological, and environmental deterioration and their effect on living conditions;
world population growth and inequitable economic growth; uncontrolled urbanization; rural

backwardness and rural dispersion; involuntary migration. Recommendations for action are grouped under the following headings: settlement policies and strategies; settlement planning as a continuing process; shelter, infrastructure, and services; land resource ownership and management; public participation; institutions and human skill management. (BPA)

Walter, J. P., "The City as a Source of Regional Economic Disparity in Latin America," Review of Social Economy, Vol. 31, No. 1, April 1973. This study attempts to show that Latin America is not characterized by a dualist economy. Rather, there is, and historically has been, a continuum between the rural and urban areas. Moreover, the city's growth has taken place at the expense of the rural area due to this historical continuum. Economic theories based on the concepts of disguised unemployment and marginal productivity are inoperable in explaining population movements from the rural to urban area as urbanization occurred before industrialization in Latin America. (JEL) (See Cebula, above)

Wheelock, Gerald C., and Young, Frank W., MACRO-SOCIAL ACCOUNTING FOR MUNICIPALITIES IN THE PHILIPPINES: Rural Banks and Credit Cooperatives, Cornell International Agriculture Bulletin 26, July 1973.

World Bank, HOUSING, Sector Policy Paper, May 1975.

World Bank, URBANIZATION, Sector Working Paper, June 1972.

World Bank, "Urban Poverty in Developing Countries: A World Bank Analysis," Population and Development Review, Vol. 1, No. 2, December 1975.

World Bank, URBAN TRANSPORT, Sector Policy Paper, May 1975.

U.S. Policy

X-REF: ASIA: Olson, BRAZIL: McCann, CHINA: Moorstein, DOMINICAN REPUBLIC: Atkins, Lowenthal, Slater, HAITI: Schmidt, INDIA: Brown, LATIN AMERICA: Grunwald, Tancer, MALAYSIA: Gould, MEXICO:

227

Fagen, Mayer, Poulson, Ross, PANAMA: Mellander,
PERU: Dye, Sharp, PHILIPPINES: Buss, PUERTO RICO:
Clark.

Blasier, Cole, THE HOVERING GIANT: U.S. Responses
to Revolutionary Change in Latin America, University of Pittsburgh Press, 1976.

Connell-Smith, Gordon, THE UNITED STATES AND LATIN
AMERICA: An Historical Analysis of Inter-
American Relations, New York, Halsted Press,
1974. The well-known author of this valuable
study of hemispheric interaction concludes that
for the United States Latin America is both a
special sphere of influence and a low-priority
area in foreign policy, whereas the true U.S.
interest would be better served by the opposite
--less significance for Latin America in theory
and more importance in practice. (FA)

Cotler, Julio, and Fagen, Richard R., eds., LATIN
AMERICA AND THE UNITED STATES: The Changing
Political Realities, Stanford, California,
Stanford University Press, 1974. These 11 extensive essays (with shorter commentaries on
each) by recognized foreign policy analysts and
social scientists, represent the agenda of the
1972 conference at the Institute of Peruvian
Studies in Lima. Topics include political,
economic, and military relations, governmental
policymaking, and multinational corporate
issues. (FA)

Green, David, THE CONTAINMENT OF LATIN AMERICA,
Chicago, Quadrangle Books, 1971. The theme:
the Good Neighbor policy failed because FDR and
Truman used it to strengthen U.S. control over
Latin American economies, thereby intensifying
nationalism and instability. The research is
good but some will doubt the conclusion. (FA)

Ferguson, Yale H., ed., CONTEMPORARY INTER-AMERICAN
RELATIONS: A Reader in Theory and Issues,
Englewood Cliffs, New Jersey, Prentice-Hall,
Inc., 1972.

Fishlow, Albert, THE MATURE NEIGHBOR POLICY: A New
United States Economic Policy for Latin Ameri-
ca, Paper No 3, Policy Papers for International
Affairs, Berkeley, University of California,
Institute of International Studies, 1977.

Kane, William Everett, CIVIL STRIFE IN LATIN AMERICA:
A Legal History of U.S. Involvement, Baltimore,
Maryland, Johns Hopkins University Press, 1972.
An excellent work, refreshing in its candor.
U.S. interventions in Latin America are seen as
primarily preemptive, based on strategic rather
than economic concern. The author hints at the
desirability of relaxing the traditional non-
intervention dogma and the manner of circum-
scribing such a liberalization. (FA)

Krause, Walter, ECONOMIC DEVELOPMENT: The Underdeveloped World and the American Interest, San
Francisco, Wadsworth Publishing, 1961.

Lodge, George C., ENGINES OF CHANGE: United States
Interests and Revolution in Latin America, New
York, Knopf, 1970. An eloquent plea for the
alignment of the United States with the forces
of nontotalitarian revolutionary change in
politics, religion and society. The proposals
for new administrative techniques and structures are helpful. (FA)

Lowenthal, Abraham F., "The United States and Latin
America: Ending the Hegemonic Presumption,"
Foreign Affairs, Vol. 55, No. 1, October 1976,
pp. 199-213.

Martin, Edwin M., and Fowler, Henry H., THE UNITED
STATES AND THE DEVELOPING COUNTRIES, Boulder,
Colorado, Westview Press, 1977. While the
recent record of U.S. development policies is
an uneven one, U.S. policy in this field of
central importance, despite the growing influence of the European Community and Japan on the
global economy. Most of the choices the U.S.
faces today concerning future development
policy must be made also by the other industrialized democracies, which share common vital
interests in the outcome of the collaborative
development process, and which have common
though not identical contributions to make to
its success. It is essential that the resources devoted to the development effort
achieve the desired outcome, and this is possible only if those resources are put to work
in ways that are mutually agreed upon. To get
the job done, the Atlantic Council Working
Group on the United States and the Developing
Countries outlines a coordinated approach

toward development, emphasizing that policymaking and policy inplementation cannot be permitted to degenerate into a "lowest common
denominator" effort. (BPA)

Martin, John Bartlow, U.S. POLICY IN THE CARIBBEAN,
Boulder, Colorado, Westview Press, 1978. John
Bartlow Martin reviews and rejects both the
activist policy of the Kennedy administration
and the passive attitude of more recent administration, and makes policy recommendations aimed
at cooperative U.S.-Caribbean relations. After
rapidly surveying the historical background of
these relations, Professor Martin focuses on
current issues vis-à-vis the Greater Antilles
(Puerto Rico, the Dominican Republic, Haiti,
Jamaica, and Cuba); Central America; Trinidad-
Tobago; and two mainland countries, Venezuela
and Guyana. (BPA)

Olson, Gary, U.S. FOREIGN POLICY AND A THIRD WORLD
PEASANT: Land Reform in Asia and Latin America, New York, Praeger, 1974.

Overseas Development Council, THE UNITED STATES AND
WORLD DEVELOPMENT: Agenda, annual publication
on the relationship between the United States
and the less developed world, with aid and
other statistics, New York, Praeger (for the
ODC), different dates.

Petersen, Gustav H., "Latin America: Benign Neglect
Is Not Enough," Foreign Affairs, Vol. 51, No.
3, April 1973.

Pike, Frederick B., THE UNITED STATES AND THE ANDEAN
REPUBLICS: Peru, Bolivia, and Ecuador, Cam-
bridge, Massachusetts, Harvard University
Press, 1977.

Slater, Jerome, "The United States and Latin America:
The New Radical Orthodoxy," Economic Development and Cultural Change, Vol. 25, No. 4, July
1977, pp. 747-761.

Smith, Ralph Stuart, THE UNITED STATES AND THE THIRD
WORLD, Washington, D.C., Department of State,
July 1976.

Tambs, Lewis A., ed., UNITED STATES POLICY TOWARD
LATIN AMERICA: Antecedents and Alternatives,

Tempe, Arizona State University, 1976. The
field covered by these 13 papers extends from
Panama and Cuba to SELA and the OAS to financial flows and technological aspects, with some
emphasis on the duality of U.S. idealism and
realpolitik, and the predominance of U.S. and
Brazilian influence. (FA)

Wagner, R. Harrison, UNITED STATES POLICY TOWARD
LATIN AMERICA: A Study in Domestic and International Politics, Stanford, California, Stanford University Press, 1970. The economic
politics of the United States toward Latin
America between World War II and the coming of
the Alliance for Progress are traced in crafts-
manlike detail, with particular reference to
the effect of American domestic considerations.(FA)

Ullman, Richard H., "Trilateralism: 'Partnership'
for What?" Foreign Affairs, Vol. 55, No. 1,
October 1976.

United States, INTERNATIONAL ECONOMIC REPORT OF THE
PRESIDENT, transmitted to Congress in January
of each year, Washington, D.C., Government
Printing Office, every year. Contains a summary of the year's policy developments.

Whitaker, Arthur P., THE UNITED STATES AND THE
SOUTHERN CONE: Argentina, Uruguay, and Chile,
Cambridge, Massachusetts, Harvard University
Press, 1977. Broad in scope, balanced and judicious, well researched, and written with clarity
and grace, this is a work of the highest quality. The period covered for each of the three
Southern Cone countries extends from 1810 to the
military takeover in Argentina in March 1976.(FA)

Wood, Bryce, THE MAKING OF THE GOOD NEIGHBOR POLICY,
New York, Columbia University Press, 1961.

World Bank

Baer, W., "The World Bank Group and the Process of
Socio-Economic Development in the Third World,"
World Development, Vol. 2, No. 6, June 1974.

Brookings Institution, "The World Bank at Quarter
Century," The Brookings Bulletin, Washington,
D.C., 1973.

231

International Bank for Reconstruction and Develop-
    ment, WORLD BANK OPERATIONS: Sectoral Programs
    and Policies, Baltimore, Maryland, Johns Hop-
    kins University Press for the International
    Bank for Reconstruction and Development, 1972.
    The papers describe "the distinctive economic
    and developmental characteristics of each
    sector and review the approach and scale of
    Bank operations in each field." The sectors
    which are analyzed are the following: agricul-
    ture, industry, transportation, telecommuni-
    cation, electric power, water supply and
    sewerage, education, population planning,
    tourism, and urbanization. No index. (JEL)

Reid, Escott, STRENGTHENING THE WORLD BANK, Chicago,
    Adlai Stevenson Institute, 1973. Decentraliza-
    tion, more money for the poorest countries,
    better ways of attacking unemployment and
    poverty and, above all, a stronger voice and
    fuller participation by developing countries in
    the management of the World Bank are among the
    recommendations of this experienced Canadian
    diplomat. A major contribution to the discus-
    sion of the future of multilateral development
    activities. (FA)

Van de Laar, A. J. M., "The World Bank and the
    World's Poor," World Development, Vol. 4, Nos.
    10/11, October-November 1976, pp. 837-851. In
    this article we analyze Bank policy statements
    and investigate how the Bank thinks it can
    implement this new strategy. It is shown that
    only very limited progress can be made because
    of project, sector, and institutional con-
    straints, while the Bank's analytical framework
    is also deficient. (JEL)

World Bank, WORLD DEVELOPMENT REPORT, 1978, Washing-
    ton, D.C., 1978. First of a series of annual
    reports on the progress and prospects of
    developing countries. Discusses policies and
    prospects for development progress in four main
    areas: sustaining rapid economic growth,
    modifying the pattern of economic growth to
    raise productivity and income of the poor,
    improving access of the poor to essential
    public services, and maintaining an inter-
    national environment supportive of development.(BPA)

World Bank, WORLD TABLES 1976, Washington, D.C.,
    World Bank, 1977.

232

Areas and Countries

Africa

X-REF: AGRARIAN REFORM: King, Land, Tuma, Un,
Uchendu, AGRICULTURAL CREDIT: Abbott, AGRICULTURAL
DEVELOPMENT: Hunter, Krishna, Uchendu, COMMODITIES:
Pearson, ECONOMIC INTEGRATION: Lomé, Rivkin, EDUCA-
TION: Damachi, EMPLOYMENT LABOR: Brownwood, Denti,
Frank, Gutkind, Hunter, Ilo, ENERGY: Emembolu,
HISTORY: Hopkins, HUNGER, NUTRITION, HEALTH: May,
MIDDLE EAST: Gale, MULTINATIONAL CORPORATIONS:
Cronje, Widstrand, POPULATION: de Walle, Morgan,
RURAL DEVELOPMENT: Apthorpe, SMALL BUSINESS:
Liedholm, TECHNOLOGY: Thomas, Uchendu, URBAN DEVEL-
OPMENT: Barnes, Ilo, Little, Obudho.

Adams, J., "The Economic Development of African
    Pastoral Societies: A Model," Kyklos, Vol. 28,
    No. 4, 1975, pp. 859-865. This paper uses a
    diagrammatic framework to discuss the develop-
    ment of african pastoral societies through
    three phases: the traditional, colonial, and
    modern. In the traditional phase the inter-
    relationship of the animal and human popula-
    tions is stressed. In the colonial period,
    population growth, rising food needs, and
    participation in the imperfect labor market are
    the major factors considered. Lastly, con-
    ditions for the integration of the modern and
    pastoral sectors are described. (JEL)

Amann, Victor F., ed., AGRICULTURAL EMPLOYMENT AND
LABOUR MIGRATION IN EAST AFRICA, Kampala,
Uganda, Makerere University, September 1974.

Amin, Samir, NEO-COLONIALISM IN WEST AFRICA, New
York, Monthly Review Press, 1975.

Arkhurst, Frederick S., AFRICA IN THE SEVENTIES AND
EIGHTIES: Issues in Development, New York,
Praeger, 1970. A number of leading students of
African affairs were invited in 1969 to project
ccontemporary economic, political and legal
problems into the 1980s. This volume includes
the resulting papers and comments by other
participants. (FA)

Arrighi, Giovanni and Saul, John S., ESSAYS ON THE
POLITICAL ECONOMY OF AFRICA, New York, Monthly
Review Press, 1973. Offers overviews of
socialism and economic development and of
nationalism and revolution, perspectives on
labor supplies and aristocracies, on multinational corporations and on African peasan-
tries and populism, and case studies of Tanzania, Rhodesia and Mozambique. No index.
(JEL)

Barratt, John, et al., eds., ACCELERATED DEVELOPMENT
IN SOUTHERN AFRICA, New York, St. Martin's
Press, 1974. Collection of 38 revised papers
plus comments presented in a March, 1972,
Johannesburg conference of experts from the
United States, United Kingdom, Germany, and
eight South African countries. Consideration
was given not only to economic but also to
social and political aspects of development in
the area, e.g., multi-ethnic societies. Introduction and three parts dealing with dimensions
of development, its international aspects, and
evaluation of future prospects, respectively.
Index. (JEL)

Bozeman, Adda B., CONFLICT IN AFRICA, Princeton, New
Jersey, Princeton University Press, 1976. This
extraordinary treatise wades in where others
have feared to tread--in examining the workings
of traditional African culture in the institutions and patterns of interaction that continue

to operate today. The author romanticizes and perhaps exaggerates certain aspects of traditional culture, but the effect of her downright approach is bracing--provoking opposition and then rethinking. Her comparison between Occidental and African views of conflict and conciliation is interesting in regard to the profound differences which often perplex (and annoy) Western diplomats in international forums, including the African emphasis on personal, situational diplomacy and persuasion rather than on legal agreements, and the power--malevolent as well as healing--of words. (FA)

Brownlie, Ian, ed., BASIC DOCUMENTS ON AFRICAN AFFAIRS, New York, Oxford University Press, 1971. With an emphasis on international relations, the editor has gathered a variety of important documents which have not been easily accessible in the past to scholars interested in African affairs. Included here are documents on African international organizations, on African economic development and investment, on the racial problems in southern Africa; on relations with non-African powers; on the situation in the Congo; etc. Index. (JEL)

Brownwood, David W., TRADE UNIONS IN AFRICA, K. I. A. Occasional Papers No. 2, Lower Kabete, Kenya, Kenya Institute of Administration, 1969.

Chibwe, E. C., AFRO-ARAB RELATIONS IN THE NEW WORLD ORDER, London, Friedmann, 1977. This study by the former Director of the Bank of Zambia emphasizes economic relations. Chibwe provides hard data and valuable information on African financial needs, Arab and OECD aid, and the workings of the Arab Bank for African Development, but tends toward hopeful prognostication rather than analysis of the issues underlying present and potential Afro-Arab relations. (FA)

Cleave, John H., AFRICAN FARMERS: LABOUR USE IN THE DEVELOPMENT OF SMALLHOLDER AGRICULTURE, book review in African Social Research, No. 21, June 1976, pp. 95-96.

Cosgrove-Twitchett, Carol, THE EUROPEAN ECONOMIC
     COMMUNITY AND THE AFRICAN ASSOCIATES, Lexing-
     ton, Massachusetts, Lexington Books, 1977.
     This book analyzes the Yaounde Association
     between the EEC and the Associated African and
     Malagasy States in terms of the effects of the
     Lome Convention of 1975 and the events that
     followed. (BPA)

Damachi, U. G., Routh, G., Ali Taha, A. E., eds.,
     DEVELOPMENT PATHS IN AFRICA AND CHINA, Boulder,
     Colorado, Westview Press, 1977. The contribu-
     tors to this work examine the development paths
     of China, Ghana, Kenya, Nigeria, the Sudan,
     Tanzania, and Zambia. (BPA)

DeGregori, Thomas R., TECHNOLOGY AND THE ECONOMIC
     DEVELOPMENT OF THE TROPICAL AFRICAN FRONTIER,
     Cleveland, Ohio, The Press of Case Western
     Reserve University, 1969. Outlines sub-Saharan
     Africa's technological history and potential;
     discusses the institutional barriers to techno-
     logical diffusion. Discusses traditional and
     Marxist theories of capital movements in the
     context of frontier economics, generally, and
     of the African economy, in particular. Finds
     that capital transfers have occurred, in many
     cases, from the less developed to the more
     developed economics in contradiction to tradi-
     tional theory. Contains data on African for-
     eign trade by country and major project.
     Bibliography. Index. (JEL)

de Walle, Etienne Van, "Trends and Prospects of
     Population in Tropical Africa," The Annals,
     Volume 432, July 1977, pp. 1-11.

Duignan, Peter and Gann, Lewis H., eds., COLONIALISM
     IN AFRICA 1870-1960, Volume 4: THE ECONOMICS
     OF COLONIALISM, New York, Cambridge University
     Press, 1975. The fourth in a five-volume
     history of Sub-Saharan Africa and the impact of
     colonialism. Based on an interdisciplinary
     approach by a group of economists, economic
     historians, historians, and sociologists, 18
     coordinated essays look at the various factors
     affecting the economic development in Africa
     under colonial rule. Index. (JEL)

Emembolu, G. E., and Pannu, S. S., "Africa: Oil and Development," in Africa Today, Vol. 22, No. 4, Fall 1975, pp. 39-47.

Fernandez, James W., "African Cultural Transformations," Items, Vol. 31, Nos. 1 and 2, March/June 1977, pp. 10-14.

Frank, Charles R., Jr., URBAN UNEMPLOYMENT AND ECONOMIC GROWTH IN AFRICA, Center Paper #120, Economic Growth Center, New Haven, Connecticut, Yale University, 1968.

Gale Research Co., AFRICA SOUTH OF THE SAHARA, 1978-79, eighth edition, Detroit, Michigan, Europa Publication, 1978. Essays on history and economic and social development; detailed articles on recent history, physical and social geography, and economy of all countries south of the Sahara. (BPA)

Gale Research Co., MIDDLE EAST AND NORTH AFRICA, 1978-79, 25th edition, Detroit, Michigan, Europa Publication, 1978.

Gale Research Co., STATISTICS--AFRICA, second edition, Detroit, Michigan, Europa Publications, 1978. Detailed information on a range of social and economic statistical sources; live and print sources cited for each country, including central statistical office, principal libraries, principal bibliographies, and major statistical publications. (BPA)

Gugler, Josef, and Flanagan, William, URBANIZATION AND SOCIAL CHANGE IN WEST AFRICA, Cambridge University Press, 1978. West Africa has experienced extremely rapid urban growth in recent decades. This book is a multidisciplinary study of this growth and of the social changes that have accompanied it. (BPA)

Hafkin, Nancy J., and Bay, Edna G., eds., WOMEN IN AFRICA: Studies in Social and Economic Change, Stanford, Stanford University Press, 1976. Viewing the changing lives of groups of women in East and West Africa through historical, anthropological, sociological and economic perspectives, the essays in this volume give concrete meaning to the theme of African women's loss of economic and political status through the workings of colonialism. (FA)

Hance, William A., POPULATION, MIGRATION, AND URBANIZATION IN AFRICA, New York, Columbia University Press, 1970. An excellent volume. Professor Hance asserts that there is a population problem in Africa, that the land cannot support the needs of the population, despite comparatively low densities in most areas of the continent. (FA)

Harris, Richard, ed., THE POLITICAL ECONOMY OF AFRICA, Cambridge, Schenkmen, 1975 (New York, Halsted, distributor). These essays on Kenya and Tanzania, Zambia, Ghana and Nigeria are unified by the common perspective of their authors, part of a growing group of social scientists basing their analyses of African development on a critique of African dependency and Western neocolonialism. (FA)

Hatch, John, THE HISTORY OF BRITAIN IN AFRICA, FROM THE FIFTEENTH CENTURY TO THE PRESENT, London, Andre Deutsch, 1969.

Hermassi, Elbaki, LEADERSHIP AND NATIONAL DEVELOP-MENT IN NORTH AFRICA: A Comparative Study, Berkeley, University of California Press, 1972. The emergence of Morocco, Algeria and Tunisia as national societies with their own institutions, elites and policies for development. The comparison is instructive, and the discussion of theory and method refreshingly skeptical. (FA)

Hopkins, A. G., AN ECONOMIC HISTORY OF WEST AFRICA, New York, Columbia University Press, 1973. This valuable survey emphasizes the indigenous economic contribution within the colonial context. (FA)

International Monetary Fund, SURVEYS OF AFRICAN COUNTRIES, Washington, D.C., Volume 1 (Cameroon, Central African Republic, Chad, Congo, Brazzaville, Gabon, 1968); Volume 2 (Kenya, Tanzania, Uganda, Somalia, 1969); Volume 3 (Benin, Ivory Coast, Mauretania, Niger, Senegal, Toga, Upper Volta, 1970); Volume 4 (Zaire, Malagasy Republic, Malawi, Mauritius, Zambia, 1973); Volume 5 (Botswana, Lesotho, Swaziland,

Burundi, Equatorial Guinea, Rwanda, 1973);
Volume 6 (Gambia, Ghana, Liberia, Nigeria,
Sierra Leone, 1975); Volume 7 (Algeria, Mali,
Morocco, Tunisia, 1977).

Kamarck, Andrew M., THE ECONOMICS OF AFRICAN DEVEL-
OPMENT, revised edition, foreword by Pierre
Moussa, New York, Praeger, 1971. A revised
edition of a well-received study of the problems and prospects of African development. The
original conclusions and forecasts are re-
examined "in the light of actual experience,"
and the course of African development is fore-
cast to the year 2000. Index. (JEL)

Killick, Tony, THE ECONOMIES OF EAST AFRICA: A
Bibliography 1963-1975, Boston, Massachusetts,
G. K. Hall and co., 1976.

Knapp, Wilfrid, NORTH WEST AFRICA: A Political and
Economic Survey, third edition, New York,
Oxford University Press, 1977. Survey of the
geography, population, economy, and foreign
relations of five African states that have come
into existence since the second World War:
Algeria, Libya, Mauritania and the Southern
Sahara, Morocco, and Tunisia. Also includes a
paper by Robin Ostle on the French and Algerian
literature of North West Africa. (JEL)

Konczacki, Z. A., THE ECONOMICS OF PASTORALISM: A
Case Study of Sub-Saharan Africa, London, Frank
Cass, Autumn 1977. The main theme of this book
is the economics and future of pastoralism in
sub-Saharan Africa. Some of the conclusions
reached may be applicable to other parts of the
world where similar conditions prevail.
Pastoralism is greatest in those African countries considered to be the least developed, and
in fact sixteen of the twenty-five least developed countries as defined by the U.N. are in
Africa. The arid climate of these countries is
the main obstacle to development, and makes
livestock raising, through pastoralism, the
main source of livelihood. (BPA)

Kraus, Jon, "African Trade Unions: Progress or
Poverty?" in African Studies Review, Vol. XIX,
No. 3, December 1976, pp. 95-108.

Krishna, K. G. V., "Smallholder Agriculture in Africa, Constraints and Potential," The Annals, Vol. 432, July 1977, pp. 12-25.

Lawson, Rowena, THE CHANGING ECONOMY OF THE LOWER VOLTA, 1954-1967, New York, Oxford University Press, 1972.

Lele, Uma, THE DESIGN OF RURAL DEVELOPMENT: Lessons from Africa, Baltimore, Maryland, Johns Hopkins, 1975.

Liedholm, Carl, RESEARCH ON EMPLOYMENT IN THE RURAL NONFARM SECTOR IN AFRICA, East Lansing, Michigan State University, African Rural Employment Paper No. 5, 1973.

Little, Kenneth, AFRICAN WOMEN IN TOWNS: An Aspect of Africa's Social Revolution, New York, Cambridge University Press, 1973. An informal, discursive account of women's social, economic and political roles (emphasizing the first category) in a variety of African urban settings. West Africa is generally more progressive than East, and educated women more equal than others. But, as in the rest of the world, they've still got a long way to go. (FA)

Lofchie, Michael F., ed., THE STATE OF THE NATIONS: Constraints on Development in Independent Africa, Berkeley, University of California Press under the auspices of the African Studies Center and the Committee on Political change, UCLA, 1971. Twelve academic scholars who have undertaken research in African studies contribute the eleven articles compiled in this volume. These are presented in two parts: 1) general perspectives on constraints on African development; 2) the parameters of political choice in Senegal, Ghana, Tanzania, and Ivory Coast. Bibliography; index. (JEL)

Markovitz, Irving Leonard, POWER AND CLASS IN AFRICA, New York, Prentice-Hall, 1977. This ambitious analysis succeeds admirably in organizing its large canvas without distorting the multitudinous details which form the African political landscape. Not dependency, but inequity and the often declining fortunes of the rural population, are seen to be the central problems. Despite his thesis, however, Markovitz exhibits

what seems to be an ambivalent enthusiasm for
the energetic pursuit of individual advantage
by African entrepreneurial types. (FA)

McLoughlin, Peter F. M., ed., AFRICAN FOOD PRODUC-
TION SYSTEMS: Cases and Theory, Baltimore,
Johns Hopkins Press, 1970. Approximately a
quarter of Africa's rural population is experi-
encing difficulty in feeding itself. Anthropologists and economists describe in detailed
and descriptive case studies the food production of seven African societies. These studies
attempt to provide the bases for the formulation of policy toward defining and solving the
problems of rural African development. Index.
(JEL)

Morgan, Robert W., "Niveaux de fécondité et évolution
de fécondité," Croissance démographique et
évolution socio-économique en Afrique de
l'ouest, 1973, pp. 253-323.

Munro, J. Forbes, AFRICA AND THE INTERNATIONAL
ECONOMY 1800-1960, Totowa, New Jersey, Rowman
and Littlefield, 1976. A compact history of
Africa's evolving role on the "margin" of the
European economies, and of the structural
shaping of the African economies by the modern
international system. (FA)

Mutharika, B. W. T., TOWARD MULTINATIONAL ECONOMIC
COOPERATION IN AFRICA, New York, Praeger, 1972.
Strong on data about agricultural and industrial commerce of African countries and the
extent of current multinational cooperation
among them; weak--and windy--on analysis of
political and economic factors affecting integration. (FA)

Nyerere, Julius K., "America and Southern Africa,"
Vol. 55, No. 4, July 1977, p. 671.

O'Conner, A. M., THE GEOGRAPHY OF TROPICAL AFRICAN
DEVELOPMENT, New York, Pergamon, 1971. A very
matter-of-fact survey of the distribution of
resources, agricultural and industrial production, trade and income among subsaharan nations; its effect is to underscore the general
conclusion that those who have will get more.
(FA)

Ogunsanwo, Alaba, CHINA'S POLICY IN AFRICA, 1958-1971, New York, Cambridge University Press, 1974. This careful study traces the evolution of Chinese policy in Africa from the halcyon period, when revolutionary ideology coincided with national interest in seeing the overthrow of existing governments as the first priority, to the more complicated present, when zeal preaches revolution but big-power state interest dictates cautious pragmatism and compromise.(FA)

Okwuosa, Emanuel A., NEW DIRECTION FOR ECONOMIC DEVELOPMENT IN AFRICA, London, Africa Books, 1976. The economic position of Africa in the new international economic order is crucial. This book relates some broad measures for breaking off Africa's satellite economic position and for setting the economy on its own path. The author, African economist Emanuel A. Okwuosa, develops his thesis that the future of Africa's economic development lies in "Communalism," an amalgam of Western capitalism and Eastern socialism. (BPA)

Raichur, Satish, "Implementation Problems of Economic Development Plans," in Africa Today, Vol. 20, No. 2, Spring 1973, pp. 67-75.

Rivkin, Arnold, AFRICA AND THE EUROPEAN COMMON MARKET: A Perspective, Denver, Colorado, University of Denver, 1964.

Robana, Abderrahman, THE PROSPECTS FOR AN ECONOMIC COMMUNITY IN NORTH AFRICA, New York, Praeger, 1973. A Survey of the meager results so far for building economic cooperation in the Maghreb, with some practical suggestions for making it a reality. (FA)

Robson, P. and Lury, D. A., THE ECONOMIES OF AFRICA, Evanston, Illinois, Northwestern University Press, 1969. Single-economy studies of Algeria, Cameroon, Ghana, Ivory Coast, Liberia, Nigeria and Sudan plus analyses of the East African and Central African economies. In addition to these separate essays by well-known economists, the editors include a general introductory analysis of the African economies. (FA)

Rothchild, Donald and Curry, Robert L., Jr., SCAR-
CITY, CHOICE, AND PUBLIC POLICY IN MIDDLE
AFRICA, Berkeley, University of California
Press, 1978. An interdisciplinary (political
science and economics) examination of the
policy alternatives available to African deci-
sion-makers and the implementation of public
policies toward achieving political, social,
and economic goals. Emphasizes the elements of
choice in relation to political and economic
resources, and presents a model of policy
analysis oriented toward problem-solving. Examines the main institutional resources of
middle African states, considers the patterns
of choice within the context of scarcity; explores policy options involved in global market
contacts; and argues that a "minimalist implementation strategy has validly become the preferred one (underlying African integration for
improved economic well-being) among decision-
makers in middle Africa." Index. (JEL)

Rout, Leslie B., Jr., THE AFRICAN EXPERIENCE IN
SPANISH AMERICA: 1502 TO THE PRESENT DAY, New
York, Cambridge University Press, 1976. The
author, a black historian, discovers and describes racial bias in Latin America--contra-
dicting those glib generalizations that often
gain acceptance through repetition. "In short,
both Afro-Americans and Spanish-speaking blacks
and mulattoes are striving to achieve a sense
of self-liberation...." (FA)

Sandbrook, Richard and Cohen, Robin, eds., THE
DEVELOPMENT OF AN AFRICAN WORKING CLASS:
Studies in Class Formation and Action, Toronto,
University of Toronto Press, 1976. Do African
unions work for the workers? Will African
workers work for the revolution? A qualified
yes to both questions emerges from this collection, whose unifying theme is the African wage-
laborer's community of interests with those
outside the modern sector--not with the bourgeoisie. (FA)

Scarritt, James R., ed., ANALYZING POLITICAL CHANGE
IN AFRICA: Applications of a New Multidimen-
sional Framework, Boulder, Colorado, Westview
Press, 1979. This volume addresses political
instability and the role of the military; also
class formation, class conflict, and prolonged

243

dependency. Eight diverse cases of African
political change are analyzed. (BPA)

Schultz, Ann, INTERNATIONAL AND REGIONAL POLITICS IN
THE MIDDLE EAST AND NORTH AFRICA, Detroit,
Michigan, Gale Research, 1978.

Seidman, Ann, PLANNING FOR DEVELOPMENT IN SUB-
SAHARAN AFRICA, Praeger Special Studies in
International Economics and Development, New
York, Praeger, 1974. A comprehensive study of
economic underdevelopment and of policy options
to promote the economic growth and development
of the area. The author analyzes the external
constraints to export expansion, the role of
class structure in economic development, and
the basic requirements for successful economic
planning in Africa. She then examines the
pattern of industrial and agricultural growth
and the basic aspects of industrial strategy
and of reform in the agricultural sector; next
she discusses the role of foreign trade in
African development and of alternative commercial policies. Finally, there is a section
on the fiscal, monetary, and income policies
necessary to further African economic development. (JEL)

Skurnik, W. A. E., SUB-SAHARAN AFRICA, Detroit,
Michigan, Gale Research Co., 1978. Annotated
subject bibliographies on readily available
books and articles, and substantive essays.
(BPA)

Simmons, Andre, ECONOMIC PLANNING IN AFRICA, a
biographical note, Michigan State University,
Business Topics, Summer, 1975, pp. 19-28.

Smock, David R. and Bentsi-Enchill, Kwamena, eds.,
THE SEARCH FOR NATIONAL INTEGRATION IN AFRICA,
New York, Free Press, 1976. This useful, low-
keyed collection of essays focuses on tools for
achieving national integration, including
government structures, economic planning and
education, language and communications. (FA)

Streeten, Paul, AID TO AFRICA: A POLICY OUTLINE FOR
THE 1970's, New York, Praeger, 1972. This
study by an experienced practitioner of development economics combines an incisive critique
of current economic indices for measuring the

244

efficacy of aid programs with specific policy
proposals. It emphasizes the need to see aid
in two contexts: in terms of the development
aims of the poor countries; and in terms of the
worldwide economic structure, created by the
advanced industrial nations. (FA)

Tregear, Peter and Burley, John, eds., AFRICAN
DEVELOPMENT AND EUROPE, New York, Pergamon,
1970. The title of this volume of papers and
short accounts of ensuing discussions is misleading, since it deals mainly with general
development problems in Africa, and only one
paper deals directly with relationships between
Europe and Africa. (FA)

Uchendu, Victor C., THE IMPACT OF CHANGING AGRICUL-
TURAL TECHNOLOGY ON AFRICAN LAND TENURE, LTC
Reprint No. 71, Madison, University of Wiscon-
sin, Land Tenure Center, 1970, from Journal of
Developing Areas, Vol. 4, July 1970, pp. 477-
485.

Uppal, J. S., and Salkever, L. R., AFRICA: Problems
in Economic Development, New York, The Free
Press, 1972.

NOTE: A further listing of 1,200 books on Africa is
available in Heffer Catalogue No. 108, AFRICA
SOUTH OF THE SAHARA, available from W. Heffer &
Sons, Ltd., 20 Trinity Street, Cambridge,
England CB2 SNG

Algeria

Horne, Alistair, A SAVAGE WAR OF PEACE: Algeria
1954-1962, New York, Viking, 1978. A masterful
narrative of the Algerian revolution and war of
independence, packed with detail yet written
with color and style and a full appreciation of
the causes and the personalities. The best
treatment in English and perhaps in any language. (FA)

Schliephake, Konrad, OIL AND REGIONAL DEVELOPMENT:
Examples from Algeria and Tunisia, New York,
Praeger, 1977. Examines how oil revenues can
contribute to regional development of countries

with large populations and favorable conditions for speedy industrialization. (BPA)

Benin

Ronen, Dov, DAHOMEY: BETWEEN TRADITION AND MODERN-
ITY, Ithaca, New York, Cornell University
Press, 1975. Dahomey's profusion of military
and civilian regimes have, according to Ronen,
operated in almost total detachment from most
of the country's people. He advocates "tradi-
tionalization of modern institutions" to fit
the attitudes and norms of the people. (FA)

Botswana

Hartland-Thunberg, Penelope, BOTSWANA: An African
Growth Economy, Boulder, Colorado, Westview
Press, 1978. When Botswana achieved full independence in 1966, informed opinion was unani-
mous in assessing the country's economic prospects as dismal. Ten years later, Botswana
celebrated a decade in which its real economic
growth averaged a remarkable 15 percent annually, its infrastructure was expanded, three
new cities and a number of new industries were
established, and government revenues increased
ten times over. This growth was wrought by an
aggressive development plan based on private
enterprise and foreign investment, aided by
generous allocations from foreign aid donors,
and directed by the country's skilled and
devoted leaders working within an environment
of political stability. (BPA)

Burundi

Lemarchand, Rene, RWANDA AND BURUNDI, New York,
Praeger, 1970. A good full-length study of the
two little-known states by a scholar now teaching at the University of Florida. The character of revolution and social change are the
underlying concerns of this largely historical
work. (FA)

World Bank, CHAD: Development Potential and Constraints, Washington, D.C., author, 1974. Report prepared by an economic mission on the
Chad economy covering economic structure, development constraints, planning and growth
prospects, financial prospects, and aid outlook. Statistical tables for data in period
1960-1972; country data. No index. (JEL)

East Africa

X-REF: AGRICULTURAL DEVELOPMENT: Amann.

Barkam, Joel D., and Okumu, John J., ed., POLITICS
AND PUBLIC POLICY IN KENYA AND TANZANIA, New
York, Praeger, 1978. Comparative in orientation, these eleven essays contrast the institutions and policies of Kenya and Tanzania,
two East African countries that have chosen
opposite models of development. The initial
essay explores Kenya's political economy of
client-patron capitalism, and Tanzania's system
of one-party socialism. Later discussions
examine the political institutions which generate public policy, and compare Kenyan and
Tanzanian approaches to such issues as urban
and rural development, education, and foreign
relations. The essays suggest that Kenya's
political unrest may result from built-in
structural inequalities, and that the slow
development of Tanzania's economy to date may
severely retard future progress. (BPA)

Chambers, Robert, MANAGING RURAL DEVELOPMENT: Ideas
and Experiences from East Africa, Uppsala,
Sweden, Scandinavian Institute of African
Studies, 1974; New York, Africana Publishing
Company, 1975. Moving swiftly beyond the now
commonplace analysis of administrative constraints shared by most LDC bureaucracies, this
study draws on numerous examples in propounding
a "how-to" approach to improving the implementation of rural development programs. (FA)

Hazlewock, Arthur, ECONOMIC INTEGRATION: The East
African Experience, New York, St. Martin's,
1975.

Institute for Development Research, DUALISM AND
RURAL DEVELOPMENT IN EAST AFRICA, Copenhagen,
Denmark, Author, 1973. Report on a 1973
seminar attended by members of the Danish
Institute for Development Research, graduate
students at the Universities of Copenhagen and
Arhus, and invited experts on rural development
in East Africa. The work consists of A.
Mafeje's "The Fallacy of Dual Economies Revisited" and summaries of supporting papers;
case studies of rural development in East
Africa by J. Boesen, B. Storgaard and A.
Mafeje, and J. Müller's "Appropriate Technology
and Technological Dualism" together with summaries of five other papers concerned with
various aspects of rural development. (JEL)

Pearson, D. S., INDUSTRIAL DEVELOPMENT IN EAST AFRI-
CA, New York, Oxford University Press, 1970. A
description of the setting and some of the
basic features of the process of economic
development in East Africa as well as a consideration of some general theoretical questions involved. (FA)

Egypt

X-REF: AGRARIAN REFORM: Abdel, Ilo.

Abed, G. T., "Labor Absorption in Industry: An
Analysis with Reference to Egypt," Oxford Economic Papers, Vol. 27, No. 3, November 1975.
This paper analyzes the link between output
growth and labor absorption in the industrial
sector of a growing economy. The analysis
focuses on price and wage distortions in the
industrial sector as a possible explanation for
the slow rate of labor absorption in industry.
Conditions in the factor and product markets
are characterizes using neoclassical specification of the production function and of output
demand equations. (JEL)

Al-Sayyid-Marsot, Afaf Luffi, EGYPT's LIBERAL
EXPERIMENT, 1922-1936, Berkeley, University of
California Press, 1977. An illuminating history of Egypt in the era of semi-independence,
nascent liberal political institutions, and
rising nationalism. The author, combining

248

careful research with personal knowledge of
Egypt's leading families of the time, draws a
fine portrait of Saad Zaghlul and his era and
throws new light on the triangular relations of
the British, the King, and the Wafd. Her
overall conclusions on the period are surprisingly positive. (FA)

Barbour, K. M., THE GROWTH, LOCATION, AND STRUCTURE
OF INDUSTRY IN EGYPT, Praeger Special Studies
in International Economics and Development, New
York, Praeger, 1972. Traces the history of the
subject. Essentially based on 1963 data though
there are some figures for later years.
Egypt's industrial pattern, structure and
concentration are analysed. The impact of the
country's industry on population, natural
resources, and urbanization is also studied.
Author of the book is a geographer. No index.
(JEL)

Blackman, Winifred S., THE FELLAHIN OF UPPER EGYPT:
Their Religious, Social and Industrial Life
(1927), with a foreword by R. R. Marett,
London, Frank Cass, 1968.

Hansen, B., "Employment and Wages in Rural Egypt,"
American Economic Review, Vol. LIX, No. 3, June
1969.

Mabro, Robert, THE EGYPTIAN ECONOMY 1952-1972:
Economies of the World, London, Oxford University Press, Clarendon Press, 1974. Reviews the
country's historical and political background
and then analyzes changes in population, resource utilization, land tenure, land use,
institutions, industry, infrastructure, employment, income distribution, and related aspects.
One distinguishing feature of this study is the
suppression of all references to Israel (even
Palestine). (JEL)

Mabro, Robert, and Radwan, Samir, THE INDUSTRIALIZA-
TION OF EGYPT, 1939-1973, New York, Oxford University Press, 1976. Based on extensive primary data this is above all a book for economists; but the historical evolution of industrial policy against a setting of changing
political-economic systems provides a case
study in development of more than local significance. (FA)

249

Makki, M. F. and Qayum, A., "Prospects for Egyptian
    Economic Development," Economia Internazionale,
    Vol. 28, Nos. 1-2, February-May 1975. Recent
    developments in the Middle East augur very well
    for the speedy growth of the Egyptian economy.
    The sudden and stunning affluence of the Arab
    countries provides a market of about 100 mil-
    lion people with purchasing power. Egypt has
    the highest absorption capacity in the region
    for the staggering amount of petro-dollars of
    oil producing countries, equipped as it is with
    a modicum of industrial infrastructure, ade-
    quate number of technical and engineering
    schools, a sizeable cadre of skilled and
    trained personnel, and a relatively small but
    most fertile land. Egyptian cautious and
    balanced evolution of international relation-
    ships is reassuring to both the Arab countries
    with billions of investable dollars and to the
    West with the advanced technology and power of
    political arbitrage. (JEL)

Radwan, Samir, AGRARIAN REFORM AND RURAL POVERTY:
    Egypt, 1952-1975, Geneva, ILO, 1977. This
    study appraises the impact on rural Egypt of a
    quarter of a century of agrarian reform. It
    also provides the first systematic and compre-
    hensive appraisal of what are known as "super-
    vised cooperatives," the most important institu-
    tion created by Egyptian agrarian reform.
    Examined are the impact of the cooperative
    system on resource allocation, the transfer of
    agricultural surpluses, the process of differ-
    entiation and the change in the socio-political
    power structure in Egyptian villages. After
    reviewing the pre-reform agrarian system, this
    report draws on a wide variety of sources to
    assess the effect of agrarian reform on the
    distribution of land and income in general, and
    the problem of rural poverty in particular.
    (BPA)

Waterbury, John, EGYPT: Burdens of the Past, Options
    for the Future, Bloomington, Indiana University
    Press, 1978. A collection of Waterbury's
    American Universities Field Staff Reports
    written during his stay in Egypt from 1973 to
    1976. They show his profound understanding of
    Egypt's economic and social problems and of the
    ways in which the government's choices have
    been progressively narrowed. (FA)

Ethiopia

X-REF: AGRARIAN REFORM: Cohen, Dunning, MULTINA-
TIONAL CORPORATIONS: Widstrand, REGIONAL DEVELOP-
MENT: Bendavid-Val.

Blaug, M., "Employment and Unemployment in Ethiopia,"
    International Labour Review, Vol. 110, No. 2,
    August 1974.

Cohen, John Michael, and Weintraub, Dov, LAND AND
    PEASANTS IN IMPERIAL ETHIOPIA: Social Back-
    ground to a Revolution, Assen, Van Gorcum,
    1975.

Gilkes, Patrick, THE DYING LION: Feudalism and
    Modernization in Ethiopia, New York, St. Mar-
    tin, 1975. This description of the feudal and
    bureaucratic structure of the Emperor's realm
    preserves in amber the moment just before the
    November 1974 storm and the subsequent acceler-
    ated dissolution of those fragile and anachro-
    nistic structures. (FA)

ILO, EMPLOYMENT AND UNEMPLOYMENT IN ETHIOPIA, Geneva,
    International Labour Organization, 1977. This
    report describes and analyzes recent economic
    and social trends in Ethiopia and maps out a
    development strategy which will eliminate un-
    employment and diminish inequalities in the
    near future. (BPA)

Tecle, Tesfai, THE EVOLUTION OF ALTERNATIVE RURAL
    DEVELOPMENT STRATEGIES IN ETHIOPIA: Implica-
    tions for Employment and Income Distribution,
    East Lansing, Michigan State University,
    Department of Agricultural Economics, 1975.

Gambia

X-REF: AFRICA: IMF.

X-REF: IMPORT SUBSTITUTION: Steel, MISCELLANEOUS:
Stewart, MULTINATIONAL CORPORATIONS: Forsyth, SMALL
BUSINESS: Hart.

Austin, D. and Lickham, R., eds., POLITICIANS AND
    SOLDIERS IN GHANA, 1966-1972, London, Frank
    Cass, 1975. Since one editor is a leading
    authority on the politics of Ghana and the
    other on military rule in Nigeria, the reader
    can expect them to produce a memorable book.
    Its main theme is the return to civilian rule
    in Ghana in 1969. (BPA)

Garlick, Peter C., AFRICAN TRADERS AND ECONOMIC DE-
    VELOPMENT IN GHANA, New York, Oxford University
    Press, 1971.

Hymer, Stephen H., ECONOMIC FORMS IN PRE-COLONIAL
    GHANA, Center Paper #146, New Haven, Connecti-
    cut, Yale University, 1970.

Killick, Tony, DEVELOPMENT ECONOMICS IN ACTION: A
    Study of Economic Policies in Ghana, New York,
    St. Martin's Press, 1978. A case study of
    Ghana in the 1960's, focusing upon the period
    1959-1966 during the leadership of Kwame
    Nkrumah, whose economic strategy was character-
    ized by the adherence to the major policy
    recommendations of mainstream economists: a
    "big push" consisting of a major investment and
    industrialization efforts; an emphasis on im-
    port-substitution, structural change and pro-
    tection; and a heavy reliance on state inter-
    vention; also discusses end of the 1960's with
    transition to more market-oriented policies.
    (JEL)

Leith, J. Clark, FOREIGN TRADE REGIMES AND ECONOMIC
    DEVELOPMENT: Ghana, New York, Columbia Univer-
    sity Press, 1974. Examination of Ghana's sys-
    tem of exchange control and the attempted
    liberalization during its first 15 years of
    independence (1957-1972). (JEL)

Steel, W. F., "Import Substitution and Excess
    Capacity in Ghana," Oxford Economic Papers,
    July 1972. Simultaneous pursuit of social
    goals and an independent, diversified economy

exceeded Ghana's financial and administrative capacities. Although industrialization began under favorable conditions, Ghana developed foreign exchange problems and import substitution (IS) policies which contributed to stagnation and inefficient manufacturing. (JEL)

Steel, William F., SMALL-SCALE EMPLOYMENT AND PRODUCTION IN DEVELOPING COUNTRIES: Evidence from Ghana, Praeger Special Studies in International Economics and Development, New York, Praeger, 1977.

Guinea

Rivière, Claude, GUINEA: The Mobilization of a People, Ithaca, New York, Cornell University Press, 1977. The subtitle is misleading; what the author is describing is the progressive immobilization of Guinean political and economic life over two decades in which the increasingly coercive mechanisms of Sekou Touré's socialism collided with the realities of underdevelopment. The author moves authoritatively across an impressive range of data, significantly enriching the rather meager literature on contemporary Guinea. (FA)

Ivory Coast

den Tuinder, Bastiaan A., and others, IVORY COAST: The Challenge of Success, Baltimore, Maryland, Johns Hopkins Press for the World Bank, 1978.

ILO, ABIDJAN: Urban Development and Employment in the Ivory Coast, Geneva, ILO, 1977.

IMF, "Ivory Coast Maintains Vigorous Growth, Has Highest Per Capita Income in Area," IMF Survey, January 22, 1979.

Masini, Jean; Ikonicoff, Moises; Jedliki, Claudio; and Lanzaroffi, Mario, MULTINATIONALS IN AFRICA: A Case Study of the Ivory Coast, New York, Praeger, 1978. Discussing the reasons behind European multinational investment abroad, this volume details the history of three firms

253

which decided to locate foreign subsidiaries in
the Ivory Coast. Technology transfer, job
creation, distribution of income, and spread of
innovation are used to assess the effect of
multinationals on development in the region.
(BPA)

Kenya

X-REF: AGRICULTURAL DEVELOPMENT: Aldington, EDUCA-
TION: Fields, ENTREPRENEURSHIP: Marris, MISCELLANE-
OUS: Stewart, MULTINATIONAL CORPORATIONS:
Widstrand, POPULATION: Powelson, RURAL DEVELOPMENT:
Bolnick, SMALL BUSINESS: Harper, TECHNOLOGY: Ilo,
URBAN DEVELOPMENT: Laurenti.

Aldington, T. J., and Smith, L. D., THE MARKETING OF
     RICE IN KENYA, Discussion Paper No. 74, Insti-
     tute for Development Studies, November 1968.

Amsden, Alice H., INTERNATIONAL FIRMS AND LABOUR IN
     KENYA 1945-1970, London, Frank Cass, 1971. A
     study of the influence exerted by international
     firms on the economic and political behaviour
     of labour in the third world, with Kenya pro-
     viding the exemplar. (BPA)

Burrows, John, KENYA: Into the Second Decade: Re-
     port of a Mission Sent to Kenya, World Bank
     Country Economic Reports, Baltimore, Maryland,
     Johns Hopkins University Press for the World
     Bank, 1975. Analyzes processes determining
     economic growth and identifies problem areas.
     Reviews the operation of selected sectors in
     the Kenyan economy. This study focuses on
     Kenya alone, ignoring the cross-effects of its
     membership to the East African community.
     Appendices, index. (JEL)

Clayton, E. S., "Agrarian Reform, Agricultural Plan-
     ning and Employment in Kenya," International
     Labour Review, Vol. 102, No. 5, November 1970.

Cole, William E. and Sanders, Richard D., "Popula-
     tion Growth and Employment: Mexico's Past and
     Kenya's Future," in The African Studies
     Review, Vol. XIX, No. 1, April 1976, pp. 151-
     163.

Davis, Robert K., SOME ISSUES IN THE EVOLUTION, OR-
GANIZATION AND OPERATION OF GROUP RANCHES IN
KENYA, LTC Reprint No. 95, Madison, University
of Wisconsin, Land Tenure Center, 1971.

Gerhart, John, THE DIFFUSION OF HYBRID MAIZE IN
WESTERN KENYA, Mexico, International Maize and
Wheat Improvement Center, 1975.

Harbeson, John W., NATION-BILDING IN KENYA: The
Role of Land Reform, Evanston, Illinois, Northwestern University Press, 1973. A detailed
history of land reform in Kenya, from before
independence until the present day. In the
author's view, Kenyatta's regime has sacrificed
African nationalism and political development
to economic growth. (FA)

Heyer, Judith; Maitha, J. K.; and Senga, W. M.;
eds., AGRICULTURAL DEVELOPMENT IN KENYA: An
Economic Assessment, Nairobi; New York; London
and Hong Kong, Oxford University Press, 1976.
Ten previously unpublished papers by economists
dealing with the subject from the colonial era
to the post-independence period of the early
1970's. Topics covered include: the agricultural sector and its achievement; agricultural
development policy; land tenure reform; the
development of small farms, large farms, and
the land range areas; water supplies and irrigation; and the marketing system. Index.
(BPA)

ILO, EMPLOYMENT, INCOMES AND EQUALITY: A Strategy
for Increasing Productive Employment in Kenya,
Geneva, ILO, 1978. Social justice and a fair
distribution of the benefits of growth have become important conditions for eradicating unemployment in developing countries. This book
focuses on inequalities in incomes and opportunities in Kenya, and how they may be remedied
to solve major employment problems. (BPA)

Kenya, INTEGRATED RURAL SURVEY, 1974-1975; Basic
Report, by Central Bureau of Statistics, Ministry of Finance and Planning, Republic of Kenya,
March 1977. Contains a wealth of data, not
usually found for less developed countries, on
household income and consumption, employment and
earnings in rural areas. (Ed)

King, Kenneth, THE AFRICAN ARTISAN: Education and
    the Informal Sector in Kenya, New York, Teach-
    ers College Press, Columbia University, 1977.

Leys, Colin, UNDERDEVELOPMENT IN KENYA: The Politi-
    cal Economy of Neo-Colonialism 1964-1971, Los
    Angeles, University of California Press, 1975.
    Analyzes the social and economic history of
    Kenya in view of the present state of the
    theory of underdevelopment--the particular
    forms of capitalist development in countries
    experiencing colonialism and neo-colonialism.
    Examines, in eight chapters, the mechanisms of
    underdevelopment in agriculture, foreign
    investment, the formation of an "African
    auxiliary bourgeoisie," the politics and
    contradictions of neo-colonialism.   Index.
    (JEL)

Moock, Peter Russell, MANAGERIAL ABILITY IN SMALL
    FARM PRODUCTION: An Analysis of Maize Yields
    in the Vihiga Division of Kenya, New York,
    Columbia University, Ph.D. Thesis, 1973.

Savage, Clayton and D., eds., GOVERNMENT AND LABOUR
    IN KENYA: 1895-1963, London, Frank Cass, 1974.
    A detailed account of British labour policy in
    colonial Kenya by two historians, one British
    and the other Canadian, on such subjects as
    porterage in early colonial times, forced
    labour and the impact of the International
    Labour Office on British colonial thinking in
    the inter-war years, or the establishment of
    the Kenyan Labour Department and its dealings
    with local trade unions immediately after the
    Second World War.   (BPA)

Slater, Charles C.; Walsham, Geoffrey; and Shah,
    Mahendra, KENSIM: A Systems Simulation of the
    Developing Kenyan Economy, 1970-1978, Boulder,
    Colorado, Westview Press, Replica Edition,
    1977. Describes the use of a simulation model
    based on systems modeling approach to identify,
    discuss, and analyze a spectrum of development
    problems in Kenya.   Model applied to pure
    forecasting for 1974-78 period and simulation
    of alternative policy options in fertilizer
    subsidy, rural-urban regulation, and trade-offs
    between modern and traditional agriculture.   No
    index.   (JEL)

Lesotho

World Bank, LESOTHO: A Development Challenge, A
    World Bank Country Economic Report, Washington,
    Author; distributed by Johns Hopkins Press,
    Baltimore. Examination of the economic situa-
    tion in Lesotho, located in Southern Africa.
    Discusses the economic setting, trends in the
    economy, operations of the government, and
    various sectors of the economy and provides an
    outlook for development. No index. (JEL)

Liberia

Maynard, G., "The Economic Irrelevance of Monetary
    Independence: The Case of Liberia," Journal of
    Development Studies, Vol. 6, No. 2, January
    1970.

Metcalf, J. P., "From Economic Growth to Total
    Development: A Strategy for Liberia," Inter-
    national Labour Review, Vol. 109, No. 2,
    February 1974.

Libya

El Fathaly, Omar I.; Palmer, Monte; and Chackerian,
    Richard, POLITICAL DEVELOPMENT AND BUREAUCRACY
    IN LIBYA, Lexington, Massachusetts, Lexington
    Books, 1977. This volume, which contrives to
    contain a good deal of repetition within its
    slim girth, relates political and economic
    changes in Libya to those of political develop-
    ment and modernization but tells little about
    political forces and personalities or how
    Qaddafi's "popular revolution" really works. A
    public opinion poll in a rural area provides
    interesting data but tends to overwhelm the
    rest of the book. (FA)

Farley, Rawle, PLANNING FOR DEVELOPMENT IN LIBYA:
    The Exceptional Economy in the Developing
    World, New York, Praeger, 1971. An economist's
    treatise on development that fits no other
    country. While the effects of the oil expan-
    sion get something less than their due, it is

clear that a capital surplus is no panacea for
problems of underdevelopment. (FA)

First, Ruth, LIBYA: The Elusive Revolution, Baltimore, Maryland, Penguin Books, 1974. The revolution remains elusive after finishing this
book, which nonetheless is a comprehensive and
objective study of the strengths and weaknesses,
as well as the contradictions, in the Qaddafi
regime's domestic and foreign policies. (FA)

Malawi

X-REF: MISCELLANEOUS: Stewart.

Gordenker, Leon, INTERNATIONAL AID AND NATIONAL DE-
CISIONS: Development Programs in Malawi,
Tanzania, and Zambia, Princeton, New Jersey,
Princeton University Press, 1976. Observing
the operation of U.N. aid programs from their
beginnings through their growth into an international industry, the author describes the
complex interactions between national governments and U.N. personnel, focusing on the
potential for development aid to foster the
U.N. goals of international integration and
cooperation. (FA)

Rotberg, Robert I., THE RISE OF NATIONALISM IN CEN-
TRAL AFRICA: The Making of Malawi and Zambia,
1873-1964, Cambridge, Massachusetts, Harvard,
1965.

Namibia

ILO, LABOR AND DISCRIMINATION IN NAMIBIA, Geneva,
1977. This study points out information concerning the segregated administrative apparatus
and separated economic structures of the terri-
tory, examines the extent of discrimination and
suggests changes to secure the welfare of the
Namibian people as a free and independent
nation. (BPA)

Thomas, Wolfgang H., ECONOMIC DEVELOPMENT IN NAMIBIA,
Mainz, Matthias-Grünewald, 1978. Assuming for
the purposes of his analysis a high degree of

economic and political rationality on the part
of any future Namibian government, the author
concludes that no matter what the outcome of an
election, the incoming regime will have to follow a moderate, vaguely social democratic path.
Despite the obviously conditional aspect of his
development strategies, the study constitutes a
bulging source book of dexterously assimilated
information about Namibia--invaluable for
scholars and perhaps for the country's future
governors. (FA)

Nigeria

X-REF: ISSUES: Bauer, MULTINATIONAL CORPORATIONS:
Widstrand, POPULATION: Morgan, URBAN DEVELOPMENT:
Smock.

Arnold, Guy, MODERN NIGERIA, London, Longman, 1977.
    Reviews the political and economic events of
    the 15 years after Nigeria's independence from
    Britain in October 1960. Focuses on the rules
    of oil, agriculture, education, transport and
    communications, labor, political corruption,
    development problems, and the Third Development
    Plan (1975-80). (JEL)

Baker, Pauline H., "Why Nigeria Collapsed," in
    Africa Today, Vol. 20, No. 1, Winter 1973, pp.
    77-84.

Callaway, Archibald, THE EMPLOYMENT PROBLEM OF SEC-
    ONDARY GRAMMAR SCHOOL LEAVERS: A Pilot Study,
    Ibadan, Nigerian Institute of Social and
    Economic Research, 1975.

Damachi, Ukandi Godwin, NIGERIAN MODERNIZATION: The
    Colonial Legacy, New York, Third Press, 1972.
    A Nigerian social scientist looks at what the
    West has wrought in his country, accepting as
    inevitable the growth of social stratification,
    the decline of family and tribal ties, the in-
    creasing urbanization. (FA)

Dean, Edwin, PLAN IMPLEMENTATION IN NIGERIA: 1962-
    1966, New York, Oxford University Press, 1974.
    Admirably eschewing professional jargon, this
    useful book explains the shortfalls in the im-
    plementation of the Nigerian National Develop-
    ment Plan, particularly in terms of a failure

to proportion the plan to the strengths and
weaknesses of executive capability in various
areas. The author notes, however, that many of
the plan's general economic goals were achieved
as a result of the performance of the private
sector. (FA)

Eicher, Carl K. and Liedholm, Carl, eds., GROWTH AND
DEVELOPMENT OF THE NIGERIAN ECONOMY, East
Lansing, Michigan State University Press, 1970.
The twenty-one essays, all specially written
for this volume, are addressed to three subjects: 1) the long-term growth process of the
Nigerian economy from 1900 until independence
in 1960, 2) the performance of the economy in
the 1960's, and 3) the leading economic policy
issues of the next decade. Bibliography. (JEL)

Ekundare, R. Olufemi, AN ECONOMIC HISTORY OF NIGERIA
1860-1960, New York, Africana, 1973. Study of
a nation's economic history designed for students at both the undergraduate and advanced
levels. The time period chosen corresponds
roughly with Nigeria's period of colonial rule:
the analysis is divided into the initial
British efforts, lasting until 1900; the colonial period until 1945; and the period of
economic change prior to political independence
in 1960. The investigation deals with such
topics as agriculture, industrial production,
transportation and communications, foreign
trade, and money and banking. A final section
deals with the post-independence years to 1972.
Index. (JEL)

Etim, B. A., and Eronini, F. N., PERSONAL INCOME
DISTRIBUTION IN NIGERIA 1969/70-1971/72, paper
delivered at the Annual Conference of Nigerian
Economic Society, 1975.

Fajana, Olufemi, THE DISTRIBUTION OF PERSONAL INCOME
IN NIGERIA, paper presented at the annual
conference of the Nigerian Economic Society,
April 1975.

Famoriyo, Segun, LAND TENURE STUDIES IN EGBA AND
ONDO AREAS OF SOUTHERN NIGERIA, Ibadan, Nigerian Institute of Social and Economic Research, 1975.

Federal Office of Statistics, RURAL ECONOMIC SURVEY
OF NIGERIA, CONSOLIDATED RESULTS OF RURAL
HOUSEHOLD ENQUIRIES, 1970, 1971, and 1972,
Lagos, Nigeria, Federal Office of Statistics,
1973.

Frank, Charles R., Jr., INDUSTRIALIZATION AND EM-
PLOYMENT GENERATION IN NIGERIA, Center Paper
#126, New Haven, Connecticut, Economic Growth
Center, 1969.

Hawbaker, George D., A CASE STUDY OF A.I.D. ASSIS-
TANCE TO NIGERIA, 1962-1971, Washington, D.C.,
Agency for International Development, December
1972.

Herskovits, Jean, "Nigeria: Africa's New Power,"
Foreign Affairs, Vol. 53, No. 2, January 1975.

Herskovits, Jean, "One Nigeria," Foreign Affairs,
Vol. 51, No. 2, January 1973.

Hill, Polly, POPULATION, PROSPERITY AND POVERTY,
Cambridge, Cambridge University Press, 1977.
This companion volume to the author's well
known Rural Hausa (C.U.P. 1972) investigates a
contrasting region (Dorayi), one that is land
poor and over-populated. Utilizing archival
and field material, the author compares and
contrasts Dorayi with the much less densely
populated village of her previous study and
attempts to interpret the present-day stability
of this overcrowded farming region in terms of
the socio-economic conditions in very early
colonial times. (BPA)

Morgan, Robert W., "A Population Dynamics Survey in
Lagos, Nigeria," Social Science and Medical
Journal, Vol. 7, 1973, pp. 1-30.

Olatunbosun, 'Dupe, NIGERIA'S NEGLECTED RURAL
MAJORITY, Ibadan, Oxford University Press,
1975.

Olayemi, J. K., FOOD MARKETING AND DISTRIBUTION IN
NIGERIA: Problems and Prospects, Ibadan,
Nigerian Institute of Social and Economic
Research, 1974.

Onitiri, H. M. A., and Olatunbosun, Dupe, THE MAR-
KETING BOARD SYSTEM, proceedings of an international conference, Ibadan, Nigerian Institute
of Social and Economic Research, 1974.

Onuorah, Gina, A LIST OF BOOKS, ARTICLES AND GOVERN-
MENT PUBLICATIONS ON THE ECONOMY OF NIGERIA,
1971-74, Ibadan, Nigerian Institute of Social
and Economic Research, 1975.

Panter-Brick, Keith, ed., SOLDIERS AND OIL: The Political Transformation of Nigeria, London,
Cass, 1978. This group of essays represents a
successful attempt to fill in broad gaps in
current analysis of postwar Nigeria; most
interesting contributions are on military
reorganization by Ian Campbell and Nigerian
"commercial capitalism" by Terisa Turner. (FA)

Parsons, Kenneth H., THE LAND REFORM PROBLEM IN
NIGERIA, Washington, D.C., U.S. Agency for In-
ternational Development, Spring Review of Land
Reform, 1970; country paper SR/OR/C-15, 1970.

Pearson, Scott R., PETROLEUM AND THE NIGERIAN ECONO-
MY, Stanford, California, Stanford University
Press, 1970. A Stanford University economist
in the Food Research Institute calculates that
the net direct and indirect benefits of foreign
investment in the petroleum industry amount to
about seven percent of prewar national income
and might increase to 18 percent of a much
larger national income within five years.
Political as well as economic implications are
assessed in this excellent study. (FA)

Post, Kenneth and Vickers, Michael, STRUCTURE AND
CONFLICT IN NIGERIA, 1960-1965, London, Heine-
mann Educational, 1973. Explores the ways in
which the politics and politicians of the First
Nigerian Republic contributed to the conditions
which led to the 1966 coups and the Nigerian
Civil War. (BPA)

Schatz, Sayre P., NIGERIAN CAPITALISM, Berkeley,
University of California Press, 1977. Examines
the development of and impact on indigenous
private enterprise by Nigerian "nurture-capital-
ism," the basic orientation of economic development policy during the early period, 1949-66,
in which private enterprise provides the thrust

in the productive sector, while the government
nurtures capitalism generally and favors indigenous enterprise specifically. Also assesses
the post-Civil War period, 1970-1975; the
period of oil affluence, 1975-80; and the
operations of an assortment of public business-
assistance measures undertaken in the period up
to the Civil War. Index. (JEL)

Smock, David R., CONFLICT AND CONTROL IN AN AFRICAN
     TRADE UNION: A Study of the Nigerian Coal
     Miners' Union, Hoover Institution Studies #23,
     Palo Alto, California, Stanford University,
     Hoover Institution Press, 1969.

Smock, David R., and Smock, Audrey C., CULTURAL AND
     POLITICAL ASPECTS OF RURAL TRANSFORMATION: A
     Case Study of Eastern Nigeria, New York, Prae-
     ger, 1972.   Three studies of the effects of
     cultural factors on economic development.   The
     first two, dealing with Ghanian businessmen and
     farmers respectively, reinforce each other's
     conclusions about the inhibiting effects of
     family structure and the need for security.
     The third book, on the other hand, emphasizes
     the effectiveness of demonstrated economic
     advantage in stimulating Ibo and Ibibio farmers
     in Nigeria to adopt new techniques and enter-
     prises.   (FA)

Tims, Wouter, NIGERIA: Options for Long-Term Devel-
     opment, World Bank Country Economic Report,
     Baltimore, Maryland, Johns Hopkins University
     Press, 1974.   One in a series of country eco-
     nomic reports which reviews "the major trends
     and policies that have characterized (Nigeria's)
     economic development to date and examines in
     more detail the current position of the economy,
     its prospects during the remaining period of
     the Second National Development Plan (1972/73-
     1973/74) and the longer-term outlook through
     the early 1980s."   No index.   (JEL)

Weidemann, W. C., A LONGITUDINAL STUDY OF DETERMI-
     NANTS OF INCOME IN NIGERIA, paper presented at
     1975 annual conference of the Nigerian Economic
     Society, 1975.

Wells, Jerome C., AGRICULTURAL POLICY AND ECONOMIC
    GROWTH IN NIGERIA 1962-1968, Ibadan, Oxford
    University Press for Nigerian Institute of
    Social and Economic Research, 1974. Undertakes
    to formulate a set of methods for evaluating a
    national agricultural policy and applies it to
    the pre-Civil War Nigerian experience (1962-68
    Plan). Provides a general background for
    understanding the agricultural sector of the
    Nigerian economy and then goes on to discuss
    investment in tree crop development and "mod-
    ernizing institutions" (including farm set-
    tlements; extension (education) programs; some
    mixed strategies including irrigation, mechani-
    cal cultivation, fisheries, and credit). (JEL)

Williams, Gavin, NIGERIA: Economy and Society,
    Totowa, New Jersey, Rowman & Littlefield, 1977.

Williams, Gavin, NIGERIA: Economy and Society, Lon-
    don, Rex Collins, Ltd., 1976.

Rwanda

X-REF: BURUNDI: Lemarchand.

Senegal

Curtin, Philip D., ECONOMIC CHANGE IN PRE-COLONIAL
    AFRICA: Senegambia in the Era of the Slave
    Trade, Madison, University of Wisconsin Press,
    1975. The first quantitative study of an Afri-
    can economy in the pre-colonial period, includ-
    ing a close view of the slave trade as seen
    from the African point of view. (BPA)

World Bank, SENEGAL: Tradition, Diversification,
    and Economic Development, a World Bank Country
    Economic Report, Washington, D.C., Author,
    1974. Part one of the study discusses the
    country's economic development, particularly
    with regard to growth performance between 1960
    and 1971. Particular attention is paid to the
    role of monetary and fiscal policies in achiev-
    ing past development objectives and the quality
    and quantity of human resources available to
    meet future growth of the economy. Part two

gives more detail of the rural and modern
sectors. Part three discusses how the objectives of economic growth and development can
be achieved, given the constraints of foreign
currency requirements and savings. (JEL)

Sierra Leone

X-REF: SMALL BUSINESS: Chuta, Liedholm.

Cartwright, John R., POLITICAL LEADERSHIP IN SIERRA
LEONE, Toronto, Canada, University of Toronto
Press, 1978. This thoughtful account of the
contrasting political styles of the traditional
conservative Dr. Milton Margai and his "bour-
geois" brother Albert, who successively led
Sierra Leone during much of the 1950s and
1960s, considers the Margais' records on political and economic development in relation to
that of other (and more "radical") African
leaders. The author concludes that the obstacles to development are so complicated and
formidable that ends and even means bear only a
tenuous relationship to results. (FA)

Spitzer, Leo, THE CREOLES OF SIERRA LEONE: Responses to Colonialism, 1870-1945, Madison,
University of Wisconsin Press, 1974. A fascinating description of the mixture of Victorian
England and Africa in the Creole life-style,
and of the attempts of this elite group to come
to terms with their African roots in face of
the increasing racial discrimination of their
British masters. (FA)

South Africa

Benbo, BLACK DEVELOPMENT IN SOUTH AFRICA: The Eco-
nomic Development of the Black Peoples in the
Homelands of the Republic of South Africa,
Pretoria, BENBO, 1976.

Bissell, Richard E. and Crocker, Chester A., eds.,
SOUTH AFRICA INTO THE 1980s, Boulder, Colorado,
Westview Press, 1979. The authors discuss South
Africa's internal situation, with particular
emphasis on the interests of competing political

parties; then they focus on the country's
ability to project influence abroad. (BPA)

Butler, Jeffrey; Rotberg, Robert I.; and Adams,
John, THE BLACK HOMELANDS OF SOUTH AFRICA: The
Political and Economic Development of Bophu-
thatswana and Kwazulu, Berkeley, University of
California Press, 1977. Striving visibly for
objectivity, this study considers the possible
contributions of the homelands to the achievement of evolutionary change in South Africa,
while at the same time thoroughly documenting
the vast physical and political constraints on
homelands development; in the conclusion, the
determined balancing becomes a sometimes
bewildering dialectic between future possibilities and present realities. An extremely
useful source. (FA)

Clark, Dick, U.S. CORPORATE INTERESTS IN SOUTH
AFRICA, Report to the Committee on Foreign
Relations, United States Senate Subcommittee on
African Affairs, Washington, D.C., January
1978.

Duggan, William Redman, A SOCIOECONOMIC PROFILE OF
SOUTH AFRICA, New York, Praeger, 1973. An excellent handbook on South Africa and a persuasive argument for the point of view of the
author, an ex-Foreign Service officer and
Africa specialist. He argues that the best
hope for change in South Africa would be in the
concerted application of a carrot-and-stick
approach by the United States and other Western
nations. (FA)

Houghton, D. Hobart, THE SOUTH AFRICAN ECONOMY,
third edition, New York, Oxford University
Press, 1973. The book explains the importance
and growth of that country's national income,
farming, population, migratory labor, mining,
manufacturing, labor force, foreign trade, and
other aspects. The author also traces the evolution of economic institutions and the 1961-
1970 economic boom. (JEL)

Leftwich, Adrian, ed., SOUTH AFRICA: Economic
Growth and Political Change, New York, St.
Martin's, 1974. The old themes are replayed
here with new data and considerable style; the
overall conclusion remains the same: economic

266

growth may alter South African society but will not seriously affect racial politics. (FA)

Lemarchand, Rene, ed., AMERICAN POLICY IN SOUTHERN AFRICA: The Stakes and the Stance, Washington, University Press, of America, 1978. Many of the chapters in this volume were written for a conference which took place in February 1976; hence the inevitably historical focus and somewhat repetitive analysis. The collection is distinguished by the contributions of Gerald Bender, William Foltz, and the editor himself. (FA)

Palmer, Robin and Parsons, Neil, eds., THE ROOTS OF RURAL POVERTY IN CENTRAL AND SOUTHERN AFRICA, Berkeley, University of California Press, 1978. This group of essays focuses on a little-known area--the pre-colonial economies and their alteration under the impact of white rule--providing a useful background for understanding development patterns today. (FA)

Shepherd, George W., Jr., ANTI-APARTHEID: Transnational Conflict and Western Policy in the Liberation of South Africa, Westport, Connecticut, Greenwood Press, 1977. This highly knowledgeable survey of the evolution of the Western anti-apartheid movement contrasts the activism of non-governmental organizations with the foot-dragging of Western governments-- particularly on the U.N. arms embargo. Shepherd, however, overextends the pessimism implicit in his material when he dismisses the possibility--and even the potential significance--of effective Western governmental action against apartheid. (FA)

Trapido, S., "South Africa in a Comparative Study of Industrialization," Journal of Development Studies, Vol. 7, No. 3, April 1971.

van Rensburg, W. C. J., and Pretorius, D. A., SOUTH AFRICA'S STRATEGIC MINERALS: Pieces on a Continental Chessboard, Pretoria, South Africa, Foreign Affairs Association, 1977. This glossy semi-official review of South Africa's minerals position reiterates its main theme from a number of ingeniously differentiated angles. South Africa's mineral resources, though pres-

ently a Western asset, are in ominous proximity
to the maw of the Russian bear. (FA)

<u>Sudan</u>

X-REF: EMPLOYMENT LABOR: Oberai.

Deng, Francis Mading, AFRICANS OF TWO WORLDS: The
    Dinka in Afro-Arab Sudan, New Haven, Connecti-
    cut, Yale University Press, 1978. As the son
    of a Paramount Chief from southern Sudan and a
    diplomat and minister in the traditionally
    northern-dominated (Arab) Sudanese government,
    Deng is well placed to understand the ethnic
    cleavages he describes and to assess the pos-
    sibilities for overcoming them. Although too
    much of the book is taken up with transcripts
    of disquisitions by southern chiefs, the first
    and final chapters perceptively analyze methods
    for integrating diverse nationalities into one
    nation. (FA)

ILO, GROWTH, EMPLOYMENT, AND EQUITY: A Compre-
    hensive Strategy for the Sudan, Geneva, 1978.
    The Sudan possesses vast areas of underuti-
    lized, fertile land with adequate rain-fall
    during parts of the year, and has a number of
    other unusual development advantages. This
    study formulates a strategy designed to exploit
    the Sudan's situation in the most productive
    way: in the first place by a major effort by
    the government in support of traditional
    agriculture and, in the second place, through
    the expansion of modern agriculture. (BPA)

Lees, Francis A. and Brooks, Hugh C., THE ECONOMIC
    AND POLITICAL DEVELOPMENT OF THE SUDAN, Boulder,
    Colorado, Westview Press, 1977. Study of the
    progress and problems encountered in the de-
    velopment process of the Sudan. Provides an
    economic overview and examines the following
    sectors: population and manpower; agriculture
    and forestry; transport, power and industry;
    and financial intermediaries. Also comments on
    external economic relations and the prospects
    for developmental planning. (JEL)

Warburg, Gabriel, SUDANESE POLITICS: Islam, Nationalism and Communism in a Traditional Society,
London, Frank Cass, 1978. This book highlights
the importance of popular Islam in Sudanese
society and politics since the turn of the century. It will be of great interest to those
studying Islamic history, emergence of religious movements and modern politics. (BPA)

Tanzania

X-REF: INCOME DISTRIBUTION PRINCIPLES: van Ginne-
ken, MALAWI: Gordenker, MULTINATIONAL CORPORATIONS:
Widstrand, RURAL DEVELOPMENT TECHNOLOGY: Ilo, URBAN
DEVELOPMENT: Amey, Ilo.

Amey, Alan, URBAN-RURAL RELATIONS IN TANZANIA: Methodology Issues and Preliminary Results, Development Studies, Discussion Paper, University
of East Anglia, December 1976.

Blue, Richard N. and Weaver, James H., A CRITICAL
ASSESSMENT OF THE TANZANIAN MODEL OF DEVELOP-
MENT, Agricultural Development Council Reprint,
No. 30, July 1977.

Clark, E., "Socialist Development in an Underdeveloped Country: The Case of Tanzania," World Development, Vol. 3, No. 4, April 1975.

Clark, W. Edmund, SOCIALIST DEVELOPMENT AND PUBLIC
INVESTMENT IN TANZANIA, 1964-1973, Toronto,
University of Toronto Press, 1977. After an
exhaustive survey of Tanzanian government
spending, which documents the disjunction
between Nyerere's rural-oriented development
strategy and the allocation of government
revenues (through 1973), Clark proposes that
the Ujamaa program be "institutionalized"
through strictly legislated guidelines for
public spending. He fails to indicate, however,
how his approach would circumvent the internal
political problems which, as he himself points
out, have thus far delayed and distorted
Nyerere's goals. (FA)

Collins, Paul, "Decentralization and Local Administration for Development in Tanzania," in Africa
Today, Vol. 21, No. 3, Summer 1974, pp. 15-25.

Cunningham, G. L., "Peasants and Rural Development in Tanzania," in Africa Today, Vol. 20, No. 4, Fall 1973, pp. 3-18.

Feldman, R., "Custom and Capitalism: Changes in the Basis of Land Tenure in Ismani, Tanzania," Journal of Development Studies, Vol. 10, No. 3-4, April-July 1974.

Finucane, James R., RURAL DEVELOPMENT AND BUREAUCRACY IN TANZANIA: The Case of Mwanza Region, Uppsala, Sweden, The Scandinavian Institute of African Studies, New York, Holmes and Meier, Africana Publishing Co., 1974. Describes the "bureaucratic pattern and some of the difficulties and contradictions which the Tanzanian leaders (Members of Parliament, specifically) have faced in attempting to alter it." Analyzes the rural development plans and experience in Tanzania under the dual objective of output growth and a "sincere" tendency toward economic quality. Discusses the nature of cooperative peasant participation in plan approval and implementation, and the still existing strong bureaucratic role. No index. (JEL)

Friedland, William H., VUTA KAMBA: The Development of Trade Unions in Tanganyika, Palo Alto, California, Stanford University, Hoover Institution Press, 1969.

Helleiner, G. K., "Socialism and Economic Development in Tanzania," Journal of Development Studies, Vol. 8, No. 2, January 1972.

Macpherson, G. and Jackson, D., "Village Technology for Rural Development: Agricultural Innovation in Tanzania," International Labour Review, Vol. 111, No. 2, February 1975.

Mwapachu, Juma Volter, "Operation Planned Villages in Rural Tanzania: A Revolutionary Strategy for Development," in The African Review, Vol. 6, No. 1, 1976, pp. 1-16.

Neerso, P., "Selected Aspects of Tanzania's Policies on Foreign Investment," World Development, Vol. 2, No. 2, February 1974.

Nellis, John R., A THEORY OF IDEOLOGY: The Tanzanian Example, New York, Oxford University Press, 1972. A schematic analysis of the Tanzanian political system through an economic "model" (in which ideology is assumed to stem from material self-interest alone). The author asserts that Nyerere's government is buying time by appealing to the masses over the heads of the self-seeking elites and concludes that this policy will eventually backfire by creating more politically aware citizens aspiring to elite prerogatives. (FA)

Nyerere, Julius K., THE ARUSHA DECLARATION TEN YEARS AFTER, Dar es Salaam, Tanzania, Tanzanian Government Printing Office, 1977. An objective assessment of the aspirations of the President of Tanzania, and a harshly frank appraisal of the shortcomings in achievement which would be surprising if it were to come from any other head of state than Nyerere (or perhaps Castro?) (Ed)

Nyerere, Julius K., "The Economic Challenge: Dialogue or Confrontation?" International Development Review, Vol. XVIII, No. 1, 1976, pp. 2-8.

Nyerere, Julius K., MAN AND DEVELOPMENT: Binadamu na Maendeleo, New York, Oxford University Press, 1974. Papers cover a five-year period (1968-73) and contain the author's views on democracy, equality, and human rights; African unity and liberation, education ahd health; economic development; and international affairs. It reaffirms "the need to recognize in action the fundamental unity and equality of all human beings, regardless of colour, race, religion, or sex." No index. (JEL)

Nyerere, Julius K., UJAMAA--ESSAYS ON SOCIALISM, New York, Oxford University Press, 1969. Nyerere's philosophy of development emerges clearly from this collection of party documents and presidential speeches. Of particular interest are the all-important Arusha Declaration of February 1967 and Nyerere's subsequent assessments of its implementation in Tanzania nearly a year later. (FA)

Nyerere, Julius K., "From Uhuru to Ujamaa," in
Africa Today, Vol. 21, No. 3, Summer 1974, pp.
3-8.

Odia, S., "Rural Education and Training in Tanzania,"
International Labour Review, Vol. 103, No. 1,
January 1971.

Omari, C. K., "Tanzania's Emerging Rural Development
Policy," in Africa Today, Vol. 21, No. 3,
Summer, 1974, pp. 9-14.

Pratt, Cranford, THE CRITICAL PHASE IN TANZANIA,
1945-1968: Nyerere and the Emergency of a
Socialist Strategy, New York, Cambridge University Press, 1976. Tanzania's devolution to
independence from British rule is presented
here as prelude to the country's further striving for national self-reliance. Nyerere's
skillful balance between the imperatives of
strong leadership and popular participation
arouse both awe and anxiety in the observer.
(FA)

Pratt, Cranford, "Nyerere on the Transition to Socialism in Tanzania," in The African Review,
Vol. v, No. 1, 1975, pp. 63-76.

Rweyemamu, Justinian, UNDERDEVELOPMENT AND INDUSTRI-
ALIZATION IN TANZANIA: A Study of Perverse
Capitalist Industrial Development, New York,
Oxford University Press, 1973. In three parts,
the author examines "the political economy of
Tanzania from a historical perspective," analyses the impact of colonialism on the industrial
development of Tanzania," and explores change
in the social structure based on the assumption
"that the formation and implementation of an
appropriate industrial strategy is essential to
the attainment of the goal of socialism and
self-reliance." Data extend through the mid-
1960's. (JEL)

Samoff, Joel, TANZANIA: Local Politics and the
Structure of Power, Madison, University of
Wisconsin Press, 1974. Critical new insights
are offered on the operations of Tanzania's
political party--TANU--while providing a model
study of local politics in the context of
national development. (BPA)

Van Hekken, P. M., Van Velzen, H. U. E. Thoden, LAND
    SCARCITY AND RURAL INEQUALITY IN TANZANIA:
    Some Case Studies from Rungwe District, Mouton
    & Co., 1972.

Tunisia

X-REF: INCOME DISTRIBUTION PRINCIPLES: van
Ginneken, URBAN DEVELOPMENT: Ilo.

Schliephake, Konrad, OIL AND REGIONAL DEVELOPMENT:
    Examples From Algeria and Tunisia, New York,
    Praeger, 1977.

Uganda

Gershenberg, Irving, "Multinationals and Development:
    Commercial Banking in Uganda," in Africa Today,
    Vol. 20, No. 4, Fall 1973, pp. 19-27.

Gwyn, David, IDI AMIN: Death-Light of Africa,
    Boston, Little, Brown, 1977. Gwyn (a pseudonym
    masking the identity of a Briton who apparently
    served in Uganda's government under colonial
    rule and through the beginning of Amin's re-
    gime) assaults the reader with a terrifying
    barrage of facts, dates, places, names, with
    modes of torture, mutilation, death. His
    extraordinary indictment is followed by the
    thoughtful reflections of Ali Mazrui on Uganda
    and the dilemma it poses for Africans regarding
    human rights in the black-ruled states of the
    continent. (FA)

Hunt, Diana, CREDIT FOR AGRICULTURAL DEVELOPMENT: A
    Case Study of Uganda, Nairobi, Kenya, East
    African Publishing House, 1975.

Parson, Jack D., "Africanizing Trade in Uganda: The
    Final Solution," in Africa Today, Vol. 20, No.
    1, Winter 1973, pp. 59-72.

Zaire

X-REF: TECHNOLOGY: Ilo.

Young, Crawford, "Zaire: The Unending Crisis," For-
    eign Affairs, Vol. 57, No. 1, Fall 1978, pp.
    169-185.

Zambia

X-REF: FINANCE: Wilson, MALAWI: Gordenker, Rotberg, REGIONAL DEVELOPMENT: Bendavid, TECHNOLOGY:
Ilo.

Anglin, Douglas G., and Shaw, Timothy M., ZAMBIA'S
    FOREIGN POLICY, Studies in Diplomacy and Depen-
    dence, Boulder, Colorado, Westview Press, 1979.
    Examines Zambia's role in the search for African
    independence, unity, and development; also
    analyzes the problems of dependence and under-
    development and their impact on foreign policy-
    making. (BPA)

Bond, George C., THE POLITICS OF CHANGE IN A ZAMBIAN
    COMMUNITY, Chicago, University of Chicago
    Press, 1976. A case study in Zambian rural
    politics around the time of independence (1963-
    65). The author views this period as a brief
    flowering of local participation, which, even
    as he watched, began to wither again. (FA)

Bostock, Mark, and Harvey, Charles, eds., ECONOMIC
    INDEPENDENCE AND ZAMBIAN COPPER: A Case Study
    of Foreign Investment, Praeger Special Studies
    in International Economics and Development, New
    York, Praeger, 1972. Contains eight original
    essays by the editors and their associates on
    the history of the Zambian economy, the mining
    industry, and the 1969 government take-over of
    that industry. Contains data through 1969 plus
    projections for the mining industry through
    1975. Includes documents related to the take-
    over. No index. (JEL)

Dodge, Doris Jansen, AGRICULTURAL POLICY AND PER-
FORMANCE IN ZAMBIA: History, Prospects, and
Proposals for Change, Research Series No. 32,
Berkeley, University of California Institute of
International Studies, 1977. A detailed analysis of government policy and performance of the
agricultural sector in Zambia during the pre-
independence (1890-1964) and post-independence
periods (1966-1976). Finds a serious diver-
gence between government aims and actual performance. A major part of the work is devoted
to the design of a new crop production and
rural incomes policy involving presentation of
the methodology and results of domestic resource
cost (DRC) calculations by crop, an econometric
estimation of the shadow price of traditional
farm labor. No index. (JEL)

Elliott, Charles, ed., CONSTRAINTS ON THE ECONOMIC
DEVELOPMENT OF ZAMBIA, New York, Oxford University Press, 1971. A book of twelve readings
about constraints on economic development in
Zambia. Seven of the articles deal with
general constraints: man-power, industrial
relations, wages, financial, fiscal, markets,
and foreign exchange. Five of the articles
deal with constraints on individual industries:
mining, agriculture, manufacturing, transport,
and construction. Index. (JEL)

Faber, M. L. O., and Potter, J. G., TOWARDS ECONOMIC
INDEPENDENCE, Papers on the Nationalisation of
the Copper Industry in Zambia, University of
Cambridge Department of Applied Economics Occasional Paper No. 23, New York, Cambridge University Press, 1971. Four papers (plus an
introduction and appendix) by the authors
dealing with the corporate structure of copper
industry in Northern Rhodesia (now Zambia) in
1963, recovery of mineral rights at Independence in 1964, the future of Zambia's copper
industry, and the proposal for the 51 percent
nationalization of the Zambian copper mines
(made by one of the authors earlier). No
index. (JEL)

Kaunda, Kenneth D., HUMANISM IN ZAMBIA AND A GUIDE
TO ITS IMPLEMENTATION, Part II, Lusaka, Division of National Guidance, 1974. Also Part I.
Part I is brief and incomplete. Part II published separately, is complete in itself; it

275

provides an insight into the social and human-
istic philosophy of Zambia's President, which
has profoundly influenced development policy.
(Ed)

Lombard, C. Stephen, THE GROWTH OF CO-OPERATIVES IN
ZAMBIA 1914-1971, book review in African
Studies, Vol. 35, No. 2, 1976, pp. 142-144.

Myers, R. J., "Rural Manpower Planning in Zambia,"
International Labour Review, Vol. 102, No. 1,
July 1970.

Pettman, Jan, ZAMBIA: Security and Conflict, New
York, St. Martin, 1974. An intelligent and
comprehensive survey of Zambia's political and
economic development since independence, somewhat marred by what hindsight reveals to be an
exaggerated view of the external--southern
African--threats to the nation's security. (FA)

Rotberg, Robert I., BLACK HEART: Gore-Browne and
the Politics of Multiracial Zambia, Berkeley,
University of California Press, 1978. A tale
well told about a British aristocrat, leader of
the white Legislative Council of Northern Rhodesia, and the evolution over more than 50
years of his rather conventional white upper-
class attitudes toward the "natives" into a
fervent support for African nationalism that
put him at political odds with virtually all
his fellow settlers. (FA)

Shaw, Timothy M., DEPENDENCE AND UNDERDEVELOPMENT:
The Development and Foreign Policies of Zambia,
Papers in International Studies, Africa Series
No. 28, Athens, Ohio University Center for
International Studies, Africa Program, 1976.

Sklar, Richard L., CORPORATE POWER IN AN AFRICAN
STATE: The Political Impact of Multinational
Mining Companies in Zambia, Berkeley, University of California Press, 1975. In this careful
and intelligent analysis of the evolving relationship between an LDC host and its multinationals, Zambian nationalism is seen to be
entirely compatible with the development of an
elite class whose interests coincide with those
of international capitalism, although the
corporations have adapted smoothly to the
expressed policies. (FA)

Wilson, Frank A., "The Role of Commercial Banks in Financing Farmers: Some Reflections on the Situation in Zambia," Agricultural Administration, Vol. 1, 1974, pp. 245-257.

Zimbabwe

Arrighi, G., "Labour Supplies in Historical Perspective: A Study of the Proletarianization of African Peasantry in Rhodesia," Journal of Development Studies, Vol. 6, No. 3, April 1970.

Blake, Robert, A HISTORY OF RHODESIA, New York, Knopf, 1978. This important account of Rhodesian political development from its earliest African settlement to the present is based on ten years of evidently painstaking research. The approach of the author (whose biography of Disraeli offered another view of Britain's imperial past) is objective in tone but one-sided: although white Rhodesia's progress to its present impasse is recounted often with striking insight, the black nationalist perspective is almost entirely absent. (FA)

Clarke, D. G., THE DISTRIBUTION OF INCOME AND WEALTH IN RHODESIA, Mambo Occasional Papers, Socio-Economic Series, No. 7, Gwelo, Rhodesia, Mambo Press, 1977. Identifies the income distribution pattern, with emphasis on the past decade and on the socioeconomic implications of the existing structure. Finds that: (1) the pattern has grown increasingly complex in recent years; (2) the existing distribution of both incomes and wealth is highly unequal; and (3) Rhodesia does not measure up well in the "international stakes" with respect to the level and distribution of incomes. (JEL)

ILO, LABOR CONDITIONS AND DISCRIMINATION IN SOUTHERN RHODESIA (ZIMBABWE), Geneva, 1978. This study is to identify labor conditions and related patterns of discrimination in Zimbabwe since "independence" was declared illegally in 1965. (BPA)

Palmer, Robin, LAND AND RACIAL DOMINATION IN RHODESIA, Berkeley, University of California Press, 1977. The author succinctly analyzes the

origins of present-day Rhodesian land tenure
and the corresponding phases in the subjugation
of the country's Africans: the ever-widening
expropriations made official in 1914, 1920, and
1930; the destruction of a flourishing agriculture; the creation of a class of African wage
labor integrated into the white economy; the
segregation of African land and agriculture and
the strict limitation of African opportunity in
the white economy. An affecting description of
the creation of African dependency and demonstration of its extreme usefulness to the European colonist. (FA)

Strack, Harry R., SANCTIONS: The Case of Rhodesia,
Syracuse, New York, Syracuse University Press,
1978. This study assesses the effectiveness of
sanctions from a variety of perspectives--
giving them mixed grades--but is most valuable
as a compendium of information on Rhodesia's
extensive international connections, overt and
covert, since sanctions were imposed. (FA)

Asia

X-REF: AGRARIAN REFORM: Foland, Ilo, King, Klein,
Ledesma, Mitchell, Querol, Smith, Tuma, Un, AGRICUL-
TURAL CREDIT: Kato, AGRICULTURAL DEVELOPMENT:
Hunter, Rao, Yamada, EDUCATION: Huq, EMPLOYMENT
LABOR: Ilo, Mehta, INCOME DISTRIBUTION PRINCIPLES:
Oshima, MULTINATIONAL CORPORATIONS: Cohen, TEXT-
BOOKS: Committee, URBAN DEVELOPMENT: Davis.

Asian Development Bank, RURAL ASIA: Challenge and
Opportunity, New York, Praeger, 1978. Assessing the critical issues confronting policy
makers in the coming decade, the Second Asian
Agricultural Survey details the essential
elements of an effective development strategy.
The Survey traces the origins of the agricultural problems currently facing rural Asia and
evaluates the impact of technology and the success of government policies. (BPA)

Badgley, John, ASIAN DEVELOPMENT: Problems and
Prognosis, New York, Free Press, 1971. Most
Asian peoples live in societies where the idea
of the nation has no organic meaning, political
authority generally lacks legitimacy and con-

278

flict is a continuing probability. This gloomy analysis leads the author to two heterodox conclusions: U.S. involvement with Asia should increase, not decline; and effective "development" is more likely through local and parochial loyalties and community development than on the national scale. (FA)

Chandavarkar, Annand G., SOME ASPECTS OF INTEREST RATE POLICIES IN LESS DEVELOPED COUNTRIES: The Experience of Selected Asian Countries, International Monetary Funds Staff Papers, Vol. 18, 1971.

Evers, Hans-Dieter, ed., MODERNIZATION IN SOUTHEAST ASIA, New York, Oxford University Press, 1973. Twelve essays which were presented at a seminar held in Singapore in 1971 under the auspices of the Institute of Southeast Asian Studies. Beyond the general topic of modernization in developing countries, the papers are divided into four groups dealing with the modernization topics of political, economic, and social development, and religion and ideology. (JEL)

Etienne, G., "Foodgrain Production and Population in Asia: China, India, and Bangladesh," World Development, Vol. 5, Nos. 5-7, May-July 1977.

Fryer, Donald W., EMERGING SOUTHEAST ASIA: A Study in Growth and Stagnation, New York, McGraw-Hill, 1970. More effective trade, aid and regional cooperation is advocated to meet Southeast Asia's pressing problems of food production and overpopulation. (FA)

Ghosh, A., DEVELOPMENT PLANNING IN SOUTH-EAST ASIA: An Input-Output Approach, in collaboration with C. Chakravarti and H. Sarkar, forword by J. Tinbergen, The Netherlands, Rotterdam University Press, distributed in the United States and Canada by International Scholarly Book Services, 1974. Demonstrates the use of input-output modeling and regression analysis techniques as they were applied by the author (a professor at Jadavpur University, Calcutta) to long-range development planning in South-East Asia--mainly in Taiwan, Korea, Malaysia, and Ceylon. This monograph provides a model and guide for planners in other countries at a similar stage of economic development. Projections are made for outputs (1960-1980) and sectoral employment. No index. (JEL)

Golay, Frank H., et al., UNDERDEVELOPMENT AND ECO-NOMIC NATIONALISM IN SOUTHEAST ASIA, Ithaca, New York, Cornell University Press, 1969. A country-by-country study of the economic and industrial resources and enterprises of the Southeast Asian nations, with emphasis on the importance of increasing the role of nationals in the ownership and control of productive assets. (FA)

Huang, Po-Wen, Jr., THE ASIAN DEVELOPMENT BANK: Diplomacy and Development in Asia, New York, Vantage, 1976. Long on describing the origins of the Bank, but short on assessing its strengths and weaknesses. (FA)

Kato, Yuzury, "Sources of Loanable Funds of Agricultural Credit Institutions in Asia," Developing Economies, Vol. 10, 1972, pp. 126-140.

Lewis, John Wilson, ed., PEASANT REBELLION AND COMMUNIST REVOLUTION IN ASIA, Stanford, California, Stanford University Press, 1974. Some conclusions on the Asian revolutions of our time: freeholding peasants are more prone to insurrection than poor tenants; people join revolutions because they have something to gain rather than nothing to lose; Asian revolutions of the twentieth century have been protracted because the revolutionaries have had to create a state to capture. (FA)

Maddison, Angus, ed., MYRDAL'S ASIAN DRAMA: An Interdisciplinary Critique, Liege, Belgium, CIRIEC, 1971. Proceedings of a conference held at Sir George Williams University in Montreal, Canada to review Gunnar Myrdal's controversial Asian Drama which is an assessment of postwar economic and social progress in eight Asian countries. The 27 participants, including Professors Chenery, Higgins, and Tinbergen, read 11 papers and deliberated on Myrdal's provocative findings for the eight countries' development. No index. (JEL)

Morgan, Theodore and Spoelstra, Nyle, eds., ECONOMIC
INTERDEPENDENCE IN SOUTHEAST ASIA, Madison,
University of Wisconsin Press (for the Center
for International Economics and Economic Development), 1969. Trends and prospects for accelerating the rate of national economic growth
and promoting trade relationships in Asia
through regional cooperation and integration of
on-going projects. (FA)

Myrdal, Gunnar, ASIAN DRAMA: An Inquiry into the
Poverty of Nations, in three volumes, New York,
Pantheon-A Division of Random House, 1968. A
monumental work, with a wealth of data and insights on the evolution of independent Asian
economies; concludes that major cultural change
is essential to successful development. (Ed)

Paauw, Douglas S., and Fei, John C. H., THE TRANSI-
TION IN OPEN DUALISTIC ECONOMIES: Theory and
Southeast Asian Experience, New Haven, Con-
necticut, Yale University Press, 1973.

Pauker, Guy J.; Golay, Frank H.; and Enloe, Cynthia
H., DIVERSITY AND DEVELOPMENT IN SOUTHEAST
ASIA: The Coming Decade, Council on Foreign
Relations, New York, McGraw-Hill, 1977. Three
studies, written by a social scientist, an
economist, and a political scientist, plus an
introduction by Catherine Gwin, on the implications of the region's diversity for national
economic and political development, regional
stability, and the solidarity of the Southeast
Asian states with that of the developing world.
(BPA)

Rao, V. K. R. V., GROWTH WITH JUSTICE IN ASIAN
AGRICULTURE: An Exercise in Policy Formulation, Geneva, United Nations Research Institute
for Social Development, 1974.

Robinson, E. A. G., and Kidron, M., eds., ECONOMIC
DEVELOPMENT IN SOUTH ASIA, proceedings of a
conference held by the International Economic
Association at Kandy, Ceylon, New York, St.
Martin's Press, 1971. A collection of 28
original papers presented at an International
Economic Association Conference. (JEL)

Rudner, Martin, ed., SOCIETY AND DEVELOPMENT IN
ASIA, Asian and African Studies, Volume 6,
Jerusalem, Israel Oriental Society, 1970. The
ten articles in this volume constitute the
proceedings of the Franz Oppenheimer Memorial
Symposium are: Development from Below, The
Social Ethics of Buddhism and the Socio-eco-
nomic Development of Southeast Asia, The State
and Commerce in Imperial China, Impediments to
'Development from Below' in India's Economic
History, The State and Peasant Innovation in
Rural Development: The Case of Malaysian
Rubber: Socioeconomic Dualism and Development,
Agricultural Development in Post-war Japan,
India's Agricultural Performance, The Taiwan
Land Reform, and The Japan Kibbutz Association.
No index. (JEL)

Schiffrin, Harold Z., ed., MILITARY AND STATE IN
MODERN ASIA, Jerusalem, Jerusalem Academic
Press, 1976. Lissak discusses the army regimes
in Thailand and Burma; the papers from the 1974
Truman Institute symposium on Military and
State in Modern Asia at the Hebrew University
range farther afield to the Middle East and
Imperial Japan. Agreement emerges, however, on
essential points: military men are better at
guns than government; and the military is not
an agent of modernization, but of "pseudo-
modernization." (FA)

Shand, R. T., AGRICULTURAL DEVELOPMENT IN ASIA,
Berkeley, University of California Press, 1969.
Ten specialists discuss the main technical,
economic and socio-political ingredients of an
effective approach to the solution of the problem of poverty in post-World War II Asia, especially food supplies. (FA)

Weidner, Edward W., DEVELOPMENT ADMINISTRATION IN
ASIA, Durham, North Carolina, Duke University
Press (in cooperation with the Comparative
Administration Group of the American Society
for Public Administration), 1970. The distinctive roles, and modification of roles, of
Asian administrators under conditions of rapid
change and development. Political and cultural
aspects are emphasized as well as those that
are strictly administrative. (FA)

Wriggins, W. Howard and Guyot, James F., eds., POPU-
LATION, POLITICS, AND THE FUTURE OF SOUTHERN
ASIA, New York, Columbia University Press,
1973. At present growth rates, populations in
southern Asia will double in 25 years. What
does this mean in political terms? The authors
predict heightened popular participation, more
demands for social welfare, intensification of
ethnic rivalries, and a situation where political leaders must either be more demagogic or
more effective. They are not optimistic about
the prospect. (FA)

Yamada, Saburo, A COMPARATIVE ANALYSIS OF ASIAN
AGRICULTURAL PRODUCTIVITIES AND GROWTH PAT-
TERNS, Asian Productivity Organization, 1975.

Aden

Kour, Z. H., THE DEVELOPMENT OF ADEN AND BRITISH
RELATIONS WITH NEIGHBOURING TRIBES, 1839-72,
London, Frank Cass, 1978.

Afghanistan

Dupree, Louis and Albert, Linette, eds., AFGHANISTAN
AND THE 1970's, foreword by Phillips Talbot,
Praeger Special Studies in International Economics and Development, New York, Praeger 1974.
Presents 14 unpublished papers on present day
social, cultural, economic, and political
trends in Afghanistan by social scientists.
Topics discussed include the problems of
peasant-tribal society, trends in Afghan
history, the constitution of 1964, foreign
relations, recent economic development (by
Marvin Brant), the modernization of rural
Afghanistan, the role of Afghan women, unification, education, and the arts. A selected
bibliography is included after each paper.
Index. (JEL)

Fry, Maxwell J., THE AFGHAN ECONOMY: Money, Finance,
and the Critical Constraints to Economic Development, Vol. 15: Social, Economic and Political
Studies of the Middle East, Leiden, Netherlands,
E. J. Brill, 1974. "First book in English,"

offering a comprehensive analysis of the economic structure of Afghanistan. The author provides an introduction to the economic, social, and geographic characteristics of Afghanistan and then focuses his attention on an examination of resource mobilization under recent development plans, the structure and role of the country's financial sector, its public finances, its foreign trade sector, and recent monetary and fiscal policies. Index. (JEL)

Bangladesh

X-REF: INDIA: Brown.

Alamgir, Mohiuddin and Rahman, Atiqur, SAVING IN BANGLADESH 1959/60-1969/70, Research Monograph No. 2, Dacca, Bangladesh Institute of Development Studies, 1974. A first attempt at determining the volume and the role of savings in the Bangladesh economy during the 1960's. The authors focus "not only on the magnitude and rate of saving, total and sectoral, but also on the intersectoral flow of funds, particularly an investigation into the financing of investment in Bangladesh." No index. (JEL)

Islam, Nurul, DEVELOPMENT PLANNING IN BANGLADESH: A Study in Political Economy, New York, St. Martin's Press, 1977. Examines the evolution of economic planning in Bangladesh, 1972-1975, evaluating it in terms of the various socio-economic groups and their influence on the political process machinery. Discusses the application of tools of economic analysis in economic planning, including models for medium-term planning and illustrating the interaction of economic, political, and administrative factors in two areas: domestic resource mobilization and the issue of the public versus the private sector. Index. (JEL)

Raper, Arthur F., et al., RURAL DEVELOPMENT IN ACTION, Ithaca, New York, Cornell University Press, 1970. A report on a decade of sustained and impressive efforts by the Academy for Rural Development at Comilla, East Pakistan, to improve the social and economic lot of the Bengalis. (FA)

Robinson, E. A. G., and Griffin, Keith, eds., THE ECONOMIC DEVELOPMENT OF BANGLADESH, Proceedings of a conference held by the International Economic Association at Dacca, New York, Halsted Press, 1974. A collection of the papers and proceedings of a conference held in early 1973. Aside from an introduction by E. A. G. Robinson, the volume has 12 articles, most of which are followed by comments and a discussion. Index. (JEL)

Robinson, E. A. G., and Griffin, Keith, eds., THE ECONOMIC DEVELOPMENT OF BANGLADESH WITHIN A SOCIALIST FRAMEWORK, New York, Halsted Press (for the International Economic Association), 1974. Bangladesh, as the editors point out, comes nearer to one's nightmares of Malthusia than almost any other country in the world. These papers, from a star-studded international group of economists convened to do some emergency thinking on a situation of endemic crisis, are stimulating and saddening: this science struggles not to be dismal, but it is an uphill battle. (FA)

Burma

X-REF: INDUSTRIAL DEVELOPMENT: Resnick.

Donnison, F. S. V., BURMA, New York, Praeger, 1970. A former Indian Civil Service officer presents a dismal view of Burma, pointing to the ineffective rule of military dictatorship, the prevailing disunion and internal strifes and hardships. His outlook for the future is equally gloomy. (FA)

Maung, Mya, BURMA AND PAKISTAN: A Comparative Study of Development, Praeger Special Studies in International Economics and Development, New York, Praeger, 1971. This book applies the principles of development economics to a comparison of development in Burma and Pakistan. The author's primary purpose is to answer the question of why certain types of economic philosophy and policy are being pursued in

these two countries, and to examine their
degree of success or failure. (JEL)

Resnick, Stephen A., "The Decline of Rural Industry
    Under Export Expansion: A Comparison Among
    Burma, Philippines, and Thailand, 1870-1938,"
    Center Paper #147, New Haven, Connecticut, Yale
    University, Economic Growth Center, 1970.

Silverstein, Josef, BURMA: Military Rule and the
    Politics of Stagnation, Ithaca, New York,
    Cornell University Press, 1977. Although this
    volume helps fill the enormous gap in analysis
    of contemporary Burma, it lacks depth. The
    author avers that those who see the military as
    modernizers will find that a study of Burma
    brings that proposition into serious question.
    But he does not go very far in helping to ex-
    plain why the Burmese regime of "socialist-
    soldiers" has been so ineffective. (FA)

China

X-REF: AFRICA: Damachi, Ogunsanwo, AGRARIAN REFORM:
Chao, Lehmann, FOREIGN AID: Barthke, Horvath, LATIN
AMERICA: Johnson.

Alexander, Garth, THE INVISIBLE CHINA: The Overseas
    Chinese and the Politics of Southeast Asia, New
    York, Macmillan, 1974. This earnest and alarm-
    ist book provides a "new key" to American Far
    East policy, the Vietnam War and the future of
    Southeast Asia: "anti-Sinitism." Unfortu-
    nately, its lurid prose, apocalyptic visions
    and drastic oversimplification form an organic
    whole in which useful insights are smothered by
    rhetoric, and fact by opinion. There is a good
    book here, which might have emerged with more
    care. (FA)

American Rural Small-Scale Industry Delegation,
    RURAL SMALL-SCALE INDUSTRY IN THE PEOPLE'S
    REPUBLIC OF CHINA, Dwight Perkins, Chairman,
    Berkeley, University of California Press, 1977.
    Based on the observations of twelve scholars,
    technologists, and administrators, headed by
    Perkins; concludes that rural industry has
    generally helped raise agricultural production

through self-reliance and has paved the way for
further advances in industrialization. (JEL)

Andors, Stephen, CHINA'S INDUSTRIAL REVOLUTION:
1949 to the Present, New York, Pantheon, 1977.
A substantial and original account of industrial organization in China which is, however,
seriously flawed by the author's ideological
biases. Most questionable are his views that
China has discovered a new path to modernization without relying on a technocratic or
bureaucratic elite and that China is the har-
binger of a "new global socialist civilization." In fact, since the end of the Cultural
Revolution, as Andors himself makes clear,
there has been "far greater stress...on the
importance of control, discipline and leadership, and much less emphasis on worker innovation and spontaneity. It is also clear that
the technical personnel who had been so thoroughly criticized during the Cultural Revolution were once again wielding significant
authority in many factories, and that great
importance was placed on statistics, on efficient and productive quotas and norms...and on
technical controls in general." (FA)

Andors, Stephen, "Urbanization and Urban Government
in China's Development: Toward a Political
Economy of Urban Community?" in Economic Development and Cultural Change, Vol. 26, No. 3,
April 1978, pp. 525-546.

Axilrod, Eric, THE POLITICAL ECONOMY OF THE CHINESE
REVOLUTION, Hong Kong, Union Research Institute, 1972. An effort by a Western economist
to assess the Chinese economic experience from
about 1911 to 1965 in terms of the "laws of
change and development" peculiar to China.
Areas of study include the "Historical Origins
of the Chinese Revolution," "The Process of
Development after the Great Land Reform," and
"The Collective Revolution and the Two Tendencies." Bibliography; no index. (JEL)

Ayers, William, CHANG CHIH-TUNG AND EDUCATIONAL RE-
FORM IN CHINA, Cambridge, Massachusetts, Harvard University Press, 1971.

Barnett, Robert W., "China and Taiwan: The Economic Issues," Foreign Affairs, Vol. 50, No. 3, April 1972.

Bennett, Gordon, CHINA'S FINANCE AND TRADE: A Policy Reader, distributed by M. E. Sharpe Inc., 1978.

Berger, R., "Economic Planning in the People's Republic of China," World Development, Vol. 3, Nos. 7 and 8, July-August 1975. The paper discusses the economic problems confronting the Chinese communists after taking power in 1949, in particular the relationship between industry and agriculture. (JEL)

Bettelheim, Charles, CULTURAL REVOLUTION AND INDUSTRIAL ORGANIZATION IN CHINA: Changes in Management and the Division of Labor, New York, Monthly Review Press, 1974. The author has let his enthusiasm for the Chinese experiment override his passion for fact and documentation. Consequently, the title's promise is somewhat misleading. There is little here about industrial organization, management, and the division of labor, but much about decentralization, small-medium enterprise, and the elimination of the town-country dichotomy. The purely theoretical and speculative considerations about the future of organization in a post-capitalist society are interesting, however, and there is a good analysis in the postscript of the difference between "ultra-leftism" and Maoist orthodoxy. (FA)

Brugger, William, DEMOCRACY AND ORGANIZATION IN THE CHINESE INDUSTRIAL ENTERPRISE, 1948-1953, New York, Cambridge University Press, 1976. Examines the new system of factory management implemented in China after 1949, focusing on the political and sociological background against which economic changes occurred. (BPA)

Bulletin of the Atomic Scientists, CHINA AFTER THE REVOLUTION, New York, Random House, 1970. An important study, made up of selections from The Bulletin of the Atomic Scientists, of how China fares today in the fields of technology, economics, politics and foreign affairs by 11 specialists who examine China's main problems:

population growth, shortage of fertile land and paucity of skills. (FA)

Burki, Shahid, A STUDY OF CHINESE COMMUNES, 1965, Cambridge, Massachusetts, East Asian Research Center, Harvard University, distributed by Harvard University Press, 1969.

Chang, John K., INDUSTRIAL DEVELOPMENT IN COMMUNIST CHINA: A Quantitative Analysis, Chicago, Illinois, Aldine Publishing Co., 1967.

Chang, Parris H., POWER AND POLICY IN CHINA, University Park, and London, The Pennsylvania State University Press, 1975.

Chao, Kuo-chun, ECONOMIC PLANNING AND ORGANIZATION IN MAINLAND CHINA: A Documentary Study 1949-1957, Vols. I and II, Cambridge, Center for East Asian Studies, Harvard University, distributed by Harvard University Press, 1959-60.

Chen, Kuan-I, and Uppal, J. S., COMPARATIVE DEVELOPMENT OF INDIA AND CHINA, New York, the Free Press, London, Collier-Macmillan, 1971. A compilation of 26 previously printed articles written by a welter of specialists and six articles written under the auspices of three offices in the Government of India. This comparative study of India and China brings out what the editors regard as the many similarities between the two countries, particularly in their physical and human resources. The outcome of these two countries' efforts in tackling their major economic, political, and social problems is bound to affect the future economic and political development of the rest of the world's underdeveloped countries. The articles are presented under six major topics: emerging patterns in economic development, development policy and planning techniques, demographic patterns and population policy, capital formation and development of human resources, international economic relations (trade and aid), and future prospects. No index. (JEL)

Clark, D., "Economic Development in Communist China," Journal of Political Economy, Vol. 84, No. 2, April 1976. This article extends a previous study, which covered the years 1930 to 1959.

Chinese population is both lower and slower-
growing than generally believed. 1971 per
capita GNP was $451. Its long-run rate of
increase has been about 2 percent per year on
either a 1930's or early 1950's base--less than
the developing country average. Inequalities
in income distribution are similar to those of
other countries. (JEL)

Dean, G., "A Note on the Source of Technical Innova-
tions in the People's Republic of China,"
Journal of Development Studies, Vol. 9, No. 1,
October 1972.

Deleyne, J., THE CHINESE ECONOMY, New York, Harper
and Row, 1973.

Dernberger, Robert F., "The Relevance of China's
Experience for Other Developing Countries,"
Items, Vol. 31, No. 3, September 1977, (SSRC).
Résumés of eight papers presented at a confer-
ence.

Dewenter, John R., "China Afloat," Foreign Affairs,
Vol. 50, No. 4, July 1972.

Domes, Jurgen, CHINA AFTER THE CULTURAL REVOLUTION,
Berkeley, University of California Press, 1977.

Eberhard, Wolfram, A HISTORY OF CHINA, Richmond,
California, University of California Press,
1977. An easy-reading, very informative, history of China, which discusses (inter alia) the
economic and social conditions of each dynastic
era. (Ed)

Eckstein, Alexander, CHINA'S ECONOMIC DEVELOPMENT:
The Interplay of Scarcity and Ideology, Ann
Arbor, University of Michigan Press, 1975.
Professor Eckstein here collects his essays on
the Chinese economy over the last 20 years and
adds a postscript based on a short first-hand
exposure to Chinese society. The latter, he
remarks, strengthened his impression of high
morale and commitment to equality, but falsi-
fied none of his earlier attempts at long-
distance Sinology. (FA)

Eckstein, Alexander, CHINA'S ECONOMIC REVOLUTION,
Cambridge, New York and Melbourne, Cambridge
University Press, 1977. Study of China's

efforts to industrialize within a socialist
framework over the past 25 years. Following a
detailed analysis of the character of the key
inputs in China's development (the resources
and constraints from the past; a broadly defined, motivating ideology, institutional
transformation in property relations controlling resource allocation; and specific planning
instruments designed to achieve the desired
outputs), the author evaluates the extent to
which the objectives of the system where attained, assessing, in particular, the economy
and its quest for stability, growth, self-
reliance, and improvements in income distribution. Index. (JEL)

Eckstein, Alexander, "China's Trade Policy and Sino-
American Relations," Foreign Affairs, Vol. 54,
No. 1, October 1975.

Eckstein, Alexander, COMMUNIST CHINA'S ECONOMIC
GROWTH AND FOREIGN TRADE, New York, McGraw-
Hill, 1966.

Fei, John C. H., THE "STANDARD MARKET" OF TRADITION-
AL CHINA, Center Discussion Paper No. 172, New
Haven, Connecticut, Yale University, Economic
Growth Center, February 1973.

Garth, Bryant G., et al., eds., CHINA'S CHANGING
ROLE IN THE WORLD ECONOMY, Praeger Special
Studies in International Economics and Develop-
ment, New York, Praeger in cooperation with the
National Council of U.S.-China Trade, 1975.
Nine papers, part of the Stanford Journal of
International Studies, that examine the eco-
nomic and political issues concerning China's
economic development, focusing on the acquisi-
tion and use of technology. No index. (JEL)

Gayn, Mark, "Who After Mao?" Foreign Affairs, Vol.
51, No. 2, January 1973.

Guillermaz, Jacques, THE CHINESE COMMUNIST PARTY IN
POWER, 1949-1976, Boulder, Colorado, Westview
Press, 1977. In less than a generation, the
People's Republic of China, starting practically from scratch, has raced to the fore-
front of the international stage. Today, it is
a first-rate power, acting in the concert of
nations with confidence and skill. This book

is the story of China's incredible rise. It is
conceived as history, but also as an account of
the contemporary situation, a broad, comprehensive, magisterial survey by one of the
world's eminent experts in the field. (BPA)

Gurley, John G., CHINA'S ECONOMY AND THE MAOIST
STRATEGY, New York and London, Monthly Review
Press, 1976. Eight essays (five previously
published) that recount the progress of the
Chinese economy from 1840 to the present, with
special emphasis on the period since 1949.
Writing for the layman, the author attempts to
impart "an understanding of Mao's economic
strategy and the ways it has been translated
into policies." (JEL)

Gurley, J. G., "Rural Development in China 1949-
1972, and the Lessons to be Learned from It,"
World Development, Vol. 3, Nos. 7 & 8, July-
August 1975. Rural development in China since
1949 has been based on land reforms, collectivization of agricultural production, mechanization of agriculture, and improved terms of
trade in favor of the countryside. The land
reforms redistributed wealth and income from
the rich to the poor, eliminated the former
ruling classes, and raised both peasant consumption and rural savings. Collectivization
raised rural output through better utilization
of labor. The mechanization of agriculture
further boosted output by raising labor productivity. Finally, rural development was
promoted by the lowering of prices paid by
peasants and raising those received by them.
(JEL)

Hardy, Randall W., CHINA'S OIL FUTURE: A Case of
Modest Expectations, Boulder, Colorado, Westview Press, 1978. The great merit of this
study is that it analyzes soberly the many
constraints on China's oil development and
comes to the conclusion that China is not the
potential oil giant that some writers have
contended it is. In fact, says Hardy, China in
the 1980s could well find itself more in need
of development capital from Japan and the U.S.
than those two nations are in need of oil from
China. (FA)

Hidasi, G., "China's Economy in the Mid-1970's and Its Development Perspectives," Acta Oeconomica, Vol. 14, No. 4, 1975. Based on scarce and scattered appearances of data in interviews, newspaper articles, and unofficial disclosures, the author makes an attempt to draw an overall picture of the development of the Chinese economy from 1949 to the present and to envisage future development by 2000. Data for industrial and agricultural development, net industrial and agricultural output, and national income are given, together with the production of certain crucial commodities. (JEL)

Howe, Christopher, EMPLOYMENT AND ECONOMIC GROWTH IN URBAN CHINA 1949-1957, New York, Cambridge University Press, 1971. Analyzes the size and determinants of urban employment change and traces the evolution of Chinese thinking about employment and the institutions of labor control that reflect this thinking in day-to-day administration. (BPA)

Howe, Christopher, WAGE PATTERNS AND WAGE POLICY IN MODERN CHINA 1919-1972, New York, Cambridge University Press, 1973. An analysis of changes in the level and structure of Chinese wages and of the economic aspects of the Cultural Revolution in which the author argues that wage policy can only be fully understood in relation to changes in the range of incentives to the work force. (BPA)

Hsiao, Gene T., THE FOREIGN TRADE OF CHINA: Policy, Law, and Practice, Berkeley, University of California Press, 1977. Particularly useful on the organization of the Ministry of Foreign Trade in China and on Sino-Japanese trade relations. (FA)

Institute for Asian/Pacific Studies, CHINA AFTER MAO: What Next? Occasional Paper No. 2, San Francisco, California, University of San Francisco, 1977.

Ishikawa, S., "A Note on the Choice of Technology in China," Journal of Development Studies, Vol. 9, No. 1, October 1972.

Karcher, Martin, "Unemployment and Underemployment in the People's Republic of China," reprinted from China Report 11, September-December 1975.

Keesing, D. B., "Economic Lessons from China," Journal of Development Economics, Vol. 2, No. 1, March 1975.

King, Frank H. H., A CONCISE ECONOMIC HISTORY OF MODERN CHINA (1840-1961), New York, Praeger, 1970. Dr. King struggles intelligently with inadequate statistical evidence to probe the important aspects of the Ch'ing economic system and the effects of the impact of Western intervention in China and Taiwan. (FA)

Kuo, Leslie T. C., AGRICULTURE IN THE PEOPLE'S REPUBLIC OF CHINA: Structural Changes and Technical Transformation, New York, Praeger, 1976. Part I reviews and interprets the social transformation of agriculture since the founding of the PRC in 1949 (farm organization, management, and ownership, means of production, distribution of income and production). Part II updates and expands the author's earlier study (1971) on the basis of post-Cultural Revolution sources. (BPA)

Lardy, Nicholas R., ECONOMIC GROWTH AND DISTRIBUTION IN CHINA, New York, Cambridge University Press, 1978. A solid study of resource allocation and income distribution in China which concludes that China has achieved both a rapid rate of growth and a relatively equitable distribution of income. But the author's most reliable data refer to the 1950s and 1960s. During the past decade, as he himself suggests, the Chinese growth model may have run into difficulties. Mao's "pro-peasant" policies were highly divisive, and brought about sharp declines in industrial output and strikes and work stoppages, some of which required army intervention to put down. This widespread worker unrest, combined with lagging technological progress, may help explain the switch to a new development strategy by the new leadership. Lardy's book, depicting the old development strategy as a success, does not. (FA)

Leng, Shao-chuan, ed., POST-MAO CHINA AND U.S.-CHINA
    TRADE, Charlottesville, University Press of
    Virginia, 1978. A solid collection of essays
    on Chinese-U.S. trade prospects. Robert Dern-
    berger is pessimistic about the likelihood of a
    significant increase in Chinese exports to the
    United States even considering the possibility
    of Chinese oil being exported to the United
    States or of China's being granted most-favored-
    nation status. (FA)

Lippitt, V. D., "Economic Development in Meiji Japan
    and Contemporary China: A Comparative Study,"
    Cambridge Journal of Economics, Vol. 2, No. 1,
    March 1978, pp. 55-81. This essay attempts to
    show that the basic pattern of economic devel-
    opment in Meiji Japan (1868-1912) was shaped by
    the interests of the property-owning classes--
    mainly landowners and capitalists--while that
    of China since liberation (1949) has been
    shaped by the interests of the direct pro-
    ducers--mainly poor peasants and workers.
    (JEL)

Lippitt, Victor D., LAND REFORM AND ECONOMIC DEVEL-
    OPMENT IN CHINA: A Study of Institutional
    Change and Development Finance, New York,
    International Arts and Sciences Press, 1974.
    "This understated but important work argues
    that land reform as practiced in China in the
    early 1950s...(shifted) the agricultural sur-
    plus away from rent payments to landlords who
    consumed and into tax payments to a state which
    invested. The statistical data are carefully
    selected and the mathematics is ingenious."
    (FA)

Liu, Ta-Chung and Yeh, Kung-Chia, "Chinese and Other
    Asian Economies: A Quantitative Evaluation,"
    American Economic Review, Vol. LXIII, No. 2,
    May 1973.

MacFarquhar, Roderick, THE ORIGINS OF THE CULTURAL
    REVOLUTION, 1: CONTRADICTIONS AMONG THE PEOPLE
    1956-1957, New York, Columbia University Press,
    1974. The first volume of a projected three-
    part history, this work deals with the first
    turn in China away from the Soviet model and
    with the period in which 100 flowers were to
    bloom, 100 schools of thought to contend. It

is gracefully written and comprehensively researched. (FA)

Meisner, Maurice, MAO'S CHINA: A History of the
People's Republic, New Jersey, New Publications, Macmillan Publishing Co., 1977. The
first full history of the Maoist era in China,
from the founding of the People's Republic on
October 1, 1949, to the death of Chairman Mao
on September 9, 1976. Exploring the country's
political, social, economic, and intellectual
development, the author covers every major
stage and campaign, personality and event in
modern China. He compares the Chinese experience with that of the Soviet Union, and illu-
minates problems central to every socialist
revolution. This is the most comprehensive
look yet at the critical first decades of one
of the most important national transformations
in this century. (FA)

Moorsteen, Richard and Abramowitz, Morton, REMAKING
CHINA POLICY: U.S.-China Relations and Govern-
mental Decisionmaking, Cambridge, Massachusetts,
Harvard University Press, 1971.

Murphey, Rhoads, THE OUTSIDERS: The Western Experience in India and China, Ann Arbor, University
of Michigan Press, 1977.

Myers, Ramon H., THE CHINESE PEASANT ECONOMY: Agricultural Development in Hopei and Shantung,
1890-1949, Cambridge, Massachusetts, Harvard
University Press, 1970. "An in-depth study of
the village economy in two North China provinces
based on detailed analyses of field surveys and
statistical data." (BPA)

Needham, Joseph, SCIENCE AND CIVILIZATION IN CHINA,
Vol. I, Chapter 5: Historical Introduction,
The Pre-Imperial Phase, Cambridge, Cambridge
University Press, 1954. This one chapter out of
a voluminous work on China, history and civilization, is of particular importance to students
of economic development. (Ed)

Orleans, L. A., "China's Experience in Population
Control: The Elusive Model," World Development, Vol. 3, Nos. 7 & 8, July-August 1975.

Orleans, Leo A., EVERY FIFTH CHILD: The Population
    of China, Stanford, California, Stanford Uni-
    versity Press, 1972. Careful sifting of avail-
    able evidence leads the author to enter a
    figure of approximately 800 million in the
    China population sweepstakes. He suggests that
    Chinese agriculture can feed this number; that
    population pressure will not be a motive for
    expansion; and that the ratio of Chinese to the
    world population total is not growing but
    declining. (FA)

Perkins, Dwight H., ed., CHINA'S MODERN ECONOMY IN
    HISTORICAL PERSPECTIVE, Stanford, California,
    Stanford University Press, 1975. The 10 papers
    in this volume were originally presented at a
    conference sponsored by the Subcommittee for
    Research on the Chinese Economy of the Joint
    Committee of Contemporary China of the Social
    Science Research Council and the American Coun-
    cil of Learned Societies, supported by the Ford
    Foundation. The authors examine the factors
    that have contributed most to the historical
    development of China from a traditional to a
    modern economy. (JEL)

Perkins, Dwight H., MARKET CONTROL AND PLANNING IN
    COMMUNIST CHINA, Cambridge, Massachusetts, Har-
    vard University Press, 1966.

Perkins, Dwight H., "Plans and Their Implementation
    in the People's Republic of China," American
    Economic Review, Vol. LXIII, No. 2, May 1973.

Prybyla, Jan S., THE CHINESE ECONOMY: Problems and
    Policies, Columbia, University of South Carolina
    Press, 1978. Specific topics of discussion
    are: population, agriculture, industry, money
    and banking, transportation and communications,
    domestic and foreign trade, and public health
    and education. A final chapter summarizes the
    record and considers the prospects for China's
    economic future in several areas, concluding
    that "perhaps in less than two decades, China
    will surely join the ranks of the world's eco-
    nomic powers." (JEL)

Prybyla, Jan S., "Industrial Development in China:
    1967-76 and 1976-78," Challenge, September/
    October 1978.

Pye, Lucian W., and Pye, Mary W., CHINA: An Introduction, Boston, Massachusetts, Little, Brown,
1972. A masterly introduction to the history
and politics of contemporary China. Pye's
clear-eyed and unsentimental analysis combines
concision and sweeping coverage, producing a
survey which will rank among the best in its
class.(FA)

Rawski, Thomas G., "Problems of Technology Absorption in Chinese Industry," The American
Economic Review, Vol. LXV, No. 2, May 1975.

Reynolds, L. G., "China as a Less Developed Economy,"
American Economic Review, Vol. LXV, No. 3, June
1975.

Richman, Barry, "Chinese and Indian Development: An
Interdisciplinary Environmental Analysis,"
American Economic Review, Vol. LXV, No. 2, May
1975, pp. 345-355.

Ridley, Charles P., CHINA'S SCIENTIFIC POLICIES:
Implications for International Cooperation,
American Enterprise, Institute for Public
Policy Research, Washington, D.C.; Hoover
Institution on War, Revolution and Peace,
Stanford University, Stanford, California,
1976.

Rifkin, S. B. and Kaplinsky, R., "Health Strategy
and Development Planning: Lessons from the
People's Republic of China," Journal of Development Studies, Vol. 9, No. 2, January 1973.

Scalapino, Robert A., "China and the Balance of
Power," Foreign Affairs, Vol. 52, No. 2, January 1974.

Schram, Stuart R., ed., AUTHORITY PARTICIPATION AND
CULTURAL CHANGE IN CHINA, Cambridge, London,
New York, and Melbourne, Cambridge University
Press, 1973.

Seybolt, Peter J., REVOLUTIONARY EDUCATION IN CHINA:
Documents and Commentary, White Plains, New
York, International Arts and Sciences Press,
1973.

Sidel, V. W. and Sidel, R., "The Development of
    Health Care Services in the People's Republic
    of China," World Development, Vol. 3, Nos. 7 &
    8, July-August 1975.

Sigurdson, Jon, RURAL INDUSTRIALIZATION IN CHINA,
    Harvard East Asian Monographs, No. 73, Cam-
    bridge, Massachusetts, and London, Harvard
    University, Council on East African Studies,
    distributed by Harvard University Press, 1977.
    Examines the Chinese experience in rural indus-
    trialization at the county, commune, and bri-
    gade levels. Points out that Chinese rural
    industrialization has involved two different
    elements: an industrial dualism strategy in a
    number of industrial sectors and an integrated
    rural development strategy involving health,
    education, and repair/manufacturing. (JEL)

Sigurdson, Jon, "Technology and Employment in China,"
    World Development, Vol. 2, No. 3, March 1974.
    China is solving the employment and man-power
    problems facing most developing countries
    through systematic development of rural areas
    and integration of agriculture with local
    industry. This approach is based on the as-
    sumption that a majority of China's population
    will have to remain in rural areas for a con-
    siderable period of time engaged in agriculture
    or agriculture-related activities. This in
    turn requires the urban/rural differential in
    income and employment opportunities, services
    and education/culture to be reduced. Rural
    industrialization and local technology systems
    have then become important instruments in
    achieving a more equal distribution of capital,
    knowledge and problem-solving capability, and,
    at the same time, improving overall efficiency
    of the economy. (JEL)

Stavis, Ben, "A Preliminary Model for Grain Produc-
    tion in China, 1974," The China Quarterly, No.
    65, March 1976.

Swamy, Subramanian, ECONOMIC GROWTH IN CHINA AND
    INDIA 1952-1970: A Comparative Appraisal,
    Chicago, and London, University of Chicago,
    Press, 1973. A comparative evaluation of the
    two development experiences occurring since
    stable political systems emerged in both coun-
    tries. The author recognizes the numerous

problems involved in such a comparison of national products--essentially those of scope,
grossness, and valuation--and proposes techniques for dealing with them. With extensive
use of quantitative data pertaining to the
period in question, the author covers the contribution of the agricultural sector, the
industrial production, and rates of growth of
national product, with related subtopics.
(JEL)

Tawney, R. H., LAND AND LABOR IN CHINA, introduction
by Barrington Moore Jr., New York, Harcourt,
Brace, 1932.

Terrill, Ross, "China and the World: Self-Reliance
or Interdependence?" Foreign Affairs, Vol. 55,
No. 2, January 1977.

United Nations, HEALTH CARE IN THE PEOPLE'S REPUBLIC
OF CHINA, Washington, D.C., 1975. Biblio-
graphic listings and abstracts of articles on
approaches taken by China to deliver health
care to its people, both rural and urban.
Includes an introduction on the significance of
the Chinese experience in health care with an
analysis of accomplishments and trends. Topics
cover disease control, education and training,
nutrition and family planning. (BPA)

U.S. Congress, Joint Economic Committee, CHINA: A
Reassessment of the Economy, a compendium of
papers submitted to the Joint Economic Committee, Congress of the United States, U.S.
Government Printing Office, Washington, D.C.,
1975.

Walker, Richard L., THE HUMAN COST OF COMMUNISM IN
CHINA, Washington, D.C., ACU Education and Research Institute, 1977.

Wang, K. P., THE PEOPLE'S REPUBLIC OF CHINA: A New
Industrial Power with a Strong Mineral Base,
Washington, D.C., Bureau of Mines, U.S. Depart-
ment of the Interior, 1975.

Weisskopf, Thomas E., "China and India: Contrasting
Experiences in Economic Development," American
Economic Review, Vol. LXV, No. 2, May 1975.

Whiting, Allen S., "Chinese Foreign Policy: A Workshop Report," Items Vol. 31, Nos. 1 & 2, March/
   June 1977, pp. 1-3.

Willmott, W. E., ECONOMIC ORGANIZATION IN CHINESE
   SOCIETY, Stanford, California, Stanford University Press, 1972.

Wong, John, CHINESE LAND REFORM IN RETROSPECT, LTC
   Reprint No. 113, Madison, University of Wisconsin, Land Tenure Center, 1973.

Wong, John Chiu Hon, LAND REFORM IN THE PEOPLE'S
   REPUBLIC OF CHINA: Institutional Transformation in Agriculture, New York, Praeger, 1973.

Wu, Silas H. L., COMMUNICATION AND IMPERIAL CONTROL
   IN CHINA: Evolution of the Palace Memorial
   System, 1693-1735, Cambridge, Massachusetts,
   Harvard University Press, 1970. "Based on a
   thorough examination of archival and published
   documents. Wu's work provides us with valuable
   insights into the decision-making process in
   the Ch'ing political system." (BPA)

Yang, C. K. A., A CHINESE FAMILY IN THE COMMUNIST
   REVOLUTION, Cambridge, Massachusetts, MIT
   Press, 1968. A study of the revolutionary
   transformation of the traditional Chinese
   society through an examination of recent modi-
   fications in its structural core, the family.
   (BPA)

Yang, C. K. A., A CHINESE VILLAGE IN EARLY COMMUNIST
   TRANSITION, Cambridge, MIT Press, 1968. A case
   study of the development of a Chinese village,
   showing the traditional pre-Communist agricultural society, the struggle during 1949-51 and
   the adjustments to new social and economic patterns imposed by the Communist regime. (BPA)

Hong Kong

Beazer, William F., THE COMMERCIAL FUTURE OF HONG
   KONG, New York, Praeger, 1978. Focuses on Hong
   Kong's relationship with Great Britain, China,
   the United States, and Japan. Describes Hong
   Kong's activities as an Asian financial center,

its financial importance to the Chinese, and its response to international recession. (BPA)

Geiger, Theodore, TALES OF TWO CITY-STATES: The Development Progress of Hong Kong and Singapore, assisted by Frances M. Geiger, National Planning Association Studies in Development Progress, No. 3, Washington, D.C., National Planning Association, 1973. Study that "endeavors to explain in nontechnical language the (unorthodox) means by which the two city-states have achieved their extraordinary economic growth and the benefits that have resulted therefrom in terms of full employment and rising living standards." The work presents an overview of development and a look at the Chinese sociocultural background of the two cities, jointly, and more extensive studies which examine the history, present economic activity, quality of life, and government of each city. Numerous tables present post World War II economic data for the cities. Index. (JEL)

Hopkins, Keith, ed., HONG KONG: The Industrial Colony, a Political, Social and Economic Survey, Hong Kong, London, and New York, Oxford University Press, 1971. Seven contributors join in presenting a volume which gives a detailed insight into Hong Kong, a city which has grown into a modern British industrial colony. This exciting Asian city--a tourist center, a free port, and a shipping center-- remains one of the few colonies left in the world. The Hong Kong economy has grown rapidly; the quality and variety of her exports have been impressive. Index. (JEL)

Riedel, James, THE INDUSTRIALIZATION OF HONG KONG, Tubingen, Germany, J. C. B. Mohr (Paul Siebeck), 1974. Describes Hong Kong's economic development over the last two decades, analyzing its development within the framework of orthodox economic theory. Specific consideration is given to industrialization in Hong Kong, the supply of labor, employment and wages, capital accumulation and technical changes, and the role of government. Neo-classical production theory is used, and interviews with business and government leaders have supplied the author with information and insights. No index. (JEL)

X-REF: AGRARIAN REFORM: Lehmann, AGRICULTURAL
CREDIT: Baker, AGRICULTURAL DEVELOPMENT: Agarwal,
Farmer, CHINA: Chen, Murphey, Richman, Swamy,
Weisskopf, EMPLOYMENT LABOR: Chakraborty, Gupta,
Sahoo, Uppal, ENTREPRENEURSHIP: McClelland, Naf-
ziger, FISCAL: Cutt, Panandikar, INCOME DISTRIBU-
TION PRINCIPLES: Dahiya, Gupta, ISSUES: Bauer,
MISCELLANEOUS: Day, PROJECT ANALYSIS: Muthoo,
TECHNOLOGY: Ilo, TERMS OF TRADE: Mathur.

Agarwal, N. L., and Kumawat, R. K., "Green Revolution and Capital and Credit Requirements of the
Farmers in Semi-arid Region of Rajasthan,"
Indian Journal of Agricultural Economics, Vol.
29, No. 1, 1974, pp. 67-75.

Appleyard, Dennis R., "Terms of Trade and Economic
Development: A Case Study of India," American
Economic Review, Vol. LVIII, No. 2, May 1968.

Baker, C. B. and Bhargava, Vinay K., "Financing
Small-Farm Development in India," Australian
Journal of Agricultural Economics, Vol. 18, No.
2, August 1974, pp. 101-118.

Banerji, Ranadev, THE DEVELOPMENT IMPACT OF BARTER
IN DEVELOPING COUNTRIES: The Case of India,
Washington, D.C., OECD, November 1977.

Bhagwati, Jagdish N. and Srinivasan, T. N., FOREIGN
TRADE REGIMES AND ECONOMIC DEVELOPMENT: India,
A Special Conference Series on Foreign Trade
Regimes and Economic Development, Vol. 6, New
York, Matopma; Bureau of Economic Research;
distributed by Columbia University Press, New
York, 1975. Examines India's foreign trade
regime's interaction with domestic policies and
objectives between 1950 and 1970, assessing its
efficiency and growth. Discusses the anatomy
of exchange control, focusing on 1956-66 and
examines 1966-70 with emphasis on the "liberalization episode," beginning with devaluation in
June 1966. Index. (JEL)

Bhagwati, Jagdish N., INDIA IN THE INTERNATIONAL
ECONOMY: A Policy Framework for a Progressive
Society, University Campus, Hyderabad, India,
Institute of Public Enterprise, 1973. Profes-

sor Bhagwati's 1973 Lal Bahadur Shastri Memorial Lecture delivered at the Delhi School of Economics. The author reviews the past and present structure of economic policy in India and suggests some new policy directions for the Fifth Five Year Plan, particularly in the light of changes in the international monetary system. (JEL)

Bhagwati, Jagdish N. and Desai, Padma, INDIA: Planning for Industrialization; Industrialization and Trade Policies since 1951, Industry and Trade in Some Developing Countries, New York, Oxford University Press for the Development Centre of the Organization for Economic Cooperation and Development, 1970. A comprehensive analysis of Indian planning and economic policies. Argues that "Indian economic policy suffered from a paradox of inadequate and excessive attention to detail": a lack of indepth programs on the one hand the proliferation of ill-conceived direct controls over investment and foreign trade on the other. Many of the data appear in comparable (over time) form for the first time. Bibliography; index. (JEL)

Bhatt, V. V., "A Decade of Performance of Industrial Development Bank of India," World Bank Reprint Series, No. 18, 1974.

Bhattacharya, D., "A Critical Survey of Indian Planning and Its Achievements," Economic Affairs, Vol. 18, No. 3, March 1973.

Broehl, Wayne G., Jr., THE VILLAGE ENTREPRENEUR: Change Agents in India's Rural Development, Cambridge, Massachusetts, Harvard University Press, 1978. Presents an entrepreneurial system model, which defines the nature and locus of entrepreneurship in less developed countries and explores the entrepreneurial role by observing the attitude and behavior of the fertilizer distributor and the rice miller. Examines economic activities in two community development blocks in the south of India. (JEL)

Brown, Norman, THE UNITED STATES AND INDIA, PAKISTAN, BANGLADESH, Cambridge, Massachusetts, Harvard University Press, 1972.

Chaudhuri, M. K., ed., TRENDS OF SOCIO-ECONOMIC
     CHANGE IN INDIA 1871-1961, Transactions of the
     Indian Institute of Advanced Study, Vol. 7,
     Simla, Indian Institute of Advanced Study,
     1969. Over 40 papers prepared by historians,
     sociologists, political scientists, and econo-
     mists presented to a 1967 seminar devoted to
     the Census Reports of india published decenially
     since 1872 and sponsored by the Institute.
     Index. (JEL)

Cohen, Benjamin I., THE INTERNATIONAL DEVELOPMENT OF
     INDIA AND PAKISTAN, Discussion Paper No. 171,
     New Haven, Connecticut, Yale University, Eco-
     nomic Growth Center, 1971.

Dandekar, V. M., and Rath, N., POVERTY IN INDIA, New
     Delhi, Ford Foundation, 1970.

Das, Nabagocal, THE INDIAN ECONOMY UNDER PLANNING,
     Calcutta, India, World Press Private Ltd.,
     1972. The author discusses the constraints on
     Indian economic growth, the history and prac-
     tice of planning in India, the various economic
     and social problems planners have had to con-
     sider, and the many socio-political and eco-
     nomic issues that India has yet to resolve.
     Index. (JEL)

Franda, Marcus F., ed., RESPONSES TO POPULATION
     GROWTH IN INDIA: Changes in Social, Political,
     and Economic Behavior, New York, Praeger, 1975.
     Investigates the ways in which India's basic
     societal institutions have responded, as com-
     pared with the drastic changes that have been
     made in response to population growth in
     China's institutional structures. (BPA)

Frankel, Francine R., INDIA'S GREEN REVOLUTION:
     Economic Gains and Political Costs, written
     under the auspices of the Center of Inter-
     national Studies, Princeton, New Jersey,
     Princeton University Press, 1971. The author
     looks into the socio-economic and political
     aspects of India's "green revolution"--a new
     strategy of rapid agricultural modernization.
     The study "...represents a preliminary as-
     sessment of the impact of modern technology,
     including the High Yielding Varieties Program,
     on patterns of income distribution among vari-
     ous classes of agriculturists; the stability of

traditional patron-client relationships between landowners and the landless; and types of political participation among the peasantry." Glossary; appendices; index. (JEL)

Gadgil, D. R., PLANNING AND ECONOMIC POLICY IN INDIA, Poona, Gokhale Institute of Politics and Economics; distributed by Orient Longman, Bombay, 1972. A series of notes, memoranda, etc., connected with planning in India and policy of government from 1955 to 1966. Employment and social policy, the public interest, big business, and monopoly and concentration are covered. (BPA)

Ghosh, R., "Achievements of Five Year Plans in India," Economic Affairs, Vol. 17, Nos. 1-2, January-February 1972.

Ghosh, B. C., "How Far Has Mixed Economy Succeeded in India?" Economic Affairs, Vol. 16, No. 12, December 1971.

ILO, GENERATING EMPLOYMENT FOR THE EDUCATED IN INDIA, A Report on a Mission to India by the Asian Regional Team for Employment Promotion, Geneva, International Labour Office, 1975.

Jannuzi, F. Tomasson, AGRARIAN CRISIS IN INDIA: The Case of Bihar, Austin, University of Texas Press, 1974. The Congress Party has talked of "agrarian reform" since independence, but land holdings are still vastly unequal, productivity low, and multitudes chronically undernourished. Professor Jannuzi suggests a minimal program to ensure water, seeds, fertilizer, electricity, credit, and security of tenure for the small farmer. But he is not hopeful about its realizations. (FA)

Joshi, Puran Chandra, LAND REFORMS IN INDIA: Trends and Perspectives, Bombay: Allied Publishers, 1975, Institute of Economic Growth, Delhi, Studies in Economic Growth, #19.

Krueger, Anne O., THE BENEFITS AND COSTS OF IMPORT SUBSTITUTION IN INDIA: A Micro-Economic Study, Minneapolis, University of Minnesota Press, 1975.

Lakshmanan, M. S., ECONOMIC DEVELOPMENT IN INDIA,
Delhi, India, Hindustan; distributed by International Scholarly Book Services, 1974. A
study of India's recent economic growth experience since 1951 with particular emphasis on the
role of the foreign sector. There is a review
of India's various economic plans since 1951,
of the behavior of the country's balance of
payments, the extent of foreign capital inflows,
the role of international economic and aid
agencies, the trends in her foreign trade, and
the nature of her commercial policy. No index.
(JEL)

Mahajan, V. S., SOCIALISTIC PATTERN IN INDIA: An
Assessment, New Delhi, S. Chand, 1974. The
core of the investigation analyzes the growth
of agriculture, industry, and the social infrastructure in the last two decades and evaluates
the contribution of each to the realization of
the socialistic organization. The study concludes that by following policies designed to
keep the country somewhere between socialism
and capitalism, "the Indian Government has
already created more frustration among the
people than won sympathies." Selected bibliography; index. (JEL)

Mandelbaum, David G., HUMAN FERTILITY IN INDIA: Social Components and Policy Perspectives,
Berkeley, University of California Press, 1974.

Mellor, John W., THE NEW ECONOMICS OF GROWTH: A
Strategy for India and the Developing World, A
Twentieth Century Fund Study, Ithaca, New York,
Cornell University Press, 1976. Advocates a
"rural-led, employment-oriented strategy of
economic growth...for India and many other
countries as well." While concerned that absolute income rises for the poor will not improve
their relative position, the author believes
that this strategy improving agricultural output, will have "a consequent multiplier effect
on growth" and will thereby expand employment
opportunities. Urges abandoning high technology for industry, accepting open trade
arrangements, accepting foreign technical
advice, and supporting minimum capital-intensive but maximum labor-intensive projects.
Index. (JEL)

307

Mellor, John W., ed., INDIA: A RISING MIDDLE POWER,
Boulder, Colorado Westview Press, 1979. A collection of essays covering the following topics: India and the U.S.; the political impact
of foreign assistance; the Congress party and
the bureaucratic state; economic growth; India's
world role; regional power in a multipolar
world; India and nuclear nonproliferation; science and technology; trade prospects; and
American aid. (BPA)

Minhas, B. S., "Rural Poverty, Land Redistribution
and Development," Indian Economic Review, Vol.
V, No. 1, April 1970.

Mishra, G. P., "Planning and Land Reform Policy in
India," Economic Affairs, Vol. 18, No. 5, May
1973.

Nafziger, E. Wayne, "Entrepreneurship, Social Mobil-
ity, and Income Redistribution in South India,"
American Economic Review, Vol. 67, No. 1,
February 1977.

Ojha, P. D. and Bhatt, V. V., "Pattern of Income
Distribution in India: 1953-55 to 1963-65,"
World Bank Reprint Series, No. 18, 1974.

Panandikar, D. H. Pai, INTEREST RATES AND FLOW OF
FUNDS, A CASE STUDY: India, Macmillan, 1973.

Repetto, Robert C., TIME IN INDIA'S DEVELOPMENT PRO-
GRAMMES, Harvard Economic Studies, Vol. 137,
Cambridge, Massachusetts, Harvard University
Press, 1971. Studies the alternative economic
decisions in the use of scarce capital resources in India, centering on the need for the application of appropriate rates of time discount. Benefit-cost comparisons of some programs are presented in this empirical study
with discount rates ranging from seven to 15
percent. Bibliography; index. (JEL)

Rosen, George, PEASANT SOCIETY IN A CHANGING ECONOMY:
Comparative Development in Southeast Asia and
India, Chicago, University of Illinois Press,
1975. Applies an interdisciplinary framework
to study development in the Philippines, Indonesia, and Thailand. Provides three interpre-
tative essays on these countries and a shorter
one on India. The author attempts "to relate

the structures of rural society to political
processes and economic policies. "The last
part of the book compares the basic similarities in the social structures of the countries
and makes suggestions for similar common
policies for economic development. Index.
(JEL)

Roy, Asishaumar, THE STRUCTURE OF INTEREST RATES IN
    INDIA, Calcutta, India, World Press, 1975.

Shenoy, Sudha R., INDIA: Progress or Poverty? A
    Review of the Outcome of Central Planning in
    India, 1951-1969, Research Monograph No. 27,
    Westminster, England, Institute of Economic
    Affairs, 1971. A monograph that evaluates the
    Five-Year Plans of the Government of India
    during the decades of the 1950s and '60s,
    bringing out "...the failure of the Indian
    plans to achieve their declared aims (and)...
    their fundamental misconception of clear con-
    cepts of the (Indian's) primary needs." This
    failure stemmed principally from the fact that
    the Indian government placed priority on indus-
    trialization over agricultural development,
    land reform, and creation of agricultural
    credit facilities. The magnitude of the food
    imports needed to feed the huge population of
    India resulted in increased trade and exchange
    deficits during the period, necessitating
    recourse to foreign aid to finance most of the
    total imports. Contains 39 tables on agricul-
    tural and economic data for India. No index.
    Note on sources. (BPA)

Singh, Tarlok, INDIA'S DEVELOPMENT EXPERIENCE,
    London: Macmillan, 1974.

Srinivasan, T. N. and Bardhan, P. K., eds., POVERTY
    AND INCOME DISTRIBUTION IN INDIA, Calcutta,
    India, Statistical Publishing Society, 1974.
    The volume presents 23 articles dedicated to
    the memory of Pitambar Pant (1919-1973), a
    senior co-worker of Professor P. C. Mahalanobis.
    Eight of the articles have been published pre-
    viously. The authors, all Indians, are con-
    cerned with the methods of eliminating poverty,
    the pattern and trends in income distribution,
    and the evaluation of policies that have been
    pursued with the reduction of inequality of in-
    comes as the objective. Discussion integrates

both quantitative information and policy aspects of income distribution. A bibliography is given after each article. No index. (JEL)

United Nations, Department of Economic and Social Affairs, POVERTY, UNEMPLOYMENT, AND DEVELOPMENT POLICY: A Case Study of Selected Issues with Reference to Kerala, New York, Author, 1975.

Veit, Lawrence A., INDIA'S SECOND REVOLUTION: The Dimensions of Development, A Council on Foreign Relations Book, New York, McGraw-Hill, 1976. Study of the economic development of India, which makes frequent reference to social and political forces, domestic and international. Investigates the derivation of political power; India's international relations with the West, Communist countries, and multinational bodies; and the making and implementation of Indian economic policy. (JEL)

Indonesia

X-REF: INCOME DISTRIBUTION PRINCIPLES: van Ginneken, INDIA: Rosen, POVERTY: Papanek, URBAN DEVELOPMENT: Ilo.

Carlson, Sevine, INDONESIA'S OIL, Westview Special Studies in Natural Resources and Energy Management, Boulder, Colorado, Westview Press, 1977. Studies the politics and economics of Indonesia's oil, emphasizing the importance of oil to the country's economic development. Discusses in particular the development of the industry, its present and future prospects, and the country's position in and attitude toward OPEC. (JEL)

Crouch, Harold, THE ARMY AND POLITICS IN INDONESIA, Ithaca, New York, Cornell University Press, 1978. Both in Indonesia and the West, there has been widespread hope that the army-dominated government, which took over when Sukarno's "Guided Democracy" collapsed in 1965, would at last open the way to prosperity and progress. Crouch's book represents one of the most complete accounts to date of why these hopes have not been realized. He portrays a struggle between the "technocrats" pursuing development

310

and the "financial" generals pursuing their own
interests and impeding development. (FA)

Fryer, Donald W. and Jackson, James C., INDONESIA,
    Boulder, Colorado, Westview Press, 1977. Pro-
    fessors Fryer and Jackson's analysis of the
    country's complex history suggests that many of
    its most intractable difficulties originated in
    the nature of Indonesian society and were com-
    pounded by the experience of the Japanese occu-
    pation and World War II. During the postwar
    decades the Sukarno regime plunged the economy
    into chaos, a situation which Suharto's New
    Order has set about repairing--in a speci-
    fically Indonesian way. The authors explore in
    detail the dichotomy between the indigenous
    agricultural and the modern economies, with
    special reference to oil, and conclude that
    Indonesia still has grave economic burdens
    ahead. (BPA)

Gautama, Sudargo (Gouwgioksiong); Allan, David E.;
    Hiscock, Mary E.; and Roebuck, Derek, CREDIT
    AND SECURITY IN INDONESIA: The Legal Problems
    of Development Finance, New York, Crane, 1973.
    First of a projected 10-volume series on law
    and development finance in Asia, this volume
    surveys the legal aspects of financing private
    development through loans. Examines the inter-
    action of Western law and native (adat) law,
    commercial practices, policies of financiers,
    and the needs of the community in an effort to
    determine the extent to which the legal system
    and security laws constrain the free flow of
    development finance. Bibliography, index.
    (JEL)

Gupta, Syamaprasad, A MODEL FOR INCOME DISTRIBUTION,
    EMPLOYMENT, AND GROWTH: A Case Study of Indo-
    nesia, assisted by Ellen Anderson and Ronald
    Padual, World Bank Staff Occasional Paper, No.
    24, Baltimore, Maryland, Johns Hopkins Univer-
    sity Press for the World Bank, 1977. Presents
    a comparatively disaggregated general equi-
    librium model, consisting of a set of nonlinear
    equations, which explores the trade-offs be-
    tween growth and equity, growth and employment,
    and growth and poverty in Indonesia within the
    long-term context of various development
    strategies. (JEL)

International Labor Organization, JAKARTA: Urban
    Development and Employment, Geneva, ILO, 1977.

Lipsky, Seth, and Pura, Raphael, "Indonesia: Test-
    ing Time for the "New Order," Foreign Affairs,
    Vol. 57, No. 1, Fall 1978, pp. 186-202.

Palmer, Ingrid, THE INDONESIAN ECONOMY SINCE 1966,
    London, Frank Cass, 1977. This book divides
    the new Indonesian economy into endogenous and
    exogenous parts to highlight the great gulf
    between 'growth' and 'development', the failure
    of the macro indicators to affect real mass
    living standards. (BPA)

Papanek, Gustav F., "The Poor of Jakarta," Economic
    Development and Culture Change, October 1975.

Sievers, Allen M., THE MYSTICAL WORLD OF INDONESIA:
    Culture and Economic Development in Conflict,
    Baltimore, Johns Hopkins University Press,
    1974. In this panorama of Indonesian society,
    an economist who doesn't mind using nonquanti-
    fiable variables argues that only fundamental
    changes in the traditional value system can
    make possible either political democracy or
    economic welfare in the abysmally impoverished
    peasant villages. The unorthodox thesis is
    presented subtly and readably. (FA)

Talmer, Ingrid, TEXTILES IN INDONESIA: Problems of
    Import Substitution, Praeger Special Studies in
    International Economics and Development, New
    York, Praeger, 1972.

Iran

X-REF: INCOME DISTRIBUTION PRINCIPLES: Looney,
MISCELLANEOUS: Farmanfermaian.

Amirsadeghi, Hossein, ed., TWENTIETH CENTURY IRAN,
    New York, Homes and Meier, 1977. Eight excel-
    lent essays on modern Iran covering such topics
    as the reigns of Riza Shah and of the (deposed)
    Shah, development of the oil industry, social
    transformation, foreign policy, and Iran's
    future strategic role. (FA)

312

Amuzegar, Jahangir, IRAN: An Economic Profile,
Washington, D.C., Middle East Institute, 1977.
The profile takes the form of a handbook con-
taining much useful information, an almost
colorless discussion of policies, and an offi-
cial glimpse into the future. The author is
Iran's Principal Resident Representative to the
IMF and World Bank. (FA)

Aresvik, Oddvar, THE AGRICULTURAL DEVELOPMENT OF
IRAN, New York, Praeger, 1976. Covers Iran's
agricultural development from 1900 to its
present oil-rich economy. Predicts the results
of abundant government funding for large-scale
agriculture, and its probable impact on the
economic and social conditions of farmers.
Shows how the "White Revolution" (land reform)
hampered the start of the Green Revolution,
that the trend is toward farm corporations,
production co-ops, and meat and dairy complexes.
(BPA)

Baldwin, George B., PLANNING AND DEVELOPMENT IN
IRAN, Baltimore, Maryland, Johns Hopkins Press,
1967.

Bharier, Julian, ECONOMIC DEVELOPMENT IN IRAN, 1900-
1970, New York, Oxford University Press, 1971.
"The aim of this book is to document the changes which have occurred in Iran since the beginning of the twentieth century, both in the
economy as a whole and in individual sectors,
and to assess their effects on development."
Starting with a composite picture of the
Iranian economy in 1900, it discusses development of the economy as a whole, the role of the
state, the problems and issues of various
sectors, and concludes with a discussion of the
state of the economy in 1970 and the prospect
for the seventies. Bibliography; index. (JEL)

Cottam, Richard W., NATIONALISM IN IRAN, second edition, Pittsburgh, Pennsylvania, University of
Pittsburgh Press, 1979. In a new forty-page
chapter, the author enlarges his earlier study
of nationalism by examining the conditions of
Iran in 1978, including the economic and political changes of recent years. He discusses in
detail the Shah's use of the Iranian security organization and his unsuccessful efforts to use

313

symbol manipulation to arouse sentiment in his
favor. (BPA)

Fesharaki, Feraidum, DEVELOPMENT OF THE IRANIAN OIL
    INDUSTRY: International and Domestic Aspects,
    New York, Praeger, 1976. Traces Iran's oil
    industry development since 1900. Shows the
    transition from a foreign-operated to a modern
    sophisticated industry that has produced eco-
    nomic growth in Iran. (BPA)

ILO, EMPLOYMENT AND INCOME POLICIES FOR IRAN, Geneva,
    International Labour Office, 1973.

Katouzian, M. A., "Land Reform in Iran--A Case Study
    in the Political Economy of Social Engineering,"
    The Journal of Present Studies, Vol. 1, No. 2,
    1974, pp. 220-239.

Lambton, A.K.S., THE PERSIAN LAND REFORM, 1962-1966,
    Oxford University Press, 1969.

Lenczowski, George, ed., IRAN UNDER THE PAHLAVIS,
    Stanford, California, Hoover Institution, 1978.

Looney, Robert E., A DEVELOPMENT STRATEGY FOR IRAN
    THROUGH THE 1980s, Praeger Special Studies in
    International Economics and Development, New
    York, Praeger, 1977. In an attempt to under-
    stand Iran's medium-term development prospects,
    the author begins by providing a long-term
    overview of the country's development efforts
    and accomplishments and by examining evolu-
    tionary patterns in key economic, social, and
    political sectors. The emphasis then shifts to
    a discussion on the sources and consequences of
    growth and the major problems that face Iran in
    the future; lessons are then drawn from other
    similar countries, namely Iraq, Venezuela,
    Algeria, and Ecuador. (JEL)

Looney, Robert E., IRAN AT THE END OF THE CENTURY:
    A Hegelian Forecast, Lexington, Massachusetts,
    Lexington Books, 1977. Iran shows a rate of
    growth that could make it a major power by the
    end of the century. Strategies and policies
    necessary to ensure such success are discussed
    in this work. The authors seek to make a long-
    run forecast of the Iranian economy by inte-
    grating the modern analytical tools of eco-
    nomics with a theory of cultural change derived

from Hegel. For the economist, the specialist
in Middle East studies, and professionals
involved with oil-related issues. Appendixes,
notes, bibliography, figures, tables. (BPA)

Wilber, Donald N., IRAN: Past and Present, Princeton, New Jersey, Princeton University Press,
1975.

Iraq

Gabbay, Rony, COMMUNISM AND AGRARIAN REFORM IN IRAQ,
London, Croom Helm, 1978. A painstaking monograph on the Iraqi Communist Party's advocacy
of and involvement with agrarian reform, and
its contribution to the radicalization of Iraqi
society, based mainly on the party's own
literature. (FA)

Jalal, Ferhang, THE ROLE OF GOVERNMENT IN THE INDUS-
TRIALIZATION OF IRAQ, 1950-1965, London, Frank
Cass, 1972. The government of Iraq has adopted
a number of policies designed to promote growth
of the industrial sector. Dr. Jalal analyses
and appraises these policies: the establishment of enterprises financed, constructed and
operated by the government, and the encourage-
ment of the expansion of private industrial
enterprise by protecting it from foreign competition. (BPA)

Khadduri, Majid, SOCIALIST IRAQ: A Study in Iraqi
Politics since 1968, Washington, Middle East
Institute, 1978. Once again Professor Khadduri
puts Western readers in his debt. In com-
pleting his trilogy on the politics of Iraq
since independence, he uses his unique quali-
fications and sources to provide a wealth of
information on the little-known recent history
of that country. With scholarly objectivity he
generally lets the documents and the main
actors--Baathists, Communists and others, many
of whom he interviewed--speak for themselves.
The result, for better or for worse, is to
present the regime almost at face value. (FA)

Penrose, Edith and E. F., IRAQ: International Relations and National Development, Boulder, Colorado, Westview Press, 1978. An excellent his-

torical and descriptive study, drawing heavily
on the work of Khadduri, Longrigg and others on
the political side and on the authors' own formidable knowledge of economics and the oil industry. Sympathetic to the Iraqi people but
coldly realistic about the failings of the political leadership and the inadequacies of
economic policy. (FA)

Israel

X-REF: MISCELLANEOUS: Kalecki, PLANNING: Lerner,
RURAL DEVELOPMENT: Don.

Chenery, Hollis B., and Bruno, Michael, DEVELOPMENT
ALTERNATIVES IN AN OPEN ECONOMY: The Case of
Israel, Research Center in Economic Growth,
Reprint #22, Stanford, California, Stanford
University, 1962.

Globerson, Ayre, HIGHER EDUCATION AND EMPLOYMENT IN
ISRAEL, New York, Praeger, 1978. The author
examines the need to gear university courses to
labor market demands, the relationship between
university location and regional development,
job satisfaction and utilization of studies at
the undergraduate and graduate levels, and the
attitudes of graduates toward occupational
training. (BPA)

Greenberg, Harold I., and Nadler, Samuel, POVERTY IN
ISRAEL: Economic Realities and the Promise of
Social Justice, New York, Praeger, 1977. Examines differences in socio-economic status
among ethnic groups, and presents extensive
data on educational levels, income, occupation,
health, mortality, family size, and nature of
social welfare programs. Explores Israeli response in terms of ethical tradition, governmental programs, assistance agencies, pressure
groups, and protest movements. Compares
Israeli problems with U.S. poverty issues,
including popular dislike of government-spon-
sored welfare, inefficiency of government
welfare programs, and constraints placed on
these programs by defense priorities. (BPA)

Horowitz, David, THE ENIGMA OF ECONOMIC GROWTH: A Case Study of Israel, Praeger Special Studies in International Economics and Development, New York, Praeger, 1972. An in-depth analysis of the forces and pattern of economic growth peculiar to Israel during the years 1950-1970. Gives special attention to Israel's unique experience in population transplantation and capital importation. No index. (JEL)

Japan

X-REF: AGRARIAN REFORM: Chao, Smith, AGRICULTURAL DEVELOPMENT: Hayami, CHINA: Lippitt, FOREIGN AID: Loutfi.

Austin, Lewis, ed., JAPAN: The Paradox of Progress, assisted by Adrienne Suddard and Nancy Remington, New Haven, Connecticut, Yale University Press, 1976. Eleven previously unpublished papers on identifying and analyzing elements likely to shape the future of Japan. The articles address one of the three areas: political variables that will affect the direction of change and the political processes, economic variables such as land, labor, capital, structure of trade, technology, and investment; and the values themselves "that will give content and direction to the process of attempted control." Index. (JEL)

Bieda, K., THE STRUCTURE AND OPERATION OF THE JAPANESE ECONOMY, New York, Wiley, 1970. Analytic clarity, a sardonic originality and a profusion of relevant and statistical data make Bieda's book the best study of the overall functioning of the modern Japanese economy yet to appear. (FA)

Boltho, Andrea, JAPAN: An Economic Survey, 1953-1973, Economics of the World, New York, Oxford University Press, 1975. Summarizes the development, structure, and performance of the Japanese economy in the period 1953-73. Analyzes the role of the government in the growth process, the importance of foreign trade, and the role of the distribution of income in Japan's growth. Selected reading list; index. (JEL)

317

Broadbridge, Seymour A., INDUSTRIAL DUALISM IN
JAPAN: A Problem of Economic Growth and Structural Change, Chicago, Illinois, Aldine Publishing Co., 1966.

CED, TOWARD A NEW INTERNATIONAL ECONOMIC SYSTEM: A
Joint Japanese-American View, by Keizai Doyukai,
New York, CED Publications, 1974. Urges the
United States, Japan and Western Europe to join
together and adopt measures that would make the
international economic system capable of easing
political tensions generated by economic differences and of accommodating conditions of
post-cold war era. The recommendations prepared jointly with the Japan Committee for Economic Development "command serious attention
from governments and the international business
community." (BPA)

Denison, Edward F. and Chung, William K., HOW JAPAN'S
ECONOMY GREW SO FAST: The Sources of Postwar
Expansion, Washington, D.C., The Brookings
Institution, 1976. This book, partly an outgrowth of work on Asia's New Giant: How the
Japanese Economy Works is an investigation of
the sources of Japanese economic growth (1953-
71) wherein the authors stress that "the extra-
ordinarily rapid growth...was made possible...
by the economic backwardness of Japan in relation to the United States at the beginning of
the (post-war) period." Compares growth with
five industrial countries and identifies the
sources and determinants of growth. Index.
(JEL) (See Patrick, below)

Doyudai, Keizai, HOW THE UNITED STATES AND JAPAN SEE
EACH OTHER'S ECONOMY: An Exchange of Views Between the American and Japanese Committees for
Economic Development, New York, CED Publications, 1974. Provides studies made by panels
from each group as a means of deepening understanding and determining differences in each
economy. "The consensus it represents is
something to reckon with...a tactfully worded,
yet mainly candid view of economic neighbors--
and rivals." (BPA)

318

Fodella, Gianni, ed., SOCIAL STRUCTURES AND ECONOMIC
DYNAMICS IN JAPAN UP TO 1980, Series on East
Asian Economy and Society, Vol. 1, Milan,
Italy, Luigi Bocconi University, Institute of
Economic and Social Studies for East Asia,
1975. Essays examine the future dynamics of
Japan's socioeconomic system, approaching
problems from anthropological, political,
sociological, international, and organizational
angles. The papers fall into one of six sections: interpersonal relations, family; labor;
society; economy, domestic; and economy, external. The contributors include sociologists,
historians, economists, writers, and government
officials. No index. (JEL)

Frank, Isaiah, ed., THE JAPANESE ECONOMY IN INTERNA-
TIONAL PERSPECTIVE, a supplementary paper of
the Committee for Economic Development, Baltimore, Maryland, Johns Hopkins University Press,
1975. Includes 10 original essays discussing
the economic institutions and policies of
Japan. Essays are concerned with aspects of
the Japanese economy affecting its external
relations. The essays cover: the economic
implications of the changing American and
Japanese security roles in Asia, Japan's industrial policy, an appraisal of the Japanese
economic policy from 1960 to 1972, Japanese
distribution of income and wealth, political
influences on the Japanese farmer, aspects of
foreign trade, Japan's fiscal incentives to
export, a comparison of raw materials policy in
the United States and Japan, Japanese foreign
direct investment, and international corporate
investment in Japan. Index. (JEL)

Hanley, Susan B. and Yamamura, Kozo, ECONOMIC AND
DEMOGRAPHIC CHANGE IN PREINDUSTRIAL JAPAN,
1600-1868, Princeton, New Jersey, Princeton
University Press, 1977. The authors suggest
that the Japanese economy grew throughout the
Tokugawa period, though slowly by modern standards and unevenly. This growth, they show,
tended to exceed the rate of population increase
even in the poorer regions, thus raising the
living standard despite major famines. (BPA)

Hatani, Kanji, THE JAPANESE ECONOMIC SYSTEM: An
Institutional Overview, Lexington, Massachusetts, Heath, Lexington Books, 1976. Describes

the institutional characteristics of the Japanese economy, including relevant political and social institutions. Includes discussions of the educational system, government bureaucracy, business organization, industrial relations and organization, money and banking, and fiscal policy. Index. (JEL)

Havens, Thomas R. H., FARM AND NATION IN MODERN JAPAN: Agrarian Nationalism, 1870-1940, Princeton, New Jersey, Princeton University Press, 1974. Japan's entry into the modern world of the bureaucratic state left much of the population resentful, nostalgic, and confused, and nurtured the ideologists of Nōhonshugi--"the farm is the basis." Havens portrays with insight and sympathy the ironic fate of this rural-romantic movement--where idealization of harmony led to violence, respect for self-rule to imperial adventures. (FA)

Henderson, Dan Fenno, FOREIGN ENTERPRISE IN JAPAN: Law and Policies, Chapel Hill, University of North Carolina Press (for the American Society of International Law), 1973. A cogent, factual volume, the fifth in a series examining the legal framework for U.S. investment in selected areas abroad. The author concludes that the widely varying American and Japanese attitudes toward law and the legal system make arbitration, not litigation, the best means of resolving disputes in cases of foreign investment. (FA)

Hirschmeier, Johannes, and Tsunehiko Yui, THE DEVELOPMENT OF JAPANESE BUSINESS, 1600-1973, Cambridge, Massachusetts, Harvard University Press, 1975.

Hirschmeier, Johannes, THE ORIGINS OF ENTREPRENEURSHIP IN MEIJI, JAPAN, Cambridge, Massachusetts, Harvard University Press, 1964.

Japan Institute of International Affairs, THE OIL CRISIS--ITS IMPACT ON JAPAN AND ASIA, Tokyo, Japan Institute of International Affairs.

Johnson, Chalmers, JAPAN'S PUBLIC POLICY COMPANIES, Washington, American Enterprise Institute/ Stanford, Hoover Institution, 1978. A provoca-

320

tive study of the government-business relationship in Japan and why it works so well. One
clue is the Japanese government's skillful use
of public corporations along the lines of the
American TVA. Such corporations are one of the
ways in which the world's second largest industrial society gets its public work done. Johnson concludes that the West could profit from
Japan's experience. The Japanese government
gets more for its money but actually spends
less than comparable governments elsewhere,
even though it plays a very active role in all
phases of economic life. (FA)

Kelly, Allen C. and Williamson, Jeffrey G., LESSONS
FROM JAPANESE DEVELOPMENT: An Analytical Economic History, Chicago, Illinois, University of
Chicago Press, 1974. Is nineteenth-century
Japan a model for growth in the Third World
today? The authors conclude that small agricultural growth and shifts to industry were the
fortuitous (and inimitable) result of a combination of high factor productivity growth,
inelastic land supply and low population pressure. Two lessons, however, can be copied:
military spending cuts income growth, and low-
income elasticity of demand for food fosters
growth. (FA)

Kershner, Thomas R., JAPANESE FOREIGN TRADE, Lexington, Massachusetts, Lexington Books, 1975. It
is almost a cliche that the Japanese economic
role in Pacific Asia may be viewed as a continuation by peaceful means of the ideal of the
Greater East Asian Co-Prosperity Sphere. The
author argues persuasively that the Japanese
surplus of capital and the Asian surplus of
materials all but require such a relationship:
if Japan did not exist, Asia would have to in-
vent her. (FA)

Kitamura, Hiroshi, CHOICES FOR THE JAPANESE ECONOMY,
London, The Royal Institute of International
Affairs, 1976. Examines the basic issues confronting the Japanese economy in the 1970's,
including the fact of the oil crisis. The
author sees Japanese economy, which had experienced an unprecedented rate of growth after
World War II, due primarily to high levels of
investment, moving to a "more balanced" growth
path in the 1970's. The author presents the

basic elements of postwar Japanese domestic development in part one. Part two presents the
international aspects of Japan's economic position and sees Japan reducing its material and
energy imports in the future and expanding its
chemical and machine exports and investments in
these industries abroad. Index. (JEL)

Kojima, Kiyoshi, JAPAN AND A NEW WORLD ECONOMIC
ORDER, Boulder, Colorado, Westview Press; London, Croom Helm, 1977. Examines the position
of the Japanese economy before and after the
oil crisis in October 1973 and Japan's attitude
towards the prospects for the Tokyo Round of
trade negotiations. Discusses the reform of
the international monetary system, noting that
managed floating exchange rates are a necessary
evil for the time being. Analyzes the characteristics of two different types of foreign
direct investments trade-oriented (the Japanese
model) and anti-trade-oriented (the American
model) and argues that the Japanese approach
contributes effectively to the gradual transfer
of manufacturing industries to developing
countries, while American foreign direct investment made from a position of comparative advantage results in balance-of-payments difficulties and trade protectionism. Index. (JEL)

Kruihara, Kenneth K., THE GROWTH POTENTIAL OF THE
JAPANESE ECONOMY, Baltimore, Maryland, Johns .
Hopkins Press, 1971. Professor Kurihara sees
the reasons for Japan's leadership in the
growth rate competition (a secular rate of
growth of national income of 42.3 percent over
the last century, highest in the world), in the
coupling of a "delicate and intricate tradition
of state paternalism" with an urgently felt and
universally shared need to "catch up." (FA)

Marsh, Robert M. and Mannari, Hiroshi, MODERNIZATION
AND THE JAPANESE FACTORY, Princeton, New Jersey
and London, Princeton University Press, 1976.
Study of the sociology of complex organizations,
relating three sets of variables--technological
modernization, the modernization of social organization, and organizational performance or
effectiveness--at the level of the manufacturing
firm and its subunits. Deals with the problem
of the validity of the paternalism-lifetime
commitment model of the Japanese factory and

322

examines the convergence theory of modernization. Bibliography; index. (JEL)

Minami, Ryoshin, THE TURNING POINT IN ECONOMIC DEVELOPMENT: Japan's Experience, The Institute of Economic Research, Hitotsubash University, Economic Research Series No. 14, Tokyo, Kinokuniya Bookstore, 1973.

Minami, Ryoshin, THE TURNING POINT IN THE JAPANESE ECONOMY, New Haven, Connecticut, Yale University, Economic Growth Center, 1968.

Minami, Ryoshin, FURTHER CONSIDERATIONS ON THE TURNING POINT IN THE JAPANESE ECONOMY, Center Paper #158, New Haven, Connecticut, Yale University, Economic Growth Center, 1970.

Nakayama, Shigeru; Swain, David L.; and Yagi, Eric, SCIENCE AND SOCIETY IN MODERN JAPAN, Cambridge, Massachusetts, MIT Press, 1973. Documents Japan's modernization (by Imperial flat), the depression, nationalistic totalitarianism, and the disastrous war against which Japanese scientists were forced to confront their relations as professionals to a society launched toward tragedy. (BPA)

Ohkawa, Kagushi; Johnson, Bruce F.; and Kaneda, Hiromitsu; eds., AGRICULTURE AND ECONOMIC GROWTH: Japan's Experience, Tokyo, Tokyo University Press and Princeton, Princeton University Press, 1968.

Ohkawa, Kazushi and Rosovsky, Henry, JAPANESE ECONOMIC GROWTH: Trend Acceleration in the Twentieth Century, Studies of Economic Growth in Industrialized Countries, Stanford, California, Stanford University Press; London, Oxford University Press, 1973. A comprehensive analysis of Japan's 20th century economic growth experiences with special emphasis on the post-World War II record. A brief historical introduction, a review of the growth of major economic aggregates, and estimation of an aggregate production function for the private sector, an analysis of sectoral growth and the role of technological progress, a study of the demand for and supply of Japanese labor, a survey of the behavior of key components of aggregate demand, and an examination of the

impact of the foreign sector on the Japanese
economy. (JEL)

Okochi, Kazuo, et al., eds., WORKERS AND EMPLOYERS
IN JAPAN: The Japanese Employment Relations
System, Princeton, New Jersey, Princeton University Press/Tokyo, University of Tokyo Press,
1974. A star-studded group of labor economists
looks at the Japanese scene with its characteristics of lifetime employment, promotion by
seniority, and the company union. They note
that collective bargaining and the strike were
legitimized by U.S. pressure but comment, in-
scrutably, "it is not clear why." The group
fudges on the question of whether "convergence"
is inevitable in the social forms of industrial
societies. (FA)

Organisation for Economic Co-operation and Development, OECD ECONOMIC SURVEYS: Japan, Paris,
1978. Annual report, reviewing recent trends
in demand, output, prices, and wages; comments
on the situation of the corporate sector; and
discusses the developments in the balance of
payments. (JEL)

Ozaki, Robert S., THE CONTROL OF IMPORTS AND FOREIGN
CAPITAL IN JAPAN, New York, Praeger, 1972.
Both U.S. and European business communities
have accused Japan of unreasonable and illegal
restrictions on foreign investment, while
deploring Japanese penetration of their own
bailiwicks. Ozaki, however, has provided a
view of the situation which is both a valuable
compendium of Japanese legislation and policy
statements and an analysis of how, under certain
circumstances, a policy of limited and strategic protectionism can work spectacularly well.
(FA)

Ozawa, Terutomo, JAPAN'S TECHNOLOGICAL CHALLENGE TO
THE WEST, 1950-1974: Motivation and Accomp-
lishment, Cambridge, Massachusetts, MIT Press,
1974. In this thoroughly documented analysis,
the author finds the key to Japanese economic
dynamism in two factors: the applicability of
the Schumpeterian model of development, where
innovation stimulates growth, and the intensity
of the national need to catch and surpass the
West. (FA)

Patrick, Hugh and Rosovsky, Henry, eds., ASIA'S NEW
    GIANT: How the Japanese Economy Works, Wash-
    ington, D.C., The Brookings Institution, 1976.
    Thirteen research studies examine the various
    facets of the management of the Japanese econo-
    my over the past 20 years. Topics include:
    economic growth and its sources; fiscal, mone-
    tary and related policies; banking and finance;
    taxation; Japan and the world economy; indus-
    trial organization; technology; labor markets;
    urbanization; politics, government and economic
    growth; and social and cultural factors in eco-
    nomic growth. (JEL)

Patrick, Hugh, ed., JAPANESE INDUSTRIALIZATION AND
    ITS SOCIAL CONSEQUENCES, assisted by Larry
    Meissner, Berkeley, University of California
    Press, 1976. Twelve previously unpublished
    papers by economists, sociologists, and anthro-
    pologists on the interrelationships between
    social and economic variables in Japan's modern
    development. The papers are divided into three
    sections on evolving economic and sociological
    aspects of the Japanese industrial workers, on
    specific industries and issues and problems
    with respect to firm size, and on certain
    social consequences of industrialization,
    including demographic transition, income in-
    equality, and poverty. Index. (JEL)

Patrick, Hugh T., THE PHOENIX RISEN FROM THE ASHES:
    Postwar Japan, Center Paper #151, New Haven,
    Connecticut, Yale University, Economic Growth
    Center, 1970.

Taira, Koji, ECONOMIC DEVELOPMENT AND THE LABOR MAR-
    KET IN JAPAN, New York, Columbia University
    Press, 1970. Taira uses sophisticated but oc-
    casionally--of necessity--speculative economic
    analyses to support his attempt at a wholesale
    debunking of received ideas about Japanese eco-
    nomic growth. He asserts, e.g., that develop-
    ment was not "quick" but "slow;" that the
    economy has not had a "dual structure;" that
    lifetime employment doesn't make the labor
    market rigid; that cultural variables play only
    a negligible role in determining Japanese
    economic patterns. A solid work which will
    stimulate controversy and raise its level.
    (FA)

Voelkner, Harold E., LAND REFORM IN JAPAN, Washington, D.C., U.S. Agency for International Development, Spring Review of Land Reform, 1970, Country paper, SR/LR/C-23.

Wakaizumi, Kei, "Japan's Role in a New World Order," Foreign Affairs, Vol. 51, No. 2, January 1973.

Yakabe, Katsumi, ed., LABOR RELATIONS IN JAPAN--FUNDAMENTAL CHARACTERISTICS, Japan, International Society for Educational Information, Inc., 1974.

Yamamoto, Noboru, THE ECONOMY AND SOCIETY OF THE NEW JAPAN, Japan, Public Information Bureau, Ministry of Foreign Affairs, 1975.

Young, Alexander, THE SOGO SHOSHA: Japan's Multinational Trading Companies, Boulder, Colorado, Westview Press, 1979. This book analyzes the basic characteristics, methods, sales and profit trends, strategies, and future prospects of these global trading conglomerates. It presents the economic and social origins of the ten largest companies, and how they differ from the pre-World War II zaibatsu, and how they resemble and differ from Western multinational corporations. (BPA)

Jordan

Aresvik, Oddvar, THE AGRICULTURAL DEVELOPMENT OF JORDAN, New York, Praeger, 1976.

Mazur, Michael P., ECONOMIC GROWTH AND DEVELOPMENT IN JORDAN, Boulder, Colorado, Westview Press, 1979. Part 1 includes statistical data, some never before published, measuring the growth performance of Jordan's prewar economy, and presents the first quantitative explanation of its concentration in the service sector. Part 2 surveys the postwar East Bank economy, including a critical analysis of statistical sources. Part 3 (the largest) covers Jordan's development policies in industry, agriculture, and planning. (BPA)

Korea

X-REF: AGRARIAN REFORM: Smith, EMPLOYMENT LABOR:
Fei, Finance, Villanueva, INCOME DISTRIBUTION PRIN-
CIPLES: Looney, MULTINATIONAL CORPORATIONS: Cohen.

Bank of Korea, SEOUL, FINANCIAL DEVELOPMENT SINCE
    INTEREST RATE REFORM, Seoul, Bank of Korea,
    1970.

Brown, Gilbert T., KOREAN PRICING POLICIES AND ECO-
    NOMIC DEVELOPMENT IN THE 1960s, Baltimore and
    London, The Johns Hopkins University Press,
    1973.

Brun, Ellen and Hersh, Jacues, SOCIALIST KOREA: A
    Case Study in the Strategy of Economic Develop-
    ment, New York, Monthly Review Press, 1976.
    Presentation of the development of the Democra-
    tic People's Republic of Korea (DPRK), estab-
    lishing a basis for understanding the scope of
    the socioeconomic transformation of Korean
    Society. Divided into three parts, the first
    describes the historical development; the
    second part identifies the forces and laws
    behind the process of rapid development as
    revealed by the Korean example; and the last
    part explores the problems of a transitional
    society, especially on the superstructural
    level, including changes in planning and man-
    agement systems, social priorities, and moti-
    vations. No index. (JEL)

Chung, Joseph Sang-Hoon, THE NORTH KOREAN ECONOMY:
    Structure and Development, Stanford, California,
    Hoover Institution Press, 1974. Assiduous re-
    search coupled with shrewd inference and extrap-
    olation to demonstrate that centralization and
    bureaucratic control have been effective in
    raising national income and living standards
    over the period 1954-67. A subsequent lag in
    growth rates is attributed either to increased
    military spending or to the inability of the
    bureaucracy to handle a more complex economy.
    (FA)

Cohen, S. I., PRODUCTION, MANPOWER AND SOCIAL PLAN-
    NING: With Applications to Korea, foreword by
    Jan Tinbergen, The Netherlands, Rotterdam
    University Press; distributed by Academic Book
    Services, Holland, 1975. Develops a model for
    development planning integrating manpower plan-
    ning and social planning with economic planning.
    The basic inter-industry model for sectoral
    production is extended to incorporate a sym-
    metrical treatment of the formal, informal, and
    noneducational sectors to evaluate the impact
    of investment. Author and subject indices.
    (JEL)

Cole, David C. and Lyman, Princeton N., KOREAN DE-
    VELOPMENT: The Interplay of Politics and Eco-
    nomics, Cambridge, Massachusetts, Harvard Uni-
    versity Press, 1971. A cherished hypothesis in
    orthodox thinking about "modernization" has it
    that economic and political development go to-
    gether. The authors demonstrate some evidence
    to support the theory in the Korea of 1963-67
    but confess their inability to be sure that
    more riches will mean more freedom in the years
    to come. (FA)

Hahm, Pyong-choon, "Korea and the Emerging Asian
    Power Balance," Foreign Affairs, Vol. 50, No.
    2, January 1972.

Hasan, Parvez, KOREA: Problems and Issues in a Rap-
    idly Growing Economy, A World Bank Country Eco-
    nomic Report, Baltimore, The Johns Hopkins Uni-
    versity Press, for the World Bank, 1976.
    Emphasizes the problems the Korean economy has
    faced and will face in sustaining its rapid
    rate of expansion, while bringing about struc-
    tural changes in the economy. The issues of
    resource mobilization, resource allocation, and
    rural-urban income disparities are the main
    topics of the book. Index. (JEL)

Hong, Wontack, FACTOR SUPPLY AND FACTOR INTENSITY OF
    TRADE IN KOREA, Seoul, Korea Development Insti-
    tute, 1976. Investigates the changes in the
    factor intensity of Korea's trade following the
    increases in Korea's aggregate capital-labor

ratio. The period examined is 1960-73, a
period marked by rapid capital accumulation and
a rapid expansion of manufactured exports. A
secondary purpose is the examination of factor
substitution in the Korean economy during this
period, associated with changes in the wage/
rental ratio, and assessing the effects of factor substitution on the factor intensity of
Korea's trade. A third purpose is to show that
a developing country (Korea) will have a
greater factor intensity differential between
"non-competitive" (nonnatural-resource-inten-
sive) imports and exports than between "competitive" imports and exports. Bibliography
and statistical references; no index. (JEL)

Hong, Wontack, and Krueger, Anne O., eds., TRADE AND
    DEVELOPMENT IN KOREA: Proceedings of a Confer-
    ence held by the Korea Development Institute,
    KDI Studies in Economics, Seoul, Korea Develop-
    ment Institute, 1975. Nine papers presented at
    the Third Korea Development Institute Interna-
    tional Symposium on Trade and Development in
    Korea held in 1974. The economic growth of
    Korea in the period 1962-73 is examined in two
    papers in the context of her export strategy as
    well as a discussion on the changing components
    of the balance of payments. Five papers inves-
    tigate the determinants of Korean comparative
    advantage, examining: factor supply and factor
    intensity of trade; employment generated by ex-
    ports; the roles of government and multina-
    tional corporations in export growth, using the
    electronics industry as a case study; growth
    rates of productivity for export and import-
    substituting industries; and the way in which
    the exporting countries of the Far East have
    increased their share of overseas markets. The
    final papers examine the optimality of the
    policies adopted for export promotion. No
    index. (JEL)

Jones, Leroy P., PUBLIC ENTERPRISE AND ECONOMIC DE-
    VELOPMENT: The Korean Case, KDI Studies in
    Economics, Seoul, Korea Development Institute,
    1975. Study of the Korean use of public enter-
    prise as a tool for achieving economic develop-
    ment. Also attempts to develop an analytical
    framework, which will provide "a basis for ex-
    tensions both outward to international compari-
    sons, and inward to performance evaluation of

individual enterprises." Bibliography; name
and subject indices. (JEL)

Kim, Joungwon Alexander, DIVIDED KOREA: The Politics
of Development, 1945-1972, Cambridge, Massachusetts, Harvard University Press, 1975. Both
North and South Korea have moved since independence toward a high literacy rate; toward increasing urbanization; and from postwar impov-
erishment to per capita incomes--at the beginning of the 1970s--of over U.S. $200. The au-
thor argues that the North, for a variety of
reasons, has established a relatively stable
polity; the South has not. (FA)

Kim, Chuk Kyo, ed., ESSAYS ON THE KOREAN ECONOMY,
Vol. 1: Planning Model and Macroeconomic
Policy Issues, Vol. 2: Industrial and Social
Development Issues, Seoul, Korea Development
Institute; distributed by the University Press
of Hawaii, Honolulu, 1977. Twenty-three papers
(previously published as monographs) by economists affiliated with the Korea Development
Institute, written in the period since 1971.
The 13 papers of Volume 1 are in four parts:
short- and long-term planning models; inflation
and savings behavior, fiscal structure, and
foreign exchange and trade policy. The remaining papers contained in Volume II consider
pricing policy and demand analysis, regional
and urban problems, and education, health, and
income distribution. No index. (JEL)

Kim, Hyong Chun, "Korea's Export Success, 1960-69,"
Finance and Development, Vol. 8, No. 1, March
1971.

Kim, K. S., "Labour Force Structure in a Dual Economy: A Case Study of South Korea," International
Labour Review, Vol. 101, No. 1, January 1970.

Kuznets, Paul W., ECONOMIC GROWTH AND STRUCTURE IN
THE REPUBLIC OF KOREA, New Haven and London,
Yale University Press, Economic Growth Center,
1977. Describes and explains the main characteristics of economic development in South
Korea from 1953 to 1972 in terms of growth
rates, sectoral share; and the major national
accounting aggregates. Examines the causes and
consequences of Korea's accelerated growth
after 1960-62. Also discusses the labor-

absorption problem, the contribution of agriculture, the rapid growth of manufacturing, prices, monetary policy, and Korea's first three five-year plans. Explains the causes of accelerated growth in terms of institutional changes and loosening of other economic and social constraints that prevented rapid growth before the 1960's. Bibliography; index. (JEL)

Lee, Chong-Sik, THE KOREAN WORKERS' PARTY: A Short History, Stanford, California, Hoover Institution, 1978. A superb interpretive history of the Korean Communist movement in little more than 100 pages. (FA)

Morrow, Robert B., and Sherper, Kenneth H., LAND REFORM IN SOUTH KOREA, Washington, D.C., U.S. Agency for International Development, Spring Review of Land Reform, 1970, Country Paper, SR/LR/C-24.

Park, Chong Kee, SOCIAL SECURITY IN KOREA: An Approach to Socio-economic Development, Seoul, Korea Development Institute, 1975. A careful survey of the policy implications of setting up a Korean national insurance system, this study is rich in statistical data and has a broadly comparative viewpoint. (FA)

Suh, Sang Chul, GROWTH AND STRUCTURAL CHANGES IN THE KOREAN ECONOMY, 1910-1940, Cambridge, Massachusetts, Council on East Asian Studies, Harvard University distributed by Harvard University Press, 1978.

Suh, Suk Tai, IMPORT SUBSTITUTION AND ECONOMIC DEVELOPMENT IN KOREA, Working Paper 7519, Seoul, Korea Development Institute, 1975. Analyzes import substitution in the development of the Korean economy from the 1870's to the 1970's and focuses on recent performance during the post-war period. Examines import substitution as an element in the growth process and makes international comparisons. No index. (JEL)

Wade, L. L., and Kim, B. S., ECONOMIC DEVELOPMENT OF SOUTH KOREA: The Political Economy of Success, New York, Praeger, 1978. An analysis of South Korean economic development since the Korean War, this volume examines Korea's remarkable success not only in expanding its GNP growth,

but also in diversifying growth and promoting
income equality. (BPA)

Watanabe, S., "Exports and Employment: The Case of
the Republic of Korea," International Labour
Review, Vol. 106, No. 6, December 1972.

Kuwait

X-REF: REGIONAL DEVELOPMENT: El Mallakh.

Demir, Soliman, THE KUWAIT FUND AND THE POLITICAL
ECONOMY OF ARAB REGIONAL DEVELOPMENT, New York,
Praeger, 1976. A survey of the Kuwait Fund,
rather sketchy but useful for basic information
and statistics and for light on the Fund's
relation both to specific Kuwait interests and
to larger Arab concerns. (FA)

El Mallakh, Ragaei, KUWAIT: Trade and Investment,
Boulder, Colorado, Westview Press, 1979. The
author delineates Kuwait's economic activities
and potential and assesses the country's impact
on the global economy. Basing his work on two
decades of research and interviews, he presents
new data. He analyzes the use of Kuwait's
capital-surplus funds with reference to the
Middle East, Europe, and the U.S. (BPA)

Malaysia

X-REF: MULTINATIONAL CORPORATIONS: Lim.

Drake, P. J., FINANCIAL DEVELOPMENT IN MALAYA AND
SINGAPORE, Canberra, Australian National University Press, 1969. Focuses on the post-World
War II period through mid-1967; Part I is devoted to an analysis of the development of the
money supply and Part II to the allocation of
credit. Includes many data; index. (JEL)

Ghee, Lim Teck, PEASANTS AND THEIR AGRICULTURAL
ECONOMY IN COLONIAL MALAYA, 1874-1941, East
Asian Historical Monographs, Juala Lumpur; New
York, Oxford University Press, 1977. Traces
chronologically the growth of Malayan peasant
society and its agricultural economy in the

states of Perak, Selangor, Negri Sembilan, and Pahang. Describes the colonial government's role in the process of change and examines who the peasants were, where they lived, what they did, and how they differed from the rest of society. Also comments on the impact on the society of British rule. (JEL)

Gould, James W., THE UNITED STATES AND MALAYSIA, Cambridge, Massachusetts, Harvard University Press, 1969. A summary of the geography, history, and culture of Malaysia, with special attention to the historical and potential roles of the United States. (BPA)

Kasper, Wolfgang, MALAYSIA: A Study in Successful Economic Development, Washington, D.C., American Enterprise Institute for Public Policy Research, 1974. A case study in development economics. The author describes the structure, overall economic performance, policy framework, industrialization policies, and other major aspects of the Malaysian economy. He attempts to explain how and why, since it gained independence fifteen years ago, Malaysian national output "has grown at more than 6 percent annually, industrial output has expanded at about 11 percent; up to 1972, the price level remained extremely stable; and there have been none of the balance-of-payments crises typical of so many other developing countries." Bibliography; index. (JEL)

Lim, David, "Do Foreign Companies Pay Higher Wages Than Their Local Counterparts in Malaysian Manufacturing," Journal of Development Economics, Vol. 4, No. 1, March 1977.

Musolf, Lloyd D. and Springer, J. Frederic, MALAYSIA'S PARLIAMENTARY SYSTEM, Representative Politics and Policymaking in a Divided Society, Boulder, Colorado, Westview Press, 1979. This study documents and interprets the interaction of legislator, party, and voter in Malaysia. It emphasizes that the traditional emphasis on collective parliamentary representation must be supplemented with discriminating attention to the activities of individual legislators. (BPA)

Rabushda, Alvin, RACE AND POLITICS IN URBAN MALAYA,
    Stanford, California, Hoover Institution Press,
    1973. This study of racial attitudes between
    Chinese and Malay raises the old question--how
    is a multiracial pluralist society possible?
    The author finds economic conflict less divi-
    sive than political, but his advice that there-
    fore government should be minimal is dubious
    and unlikely to be followed. (FA)

Tham, Seong Chee, THE ROLE AND IMPACT OF FORMAL AS-
    SOCIATIONS ON THE DEVELOPMENT OF MALAYSIA,
    Clearing House for Social Development in Asia;
    Formal Associations and National Development,
    No. 2, Bangkok, Friedrich-Ebert-Stiftung, 1977.
    Describes the role and impact of Malay, Chinese,
    and Indian communal associations on rational
    development in Malaysia. Based partially on
    interviews of members of the various associa-
    tions, the author finds that associations or-
    ganized along communal lines play a necessary
    role and that they are not inherently divisive
    or disintegrative. Also finds that the policies
    of the Malaysian Federal Government in national
    development since independence have emphasized
    the role of communal consciousness and communal
    associations as the key to national development
    and integration at this stage. (JEL)

Thoburn, John T., PRIMARY COMMODITY EXPORTS AND ECO-
    NOMIC DEVELOPMENT: Theory, Evidence, and a
    Study of Malaysia, New York, Wiley, 1977. What
    is the role of specific primary commodity
    exports in the development process of Third
    World countries? Examining this question in
    depth, the book stresses the differences in
    development effects between different export
    products. (BPA)

Middle East

X-REF: AGRARIAN REFORM: Warriner, MODERNIZATION:
Lerner, SMALL BUSINESS: Unido, TECHNOLOGY: Nader.

Amin, Galal A., THE MODERNIZATION OF POVERTY: A
    Study in the Political Economy of Growth in
    Nine Arab Countries, 1945-1970, Leiden, Brill,
    1974. An Egyptian economist's critical study
    of widespread shortcomings in postwar Arab eco-

nomic planning and performance: lack of a common market, huge defense expenditures, low
rates of saving, income inequality, too rapid
urban growth, neglect of agriculture. (FA)

Askari, Hossein and Cummings, John Thomas, MIDDLE
EAST ECONOMIES IN THE 1970's: A Comparative
Approach, Praeger Special Studies in International Economics and Development, New York and
London, Praeger, 1976. Sectoral study of the
economics of the Middle East since 1970, which
uses a comparative approach in assessing the
advantages and bottlenecks in economic development found in varying degrees in the region.
Focusing on Middle East petroleum countries
plus Libya and Egypt; in some sections discuss
Israel, Jordan, Lebanon, and Yemen. Bibliography; index. (JEL)

Cooper, Charles S. and Alexander, Sidney S., eds.,
ECONOMIC DEVELOPMENT AND POPULATION GROWTH IN
THE MIDDLE EAST, New York, American Elsevier,
1972. A volume in a series covering a wide
spectrum of the area's problems. The conclusions are cautious, but they stress the potential for vigorous economic growth. On population, the analysis suggests a non-Malthusian
interpretation even though present Arab birth
rates are high. (FA)

El Mallakh, R. E.; Kadhim, M.; and Poulson, B.;
CAPITAL INVESTMENT IN THE MIDDLE EAST: The Use
of Surplus Funds for Regional Development,
Praeger Special Studies in International Economics and Development, New York, Praeger,
1977. Reviewing capital investment in the
Middle East, this volume traces the problems
and prospects of regional economic cooperation
among the Arab countries. It confirms that
regional approaches to development greatly
enhance economic growth in oil-poor Arab nations, and measures the capacity of the Arab
countries to absorb surplus funds through 1990.
(BPA)

335

Fatemi, Ali Mohammad S.; Amirie, Abbas; Kokoropoulos, Panos; and Shaul, Marnie; POLITICAL ECONOMY OF THE MIDDLE EAST: A Computerized Guide to the Literature, a publication of International Develop-Economics Awareness Systems (IDEAS), Akron, Ohio, University of Akron, Department of Economics, 1970. First of a series of publications based on a computer information retrieval system developed by the International Development-Economics Awareness System at the University of Akron, Ohio, it lists the titles of books, articles, etc. on the political economy of the Middle East. Includes a User's guide, author index and subject index. (JEL)

Gale Research Co., MIDDLE EAST AND NORTH AFRICA, 1978-79, 25th edition, a Europa publication, Detroit, Michigan, 1978. A review of the year's developments; physical and social geography, climate, racial and linguistic groupings, religious, agriculture, and natural resources; list of regional organizations and research institutes. (BPA)

Goldschmidt, Arthur, Jr., A CONCISE HISTORY OF THE MIDDLE EAST, Boulder, Colorado, Westview Press, 1979. Traces the history from the beginnings of Islam to the present. (BPA)

Hershlag, Z. Y., THE ECONOMIC STRUCTURE OF THE MIDDLE EAST, Leiden, Brill, 1975. Building on his earlier work, Hershlag gives a composite picture of the Middle East economy (including Israel) that is both broad in scope and rich in detail, straddling rather successfully the dilemma of the topical versus the country approach. He shows how a "dual" economy has emerged with the growing inequality of nations consequent on the oil boom. (FA)

Hottinger, Arnold, "The Depth of Arab Radicalism," Foreign Affairs, Vol. 51, No 3, April 1973.

Kapoor, Ashok, ed., INTERNATIONAL BUSINESS IN THE MIDDLE EAST, Boulder, Colorado, Westview Press, 1979. A book of case studies, revealing that few foreign companies prepare adequately for project development and implementation. Several dimensions of business development in the Middle East are distinguished. (BPA)

Kedouri, Elie, ed., THE MIDDLE EASTERN ECONOMY: Studies in Economic and Economic History, London, Cass; Forest Grove, Oreg.: Cass, c/o International Scholarly Book Services, 1976. Seven essays, previously published in a special issue of Middle Eastern Studies, Vol. 12, No. 3, dealing with current economic issues and the economic history of the Middle East in the nineteenth and twentieth centuries. Index. (JEL)

Lenczowski, George, MIDDLE EAST OIL IN A REVOLUTIONARY AGE, Washington, D.C., American Enterprise Institute for Public Research, 1976.

Sayigh, Yusif A., THE ECONOMIES OF THE ARAB WORLD: Volume 1: Development Since 1945, Volume 2: The Determinants of Arab Economic Development, New York, St. Martin's Press, 1978.

Schultz, Ann, INTERNATIONAL AND REGIONAL POLITICS IN THE MIDDLE EAST AND NORTH AFRICA, Detroit, Michigan, Gale Research, 1978. Regional issues, foreign policies, external powers, the Arab-Israeli conflict, and petroleum. Annotated listings of English-language books and articles. (BPA)

Sherbiny, Naiem A., and Tessler, Mark A., ARAB OIL: Impact on Arab Countries and Global Implications, New York, Praeger, 1976. Explores the impact of Arab oil on the Middle East (industrialization of Arab countries, production and pricing of oil, democratization and public administration modernization and cultural change) and on the industrial world in general (world energy needs, big-power relationships, increased flow of funds to Arab countries. MNCs and the Arab-Israeli conflict). (BPA)

Stone, Russell A., OPEC AND THE MIDDLE EAST: The Impact of Oil on Societal Development, New York, Praeger, 1977. Examines the impact of income from petroleum on political, economic, and social developments in the Middle East as a whole and focuses specifically on changes in Kuwait, Egypt, Iraq, Algeria, and Syria. (BPA)

Waterbury, John and El Mallakh, Ragaei, THE MIDDLE
    EAST IN THE COMING DECADE: From Wellhead to
    Well-being, 1980's Project Studies/Council on
    Foreign Relations, New York, McGraw-Hill Book
    Co., 1978.

Nepal

X-REF: AGRICULTURAL CREDIT: Caplin.

Pakistan

X-REF: INCOME DISTRIBUTION PRINCIPLES: van
Ginneken, INDIA: Brown, Cohen, TRADE: Islam,
URBAN DEVELOPMENT: Ilo.

Brecher, Irving and Abbas, S. A., FOREIGN AID AND
    INDUSTRIAL DEVELOPMENT IN PAKISTAN, New York,
    Cambridge University Press, 1972. Well aware
    of the complexity of the issues and the limits
    of their study, Professor Brecher of McGill and
    Mr. Abbas of UNCTAD convincingly demonstrate
    the substantial contribution aid made to Pakis-
    tan's industrial growth in the 1960's. (FA)

Falcon, Walter P. and Papanek, Gustav F., DEVELOP-
    MENT POLICY II: The Pakistan Experience,
    Cambridge, Massachusetts, Harvard University
    Press, 1971. A collection of papers based on
    the experiences of Harvard advisors in Pakistan
    from 1954-1970. (BPA)

Griffin, Keith and Khan, Azizur Rahman, eds., GROWTH
    AND INEQUALITY IN PAKISTAN, New York, St. Mar-
    tin's Press, 1972. A collection of ten arti-
    cles dealing with economic growth and inequal-
    ity in Pakistan. The articles are grouped into
    four sections: I, Post-Independence Develop-
    ment and Strategy; II, Stagnation and Growth in
    Agriculture; III, Industry and Trade; IV,
    Wages, Income Distribution, and Savings.
    Introduction and commentaries by the editors.
    Index. (JEL)

Gustafson, W. Eric, A REVIEW OF THE PAKISTANI ECONO-
    MY UNDER BHUTTO, Working Paper Series No. 100,
    University of California at Davis, March 1978.

338

Herring, Ronald and Chaudhey, M. Ghaffar, THE 1972 LAND REFORMS IN PAKISTAN AND THEIR ECONOMIC IMPLICATIONS: A Preliminary Analysis, LTC Reprint No. 126, Madison, University of Wisconsin, Land Tenure Center, 1974.

Islam, Nurul, COMMENTS ON PLANNING EXPERIENCE IN PAKISTAN, Center Paper #130, New Haven, Connecticut, Yale University, Economic Growth Center, 1969.

Islam, Nurul, EXPORT POLICY IN PAKISTAN, Center Paper #137, New Haven, Connecticut, Yale University, Economic Growth Center, 1969.

Jahan, Rounaq, PAKISTAN: Failure in National Integration, New York, Columbia University Press, 1972. Many social scientists see economic development as more urgent than political development. In this postmortem on Ayub Khan's Pakistan, economic growth did not unite but divided; nationhood, long denied, required war and revolution to bring it to birth. (FA)

Khan, Akhter Hameed, THREE ESSAYS: Land Reform, Rural Works, and The Food Problem in Pakistan, South Asia Series, #20, East Lansing, Michigan, Asian Study Center, Michigan State University, 1973.

Khan, Mahmood, THE ECONOMICS OF THE GREEN REVOLUTION IN PAKISTAN, New York, Praeger, 1975. Using primary data, deals with central policy issues and the often disturbing consequences emanating from new technology involved in the "green Revolution." Viewed from the farm- or micro-level of production patterns, input costs, farm values, net farm incomes, and other variables on different size farms in the Punjab and Sind provinces. (BPA)

Lewis, Stephen R., ECONOMIC POLICY AND INDUSTRIAL GROWTH IN PAKISTAN, Cambridge, Massachusetts, MIT Press, 1969. A quantitative and analytical study of how a spectacular industrial growth can occur in an otherwise stagnant economy. (FA)

Lewis, Stephen R., Jr., PAKISTAN: Industrialization and Trade Policies, Industry and Trade in Some Developing Countries, New York, Oxford University Press for the Development Centre of the Organisation for Economic Co-operation and Development, 1970. Analysis of the structure and performance of the manufacturing sector, with focus on economic policy making. Concludes that "the time is somewhat overdue for Pakistan to begin emphasizing a structure of relative prices within manufacturing, and between manufacturing and agriculture, that will induce manufacturers and potential investors in manufacturing industry to adopt technologies and to improve productivity to a degree more consistent with Pakistan's real resource availabilities." Includes many data, bibliography; and index. (JEL)

MacEwan, Arthur, DEVELOPMENT ALTERNATIVES IN PAKISTAN: A Multisectoral and Regional Analysis of Planning Problems, Harvard Economic Studies No. 134, Cambridge, Massachusetts, Harvard University Press, 1971. The author examines the full implications of several alternative development programs for Pakistan's Third and Fourth Plans. MacEwan applies a multi-sectoral, regional linear programming planning model to determine the relationship between industrial priorities and macroeconomic variables. Index. (JEL)

Stern, Joseph J., and Falcon, Walter, P., GROWTH AND DEVELOPMENT IN PAKISTAN, 1955-1969, Occasional Papers in International Affairs, No. 23, Cambridge, Massachusetts, Center for International Affairs, Harvard University, 1970. Surveys quantitatively Pakistan's growth experience and development strategy; indicates the directions which planning might take in the future. Revision of a study prepared for the Pearson Commission on International Development. No index. (JEL)

White, Lawrence J., INDUSTRIAL CONCENTRATION AND ECONOMIC POWER IN PAKISTAN, Princeton, New Jersey, Princeton University Press, 1974. The author suggests that the pattern of economic domination by a small number of family groups in Pakistan, a pattern common to many developing nations, is not only politically corrupting but economically inefficient. Realistic reme-

dies, he argues, are few; but an open international trade sector and progressive taxation
are tentatively offered. (FA)

Ziring, Lawrence; Braibanti, Ralph; and Wriggins, W.
Howard, eds., PAKISTAN: The Long View, Durham,
North Carolina, Duke University Press, 1977.
An excellent collection of essays on Pakistan.
Ziring's introduction is particularly thoughtful. He points to "a significant limitation of
Pakistan's leaders," namely their "tendency to
provoke but not control sub-national ethnic,
regional and religious group controversy."
Others also point to the failure of national
integration. In a refreshingly candid appraisal of Pakistan's foreign policy, William
Barnds notes how surprising it is that so poor
a country should have sought security through
confrontation rather than accommodation with a
neighbor several times its size. (FA)

Philippines

X-REF: AGRARIAN REFORM: Smith, AGRICULTURAL DEVEL-
OPMENT: Ruttan, BURMA: Resnick, EMPLOYMENT LABOR:
Ilo, Ranis, FINANCE: Villanueva, INDIA: Rosen,
INDUSTRIAL DEVELOPMENT: Resnick, TECHNOLOGY: Ilo,
Mason.

Averch, Harvey A., et al., THE MATRIX OF POLICY IN
THE PHILIPPINES, Princeton, New Jersey, Princeton University Press, 1971. AID and the Department of Defense sponsored the aggressively
quantitative research reported by the three
RAND authors here. They make a fervent case
for more statistical analysis in U.S. organizational intelligence. Their own conclusions,
adduced to make the point, will convince those
who like to look on the bright side: Philippine
political life is basically stable, the economy
will continue to grow, the crime problem has
been overestimated, and the Huks are not a
serious threat. (FA)

Baldwin, Robert E., FOREIGN TRADE REGIMES AND ECO-
    NOMIC DEVELOPMENT: The Philippines, A Special
    Conference Series on Foreign Trade Regimes and
    Economic Development, Vol. V, New York, Na-
    tional Bureau of Economic Research; distributed
    by Columbia University Press, New York and
    London, 1975. Describes and analyzes both the
    trade and payments policies and fiscal and
    monetary policies followed by the Philippines
    during the past 25 years. Attempts to quantify
    the differential levels of protection these
    combined policies offered to various sectors of
    the economy. Also examines the effects of
    different exchange-control methods and various
    development policies on industrial allocation
    of resources, the distribution of income, and
    the rate of growth of the economy. Index.
    (JEL)

Buss, Claude A., THE UNITED STATES AND THE PHILIP-
    PINES, Washington, American Enterprise Insti-
    tute, 1977. A competent if somewhat unfocused
    and superficial review of U.S. relations with
    the Philippines. (FA)

Cheetham, Russell J., and Hawkins, Edward K., THE
    PHILIPPINES: PRIORITIES AND PROSPECTS FOR
    DEVELOPMENT: Report of a Mission Sent to the
    Philippines by the World Bank, a World Bank
    Country Economic Report, Washington, D.C., The
    World Bank, 1976. Comprehensive report on the
    economy of the Philippines. Attention is given
    to: agriculture, urban and rural development,
    agrarian reform, industry, power, and human re-
    sources. Also examines financial and resource
    aspects of the development process, quantifying
    the financial requirements of growth and devel-
    opment. Argues that "dependence on foreign in-
    flows can be diminished only if sufficient at-
    tention is paid to export promotion and prudent
    management of the balance of payments." Index.
    (JEL)

Gupta, M. L., "Patterns of Economic Activity in the
    Philippines and Some Methodological Issues In-
    volved," International Labour Review, Vol. 101,
    No. 4, April 1970.

Hackenberg, Robert A., FALLOUT FROM THE POVERTY EX-
    PLOSION: Economic and Demographic Trends in
    Davao City, 1972-1974, 2nd Davao City Survey
    Report, Davao Action Information Center, 1974.

ILO, SHARING IN DEVELOPMENT: A Programme of Employ-
    ment, Equity, and Growth for the Philippines,
    Report of a team financed by the United Nations
    Development Programme and International Labour
    Office, Geneva, 1974.

Kann, Peter R., "The Philippines Without Democracy,"
    Foreign Affairs, Vol. 52, No. 3, April 1974.

Koone, Harold D., and Gleeck, Louis E., LAND REFORM
    IN THE PHILIPPINES, Washington, D.C., U.S.
    Agency for International Development, Spring
    Review of Land Reform, 1970, Country Paper
    SR/LR/C-26.

Medina, Jose C., THE PHILIPPINE EXPERIENCE WITH LAND
    REFORM SINCE 1972: An Overview, New York, Asia
    Society, 1975, Seadag Papers on Problems of De-
    velopment in South East Asia, #75-3.

Power, John H., and Sicat, Gerardo, THE PHILIPPINES:
    Industrialization and Trade Policies, published
    in a single volume together with Hsing, Mo-
    Huan, TAIWAN: Industrialization and Trade
    Policies, Oxford, for O.E.C.D., 1971.

Ranis, G., "Employment, Equity and Growth: Lessons
    from the Philippine Employment Mission," Inter-
    national Labour Review, Vol. 110, No. 1, July
    1974.

Resnick, Stephen A., THE DECLINE OF RURAL INDUSTRY
    UNDER EXPORT EXPANSION: A Comparison Among
    Burma, Philippines, and Thailand, 1870-1938,
    Center Paper #147, New Haven, Connecticut, Yale
    University, Economic Growth Center, 1970.

Rodgers, Gerry; Hopkins, Mike; and Wery, Reny; POPU-
    LATION, EMPLOYMENT, AND INEQUALITY: The Bachue
    Model Applied to the Philippines, New York,
    Praeger, 1978. The Bachue model, an econo-
    metric model that will be used for studies of
    developing countries, is applied to the Philip-
    pines in this work to project the development
    of its economic-demographic system over the
    next 50 years. The study examines various

343

policies that could be implemented in the
Philippines. (BPA)

Ruprecht, Theodore K., RAPID POPULATION GROWTH AND
MACRO ECONOMIC DEVELOPMENT: The Philippines
Case, Studies in Institutional Development and
Modernization, Bloomington, Indiana University,
International Development Research Center,
1975. Investigates quantitative relationship
between economic development and population
change in the Philippines, making projections
to the year 2000. Various demographic alternatives are used for each simulation of the
annual behavior of the economy. The results of
the simulations in terms of the particular
variables (output per person, consumption per
equivalent adult, savings rates, and economic
structure) are then compared. Bibliography; no
index. (JEL)

Wheelock, Gerald C. and Young, Frank W., MACROSOCIAL
ACCOUNTING FOR MUNICIPALITIES IN THE PHILIP-
PINES: Rural Banks and Credit Cooperatives,
Cornell International Agriculture Bulletin #26,
July 1973.

World Bank, THE PHILIPPINES: Priorities and Prospects for Development, National Economic and
Development Authority, Republic of the Philippines, 1976.

Saudi Arabia

Ali, Sheikh Rustum, SAUDI ARABIA AND OIL DIPLOMACY,
New York, Praeger, 1976.

Cleron, Jean Paul, SAUDI ARABIA 2000: A Strategy
for Growth, New York, St. Martin's Press, 1978.
Assesses, within a planning framework, long-
term strategies of development on the basis of
assumptions referring to policy decisions,
structural changes, and behavioral patterns.
Uses a dynamic simulation model incorporating
mechanisms that both favor and constrain economic development. Index. (JEL)

Crane, Robert D., PLANNING THE FUTURE OF SAUDI
ARABIA: A Model for Achieving National Priorities, New York, Praeger, 1978. Pioneering a

344

new system of "national goals management," this
volume adapts the techniques of zero-based
budgeting and management by objectives to long
range planning in Saudi Arabia and the Arabian
Peninsula in general. (BPA)

Knauerhase, Ramon, THE SAUDI ARABIAN ECONOMY, Praeger
Special Studies in International Economics and
Development, New York, Praeger, 1975. Analyzes
the growth of the Saudi Arabian economy over
the past 25 years and "the real progress that
has been made in the Kingdom's economic development." (JEL)

United States-Saudi Arabian Joint Commission on Economic Cooperation, SUMMARY OF SAUDI ARABIAN
FIVE YEAR DEVELOPMENT PLAN, 1975-1980, Department of the Treasury, 1975.

Wells, Donald A., SAUDI ARABIAN DEVELOPMENT STRATEGY,
National Energy Study No. 12, Washington,
American Enterprise Institute for Public Policy
Research, 1976. Examines Saudi Arabia's plan
for economic development, calling for diversification of economic activity, increasing labor
productivity through manpower programs, and
distribution of the growth in activity among
five regions. Considers Saudi Arabia's previous experience, discusses the plan for 1975-80,
and evaluates the new plan. No index. (JEL)

Singapore

X-REF: HONG KONG: Geiger, MALAYSIA: Drake,
MULTINATIONAL CORPORATIONS: Cohen.

Wilson, Dick, THE FUTURE ROLE OF SINGAPORE, London,
Oxford University Press (for the Royal Institute
of International Affairs), 1972. One of the
best of the seasoned Southeast Asia correspon-
dents ponders the economic, social and political
quantities in the Singapore equation. His
solution: Singapore must become a "global
city," a neutral mercantile and diplomatic
entrepot for all the powers in Asia. (FA)

Yoshihara, Kunio, FOREIGN INVESTMENT AND DOMESTIC
    RESPONSE: A Study of Singapore's Industriali-
    zation, Singapore; Kuala Lumpur and Hong Kong,
    Eastern Universities Press in association with
    the Institute of Southeast Asian Studies, 1976.
    Deals with the role of foreign participation
    and domestic response in the industrialization
    of Singapore. Examines the foreign investments
    by Japan, the United States, European coun-
    tries, Australia, Hong Kong, and Taiwan in
    terms of the time pattern of investment, its
    characteristics, the rate of returns, the
    distribution of equity shares, and the profile
    of foreign investors. No index. (JEL)

Sri Lanka

X-REF: AGRICULTURAL DEVELOPMENT: Farmer, EMPLOYMENT
LABOR: Ilo, INDICATORS: Pyatt.

de Silva, K. M., ed., SRI LANKA: A Survey, Boulder,
    Colorado, Westview Press, 1977. A group of Sri
    Lankan scholars provides a systematic analysis
    of the island's economy and politics and a use-
    ful survey of demography, education, religions,
    literature, and the arts. Included is an up-
    to-date statistical appendix specially compiled
    for this work. (BPA)

Ganewatte, P., FRAGMENTATION OF PADDY LAND: A Case
    Study of a Cluster of Five Purana Villages in
    Anuradhapura District, Colombo, Sri Lanka,
    Agrarian Research and Training Institute, 1974.

Ganewatte, P., "THATTUMARU" AND "KATTIMARU" SYSTEMS
    OF ROTATION OF CULTIVATION OF PADDY LAND: A
    Case Study in the Village of Unduruwa Halmil-
    lawewa Anuradhapura District, Colombo, Sri
    Lanka, Agrarian Research and Training Institute,
    1974.

Gold, Martin E., LAW AND SOCIAL CHANGE: A Study of
    Land Reform in Sri Lanka, University of Cam-
    bridge, Massachusetts Series, New York, Nellen;
    distributed by Frederick Fell, New York, 1977.
    Interdisciplinary study of land reform in Sri
    Lanka, with emphasis on issues related to law
    and modernization. Drawing on legislative
    documents, government files, and newspaper

reports, the author, a practicing lawyer,
considers the power situation both at the
center and in the outer regions and localities.
Examines in particular: the 1958 Paddy Lands
Act, colonization schemes, cultivation committees, problems of subdivision and fragmentation, land tenure, the economics of tenancy
reform and the unorganized peasantry. (JEL)

Gooneratne, Wilbert; Gunawardena, Tilak; and Ronner,
Igle; THE ROLE OF CULTIVATION COMMITTEES IN
AGRICULTURAL PLANNING AT VILLAGE LEVEL, Colombo,
Sri Lanka, Agrarian Research and Training
Institute, 1974.

ILO, MATCHING EMPLOYMENT OPPORTUNITIES AND EXPECTA-
TIONS: A Programme of Action for Ceylon, the
report of an Inter-Agency Team organized by the
International Labour Office, Geneva, International Labour Office, 1971.

Izumi, K., and Ranatunga, A. S., ENVIRONMENTAL AND
SOCIAL CONSTRAINTS ON PADDY PRODUCTION UNDER
EXISTING CONDITIONS: A Case Study in Hambantota
District, Colombo, Sri Lanka, Agrarian Research
and Training Institute, 1974.

Karunatilake, H. N. S., ECONOMIC DEVELOPMENT IN CEY-
LON, Praeger Special Studies in International
Economics and Development, Praeger, New York,
1971. An analysis of economic development in
Ceylon from 1950 through 1970. Gives a detailed account of public policy and progress in
the agricultural, industrial, and manpower
sectors. Deals with the Ceylonese planning
experience in the last 15 years and why the
"attempt to plan long-term economic development
ended in dismal failure." Highlights the
"difficulties that a country committed to high
level of consumption expenditure has to face to
achieve a higher rate of growth." Bibliography;
no index. (JEL)

Sirisena, N. L., A MULTISECTORAL MODEL OF PRODUCTION
FOR SRI LANKA, Central Bank of Ceylon Research
Series, Ceylon, Central Bank of Ceylon, 1976.
Develops a multisector planning model of the
Sri Lanka economy, with special emphasis on the
agricultural sector. Input-output models are
used to analyze social accounting, intersec-
toral linkages, and an import substitution

347

scheme. Linear programming is applied to a
production model of agriculture, concluding
that land-augmenting technology, particularly
selective mechanization, should be stressed in
agricultural planning. No index. (JEL)

Taiwan

X-REF: AGRARIAN REFORM: Chao, Smith, AGRICULTURAL
DEVELOPMENT: Ho, Ruttan.

Chang, J. L. Y., "Export as Leading Sector: A Case
of Post-Aid Economic Growth," Economia Internazionale, Vol. 24, No. 2, May 1971. Following
a fifteen-year record of high rate of economic
growth under United States aid, Taiwan (Republic of China) has managed to maintain a continued, self-propelled, and even slightly accelerated pace of gains of per capita output since
1965. Until then a part of her growth was
undoubtedly directly or indirectly attributable
to the resources which she received under the
aid program. What then accounts for her per-
sistently successful performance since 1965?
This paper attempts to offer an explanation to
this question with an analytical framework
which assigns a weight to the role of aggregate
demand as much as it does to the importance of
productive capacity. (JEL)

Gordon, Leonard H. D., TAIWAN: Studies in Chinese
Local History, New York, Columbia University
Press, 1970.

Ho, Samuel P. S., ECONOMIC DEVELOPMENT OF TAIWAN,
1860-1970, A Publication of the Economic Growth
Center, New Haven, Connecticut, Yale University
Press, 1978. Focuses upon the roles of peasant
agriculture, manufacturing, and government in
the economic development of Taiwan, especially
in the period from 1900 to 1970. Discusses the
traditional agricultural economy before 1895;
describes the pattern and impact of colonial
development prior to World War II; analyzes the
effects of government policy, foreign aid, and
savings and investment on the pace and pattern
of industrial growth after 1952; and concludes
with an assessment of the lessons and prospects

of Taiwan's economic development. Selected
bibliography; index. (JEL)

Hsing, Mo-Huan, TAIWAN: Industrialization and Trade
Policies, published in a single volume together
with Power and Sicat, THE PHILIPPINES: Industrialization and Trade Policies, Oxford, England
for O.E.C.D., 1971.

Jacoby, Neil H., U.S. AID TO TAIWAN: A Study of
Foreign Aid, Self-Help, and Development, New
York, Praeger, 1966.

Koo, Anthony Y. C., "Agrarian Reform, Production and
Employment in Taiwan," International Labour Review, Vol. 104, No. 1-2, July-August 1971.

Koo, Anthony Y., LAND REFORM IN TAIWAN, Washington,
D.C., U.S. Agency for International Development,
Spring Review of Land Reform, 1970, Country
Paper, SR/LR/C-25.

Li, K. T., THE EXPERIENCE OF DYNAMIC ECONOMIC GROWTH
ON TAIWAN, Taipei and New York, Mei Ya, 1976.
Twenty-eight previously unpublished speeches
and essays written between 1959 and 1975 on
various aspects of the Republic of China's
economic development achievements in the past
25 years. Papers arranged in seven categories:
development and planning, economic cooperation,
manpower development and population, industrial
development, agricultural development, engineering, and fiscal policy. No index. (JEL)

Manzhuber, Albert, "Economic Development of Taiwan,"
in Industry of Free China, Vol. XXXIII, No. 4,
May 1970.

Mueller, Eva, "The Impact of Demographic Factors on
Economic Development in Taiwan," Population and
Development Review, Vol. 3, Nos. 1 & 2, March
and June 1977, pp. 1-22.

Speare, Alden Jr., "Urbanization and Migration in
Taiwan," Economic Development and Cultural
Change, Vol. 22, No. 2, January 1974.

Wu, Rong-I., THE STRATEGY OF ECONOMIC DEVELOPMENT:
A Case Study of Taiwan, Louvain, Belgium,
Vander, 1971.

X-REF: AGRICULTURAL DEVELOPMENT: Ruttan, BURMA:
Resnick, CHINA: Barnett, King, EMPLOYMENT LABOR:
Fei, FISCAL: Krzyzaniak, INCOME DISTRIBUTION PRINCI-
PLES: Fei, INDIA: Rosen, INDUSTRIAL DEVELOPMENT:
Resnick, MODERNIZATION: Murray, MULTINATIONAL COR-
PORATIONS: Cohen, POPULATION: Mueller, REGIONAL
DEVELOPMENT: Bendavid, TECHNOLOGY: Ilo.

Anderson, Dole A., MARKETING AND DEVELOPMENT: The
    Thailand Experience, MSU International Business
    and Economic Studies, East Lansing, Michigan
    State University, 1970. Studies the growth of
    the national market for consumer goods in Thai-
    land. Part one reviews the Thai ecological
    matrix: history, geography, religion, educa-
    tion, and other characteristics unique to its
    society. Part two examines the marketing
    structure and the development of the national
    market particularly through transportation
    improvements. Index. (JEL)

Baldwin, W. Lee and Maxwell, W. David, eds., THE
    ROLE OF FOREIGN FINANCIAL ASSISTANCE TO THAI-
    LAND IN THE 1980's, Lexington, Massachusetts,
    Heath, Lexington Books, 1975. Edited papers
    and proceedings of a conference of the South-
    east Asia Development Advisory Group held at
    Chieng Mai, Thailand, in June 1974. (JEL)

Caldwell, J. Alexander, AMERICAN ECONOMIC AID TO
    THAILAND, Lexington, Massachusetts, Lexington
    Books, 1974. The author, with AID in Thailand
    from 1967-1969 and now with Morgan Guaranty
    Trust, argues that Thai society is stable and
    resilient and can absorb increased amounts of
    U.S. assistance. He suggests that aid should
    foster political development and "create coher-
    ent political forces," but that it should not
    be used to fight communism; that development
    can result in village discontent, but need not
    lead to lessened loyalty. (FA)

Ingram, James C., ECONOMIC CHANGE IN THAILAND 1850-
    1970, Stanford, Connecticut, Stanford Univer-
    sity Press, 1971. The author presents two new
    chapters describing and analyzing Thailand's
    recent experience (1950-1970). The 1955 edition
    Economic Change in Thailand Since 1850 remains

otherwise unchanged with the description of the
major economic changes in Thailand since mid-
19th century when this country was known as
"Siam." Covers the rice industry and home-mar-
ket industries, other exports, currency and exchange, government revenues and government expenditures, and development of an exchange
economy. Appendices; selected bibliography;
index. (JEL)

Inukai, I., "Farm Mechanisation, Output and Labour
Input: A Case Study in Thailand," International Labour Review, Vol. 101, No. 5, May
1970.

Jacobs, Norman, MODERNIZATION WITHOUT DEVELOPMENT:
Thailand as an Asian Case Study, Praeger Special Studies in International Economics and
Development, New York, Praeger, 1971. Describes and analyzes Thai society by focusing
on the institutional characteristics of authority, the economy, occupations, stratification,
kinship and descent, religion, and social order
and legitimate change for the purpose of understanding how the structures, operating rules,
and goals of these institutions facilitate the
modernization, yet impede the development of a
"typical" mainland Asian society. No index.
(JEL)

Marzouk, G. A., ECONOMIC DEVELOPMENT AND POLICIES:
Case Study of Thailand, Foreword by Jan Tinbergen, Rotterdam, Rotterdam University Press,
1972. A broad analytical coverage of the
factors contributing to Thailand's sustained
(two decades) high rate of economic growth,
containing a theoretical framework as well as
considerable detailed statistical data. Discusses ad seriatum demography, trends in income
growth and distribution, the rice economy and
other agricultural activities, agricultural
productivity and efficacy, changes in the
manufacturing sector and the policies affecting
it, foreign trade and exchange topics, domestic
monetary policy and events, fiscal policy, and
planning methods and their implementation.
Index. (JEL)

Ray, Jayanta Kumar, PORTRAITS OF THAI POLITICS, New
Delhi, Orient Longman, 1972. Political memoirs
of three Thai civilian leaders, collected and

351

introduced by one of the doyens of Indian political science, which bear out the editor's comment that Thai politics are hobbled by an endemic climate of mistrust and a lack of consensus on shared values. (FA)

Turkey

Cohn, Edwin J., TURKISH ECONOMIC, SOCIAL AND POLI-
    TICAL CHANGE: The Development of a More Pros-
    perous and Open Society, Praeger Special
    Studies in International Economics and Develop-
    ment, New York, Praeger, 1970. Reviews the
    major trends in Turkey's economic and political
    development since World War II, emphasizing the
    social and cultural obstacles to development.
    Author was an AID economic advisor to Turkey
    between 1960 and 1968. Bibliography; no index.
    (JEL)

Fry, Maxwell, J., FINANCE AND DEVELOPMENT PLANNING
    IN TURKEY, Social, Economic and Political
    Studies of the Middle East, Vol. V., Leiden,
    Netherlands, E. J. Brill, 1972. This book at-
    tempts "to illustrate the importance of the
    financial side of planned economic development
    in a mixed economy." Focusing on Turkey during
    the 1960s, the author describes the country's
    financial system first within an institutional
    framework and then with econometric models.
    Main differences in the techniques used in tra-
    ditional monetary policy and financial planning
    are also discussed and illustrated. The first
    five-year development plan (1963-67) is de-
    scribed in the second chapter. Index. (JEL)

Hatiboglu, Zeyyat, AN UNCONVENTIONAL ANALYSIS OF
    TURKISH ECONOMY: An Essay on Economic Develop-
    ment, Istanbul, Aktif Buro Basim Organizasyon,
    1978. Arguing that the conventional method of
    analysis is not appropriate to the Turkish
    economy, the author undertakes "an unconven-
    tional analysis of the Turkish economic growth
    and the level of national income" since the
    1950's. The first half of the book describes
    the economic events and policies of the Turkish
    economy for the past 25 years. The second half
    discusses "the irrelevance of the conventional
    analysis" of industrialization, unemployment,

income distribution, international trade, and money. Index. (JEL)

Krueger, Anne O., FOREIGN TRADE REGIMES AND ECONOMIC DEVELOPMENT: Turkey, A Special Conference Series on Foreign Trade Regimes and Economic Development, Vol. I, New York, National Bureau of Economic Research; distributed by Columbia University Press, New York, 1974. This volume is the first of a series, sponsored by the National Bureau of Economic Research. Examines the relationship between the foreign trade and balance of payments experience in Turkey and the country's economic growth. Appendices; index. (JEL)

Krzyzaniak, Marian, and Ozmucur, Suleyman, THE DIS-TRIBUTION OF INCOME AND THE SHORT-RUN BURDEN OF TAXES IN TURKEY, 1968, Houston, Texas, Rice University Paper No. 28, Fall 1972.

Paine, Suzanne, EXPORTING WORKERS: The Turkish Case, New York, Cambridge University Press, 1974. An in-depth study of the Turkish experi-ence in exporting labor to Western Europe, mainly the effects on the Turkish economy. The author concludes that its results have not all been as favorable as have commonly been pre-sented. (FA)

World Bank, TURKEY: Prospects and Problems of an Expanding Economy, Washington, D.C.; Author, 1975. A report discussing the development and growth strategy between 1950 and 1972, and analyzing the Third Plan and assessing medium and long-term prospects. No index. (JEL)

Viet Nam

Hung, G. Nguyen Tien, ECONOMIC DEVELOPMENT OF SOCIAL-IST VIETNAM: 1955-80, New York, Praeger, 1977. After describing North Vietnam's economy prior to the 1954 partition, this study assesses the economic performance and structural changes initiated by the Communist regime. It suggests that the North participated in the Vietnam War in order to restore access to the South's food supply, without which North Vietnam could not build a viable socialist economy. The final

353

chapters discuss the measures taken by the
South's new government after the collapse of
Saigon; identify the problems encountered in a
unified economy, and explore the implications
of reunification. (BPA)

Woodside, Alexander B., COMMUNITY AND REVOLUTION IN
MODERN VIETNAM, Boston, Houghton Mifflin, 1976.
An intellectual and political history of modern
Vietnam which traces in fascinating and erudite
detail the development of the idea of "society"
in a traditional milieu, and its revolutionary
consequences. (FA)

Latin America

X-REF: AFRICA: Rout, AGRARIAN REFORM: Alexander,
Barraclough, Dorner, Duncan, Foland, King, Lands-
berger, Stavenhagen, Tuma, Un, University, AGRICUL-
TURAL DEVELOPMENT: Carroll, Rice, Thiesenhusen,
Yudelman, DEPENDENCY: Chilcote, Frank, Jenkins,
Kahl, Stein, Tancer, ECONOMIC INTEGRATION: Council,
Krause, Milenky, Morawetz, Muritano, Switzer, Urquidi,
Wionczek, Yudelman, EMPLOYMENT LABOR: Alba, Bass,
Davis, Eriksson, Ilo, Ramos, Thiesenhusen, ENERGY:
Robichek, FISCAL MONETARY INFLATION: Baer, Geithman,
Joint, Pazos, Randall, Sommerfeld, Vogel, Wachter,
FOREIGN AID: Loehr, Oas, FOREIGN INVESTMENT: Basch,
Behrman, Dell, Swansbrough, HISTORY: Cortes, Furta-
do, Herring, IMPORT SUBSTITUTION: Baer, Bruton,
INCOME DISTRIBUTION PRINCIPLES: Cline, Foxley, Un,
INDUSTRIAL DEVELOPMENT: Carnoy, Collier, MILITARISM:
Johnson, Lieuwen, Schmitter, Solaun, MISCELLANEOUS:
Powelson, MULTINATIONAL CORPORATIONS: Behrman,
Bernstein, Council, Hirschman, Irish, Lauterbach,
Ledogar, Swansbrough, Vernon, PLANNING: Oas, POLI-
TICAL DEVELOPMENT: Alexander, Fagen, Harris, Jagu-
aribe, Johnson, Jorrin, Petran, Sigmund, van Niekerk,
POPULATION: Chaplin, Sanchez, TECHNOLOGY: Bruton,
Davis, Street, Thebaud, TRADE: Bell, Walter, Wil-
kinson, UNITED STATES POLICY: Blasier, Connell,
Cotter, Green, Ferguson, Fishlow, Kane, Lodge,
Lowenthal, Olson, Peterson, Pike, Slater, Tambs,
Wagner, Whitaker, Wood, URBAN DEVELOPMENT: Beyer,
Cebula, Fox, Miller, Morse, Portes, Walter.

Adams, Richard N., ed., SOCIAL CHANGE IN LATIN
AMERICA TODAY, New York, Harper and Brothers,
1960. A book of essays on Latin America, in-

cluding a description, by Allen Holmberg, of
the now-famous agrarian reform undertaken privately by Cornell anthropologists at Vicos.
(Ed)

Alexander, Robert J., TROTSKYISM IN LATIN AMERICA,
Stanford, California, Hoover Institution Press,
1973. The first full-length analysis of this
"small but persistent force in Latin American
left-wing politics for over forty years," by a
veteran observer of the political scene who has
extensive personal connections with knowledgeable sources. (FA)

Andreski, Stanislav, PARASITISM AND SUBVERSION: The
Case of Latin America, New York, Schocken
Books, 1969. Andreski advances an internal
type of explanation for the failure of development in Latin America citing social and political factors. The author integrates this
latter factor into a sociological theory of
parasitism--internal vicious circles of waste--
and shows how urban-rural problems, militarism,
"kleptocracy," unjust tax systems, etc. are
originated and promoted. Index. (JEL)

Bell, Harry H., TARIFF PROFILES IN LATIN AMERICA:
Implications for Pricing Structures and Economic Integration, New York, Praeger, 1971. An
interesting contribution to the growing discussion of the impact of tariffs and other import
restrictions on development. Half the book is
a technical examination linking effective protection and prices and the other half a more
broadly based discussion of the implications of
the findings for comparative advantage, special-
ization and economic integration in Latin
America. The author is a former Foreign Service Officer. (FA)

Bernstein, Marvin D., ed., FOREIGN INVESTMENT IN
LATIN AMERICA: Cases and Attitudes, State Uni-
versity of New York at Fredonia, Alfred A.
Knopf, 1966.

Betancourt, Roger R.; Sheehey, Edmund J.; and Vogel,
Robert C.; "The Dynamics of Inflation in Latin
America," The American Economic Review, Vol.
66, No. 4, September 1976.

Blachman, Morris J., and Hellman, Ronald G., eds.,
TERMS OF CONFLICT: IDEOLOGY IN LATIN AMERICAN
POLITICS, Philadelphia, Institute for the Study
of Human Issues, 1977. Discusses the principal
currents of ideology that have shaped the politics of contemporary Latin America: Corporatism, Liberalism, Marxism, and Christian Democracy: for example, Christian Democracy and
Marxism in Chile, Corporatism in Argentina and
Uruguay, and Liberalism in Brazil, relating
systems of ideas to political developments.
(BPA)

Blasier, Cole, THE HOVERING GIANT: U.S. Responses
to Revolutionary Change in Latin America,
Pittsburgh, Pennsylvania, University of Pittsburgh Press, 1976. Dr. Blasier, who possesses
both diplomatic and academic credentials,
defines three stages of revolutionary change
and investigates the U.S. response to each of
them in the cases of Mexico, Bolivia, Guatemala
and Cuba. He also refers to U.S. policy in
Peru, Chile and the Dominican Republic, and
provides a detailed description of Latin American seizures of U.S. property. (FA)

Bobbs-Merrill Company, Inc., ENCYCLOPEDIA OF LATIN
AMERICAN HISTORY, Indianapolis; New York, a
subsidiary of Howard W. Sams & Co., 1968.

Bruton, H. J., "Productivity Growth in Latin America," American Economic Review, Vol. LVII, No.
5, December 1967.

Burnell, Elaine H., ed., ONE SPARK FROM HOLOCAUST:
The Crisis in Latin America, New York, Interbook for The Center for the Study of Democratic
Institutions, 1972. A collection of essays on
contemporary Latin America, especially on its
economic and social problems as well as on its
relations with the United States. The essays,
which grew out of a 1969 conference held in
Mexico City (and was sponsored by the Center
for the Study of Democratic Institutions) are
by a number of economists, lawyers, politicians,
and other experts from both Latin America and
the United States. Index. (JEL)

Butland, Gilbert J., LATIN AMERICA: A Regional
Geography, third edition, London, Longman Group
Limited, 1972.

356

Cabal, Hugo Latorre, THE REVOLUTION OF THE LATIN
AMERICAN CHURCH, Norman, University of Oklahoma
Press, 1978. The emergence of a radicalized
"young church" out of recent Roman Catholic
turmoil is described through brief resumes,
country by country, with accounts of important
radical events and personalities. The tone
throughout is polemical and quite unencumbered
by objectivity. (FA)

Cardoso, F. Henrique, THE ORIGINALITY OF THE COPY:
ECLA and the Idea of Development, Centre of
Latin American Studies, Working Paper No. 27,
University of Cambridge, June 1977.

Carlton, Robert J., ed., SOVIET IMAGE OF CONTEMPO-
RARY LATIN AMERICA, compiled and translated by
J. Gregory Oswald, Austin, University of Texas
Press, 1971. This compilation of translated
Soviet Russian writings on the contemporary
Latin American scene presents a cross-section
of various official and academic viewpoints.
(BPA)

CED, ECONOMIC DEVELOPMENT ISSUES: Latin America,
New York, CED Publications, 1967. Latin Ameri-
can economists analyze the successes and fail-
ures of their respective countries in attempt-
ing to achieve economic development. Roberto
Alemann (Argentina); Mario Henrique Simonsen
(Brazil); Sergio Undurraga Saavedra (Chile);
Hernan Echevarria (Colombia); Gustavo Romero
Kolbeck (Mexico); Romulo A. Ferrero (Peru).
(BPA)

Chalmers, Douglas A., CHANGING LATIN AMERICA: New
Interpretations of its Politics and Society,
Proceedings of the Academy of Political Science,
Vol. 30, No. 4, New York, The Academy of Political Science, Columbia University, 1972. A
first set of essays discusses important events
which have recently taken place in Latin
America (e.g., agrarian reform, the radical
priesthood, the population explosion, socialism
in Chile, etc.). No index. (JEL)

Council of the Americas, ANDEAN PACT: Definition,
Design, and Analysis, New York, Council of the
Americas, 1973. Analyzes and evaluates development of the Andean Common Market (Ancom) and
its importance to the business community as an

emerging pattern of regional development.
Papers on directions and significance of Ancom,
Andean Pact and business opportunity, joint
ventures, and competitive forces within Ancom.
(BPA)

Davis, Harold Eugene, LATIN AMERICAN THOUGHT: A
HISTORICAL INTRODUCTION, Baton Rouge, Louisiana
State University Press, 1972. Intellectual
history is one of the stepchildren of Latin
American studies; this highly competent work,
reaching back to pre-Columbian antecedents, is
therefore a welcome addition. The emphasis, in
this case, is on social philosophy and its
revolutionary essence. (FA)

Davis, Harold Eugene, and Wilson, Larman C., LATIN
AMERICAN FOREIGN POLICIES, An Analysis, Balti-
more and London, The Johns Hopkins University
Press, 1975.

Davis, Stanley M., and Goodman, Louis W., eds.,
WORKERS AND MANAGERS IN LATIN AMERICA, Lexington, Massachusetts, Lexington Books, 1977.

Delpar, Helen, ed., ENCYCLOPEDIA OF LATIN AMERICA,
New York, McGraw-Hill Book Company, 1974.

Diaz-Alejandro, Carlos F., "Planning the Foreign
Sector in Latin America," American Economic
Review, Vol. LX, No. 2, May 1970.

Duff, Ernest A. and McCamant, John F., (with W. Q.
Morales), VIOLENCE AND REPRESSION IN LATIN
AMERICA: A Quantitative and Historical Analysis, New York, Free Press, 1976. Quantitative
analysis is applied to variations in violence
and repression that can be traced in numerous
Latin American settings, in order to postulate
and explore theoretical relationships. These,
in turn, are compared to the historical record.
(FA)

Edel, Matthew, FOOD SUPPLY AND INFLATION IN LATIN
AMERICA, Praeger Special Studies in Interna-
tional Economics and Development, New York,
Praeger, 1969. Uses data from eight countries
(Argentina, Brazil, Chile, Colombia, Mexico,
Peru, Uruguay and Venezuela) to test the struc-
turalist hypothesis that agricultural stagna-
tion is a major factor in inflation in the

area. His conclusion is that the data fail to uphold the structuralist agreement. No index. (JEL)

Einaudi, Luigi R., ed., BEYOND CUBA: Latin America Takes Charge of its Future, New York, Crane, Russak, 1974. Latin American prospects in this decade are explored in 15 essays devoted to broad trends in politics, economics, institutions, and international relations. The unifying theme that emerges, a tendency toward "increasingly stable and sophisticated institutions...often providing determined leadership for reform," may be seen as an attempt to combine the revolutionary and the conservative images of development. (FA)

Ellis, Howard S. and Wallich, Henry C., ed., ECONOMIC DEVELOPMENT FOR LATIN AMERICA, Proceedings of a conference held by the International Economic Association, St. Martin's Press Inc., 1961.

Farley, Rawle, THE ECONOMICS OF LATIN AMERICA: Development Problems in Perspective, New York, Harper & Row, 1972. A comprehensive and overall look at the economic development problems of Latin America, including current conditions, past achievements, and the issues yet to be successfully-dealt with. The author discusses such varied topics as demography, housing, education, agricultural development, land tenure, industrialization, capital formation, external financing, economic integration, and the political variables in Latin American economic development. Index. (JEL)

Ffrench-Davis, R., "The Andean Pact: A Model of Economic Integration for Developing Countries," World Development, Vol. 5, Nos. 1 & 2, January-February 1977.

Field, Arthur J., ed., CITY AND COUNTRY IN THE THIRD WORLD: Issues in the Modernization of Latin America, Cambridge, Massachusetts, Schenkman Publishing Co., 1970. Contains eleven essays which are revised papers prepared for the International Symposium on Work and Urbanization in Modernizing Societies which was held in November of 1967 in the Virgin Islands. The essays are organized into 4 parts which focus on: 1) issues in the uses of research; 2)

359

issues in political change; 3) issues in rural and urban labor; and 4) issues in urbanization. No index. (JEL)

Foxley, Alejandro, ed., INCOME DISTRIBUTION IN LATIN AMERICA, New York, Cambridge University Press, 1976. That economic growth fails to achieve the desired redistributive objective is one of the conclusions of this assessment of industrial progress in the last decade, and its effect on money income and real consumption. For technically informed readers. (FA)

Furtado, Celso, ECONOMIC DEVELOPMENT OF LATIN AMERICA: Historical Background and Contemporary Problems, second edition, Cambridge Latin American Studies, No. 8, New York, Cambridge University Press, 1970; 1976. Introductory survey in eight parts: early history of Latin America up to the formation of nation-states; entry into the system of international division of labor; traditional structural pattern; industrialization process characteristics; recent reorganization of development; international relations; intraregional relations; and structural reconstruction policies. Many of the chapters in this edition have been rewritten. Includes data on trade and development indicators. Bibliography; index. (JEL)

Geithman, David T., ed., FISCAL POLICY FOR INDUSTRIALIZATION AND DEVELOPMENT IN LATIN AMERICA, Gainesville, The University Presses of Florida, 1974.

Geyer, Georgie Anne, THE NEW LATINS: Fateful Change in South and Central America, Garden City, New Jersey, Doubleday, 1970. The author describes social and psychological change in Latin America, in a vividly written first-hand account. There are many sound analyses of character, though a few errors and exaggerations of fact. (FA)

Goldhamer, Herbert, THE FOREIGN POWERS IN LATIN AMERICA, Princeton, New Jersey, Princeton University Press (for the RAND Corporation), 1972. A particular virtue of this detailed and scholarly volume is its analysis of the impact on Latin America of the important non-Hemipheric powers as well as the United States. (FA)

360

Gordon, Wendell C., THE POLITICAL ECONOMY OF LATIN
    AMERICA, New York and London, Columbia Univer-
    sity Press, 1965.

Griffin, Keith, ed., FINANCING DEVELOPMENT IN LATIN
    AMERICA, Problems in Focus Series, London,
    Macmillan; New York, St. Martin's Press, 1971.
    A collection of eight original essays on Latin
    America's development finance, focused on do-
    mestic rather than foreign investment. After
    an introduction by Keith Griffin, the essays
    examine development finance in relation to
    basic principles (Lester D. Thurow), surplus
    and the budget (Jorge Arrate and Lucio Geller),
    the public sector activities (Laurence White-
    head), agricultural taxation (Arthur L. Domike
    and Victor E. Tokman), private savings (Timothy
    King), inflation (Rosemary Thorp), and foreign
    capital (Keith Griffin). The main thesis is
    that a large proportion of the economic surplus
    is diverted into relatively "unproductive"
    uses. (JEL)

Griffin, Keith, UNDERDEVELOPMENT IN SPANISH AMERICA:
    An Interpretation, London, Allen and Unwin,
    1969. A study of the recent development prob-
    lems of a homogeneous economic region compris-
    ing nine Latin American countries. The author's
    argument is that "the essence of development is
    institutional reform." Offers a number of hy-
    potheses regarding the role of national and
    international institutions in impeding the
    development process. Index. (JEL)

Grunwald, Joseph, ed., LATIN AMERICA AND WORLD ECON-
    OMY: A Changing International Order, Beverly
    Hills, Sage (for the Center for Inter-American
    Relations), 1978. Fourteen essays by well-
    known contributors are organized into five
    sections: Latin American relations with indus-
    trial countries, chapters on Mexico and Brazil,
    regional integration and Third World relations,
    financing and multinational corporations, and
    commentary. The quality is high. (FA)

Grunwald, Joseph, and others, LATIN AMERICAN ECO-
    NOMIC INTEGRATION AND U.S. POLICY, Washington,
    Brookings Institution, 1972. A useful overview
    of the various economic integration schemes,

and the relationship to them of U.S. policy,
buttressed by extensive text and appendix
tables. (FA)

Grunwald, Joseph and Musgrove, Philip, NATURAL RE-
SOURCES IN LATIN AMERICAN ECONOMIC DEVELOPMENT,
Baltimore, Maryland, Johns Hopkins Press for
Resources for the Future, 1970.

Guevara, Che, "Diary," in Ramparts, July 27, 1968.

Harris, Richard, DEATH OF A REVOLUTIONARY: Che
Guevara's Last Mission, New York, Norton, 1970.
An account of the controversial revolutionary,
written from a viewpoint partial to armed
uprising. (FA)

Heath, Dwight B. and Adams, Richard N., ed., CON-
TEMPORARY CULTURES AND SOCIETIES OF LATIN
AMERICA, Random House, Inc., 1965.

Hellman, Ronald G. and Rosenbaum, Jon H., eds.,
LATIN AMERICA: The Search for a New International Role, Beverly Hills, California, Sage,
1975. The Center for Inter-American Relations
is sponsoring a series of studies of Latin
American international relations, a field not
overly researched. In this first volume, 13
well-known authorities describe inter-American
relations, domestic factors in inter-American
foreign policy-making, and intra-Latin American
relations. (FA)

Herman, Donald L., ed., THE COMMUNIST TIDE IN LATIN
AMERICA: A Selected Treatment, Austin, University of Texas Press, 1973. The stress is
upon the diversity and distinctions that have
come to replace the original monolithic Communist ideology, and the resulting need for a
more discriminating U.S. response. (FA)

Hildebrand, John Raymond, ECONOMIC DEVELOPMENT: A
Latin American Emphasis, Austin, Texas, The
Pemberton Press, 1969.

Hirschman, Albert O., A BIAS FOR HOPE: Essays on
Development and Latin America, New Haven, and
London, Yale University Press, 1971. A collection of 16 of the author's previously published
essays on the interaction of economic and political forces in the process of economic devel-

362

opment and social change in the developing
Latin American countries. These short essays,
written within the span of 18 years, are repro-
duced without change and are divided into three
parts: 1) elaboration of the strategy of
economic development, 2) critique and appeals
addressed to the rich countries, and 3) addressed to the developing countries. Index.
(JEL)

Hirschman, Albert O., JOURNEYS TOWARD PROGRESS:
    Studies of Economic Policy-Making in Latin
    America, New York, The Twentieth Century Fund,
    1963.

Hoijer, Harry and Goldschmidt, Walter, eds., THE
    SOCIAL ANTHROPOLOGY OF LATIN AMERICA: Essays
    in Honor of Ralph Leon Beals, Los Angeles, UCLA
    Latin American Center, 1970. The essay topics
    include cultural evolution in South America,
    provincial power structure in Guatemala, eth-
    nicity and social mobility in Peru, labor
    migration and family structure in Mexico,
    Tarascan folk religion, the mechanisms of
    culture change, and the effects of urbanization
    on a traditional market system. (BPA)

Horowitz, Irving Louis, ed., MASSES IN LATIN AMERICA,
    New York, Oxford University Press, 1970. The
    theoretical framework developed by Horowitz is
    in the first essay; he argues that "Social sci-
    ence must always study Latin America so as to
    consider the interaction of masses and elites."
    The papers are organized into three sections on
    the mobilization, urbanization, and politicali-
    zation of the masses. (JEL)

Hunter, John M. and Foley, James W., ECONOMIC PROB-
    LEMS OF LATIN AMERICA, Boston, Massachusetts,
    Houghton Mifflin, 1975. Text for undergraduate
    students in economic development and Latin
    American studies concentrating on economic
    problems, but including social, political, and
    cultural factors where these are relevant. The
    emphasis is on the nature of the problems of
    underdevelopment and the requirements for their
    solution. No mathematical economic techniques
    or models are used. Tables of data for various
    years 1929-73. Index. (JEL)

Inter-American Development Bank, LATIN AMERICA IN
THE WORLD ECONOMY: Recent Developments and
Trends, Inter-American Development Bank, Economic and Social Development Department, March
1975.

Johnson, Cecil, COMMUNIST CHINA AND LATIN AMERICA,
1959-1967, New York, Columbia University Press,
1970. A major effort was made by the Chinese,
especially during the years 1959-1967, to
become an important force in the Latin American
scene. This book, based on Chinese and Latin
American materials, is the story of that effort.
Professor Johnson critically analyzes and
compares the Maoist theory of "people's war"
now proclaimed by the Chinese as the only
reliable strategy for revolutionaries in Latin
America and elsewhere, with the strategy articulated by Regis Debray, Che Guevara, and Fidel
Castro. He examines the Sino-Cuban ideological
conflict in the context of the Sino-Soviet
controversy and the global struggle with the
United States. Another major topic is the
Chinese effort to establish pro-Chinese parties
and movements to implement their views. (BPA)

Johnson, John J., THE MILITARY AND SOCIETY IN LATIN
AMERICA, Stanford Press, 1974.

José, James R., AN INTER-AMERICAN PEACE FORCE WITHIN
THE FRAMEWORK OF THE ORGANIZATION OF AMERICAN
STATES, Metuchen, New Jersey, Scarecrow Press,
1970. The concept of the often-mooted Peace
Force is examined from every angle. The author
concludes that it is not likely to be conjured
into early existence. (FA)

Kohl, James and Litt, John, URBAN GUERRILLA WARFARE
IN LATIN AMERICA, Cambridge, Massachusetts, MIT
Press, 1974. The historical and political
background of guerrilla movements in Brazil,
Uruguay and Argentina: the theories of guerrilla warfare formulated by Carlos Marighella
and other theoreticians and personal accounts
by typical guerrillas of military actions in
which they engaged and what motivated them.
(BPA)

Liebman, Arthur and others, LATIN AMERICAN UNIVERSITY
STUDENTS: A Six Nation Study, Cambridge,
Harvard University Press (for the Center for
International Affairs), 1972. A comparative
study of student movements and attitudes in six
countries selected for their diverse political
and university systems: Colombia, Panama,
Paraguay, Puerto Rico, Uruguay and Mexico.
(FA)

Martin, John Bartlow, UNITED STATES POLICY IN THE
CARIBBEAN, Boulder, Colorado, Westview Press,
for the Twentieth Century Fund, 1978. The ex-
Ambassador to the Dominican Republic argues for
a special Caribbean-U.S. relationship, with
preferential market access and aid policies.
He also favors political pluralism and insula-
tion of the Caribbean from U.S. global policies
and interests. He therefore urges noninterven-
tion, but, recognizing its difficulties and
ambiguities, he adds "...in most times and at
most places." And he supports a strong U.S.
naval presence and military training assistance
programs. (FA)

Mesa-Lago, Carmelo, SOCIAL SECURITY IN LATIN AMERICA:
Pressure Groups, Stratification, and Inequality,
Pittsburgh, Pennsylvania, University of Pittsburgh Press, 1978. This book is a comprehensive and sophisticated study of the relationship between social security policy and inequality in Latin America. The introduction provides a good historical background to the
problem and clearly lays out the theoretical
approach. The five succeeding chapters present
individual case studies of Chile, Uruguay,
Peru, Argentina, and Mexico. (BPA)

Morner, Magnus, ed., RACE AND CLASS IN LATIN AMERICA,
New York, Columbia University Press, 1970.
Thirteen papers of professional quality assess
race relations, slavery and social classes in
selected countries and time periods. (FA)

Musgrove, Philip, CONSUMER BEHAVIOR IN LATIN AMERICA,
Washington, D.C., Brookings Institution, 1978.
Analyzes new and fairly uniform household bud-
get data collected in ten cities in five countries; describes the distribution of incomes
among families, the portion they spend, and
what they spend it on. Income disparities

strongly associated with disparities in education, less strongly with age and occupation; income and family composition are the chief determinants of decisions to spend and to save. (BPA)

Mutchler, David E., THE CHURCH AS A POLITICAL FACTOR IN LATIN AMERICA, New York, Praeger, 1971. The Church, seeking survival, has tended in the author's opinion to serve the interests of U.S. and European policies, thereby weakening reformist and populist movements. (FA)

Nisbet, Charles T., ed., LATIN AMERICA: Problems in Economic Development, New York, Free Press, 1969. Reprints seventeen articles, written since 1960, addressed to teachers and graduate students interested in the economic development of Latin America. (JEL)

Odell, Peter R., and Preston, David A., ECONOMIES AND SOCIETIES IN LATIN AMERICA: A Geographical Interpretation, New York, Wiley, 1973. Emphasizing the influence of the spatial structures of Latin American economies and societies as a defining source of human activity, the authors have produced a stimulating and useful work. (FA)

Oswald, Gregory J., (compiled and translated) and Carlton, Robert G. (ed.), SOVIET IMAGE OF CONTEMPORARY LATIN AMERICA: A Documentary History, 1960-1968, Austin, University of Texas Press (for the Conference on Latin American History), 1971. A compilation and translation of recent (1960s) Soviet writings on Latin America, including the "national-liberation movement." (FA)

Pearce, Andrew, THE LATIN AMERICAN PEASANT, London, Frank Cass, 1975. Utilizing field material from nine countries (Cuba is included; Venezuela and Argentina are not), a British sociologist describes and analyzes land tenure, peasant and labor force organizations, rural life patterns, activism, production, and related topics. (FA)

Pescatello, Ann, ed., FEMALE AND MALE IN LATIN AMERICA: Essays, Pittsburgh, Pennsylvania, University of Pittsburgh Press, 1973. A miscellany, assembled out of literature, history

366

and political science, covering a subject generally neglected in Latin American scholarship. (FA)

Pinto, Anibal, and Kankal, Jan, AMERICA LATINA Y EL CAMBIO EN LA ECONOMIA MUNDIAL, Lima, Peru, Instituto de Estudios Peruanos, 1973.

Powelson, John P., LATIN AMERICA: TODAY'S ECONOMIC AND SOCIAL REVOLUTION, New York, McGraw-Hill Book Company, 1964. A book on Latin American issues, based on communications the author had with left-wing university students in Bolivia; what they said to him, what he said to them, and what he would have said if he had thought about it at the time. (Ed)

Prebisch, Raul, CHANGE AND DEVELOPMENT--Latin America's Great Task, Washington, D.C., Inter-American Development Bank, July 1970.

Quintana, Carlos, DEVELOPMENT PROBLEMS IN LATIN AMERICA, an analysis by the United National Economic Commission for Latin America, The University of Texas Press, Austin and London, 1970.

Randall, Laura, ed., ECONOMIC DEVELOPMENT: Evolution or Revolution?, Boston, Massachusetts, D. C. Heath and Company, 1964.

Salera, Virgil, "Prebisch on 'Change and Development,' Latin America's Great Task," Inter-American Economic Affairs, Vol. 24, No. 4, Spring 1971.

Sauvage, Leo, CHE GUEVARA: The Failure of a Revolutionary, Englewood Cliffs, New Jersey, Prentice-Hall, 1973. A journalist with a leftward emotional tilt describes in non-ideological prose the inability of the mythified and fanatical Guevara to achieve any of his major aims. In the process, Sauvage casts serious doubt upon Che's qualities of humanity and compassion. (FA)

Silvert, Kalman H., ESSAYS IN UNDERSTANDING LATIN AMERICA, Philadelphia, Pennsylvania, Institute for the Study of Human Issues, 1977. These 15 essays, arranged by the author before his recent death to show the progression of his

thought, may be taken as another memorial to
his career. Silvert's principal concerns include the broad themes of nation and class,
freedom and democracy, the nature and consequence of dependency, and the role of ideas in
social and political behavior. (FA)

Smith, T. Lynn, THE RACE BETWEEN POPULATION AND FOOD
SUPPLY IN LATIN AMERICA, Albuquerque, University of New Mexico Press, 1976. Concentrated
for the most part on conditions in Brazil and
Colombia, these demographic studies are cen-
tered on population trends, migration, and
restraints on expansion of the agricultural
sector. (FA)

Smith, T. Lynn, STUDIES OF LATIN AMERICAN SOCIETIES,
Garden City, New York, Anchor Books, Doubleday
& Company, Inc., 1970.

Swansbrough, Robert H., "The American Investor's
View of Latin American Economic Nationalism,"
Inter-American Economic Affairs, Vol. 26, No.
3, Winter 1972.

Swift, Jeannine, ECONOMIC DEVELOPMENT IN LATIN
AMERICA, New York, St. Martin's Press, 1978.
Textbook. Views issues in Latin American development as problems rooted in the history and
institutional setting of each country. Emphasizes the notion of underdevelopment as a process rather than as a stage of growth, and
thereby examines the forces that in some cases
lead to distorted growth or deterioration.
Author views radical social change in political
institutions as a necessary correlate of economic development that will benefit the masses
of people. (JEL)

Tamagna, Frank, STUDIES OF CENTRAL BANKING IN LATIN
AMERICA, Centro De Estudios Monetarios Latinoamericanos, Mexico, 1965.

Tancer, Shoshana B., ECONOMIC NATIONALISM IN LATIN
AMERICA: The Quest for Economic Independence,
Praeger Special Studies in International Economics and Development, New York, Praeger,
1976. Emphasizes the interrelationship between
the attempts of Latin American nations to
assert themselves as political entities and to
develop their economies. Discusses these

manifestations of Latin American economic
nationalism: the drive for industrialization,
increased trade, control over natural resources,
their perception of the role of international
lending, and the hopes for regional integration.
Attention has been given to the United States
and its policies vis-à-vis the Latin American
nations. Index. (JEL)

Tax Institute of America, TAX POLICY ON UNITED
    STATES INVESTMENT IN LATIN AMERICA, Princeton,
    New Jersey, Tax Institute of America, 1963.

Thebaud, Schiller, STATISTICS ON SCIENCE AND TECH-
    NOLOGY IN LATIN AMERICA: Experience with
    UNESCO Pilot Projects 1972-1974, statistical
    reports and studies, Paris, France, The UNESCO
    Press, 1976.

Theberge, James D. and Fontaine, Rober W., eds.,
    LATIN AMERICA: Struggle for Progress, Critical
    Choices for Americans, Vol. XIV, Lexington,
    Lexington Books, 1977. This overview presents
    condensed, no-nonsense summaries of Latin
    American problems and choices, and their signi-
    ficance in terms of U.S. interests. The book
    is organized under such headings as Critical
    Problems, Options, Background, U.S. Policy.
    (FA)

Theberge, James D., THE SOVIET PRESENCE IN LATIN
    AMERICA, New York, Crane, Russak & Company,
    1974.

Thurber, Clarence E. and Graham, Lawrence S., eds.,
    DEVELOPMENT ADMINISTRATION IN LATIN AMERICA,
    Comparative Administration Group Series, Dur-
    ham, North Carolina, Duke University Press for
    Comparative Administration Group of the Ameri-
    can Society for Public Administration, 1973.
    A collection of sixteen previously unpublished
    papers written mostly by members of the Ameri-
    can Society for Public Administration's Latin
    American Development Administration Committee
    and dealing with various aspects of administra-
    tive reform, policy making, and institution
    building in Latin America. Index. (JEL)

Tulchin, Joseph S., ed., LATIN AMERICA IN THE YEAR
    2000, Reading Massachusetts, Addison-Wesley
    Publishing Company, 1975.

Turner, Frederick C., CATHOLICISM AND POLITICAL DE-
VELOPMENT IN LATIN AMERICA, Chapel Hill, University of North Carolina Press, 1971. A competent and scholarly description of current
attitudes toward social change currently held
by progressive Roman Catholic leaders and their
movements. Much use is made of pastoral mes-
sages and other ecclesiastical materials. (FA)

United Nations, Economic Commission for Latin
America, DEVELOPMENT PROBLEMS IN LATIN AMERICA:
An Analysis by the United Nations Economic
Commission for Latin America, Austin, University of Texas Press (for the Institute of Latin
American Studies), 1970. The first two decades
of ECLA's achievements are summarized through
reproduction of that body's more important
studies.(FA)

United Nations, SMALL-SCALE INDUSTRY IN LATIN
AMERICA, New York, United Nations, 1969.

Urquidi, Victor L., THE CHALLENGE OF DEVELOPMENT IN
LATIN AMERICA, New York, Praeger, 1962.

Urquidi, Victor L. and Thorp, Rosemary, ed., LATIN
AMERICA IN THE INTERNATIONAL ECONOMY, New York,
Halsted Press, 1973. Thirteen papers, submitted at a conference held by the International
Economic Association in Mexico City in December
1971, devoted to full analysis of Latin America's economic dependence and its trade and
financial relations with the rest of the world.
A valuable feature: each paper is followed by
a useful summary of the discussions it invoked.
(FA)

Vaseña, Adalbert Krieger, and Pazos, Javier, LATIN
AMERICA: A Broader World Role, Totowa, New
Jersey, Rowman and Littlefield (for the Atlantic Institute for International Affairs), 1973.
In this significant analysis of Latin American
development, the theme is basically hopeful,
but the authors make heavy demands upon optimism; semi-development, with its problems of
population growth, urbanization, income distribution and unemployment, can be rectified only
by adequately planned, outward-looking expansion of production, combined with closer intraregional and worldwide economic ties. (FA)

Veliz, Claudio, LATIN AMERICA AND THE CARIBBEAN: A
Handbook, New York, Praeger, 1968. A monumental
handbook covering many topics and countries.
(Ed)

Veliz, Claudio, OBSTACLES TO CHANGE IN LATIN AMERICA,
New York, Oxford University Press, 1965.

Veliz, Claudio, THE POLITICS OF CONFORMITY IN LATIN
AMERICA, New York, Oxford University Press,
1970.

Vernon, Raymond, ed., HOW LATIN AMERICA VIEWS THE
U.S. INVESTOR, New York, Praeger, 1966.

Vogel, Robert C., "The Dynamics of Inflation in
Latin America, 1950-1969," The American Economic Review, Vol. LXIV, No. 1, March 1974.

Weiskoff, Richard, and Figueroa, Adolfo, "Traversing
the Social Pyramid: A Comparative Review of
Income Distribution in Latin America," Latin
American Research Review, Vol. XI, No. 2, 1976.

Wolf, Eric R. and Hansen, Edward C., THE HUMAN CON-
DITION IN LATIN AMERICAN, New York, Oxford University Press, 1972.

Wynia, Gary W., THE POLITICS OF LATIN AMERICAN DE-
VELOPMENT, New York, Cambridge University
Press, 1978. Viewing politics as a game with
rules, players, contests for power, and winners
and losers, Professor Wynia combines a concise
survey of Latin American political processes
with a detailed analysis of the four types of
political systems that have dominated life in
the region in recent years: the populist,
democratic reformist, military authoritarian,
and revolutionary. (BPA)

Argentina

X-REF: FISCAL MONETARY INFLATION: Tanzi.

Aizcorbe, Roberto, ARGENTINA: The Peronist Myth,
Hicksville, New York, Exposition Press, 1975.
The author, an Argentine journalist, suggests
that the vexatious national ills trace back to
the infiltration of leftist and collectivist

influences, as a consequence of the disorders, weaknesses, and violence that followed Perón's first administration. (FA)

Alexander, Robert J., JUAN DOMINGO PERON, Boulder, Colorado, Westview Press, 1979. After reviewing Perón's life, the author concludes that his political errors prevented him from realizing his dreams for Argentina; he was a tragic figure. (BPA)

Chu, Ke-young, and Feltenstein, Andrew, "Relative Price Distortions and Inflation: The Case of Argentina," I.M.F. Staff Papers, September 1978.

Ciria, Alberto, PARTIES AND POWER IN MODERN ARGENtina, (1930-1946), Albany, State University of New York Press, 1974. The enigma of Argentina during the more than four decades of confusion that have passed since the fall of Yrigoyen receives yet another analysis. The emphasis here is upon the influential pressure groups whose rising power is contrasted with the decline and impotence of the traditional political parties. (FA)

DeHaven, R. K., "Economic Development Policy in Perón's Argentina," Economic Affairs, Vol. 17, No. 1-2, January-February 1972.

de Pablo, J. C., "Relative Prices, Income Distribution and Stabilization Plans' The Argentine Experience, 1967-1970," Journal of Development Economics, Vol. 1, No. 3, December 1974, pp. 167-189.

Ferrer, Aldo, THE ARGENTINE ECONOMY, University of California Press, Berkeley and Los Angeles, 1967.

Hodges, Donald C., ARGENTINA, 1943-1976, Albuquerque, University of New Mexico Press, 1976. A professor of philosophy, with a revolutionary and Marxist view, assesses the factions contending within the Argentine Far Left with numerous comments and comparisons pertaining to Cuban and other radical precedents. A restructured Peronist movement of the Left is discussed. A bit theoretical, but not technical. (FA)

372

Imaz, José Luis De, LOS QUE MANDAN, (Those Who
        Rule), State University of New York Press,
        Editorial Universitaria de Buenos Aires, 1964.
        A descriptive analysis of the elite in Argen-
        tina and their dominant role in political and
        economic processes. (Ed)

Jefferson, Mark S. W., PEOPLING THE ARGENTINE PAMPA,
        Port Washington, New York, Kennikat Press,
        1971. A geographer draws upon first-hand
        experience to portray the Pampa as an Argentine
        frontier, and to describe the effects of Euro-
        pean immigration on the 19th century Creole way
        of life. (BPA)

Kirkpatrick, Jeane, LEADER AND VANGUARD IN MASS
        SOCIety: A Study of Peronist Argentina, Cam-
        bridge, Massachusetts, MIT Press, 1971. The
        relevance of the apparently timeless attrac-
        tions of Peronism to forthcoming political
        events in Argentina lends interest to this
        well-researched study in depth. (FA)

Mallon, R. D., and Sourrouille, J. V., ECONOMIC
        POLICYMAKING IN A CONFLICT SOCIETY: The Argen-
        tine Case, Cambridge, Massachusetts, Harvard
        University Press, 1975.

Milenky, Edward S., ARGENTINA'S FOREIGN POLICIES,
        Boulder, Colorado, Westview Press, 1978.
        Edward Milenky examines and analyzes the for-
        eign policies of Argentina as an independent
        actor in world affairs, taking into account
        both the policymaking process and the content
        of diplomacy. Presenting Argentina as a case
        study of the Latin American countries' changing
        role in international politics and the implica-
        tions of these changes for U.S. foreign policy
        and the international system, the author con-
        cludes that while Argentina is a nearly devel-
        oped country economically, it is politically
        immature. He explains both international
        behavior and domestic political upheaval in
        terms of the conflict between efforts to con-
        struct the classic, self-sufficient nationstate
        and the arrival of an age of interdependence in
        which this goal may well be unachievable at an
        acceptable price. (BPA)

373

Randall, Laura, AN ECONOMIC HISTORY OF ARGENTINA IN
    THE TWENTIETH CENTURY, New York, Columbia Uni-
    versity Press, 1977. Randall asserts that fre-
    quent changes in domestic economic policies
    account for Argentina's economic performance.
    She shows that, countrary to widespread belief,
    agriculture accounts for only a small per-
    centage of Argentina's production. (BPA)

Reina, Ruben E., PARANA: Social Boundaries in an
    Argentine City, Austin, University of Texas
    Press, 1973. The human and social configura-
    tions that shape the political process are in-
    tensively researched in the narrow focus of a
    single Argentine city. The full essence of
    urban life is summoned from church and plaza;
    from clubs, schools, almacenes; and from class
    structure and behavioral norms. Ortega y
    Gasset's warning of Argentine estrangement and
    lack of cohesion is vindicated. Excellent.
    (FA)

Rock, David, ed., ARGENTINA IN THE TWENTIETH CENTURY,
    Pittsburgh, Pennsylvania, University of Pitts-
    burgh Press, 1975. Eight commissioned essays
    analyze Peronism, past and present, and probe
    the murky sources of Argentine political and
    economic instability. There are interesting
    observations on correlations between the poli-
    tical fortunes of Peronism and the performance
    of the national economy. (FA)

Scobie, James R., "Buenos Aires of 1910: The Paris
    of South America That Did Not Take Off," Inter-
    American Economic Affairs, Vol. 22, No. 2,
    Autumn 1968.

Smith, Peter H., ARGENTINA AND THE FAILURE OF DE-
    MOCRACY: Conflict Among Political Elites,
    1904-1955, Madison, University of Wisconsin
    Press, 1974. The riddle of Argentina is ap-
    proached through a novel quantitative metho-
    dology applied to voting records in the Chamber
    of Deputies, in an effort to probe the politi-
    cal transformations of this century. The
    statistical treatment will appeal to special-
    ists. (FA)

Solberg, Carl E., OIL AND NATIONALISM IN ARGENTINA:
    A History, Stanford, California, Stanford
    Press, 1978. A case study of YPF, the world's

first state-owned oil company, this work traces
the development of Argentina's nationalistic
petroleum policy from the discovery of oil on
state-owned land in 1907 to the present. The
focus is on the period prior to 1930, when the
institutions and ideologies that have shaped
Argentine petroleum affairs became firmly
established. A final chapter summarizes developments since 1930, with emphasis on the impact
the Argentine experience has had on other oil-
producing countries in Latin America. (BPA)

Torres, Juan C., and Corradi, Juan E., eds., ARGEN-
TINA: The Second Peronist Era, Philadelphia,
Pennsylvania, ISHI Publications, not yet published. A group of Argentine scholars examine
what Perón's movement has meant for Argentina,
focusing especially on the reasons for its re-
surgence in the 1970's. (BPA)

Bolivia

X-REF: UNITED STATES POLICY: Pike, MISCELLANEOUS:
Kalecki, MULTINATIONAL CORPORATIONS: Ingram.

Andrade, Victor, MY MISSIONS FOR REVOLUTIONARY BOLI-
VIA, 1944-1962, Pittsburgh, Pennsylvania, Uni-
versity of Pittsburgh Press, 1976. The former
Bolivian Foreign Minister and Ambassador to the
United Nations presents his well-written,
chatty reminiscences of MNR activities, Paz
Estenssoro, the politics of tin, and the assort-
ed turbulences of his two decades of service.
(FA)

Burke, Melvin, "Does 'Food for Peace' Assistance
Damage the Bolivian Economy?" Inter-American
Economic Affairs, Vol. 25, No. 1, Summer 1971.

Burke, Melvin, LAND REFORM IN THE LAKE TITACACA RE-
GION, LTC Reprint No. 110, Madison, University
of Wisconsin, Land Tenure Center, 1971.

Clark, Ronald J., LAND REFORM AND PEASANT MARKET
PARTICIPATION ON THE NORTHERN HIGHLANDS OF
BOLIVIA, LTC Reprint No. 42, Madison, Univer-
sity of Wisconsin, Land Tenure Center, 1968.

Heath, Dwight B.; Erasmus, Charles J.; and Buechler, Hans C.; LAND REFORM AND SOCIAL REVOLUTION IN BOLIVIA, New York, Praeger, 1969.

Heath, Dwight B., NEW PATRONS FOR OLD: Changing Patron-Client Relationships in the Bolivian Yungas, LTC Reprint No. 101, Madison, University of Wisconsin, Land Tenure Center, 1973.

Heyduk, Daniel, "Bolivia's Land Reform Hacendados," Inter-American Economic Affairs, Vol. 27, No. 1, Summer 1973.

Heyduk, Daniel, THE HACIENDA SYSTEM AND AGRARIAN RE-FORM IN HIGHLAND BOLIVIA: A Re-Evaluation, LTC Reprint No. 117, Madison, University of Wisconsin, Land Tenure Center, 1974.

Klein, Herbert S., PARTIES AND POLITICAL CHANGE IN BOLIVIA, 1880-1952, New York, Cambridge University Press, 1970. The author traces in full detail the antecedent forces of the 1952 revolution. The comments on the seminal function of the Chaco war are particularly interesting. (FA)

Lora, Guillermo, A HISTORY OF THE BOLIVIAN LABOUR MOVEMENT 1848-1971, edited and abridged by Laurence Whitehead and translated by Christine Whitehead, New York, Cambridge University Press, 1977. This abridgement and translation of Guillermo Lora's five-volume history covers the strengthening and radicalization of Bolivia's organized labor movement which culminated in the drastic revolutionary changes of the 1950's. In spite of the military control that took place in the sixties the labor movement has continued to oppose and resist certain issues and policies. The author's analysis of such radical objectives as direct property seizures, union nominated ministers and union, military and work control will interest Latin American scholars working on socio-economic problems. Guillermo Loa, secretary of the small Trotskyist Partido Obrero Revolucionario and miner leader, was elected to the Bolivian Congress in 1948, but was jailed during the civil war of 1949 and later went into exile. (BPA)

Malloy, James M., and Thorn, Richard S., eds.,
    BEYOND THE REVOLUTION: Bolivia Since 1952,
    Pittsburgh, Pennsylvania, University of Pitts-
    burgh Press, 1971. A comprehensive book on the
    Bolivian Revolution, concentrating on the
    period 1952-64. Nine authors cover all signi-
    ficant aspects of the Revolution: antecedents;
    the revolutionary take-over, relations with the
    United States; politics; economic transforma-
    tion; public expenditure; agrarian reform in
    general, among the Yungas Indians and the Lake
    Titicaca area; and the social novel. Appendix,
    tables, glossary, and index. (JEL)

Malloy, James M., BOLIVIA: The Uncompleted Revolu-
    tion, Pittsburgh, Pennsylvania, University of
    Pittsburgh Press, 1970. The author believes
    that Bolivia has been continuously in a revolu-
    tionary situation since 1936. Political and
    economic events are traced to 1964, with empha-
    sis upon the "will, capacities and orientation
    of the active contestants." (FA)

McEwen, William J., CHANGING RURAL SOCIETY: A Study
    of Communities in Bolivia, Oxford University
    Press, 1975.

Mitchell, Christopher, THE LEGACY OF POPULISM IN
    BOLIVIA: From the MNR to Military Rule, New
    York, Praeger, 1977. The author finds the MNR
    fundamentally flawed, after its initial success-
    es in 1952-53, by its underlying identification
    with the middle class, which turned conserva-
    tive within a short time. This tendency was
    accentuated after the 1964 coup by the alliance
    between the military and moderate civilian
    elements. (FA)

Wilkie, James W., THE BOLIVIAN REVOLUTION AND U.S.
    AID SINCE 1952, Los Angeles, University of
    California, Latin American Center, 1969. An
    incisive study of state policy in a "Marxist
    but non-Communist" revolution, by UCLA profes-
    sor Wilkie, winner of the 1968 Bolton Prize for
    history. A detailed budgetary analysis that
    penetrates the financial realities behind Boli-
    via's complex political scene and offers a
    rational methodology for examining state policy
    in relation to U.S. influence in a developing
    country. Includes more than 30 tables and
    graphs of social and economic statistics. (BPA)

X-REF: AGRICULTURAL CREDIT: Adams, DEPENDENCY:
Frank, IMPORT SUBSTITUTION: Morley, Tyler, INCOME
DISTRIBUTION PRINCIPLES: Fields, Looney, MODERNIZA-
TION: Kahl, MULTINATIONAL CORPORATIONS: Council,
Morley, Ledogar, URBAN DEVELOPMENT: Gardner.

Adams, Dale W.; Davis, Harlan; and Bettis, Lee; "Is
    Inexpensive Credit a Bargain for Small Farmers?
    The Recent Brazilian Experience," Inter-Ameri-
    can Economic Affairs, Vol. 26, No. 1, Spring
    1972.

Bacha, E. L., "Issues and Evidence on Recent Brazil-
    ian Economic Growth," World Development, Vol.
    5, Nos. 1 & 2, January-February 1977.

Baer, Werner, INDUSTRIALIZATION AND ECONOMIC DEVEL-
    OPMENT IN BRAZIL, New Haven, Connecticut, Yale
    University, The Economic Growth Center, 1965.

Baer, Werner; Newfarmer, Richard; and Trebat, Thomas;
    "On State Capitalism in Brazil: Some New
    Issues and Questions," Inter-American Economic
    Affairs, Vol. 30, No. 3, Winter 1976.

Baklanoff, Eric N., ed., THE SHAPING OF MODERN
    BRAZIL, Baton Rouge, Louisiana State University
    Press, 1969. Seven essays on the growth and
    development of Brazil from its origin as a
    Portuguese colony to the present; a prediction
    of the probable pattern of the Brazilian land-
    scape in 1980 and 2000. (BPA)

Bergsmen, Joel, BRAZIL: Industrialization and Trade
    Policies, Industry and Trade in Some Developing
    Countries, New York, Oxford University Press
    for the Development Centre of the Organization
    for Economic Co-operation and Development,
    1970. Description, analysis, and evaluation of
    Brazil's infant industry policies in the post-
    war era. Concludes that "Brazilian policies
    have paid too little attention to future com-
    petitiveness, and the results show that too
    little has been achieved." Index. (JEL)

Burns, E. Bradford, A HISTORY OF BRAZIL, New York,
    Columbia University Press, 1971. A scholarly
    history that brings the Brazilian narrative up

to 1970. The author is not partial to developments since the advent of military rule in 1964. (FA)

Cehelsky, Marta, LAND REFORM IN BRAZIL: The Management of Social Change, Boulder, Colorado, Westview Press, 1978. This volume documents the disintegration of Brazilian democracy and identifies the major reasons for its instability and its tendency to revert to authoritarian rule. The author explores the significance and treatment of land reform under democratic and authoritarian rule and assesses the overall impact of a measure originally intended to produce social reform. Viewed analytically, the management of the land reform issue in Brazil attests to the resilience of the traditional elites and their power to determine substantially the nature and rate of accommodation of social and economic change. (BPA)

Cline, William R., ECONOMIC CONSEQUENCES OF A LAND REFORM IN BRAZIL, Contributions to Economic Analysis, Vol. 67, Amsterdam and London, North-Holland Publishing Co., 1970. One in a series of studies in economic analysis; the author examines the effect of the theory of land reform on agricultural production in Brazil. The study has important policy implications for Brazil and other low-income countries with unequal land distribution. Statistical appendices; bibliography; index. (JEL)

Conrad, Robert, THE DESTRUCTION OF BRAZILIAN SLAVERY, 1850-1888, Berkeley, University of California Press, 1972.

Daly, Herman E., THE POPULATION QUESTION IN NORTHEAST BRAZIL: Its Economic and Ideological Dimensions, Center Paper #157, New Haven, Connecticut, Yale University, Economic Growth Center, 1970.

Davis, Shelton H., VICTIMS OF THE MIRACLE: Development and the Indians of Brazil, New York, Cambridge University Press, 1977. An anthropologist describes the social and environmental effects, and the human costs to the indigenous Indians, of the Amazon development program. (FA)

De Barros, José Roberto Mendonca, and Graham, Douglas H., "The Brazilian Economic Miracle Revisited: Private and Public Sector Initiative in a Market Economy," Latin American Research Review, Vol. XIII, No. 2, 1978.

Donges, Juergen B., BRAZIL'S TROTTING PEG: A New Approach to Greater Exchange Rate Flexibility in Less Developed Countries, Special Analysis No. 7, Washington, D.C., American Enterprise Institute for Public Policy Research, August 1971.

Dulles, John W. F., ANARCHISTS AND COMMUNISTS IN BRAZIL, 1900-1935, Austin, University of Texas Press, 1973. Vast and thorough, erected on a foundation of broadly diversified sources and devoted to the radical components of the Opposition from pre-Vargas times to the abortive Communist revolution of 1935. (FA)

Dulles, John W. F., UNREST IN BRAZIL: POLITICAL-MILITARY CRISES 1955-1964, Austin, University of Texas Press, 1970. An interesting, well-written and elaborate description of Brazilian political factions and struggles, from the suicide of Vargas to the coming of the military government. (FA)

Ellis, Howard S., ed., THE ECONOMY OF BRAZIL, Foreword by Lincoln Gordon, Berkeley, University of California Press, 1969. Contains thirteen essays by the following Brazilian and American economists: A. Abouchar, W. Baer, D. W. Baerresen, J. Bergsman and A. Candal, J. Chacel, O. de Gouveia Bulhoes, E. Gudin, S. A. Morley, R. de Oliveira Campos, W. van Rijckeghem, M. H. Simonsen, G. W. Smith, and the editor. Together they cover the broad aspects of Brazil's development; 132 tables and statistics through 1965. Index. (JEL)

Evans, P. B., "Foreign Investment and Industrial Transformation: A Brazilian Case Study," Journal of Development Economics, Vol. 3, No. 2, July 1976, pp. 119-139.

Erickson, Kenneth Paul, THE BRAZILIAN CORPORATIVE STATE AND WORKING-CLASS POLITICS, Berkeley, University of California Press, 1978. This is a valuable account of the political power of labor leaders, its limitations, the participation of labor in public life, and the effectiveness of corporatism in bringing the urban working class into social and political activity with a minimum of disruption. Populism never became revolutionary because the purpose of Brazilian corporatism is a conservative one: preservation of the status quo through assimilation of emergent social forces. (FA)

Fields, Gary S., "Who Benefits from Economic Development?--A Reexamination of Brazilian Growth in the 1960's," The American Economic Review, September 1977, p. 570.

Fishlow, Albert, "Brazilian Size Distribution of Income," American Economic Review, Vol. LXII, No. 2, May 1972.

Flynn, Peter, BRAZIL: A Political Analysis, Boulder, Colorado, Westview Press, 1978. Extending back to monarchical times, this lengthy review concludes that the preeminent influence in shaping Brazilian political institutions and in explaining the "bonapartist" intervention of the armed forces since 1964 has been the contention among social class interests. The author also finds that the post-1964 economic model and a repressive political system are linked, and that there is no necessary correlation between an authoritarian system and economic growth and control over inflation. (FA)

Forman, Shepard, THE BRAZILIAN PEASANTRY, New York, Columbia University Press, 1975. The peasant (caboclo or sertanejo) is the 'man with the hoe,' the forgotten man of Brazil forced by the social and economic system to produce for a society which denies him an equitable share. Ever-expanding latifundia continue to encroach on independent small holdings as commercialization of agriculture turns small-scale producers into a nomadic rural proletariat. A capitalist export-oriented economy, provisioned for centuries by slaves and miserable peasants, has created social pressures that can only, with increasing difficulty, be contained by military repression. (BPA)

Freyre, Gilberto, THE MASTERS AND THE SLAVES: A
    Study in the Development of Brazilian Civiliza-
    tion, New York, Alfred A. Knopf, 1956.

Freyre, Gilberto, ORDER AND PROGRESS: Brazil from
    Monarchy to Republic, New York, Knopf, 1970.
    Brazil's famous social historian adds to his
    luster with a work delineating all facets of
    his country's transition to republican forms.
    The treatment, extending to approximately the
    era of World War I, illuminates the persistence
    of traditional social forms and practices.
    (FA)

Furtado, Celso, THE ECONOMIC GROWTH OF BRAZIL: A
    Survey from Colonial to Modern Times, Berkeley
    and Los Angeles, University of California
    Press, 1963.

Goodman, David E., and Cavalcanti de Albuquerque,
    Roberto, INCENTIVOS A INDUSTRIALIZACAO E DESEN-
    VOLVIMENTO DO NORDESTE, IPEA, Instituto de
    Planejamento Economico e Social Instituto de
    Pesquisas--INPES Relatorio de Pesquisa N. 20,
    Rio de Janeiro, 1974.

Ianni, Octavio, CRISIS IN BRAZIL, New York, Columbia
    University Press, 1970. A study of the politi-
    cal and economic developments in Brazil in
    order to explain the 1964 coup d'état. Author
    sees the 1964 coup as boundary between the era
    of popular democracy and the present stage of
    dependency relations in the capitalistic sys-
    tem. The date and interpretations for relating
    the doctrine of interdependence with new forms
    of political, economic, and military dependence
    are analyzed. In support of his analysis, the
    author reconstructs historical perspective for
    recent political and economic crisis in Brazil,
    describing the formation, development, and
    crisis of the popular movement in its various
    forms. He examines the manifestations of
    nationalism as well as the rule of the masses,
    indicating how the birth of rural labor move-
    ments was one of the pretexts for overthrow of
    Goulart government in 1964. (BPA)

ILO, SAO PAULO: Urban Development and Employment,
    Geneva, 1976. This World Employment Programme
    case study analyzes the rapid urbanization and
    the employment situation of Greater Sao Paulo,

382

Brazil. It reviews the history of the growth of Sao Paulo's economy and labor force; the role of migration; the urban informal sector; urban infrastructure and public sector investments; and suggests potential policy measures for increasing employment opportunities. (BPA)

IPEA, Instituto de Planejamento Economico e Social, Brazilian Economic Studies, Rio de Janeiro, Brazil, 1975.

Johnson, Allen W., SHARECROPPERS OF THE SERTAO: Economics and Dependence on a Brazilian Plantation, Stanford, California, Stanford University Press, 1971. An ethnographic account of the present conditions of resident workers on a fazenda in the semi-arid backlands of northeastern Brazil. Based primarily on the author's field work, the book explores the relationship of the ecological environment to the worker's material and social needs and development. Details some aspects (crops, skills, etc.) of the subsistence economy, and horizontal and vertical economic relations. Index. (JEL)

Kahil, Raouf, INFLATION AND ECONOMIC DEVELOPMENT IN BRAZIL 1946-1963, Oxford, Clarendon Press; distributed by Oxford University Press, 1973. Investigates the relationship between Brazil's rapid development and inflation in terms of the structuralist/monetarist controversy. The author accepts the "fundamental validity of... [the structuralist's] main thesis: that, because of structural weaknesses, backward economies are particularly vulnerable to monetary instability. (JEL)

Knight, Peter T., BRAZILIAN AGRICULTURAL TECHNOLOGY AND TRADE: A Study of Five Commodities, Praeger Special Studies in International Economics and Development, New York, Praeger, 1971. "...a study of technological change, public policy, and economic behavior in Brazil's agricultural sector, with emphasis on their implications for international trade." Five agricultural commodities important in international trade are studied to provide answers to broad questions of Brazilian development planners in formulating policy regarding export performance, import substitution, productivity increases, and marketing systems for principal

383

agricultural commodities. Appendix; bibliography; index. (JEL)

Kutcher, Gary P. and Scandizzo, Pasquale L., "A Partial Analysis of Sharetenancy Relationships in Northeast Brazil," World Bank Reprint Series, No. 40, reprinted from the Journal of Development Economics 3, 1976.

Leal, Victor Nunes, CORONELISMO: The Municipality and Representative Government in Brazil, New York, Cambridge University Press, 1977. Dr. Nunes Leal's material is the history of Brazil, the laws of Brazil and the Brazil of 1949; his investigation covers the nexus between superior government and locality, the boundaries of private and public power and their inter-dependence, the imperfections and constraints of democracy at its not-very-fertile root. (BPA)

Leff, Nathaniel H., THE BRAZILIAN CAPITAL GOODS INDUSTRY, 1929-1964, Cambridge, Massachusetts, Harvard University Press, 1968.

Leff, Nathaniel H., ECONOMIC POLICY-MAKING AND DEVELOPMENT IN BRAZIL, 1947-1964, New York, John Wiley & Sons, Inc., 1968.

Levine, Robert M., THE VARGAS REGIME: The Critical Years, 1934-1938, New York, Columbia University Press, 1970. Getulio Vargas governed Brazil twice, from 1930 to 1945 and again from 1950 to 1954. This book is the first to deal critically with the middle years of the first regime. Professor Levine focuses on the political and ideological development of the Vargas regime, its changing constituency, and its role as a conservative, modernizing force, one which championed national unity at the expense of formerly cherished concepts of liberal democracy. He closely analyzes the growing crises in the states, tensions within the federal armed forces, and the growth of the two movements which challenged Vargas' control of the system from opposite ends of the ideological spectrum: the green-shirted fascist integralistas, and the anti-fascist, popular Alliance Nacional Libertadora. (BPA)

Lowinger, T. C., "Import Substitution, Export Promotion and the Structure of Brazil's Protection," Journal of Development Studies, Vol. 10, Nos. 3 & 4, April-July 1974.

Mahr, Dennis A., FRONTIER DEVELOPMENT POLICY IN BRAZIL, New York, Praeger, expected 1979. Recognizing that Brazil's future economy depends on the successful development of the vast, untapped resources of the Amazonia region, this study measures the impact of public policy in this area, and makes recommendations for more effective future.

Malan, P. S. and Bonelli, R., "The Brazilian Economy in the Seventies: Old and New Developments," World Development, Vol. 5, Nos. 1 & 2, January-February 1977.

Malloy, James M., THE POLITICS OF SOCIAL SECURITY IN BRAZIL, Pittsburgh, Pennsylvania, University of Pittsburgh Press, 1979. This study follows the progressive evolution of social insurance policy through four alternating periods of democratic and authoritarian government: oligarchic democracy (1889-1930), organic authoritarianism (1930-1945), populist democracy (1945-1964), and bureaucratic authoritarianism (1964 to present). (BPA)

McCann, Jr., Frank D., THE BRAZILIAN-AMERICAN ALLIANCE, 1937-1945, Princeton, New Jersey, Princeton University Press, 1973. Those who seek authoritative analysis of the historical background to U.S. relations with the most important Latin American nation will find it in this work, which manages to combine thorough research with lively readability. (FA)

Morley, S. A. and Smith, G. W., "Import Substitution and Foreign Investment in Brazil," Oxford Economic Papers, Vol. 23, No. 1, March 1971. This paper develops a new measure of IS which captures the backward linkage effects of substitution in key sectors and uses it to show the great importance of IS in postwar industrial growth. It then investigates the hypothesis that protection induced IS is likely to cause the establishment of foreign branch plants to produce goods which were formerly imported; this is found to be true in all the

high growth, high protection sectors except
where forestalled by newly created government
enterprises. (JEL)

Overholt, William H., ed., THE FUTURE OF BRAZIL,
Boulder, Colorado, Westview Press, 1979. A
collection of essays covering foreign relations;
the political future; the economy; the role of
the State in economic development; the debt burden; and treatment of the foreign investor.
(BPA)

Pedreira, Fernando, "Decompression in Brazil?"
Foreign Affairs, Vol. 53, No. 3, April 1975,
pp. 498-512.

Raine, Philip, BRAZIL: Awakening Giant, Washington,
Public Affairs Press, 1974. The Brazilian
present and future are analyzed in a funda-
mentally optimistic vein: "Brazil will...be-
come the world's first great tropical nation of
modern times." The sensitivity of the analysis
and the author's grasp of nuance and human
intangibles are first-rate. (FA)

Randall, Laura, A COMPARATIVE ECONOMIC HISTORY OF
LATIN AMERICA 1500-1914, Vol. 3: Brazil, pub-
lished for Institute of Latin American Studies,
Columbia University by University Microfilms
International, 1977.

Robock, Stefan H., BRAZIL: A Study in Development
Progress, Lexington, Massachusetts, Heath,
Lexington Books, 1975. Provides a long-run
overview of Brazil's development, examining:
evolutionary patterns in economic, social, and
political sectors; sources of growth; and
future problems. Attributes much of success in
1950's and early 1960's to: (1) defining broad
areas of development priority, decentralized
decision-making, and incentives rather than
directives to stimulate enterprise; (2) extensive use of the market for decision-making and
implementation; and (3) welcoming foreign
investment in areas that are identified as
important to development. Index. (JEL)

Roett, Riordan, ed., BRAZIL IN THE SEVENTIES,
Studies in Foreign Policy, No. 1, AEI Studies,
No. 132, Washington, American Enterprise Insti-
tute for Public Policy Research, 1976. Four

essays dealing with the international aspects of Brazilian development: the changing role in the international political system; the extent to which economic growth 1964-1975 produced socioeconomic development and the crises of the 1975 decline; the development of the foreign economic sector; and the application of the dependency theory to Brazil. The authors suggest that Brazil has grown less dependent since 1964, that the long-run prospects for Brazilian exports are strong, and that economics will determine the foreign policy of Brazil for the foreseeable future. No index. (JEL)

Roett, Riordan, BRAZIL: Politics in a Patrimonial Society, New York, Praeger, 1978. Examines the role of the armed forces in Brazil's national politics; discusses the expansion and institutionalization of the patrimonial regime in Brazil, which has resulted in elite rule, limited political participation, and a low level of national integration. The author maintains that while the military regime has fostered rapid industrial and technological development, it has always acted to preserve the political and social structure. (BPA)

Sahota, Gian Singh, BRAZILIAN ECONOMIC POLICY: An Optimal Control Theory Analysis, Praeger Special Studies in International Economics and Development, New York, Praeger, 1975. Uses an optimal control theory approach to evaluate the quantitative effects of different public policy instruments on major macroeconomic objectives in Brazil. Objectives examined include income distribution, growth, economic stabilization, and revenues for the public supplies of goods and services. Bibliography; index. (JEL)

Saunders, John, ed., MODERN BRAZIL: New Patterns and Development, Gainesville, University of Florida Press, 1971. Brazil's progress on the road to great-power status is considered in 13 studies by competent professionals. The fields covered include economics, agriculture, sociology, culture, education and politics. (FA)

Schmitter, Philippe C., INTEREST CONFLICT AND POLITICAL CHANGE IN BRAZIL, Stanford, California, Stanford University Press, 1971.

Schneider, Ronald M., BRAZIL: Foreign Relations of a Future World Power, Boulder, Colorado, Westview Press, 1977. This is a thorough and scholarly work. It begins with a full account of current circumstances in Brazil, and continues with an analysis of the foreign policy-making process, the part played by governmental and military institutions, and the factors both facilitating and constraining Brazil's ability to assume a more prominent role as an international power. (FA)

Selcher, Wayne A., BRAZIL'S MULTILATERAL RELATIONS: Between First and Third Worlds, Boulder, Colorado, Westview Press, 1978. Based on documentary research, scores of interviews, and the literature on international organization, this book delineates Brazil's position on a variety of multilateral issues and shows how Brazil's diplomatic style and strategy reflect its interests and international position. Multilateral relations are placed functionally within the full range of the country's foreign policy concerns and efforts, revealing why a given issue is accorded the particular balance of bilateral-multilateral treatment it receives. Conclusions are ventured about the interrelationships between the two types of diplomacy, with a chapter on relations with Africa to illustrate how multilateral and systemic goals are inherent in Brazil's bilateral outreach across the South Atlantic. Multilateral relations with other developing countries are given thorough consideration. (BPA)

Silveira, Antonio Maria da, STUDIES OF MONEY AND INTEREST RATES IN BRAZIL, Ann Arbor, University of Michigan micro-films, 1971, 139 pages. Dissertation at Carnegie-Mellon University, Pittsburgh.

Skidmore, Thomas E., BLACK INTO WHITE: Race and Nationality in Brazilian Thought, New York, Oxford University Press, 1974. This excellent and thorough volume traces the pre-1930 era of scientific racism, the phase of moral superiority from 1930 to 1950, the cult of "whitening" as an unadmitted reality, and the effect of world movements on Brazilian thought. A good antidote to various simplistic assumptions that are often encountered. (FA)

Smith, T. Lynn, BRAZILIAN SOCIETY, Albuquerque, University of New Mexico Press, 1975. A clear summary of sociological conditions and tendencies, encompassing population, religious structures, urbanization, and other aspects. Just the right balance of brevity and completeness for the general reader. (FA)

Steele, John and Kanel, Don, THE AGRICULTURAL LADDER IN A BRAZILIAN COMMUNITY, LTC Reprint No. 110, Madison, University of Wisconsin, Land Tenure Center, December 1976.

Stepan, Alfred, ed., AUTHORITARIAN BRAZIL: Origins, Policies, and Future, New Haven and London, Yale University Press, 1973; 1976. Seven previously unpublished essays from a workshop on contemporary Brazil held at Yale University in April 1971, which evaluate some of the major political and economic characteristics of the development process in Brazil 1964-71. (JEL)

Stepan, Alfred, THE MILITARY IN POLITICS: Changing Patterns in Brazil, Princeton, New Jersey, Princeton University Press, 1971. The most noteworthy conclusion of this scholarly study suggests that "the mode of military involvement in Latin American politics may well shift increasingly from that of system-maintenance to that of system-transformation." (A RAND Corporation Research Study.) (FA)

Syvrud, Donald E., FOUNDATIONS OF BRAZILIAN ECONOMIC GROWTH, AEI-Hoover Research Publications 1, Stanford, California, Hoover Institution Press; distributed by American Enterprise Institute for Public Policy Research, 1974. Covers economic policies and performance of Brazilian economy from 1947 to 1972. Organized in three parts: (1) an assessment of the import substitution strategy prior to 1964 and the more balanced growth strategy after 1964, (2) the economic policy instruments available to Brazilian authorities (with comparisons of their use under the strategies prior to and after 1964), and (3) a summary of the major programs and institutions used to mobilize savings in priority sectors and regions. Bibliography; index. (JEL)

Tendler, Judith, ELECTRIC POWER IN BRAZIL: Entre-
    preneurship in the Public Sector, Cambridge,
    Massachusetts, Harvard University Press, 1968.
    This study traces the growth of the power in-
    dustry from a bottleneck to a leading sector.
    It also points out the social and economic op-
    tions generated by technology. (BPA)

Tyler, W. G., "Brazilian Industrialization and
    Industrial Policies: A Survey," World Develop-
    ment, Vol. 4, Nos. 10/11, October-November
    1976. This paper surveys the professional
    literature and current understanding of recent
    Brazilian industrialization. Since the mid-
    1960's the high rates of observed growth can be
    greatly attributed to a general policy strategy,
    within the framework of capitalist institu-
    tions, of (1) fortifying markets and improving
    the functioning of the price system and (2)
    impressive growth during nearly all the post-
    war period, although lingering socio-economic
    problems remain, frequently exacerbated by
    economic policies designed to spur industrial
    growth. (JEL)

Tyler, William G., MANUFACTURED EXPORT PROMOTION IN
    A SEMI-INDUSTRIALIZED ECONOMY: The Brazilian
    Case, reprint from Journal of Development
    Studies, Kiel University, Kiel Institute of
    World Economics, 1973.

Wagley, Charles, AN INTRODUCTION TO BRAZIL, New
    York, Columbia University Press, 1971.

Wirth, John D., THE POLITICS OF BRAZILIAN DEVELOP-
    MENT, 1930-1954, Stanford, California, Stanford
    University Press, 1970. A study of economic
    policy-making during the Vargas era, with par-
    ticular reference to steel, petroleum and for-
    eign trade. Authoritative but blessedly free
    of didacticism and jargon. (FA)

Yap, L., "Internal Migration and Economic Develop-
    ment in Brazil," Quarterly Journal of Eco-
    nomics, Vol. 90, No. 1, February 1976. Rapid
    rural-urban migration in less developed coun-
    tries has both positive and negative effects on
    economic growth. This paper shows that for
    Brazil, rapid urban population growth in the
    postwar period has had a positive effect on
    balance. These results were derived from

simulations, using a three-sector model of the
economy to generate different growth paths for
various levels of migration. (JEL)

Caribbean

X-REF: UNITED STATES POLICY: Martin.

Ameringer, Charles D., THE DEMOCRATIC LEFT IN EXILE:
The Antidictatorial Struggle in the Caribbean,
1945-1959, Coral Gables, University of Miami
Press, 1974. The political generation of
Betancourt, Figueres, Muñoz Marin, Juan Bosch,
the Cuban Auténticos, and the Caribbean Legion
is depicted on a broad canvas by an author who
benefited in many instances from personal
access to important sources. (FA)

Beckford, George L., ed., CARIBBEAN ECONOMY: Dependence and Backwardness, Mona, Kingston,
Jamaica, Institute of Social and Economic
Research, University of the West Indies, 1975.
A collection of seven papers (one previously
published) emphasizing that the underdevelopment in the Caribbean is associated with
dependence. Index. (JEL)

Corkran, Jr., Herbert, PATTERNS OF INTERNATIONAL CO-
OPERATION IN THE CARIBBEAN 1942-1969, Dallas,
Southern Methodist University Press, 1970.
Currently active regional integration strate-
gies and alignments are depicted against the
background of earlier Caribbean organizations.
(FA)

Crassweller, Robert D., THE CARIBBEAN COMMUNITY, New
York, Praeger (for the Council on Foreign Relations), 1972. A policy study, whose author
urges the development of a "Caribbean Community" characterized by greatly increased
regional coordination and joint action over a
wide range of economic and social activities.
(FA)

Demas, William G., ESSAYS ON CARIBBEAN INTEGRATION
AND DEVELOPMENT, Introduction by Alister McIn-
tyre, Kingston, Jamaica, University of West
Indies, Institute of Social and Economic
Research, 1976. Twelve (6 previously unpub-

391

lished) "non-technical" essays and addresses written since 1960 on the Caribbean economy and some of the dynamic effects of integration. The author, Chancellor of the University of Guyana, stresses the importance of economic integration among the Caribbean countries for the economic development of the area. Index. (JEL)

Kadt, Emanuel de, ed., PATTERNS OF FOREIGN INFLUENCE IN THE CARIBBEAN, New York, Oxford University Press (for the Royal Institute of International Affairs), 1972. Interesting essays on geopolitical relationships and the U.S. role in the Caribbean accompany studies of Jamaica, Cuba, Guatemala and the Dutch and French Caribbean. The treatment is short but concentrated. (FA)

Munro, Dana G., THE UNITED STATES AND THE CARIBBEAN REPUBLICS, 1921-1933, Princeton, New Jersey, Princeton University Press, 1974. With customary solidity and craftsmanship, the notable author traces the evolution of U.S. policies with respect to Cuba, the Dominican Republic, Haiti, and the five Central American countries between the end of the interventionist Wilson era and the coming of the Good Neighbor Policy. (FA)

Palmer, Ramsford W., CARIBBEAN DEPENDENCE ON THE UNITED STATES ECONOMY, New York, Praeger, expected 1979. Analyzes the increase in Caribbean exports and migration to the United States and the volume of capital flows from the United States to the Caribbean. (BPA)

Szulc, Tad, ed., THE UNITED STATES AND THE CARIBBEAN, Englewood Cliffs, Prentice Hall, 1971. These uneven papers by Caribbean specialists were prepared for the thirty-eighth American Assembly in October-November 1970. Some report on social phenomena region-wide; others are sub-regional in scope. (FA)

Theberge, James D., ed., SOVIET SEAPOWER IN THE CARIBBEAN: Political and Strategic Implications, New York, Praeger (in cooperation with the Center for Strategic and International Studies, Georgetown University), 1972. A useful volume, of particular interest in the

light of recent dramatic developments in U.S.-
Russian relations. (FA)

Central America

X-REF: ECONOMIC INTEGRATION: McClelland.

Best, M. H., "Political Power and Tax Revenues in
    Central America," Journal of Development Eco-
    nomics, Vol. 3, No. 1, March 1976.

Cohen Orantes, Isaac, REGIONAL INTEGRATION IN CEN-
    TRAL AMERICA, LEXINGTON, Massachusetts, Lexing-
    ton Books, D. C. Heath and Company, 1972.

Cline, William R., and Delgado, Enrique, eds., ECO-
    NOMIC INTEGRATION IN CENTRAL AMERICA, Washing-
    ton, The Brookings Institution, 1978. Ushered
    in by masses of detailed statistics and mathe-
    matical calculations, certain conclusions
    emerge clearly: total net economic benefits of
    the Central American Common Market have been
    substantial; the most important were foreign
    exchange savings and stimulus to investment.
    Economics of scale and employment effects have
    also been significant, though less so; struc-
    tural transformation benefits were minimal.(FA)

Durham, William H., SCARCITY AND SURVIVAL IN CENTRAL
    AMERICA: Ecological Origins of the Soccer War,
    Stanford, California, expected in 1979. Look-
    ing at both population and land tenure dynamics
    in their historical context, this study chal-
    lenges the view that the 1969 conflict between
    El Salvador and Honduras was primarily a re-
    sponse to population pressure. The author
    demonstrates that land scarcity, a principal
    cause of the war, was largely a product of the
    concentration of land holdings. The analysis
    focuses on the emigration of 300,000 Salvador-
    eans to Honduras in the years before the war,
    inquiring into the reasons for the emigration,
    its impact on local agricultural economies, and
    its relation to the conflict. (BPA)

McClelland, Donald H., THE CENTRAL AMERICAN COMMON
    MARKET: Economic Policies, Economic Growth,
    and Choices for the Future, New York, Praeger,
    1972.

393

Shaw, Royce Q., CENTRAL AMERICA: Regional Integration and National Political Development,
Boulder, Colorado, Westview Press, 1978. This
study challenges several widely held assumptions about Central American economic integration, arguing that the key to understanding the
failure of the integration program lies in
neither advanced economic nor regional integration theory, but in the domestic politics of
the member states. Thus, the author contends
that the Common Market was not the cause of the
balance-of-payments and balanced-growth crises
in Central America; rather, domestic political
forces were the major factor in the collapse of
the market and the subsequent attempts at restructuring. (BPA)

Willmore, L. N., "Trade Creation, Trade Diversion
and Effective Protection in the Central American
Common Market," Journal of Development Studies,
Vol. 12, No. 4, July 1976.

Wunia, Gary W., POLITICS AND PLANNERS: Economic Development Policy in Central America, Madison,
University of Wisconsin Press, 1972. The role
of the técnicos in relation to the Central
American Common Market and regional development
in the Isthmus area, their successes and failures, receives fuller treatment here than has
been accorded elsewhere. (FA)

Chile

X-REF: AGRARIAN REFORM: Lehmann, Shaw, COMMODITIES:
Girvan, DEPENDENCY: Frank, FOREIGN INVESTMENT:
Baklanoff, INCOME DISTRIBUTION PRINCIPLES: Foxley,
MULTINATIONAL CORPORATIONS: Ingram, TECHNOLOGY:
Ilo, URBAN DEVELOPMENT: Robin.

Allende, Salvador, DEMOCRATIC SOCIALISM: The Political Ideology of Salvador Allende, Philadelphia, Pennsylvania, ISHI, 1977. This work is a
collection and translation into English of the
principal public statements of President
Allende during the period from his election in
1970 to his death in 1973. (BPA)

Angell, Alan, POLITICS AND THE LABOUR MOVEMENT IN
CHILE, New York, Oxford University Press (for
the Royal Institute of International Affairs),
1972. An account of the contributions of
Chile's deeply politicized labor unions to the
"revolution in liberty." The author concludes
that the unions have gone beyond the function
of conflict regulation and have provided direct
support for political "revolutionary activity,"
however defined. (FA)

Barraclough, S., "Agrarian Reform and Structural
Change in Latin America: The Chilean Case,"
Journal of Development Studies, Vol. 8, No. 2,
January 1972.

Behrman, Jere R., FOREIGN TRADE REGIMES AND ECONOMIC
DEVELOPMENT, Vol. VIII: Chile, New York, National Bureau of Economic Research, Columbia
University Press, 1976. The impact of policy
on trade and payments and the problems of
sustaining liberalization of foreign transactions provide the focus for this excellent
addition to a major series that is approaching
completion. (FA)

Behrman, Jere R., MACROECONOMIC POLICY IN A DEVELOP-
ING COUNTRY: The Chilean Experience, Contributions to Economic Analysis, No. 109, New York,
Elsevier North-Holland, Amsterdam and Oxford,
North-Holland, 1977. An empirical study of the
economic structure and the impact of macroeconomic policies in Chile during the postwar
period (1946-70). Provides a historical and
institutional analysis of major postwar Chilean
stabilization attempts; estimates the sectoral
relationships and discusses their practical
equilibrium implications; and analyzes the complete model of the Chilean economy and simu-
lates the policy alternatives. No index.
(JEL)

Burnett, Ben G., POLITICAL GROUPS IN CHILE, Austin,
University of Texas Press (for the Institute of
Latin American Studies), 1970. This craftsman-
like analysis of the sources of radical sentiment and political change during the last
decade includes much comment on parties and interest groups. The recent Allende victory is
noted in a brief postscript. (FA)

395

Caviedes, César, THE POLITICS OF CHILE, A Socio-Geographical Assessment, Boulder, Colorado, Westview Press, 1979. Chile's road to socialism was not linear. In the last twenty years political parties of an astonishingly wide range of opinions participated in the administration of the country, with shifting preferences of the voting population. Disobedience, dissent, and confrontation with the government or party officials were frequent; and the struggle between centralism and provincial aspirations was a continuing fact of Chilean political life. (BPA)

Chile, A CRITICAL SURVEY, Institute of General Studies, Santiago, Chile, 1972.

Cleaves, Peter S., BUREAUCRATIC POLITICS AND ADMINISTRATION IN CHILE, Berkeley, University of California Press, 1974. Specialists in organizational theory as applied to governmental operations in third-world nations will do well to consult this examination of economic planning and administration, housing, budgeting, agriculture, and related fields, under Frei and Allende. (FA)

Crosson, Pierre R., AGRICULTURAL DEVELOPMENT AND PRODUCTIVITY: Lesson From The Chilean Experience, Baltimore, Maryland, Johns Hopkins University Press for Resources for the Future, Inc., 1970. Chile has failed to develop her agricultural output to a level which would support her population growth. The author investigates the reasons for this failure and analyzes and interprets resource use patterns and potential in Chile; he provides economists and policy-makers with more factual and statistical evidence that the problems of underdevelopment cannot be solved without a solution to the problems of agricultural stagnation. Appendix; index. (JEL)

Debray, Regis, THE CHILEAN REVOLUTION: Conversations with Allende, New York, Pantheon Books, 1972. A long introduction by Debray, the theorist of revolution, and a postscript by President Allende round out the recorded conversations in which these famous leftists discuss the nature of the new regime in Chile. (FA) de Vylder, Stefan, ALLENDE'S CHILE: The Political Economy of the Rise and Fall of the Unidad Popular, Cambridge Latin American Studies, No. 25, Cambridge; New York, Cambridge University Press, 1976. A study analyzing the Chilean economy under Allende's Unidad Popular administration and the economic factors in their failure to remain in power. After an introduction to the economic background, the book deals with the political conditions and the party's rise to power, and theoretical prospects of the Chilean road to socialism through the ballot box. Allende's short-term economic programs are discussed, with the economic developments in 1971 and the problems of stagnation and inflation during the following two years. Finally, the agrarian sector is analyzed, illustrating reasons for the government's failure to carry out a viable land reform. No index. (JEL)

de Vylder, Stefan, FROM COLONIALISM TO DEPENDENCE: An Introduction to Chile's Economic History, Development Studies 3/74, Stockholm, Swedish International Development Authority, 1974. This study's purpose is to give a brief economic and political background to more recent events in Chile and surveying Chilean history from the 16th century, as an overview of how the present structure of the Chilean economy has evolved. At least half the study focuses on the patterns of growth in the 1950's and 1960's, stressing the perpetuation of under-development and the increasing foreign dependence of Chile, in particular, reliance on the United States. No index. (JEL)

Drake, Paul W., SOCIALISM AND POPULISM IN CHILE, 1932-52, Urbana, University of Illinois Press, 1978. A sympathetic and detailed study of left-wing political movements and parties in Chile. In an epilogue covering 1952-1973, he writes of the rapid process of polarization that erupted drastically in 1973. "By 1973," he says, "the level of social and political mobilization reached by the masses since the 1930s was sufficient to invite extreme oppression but insufficient to prevent it...." (FA)

Eckaus, Richard S., et al., eds., ANALYSIS OF DEVEL-
OPMENT PROBLEMS: Studies of the Chilean Economy, Amsterdam, North-Holland Publishing Co.;
New York, American Elsevier Publishing Co.,
1973.

Espinosa, Juan G. and Zimbalist, Andrew S., ECONOMIC
DEMOCRACY: Workers' Participation in Chilean
Industry 1970-1973, New York, Academic Press,
Inc., 1978.

Fagan, Richard R., "The United States and Chile:
Roots and Branches," Foreign Affairs, Vol. 53,
No. 2, January 1975.

Ffrench-Davis, Ricardo, POLITICAS ECONOMICAS EN
CHILE: 1952-1970, Santiago, Ediciones Nueva
Universidad, 1973. An analysis of Chile's economic policies during the 1952-1970 period. The
author first examines the stabilization policies
pursued by various Chilean administrations during this time and then centers his attention on
the evolution of foreign trade, monetary, fiscal, and incomes policies. Bibliography. (JEL)

Fox, Robert W., URBAN POPULATION GROWTH IN CHILE,
Report #2, IDB Technical Department, Urban
Population Growth Series, October 1972.

Foxley, A. and Muños, O., "Income Redistribution,
Economic Growth and Social Structure: The Case
of Chile," Oxford Bulletin of Economics and
Statistics, Vol. 36, No. 1, February 1974. The
process of development in Chile during 1970-73
provides an appropriate case study on this subject. Drastic redistribution was supposed to
take place between a "minority" of high income
groups and a "majority" constituted by the rest
of the population. The paper attempts to analyze and give preliminary answers to the following questions. What determines how much of
the national income can be so redistributed
without jeopardizing the possibilities of
raising the investment rate? Which groups are
in the most underprivileged position and what
are their characteristics? What constraints
does this situation impose upon the traditional
instruments of redistribution? (JEL)

Gil, Federico G.; Lagos, E. Ricardo; and Landsberger,
Henry A., eds., CHILE AT THE TURNING POINT:
Lessons of the Socialist Years, 1970-73, Philadelphia, ISHI Publications, 1979. The contributors to the volume, participants in the
Unidad Popular as well as qualified "observers,"
focus their essays on four main themes: what
happened in Chile during the 1970-1973 period;
the "causes" of the failure; the nature of the
resulting military regime; and possible effects
of the events on other political settings.
(BPA)

Hervey, Maurice H., DARK DAYS IN CHILE: An Account
of the Revolution of 1891, Philadelphia, Pennsylvania, ISHI Publications, 1978. The Revolution of 1891 was of enormous significance to
Chilean history. The overthrow of President
Balmaceda led directly to the elimination of
local challenges to foreign control of Chilean
nitrates. The revolt also marked the beginning
of the parliamentary era, the last stand of
Chilean oligarchs against the spectre of mass
political participation. (BPA)

Horne, Alistair, SMALL EARTHQUAKE IN CHILE: Allende's South America, New York, Viking, 1972.

IDOC, CHILE: The Allende Years, the Coup Under the
Junta, New York, IDOC/North American Edition,
1973.

IDOC, Chile: Under Military Rule, a dossier of
documents and analysis compiled by the staff of
IDOC, New York, International Documentation,
1974.

ITT, DOCUMENTOS SECRETOS DE LA ITT, Santiago,
Empresa Editorial Nacional Quimantu Ltds.,
1972. Photostatic copies of the ITT documents
that were leaked to columnist Jack Anderson to
expose the plot, officially sponsored by the
U.S. Government, to prevent Allende, by illicit
means, from taking office as President in 1970.
Translations into Spanish are provided on facing pages. (Ed)

Institute of General Studies, CHILE: A Critical
Survey, Santiago, Institute of General Studies,
1972. The darker side of (Popular Unity) is
convincingly depicted in these detailed and

careful studies, whose combined scope covers the entire national life. The 16 authors are respected scholars and others prominent in public affairs. (FA)

Kaufman, Robert R., THE POLITICS OF LAND REFORM IN CHILE, 1950-1970, Cambridge, Massachusetts, Harvard University Press, 1972. In this study, the author traces with scholarly competence the impact of land-reform pressures upon Christian Democratic reforms and upon the balance of established social forces during the two decades prior to Allende's election. (FA)

Kirsch, Henry W., INDUSTRIAL DEVELOPMENT IN A TRADITIONAL SOCIETY: The Conflict of Entrepreneurship and Modernization in Chile, Latin American Monographs, Second Series, No. 21, Gainesville, University Presses of Florida, 1977. Examines the social and economic development of Chile from the late nineteenth century to the Great Depression. Argues that Chilean industrialization was fully active by the late nineteenth century and attempts to explain the failure of Chilean industry to fulfill the developmental role. (JEL)

Kusnetzoff, Fernando, "Housing Policies or Housing Politics: An Evaluation of the Chilean Experience," Journal of Interamerican Studies and World Affairs, Vol. 17, No. 3, August 1975.

Lau, Stephen F., THE CHILEAN RESPONSE TO FOREIGN INVESTMENT, New York, Praeger, 1972.

Lehmann, David, "The Political Economy of Armageddon: Chile, 1970-1973," Journal of Development Economics, Vol. 5, No. 2, p. 107-123.

Lioi, Vittorio Corbo, INFLATION IN DEVELOPING COUNTRIES: An econometric Study of Chilean Inflation, Contribution to Economic Analysis 84, Amsterdam and Oxford, North-Holland, New York, American Elsevier, 1974. An attempt toward building a macroeconomic model to study the interaction among the main macroeconomic variables in the creation of inflation in a developing country. The first part deals with monetarism, structuralism, and past studies of Chilean inflation. The second part discusses a quarterly model for industrial prices, industrial

wages, and inflation. The last part is devoted
to the specification, estimation, and simulation of an annual econometric model of the
Chilean economy. Appendices; references;
index. (JEL)

Loveman, Brian, STRUGGLE IN THE COUNTRYSIDE: Politics and Rural Labor in Chile, 1919-1973,
Bloomington, Indiana University Press, 1976.
The subject is the transformations of property
in the countryside and rural activism and labor
conflict. "...it was the radical alterations
of the political meaning of property in rural
land from 1964 to 1973 that destroyed the foundations of Chilean formal democracy--a democracy that rested heavily on the luck of the
Chilean campesino." (FA)

MacEoin, Gary, NO PEACEFUL WAY: Chile's Struggle
for Dignity, New York, Sheed and Ward, 1974. A
passionate analysis of the Allende drama from a
radical and worshipful perspective. Rarely has
black been so black, and white so white, as in
this Manichean vision. (FA)

Mamalakis, Markos, AN ANALYSIS OF THE FINANCIAL AND
INVESTMENT ACTIVITIES OF THE CHILEAN DEVELOP-
MENT CORPORATION: 1939-1964, Center Paper
#132, New Haven, Connecticut, Yale University,
Economic Growth Center, 1969.

Mamalakis, Markos J., THE GROWTH AND STRUCTURE OF
THE CHILEAN ECONOMY: From Independence to
Allende, New Haven and London, Yale University
Press, Economic Growth Center, 1976. Investigation of the economic development of Chile
between 1840 and 1973, concentrating on identifying the features of production, distribution,
and capital formation and the interactions
among them. Also examines: export production,
resource distribution, monetary and fiscal
policy, and the service sector. Index. (JEL)

McBride, George M., CHILE: Land and Society, New
York, American Geographical Society, 1936. An
analysis of Chile's traditional agrarian problems, with emphasis on historical origins and
social consequences in each of the nation's
principal regions. (BPA)

Moran, Theodore H., MULTINATIONAL CORPORATIONS AND
     THE POLITICS OF DEPENDENCE: Copper in Chile,
     Princeton, New Jersey, Princeton University
     Press, 1974. Chilean copper policy from World
     War II to the fall of Allende is analyzed in
     terms of the interactions between the multina-
     tional copper companies and domestic interest
     groups, and the dependencia created by a mass-
     ive foreign presence. The treatment is compe-
     tent and judicious. (FA)

Moss, Robert, CHILE'S MARXIST EXPERIMENT, New York,
     Halsted Press, 1974. A searching examination
     into the social and economic consequences of
     the Allende experiment, and the reasons for its
     dramatic decline and fall. The author finds
     little that will support a Left-leaning mytholo-
     gy of betrayed innocence and virtue. (FA)

Mutchler, David, THE CHURCH AS A POLITICAL FACTOR IN
     LATIN AMERICA WITH PARTICULAR REFERENCE TO
     COLOMBIA AND CHILE, New York, Praeger, 1971.

Nowak, Norman D., TAX ADMINISTRATION IN THEORY AND
     PRACTICE: With Special Reference to Chile, New
     York, Praeger, Special Studies in International
     Economics and Development, 1970.

O'Brien, Philip, ed., ALLENDE'S CHILE, Praeger
     Special Studies in International Politics and
     Government, New York and London, Praeger, 1976.
     Eleven original articles growing out of a
     series of specialist post-September 1973 coup
     seminars held at the University of Glasgow,
     which analyze Chilean class structure and class
     politics. All the papers bring out the his-
     torical developments leading to the particular
     problems of the Popular Unity period, falling
     into four main parts: analysis of the policies
     of the Popular Unity Government; the response
     of the working classes; the tactics and strate-
     gy of those opposed to the Popular Unity Gov-
     ernment; and Chile since the coup and the main
     lessons of Chile. No index. (JEL)

Orrego Vicuna, Francisco, ed., CHILE: The Balanced
     View: A Recopilation (sic) of Articles About
     the Allende Years and After, Santiago, Univer-
     sity of Chile, Institute of International
     Studies, 1975. Eighteen articles, essays, and
     statements, some published previously, examin-

ing the government of Salvador Allende and the
political and economic consequences of its
overthrow in 1973. The articles analyze the
political situation in Chile before and after
the overthrow, the economic policies of the
United States and international lending agencies toward Chile under Allende's presidency,
the economic outlook for Chile under its new
government, and future U.S.-Chile relations.
No index. (JEL)

Petras, James and Merino, Hugo Zemelman, PEASANTS IN
REVOLT: A Chilean Case Study, 1965-1971,
Austin, University of Texas Press (for the
Institute of Latin American Studies), 1972.
Three more additions to the swelling wave of
studies of the Andes and Chile since Allende,
each in a sense characteristic of one type of
approach to the traumatic upheaval. The Horne
volume presents a relatively balanced and
colorful account by a keen observer, marked by
firsthand intimacy; Morris contributes a traditional general appraisal that is partial to the
Allende goals; Petras and Merino offer sociological analysis. (FA)

Petras, James, POLITICS AND SOCIAL FORCES IN CHILEAN
DEVELOPMENT, Berkeley, University of California
Press, 1970. The author gives an analysis and
interpretation of Chilean development by examining the interrelation between industrialization, modernization, social structure, and
political organization in this Latin American
country. Appendices; bibliography; index.
(JEL)

Petras, James and Morley, Morris, THE UNITED STATES
AND CHILE: Imperialism and the Overthrow of
the Allende Government, New York, Monthly
Review Press, 1975. An examination of the overthrow undertaken by partisans of Popular Unity,
who place the blame squarely on the United
States. (Ed)

Pike, Frederick B., "Chilean Local Government and
Some Reflections on Dependence," Inter-American
Economic Affairs, Vol. 31, No. 2, Autumn 1977.

Powelson, John P., "What Went Wrong in Chile?" Cultures et Developpement, Vol. VI, No. 3, 1974,
pp. 403-500. A critical review of the Allende

years by a sympathizer with Popular Unity goals
who nevertheless argues that the overthrow
would have occurred anyway, despite U.S. intervention, because of the internal dissension
within Popular Unity, polarization in Chile,
and bad economic policy. (Ed)

Raptis, Michael, REVOLUTION AND COUNTER-REVOLUTION
IN CHILE, New York, St. Martin, 1975. A former
Secretary of the Fourth International describes
the Allende period from the point of view of
worker management and participation, as em-
bodied in the operations of worker and communal
councils. (FA)

Roxborough, Ian; O'Brien, Philip and Roddick,
Jackie; CHILE: THE STATE AND REVOLUTION, New
York, Holmes & Meier, 1977. Criticizing the
Allende administration from the Left, the
authors attribute its failure to the basic
error of trying to use the existing state
apparatus to create a workers' state. Armed
insurrection was necessary. It follows that
the U.S. role, while important, was subsidiary,
since the middle-class opposition to Unidad
Popular was inevitable anyway. (FA)

Seton, Francis, SHADOW WAGES IN THE CHILEAN ECONOMY,
Paris Development Centre of the Organization
for Economic Cooperation and Development, 1972.

Sigmund, Paul E., THE OVERTHROW OF ALLENDE AND THE
POLITICS OF CHILE, 1964-1976, Pittsburgh,
Pennsylvania, University of Pittsburgh Press,
1977. This is the most complete and thoughtful
analysis yet made of the Allende and Frei
Administrations. The reader is further reward-
ed by meditations upon related themes, such as
the relation of equity to liberty. Sigmund
concludes that Allende moved, not too slowly as
the Left believes, but too rapidly in pursuit
of "irreversible" changes. "The result was to
reverse the advances that had been made for the
last thirty years...." (FA)

Silvert, Kalman H., and Jutkowitz, Joel M., EDUCA-
TION, VALUES AND THE POSSIBILITIES FOR SOCIAL
CHANGE IN CHILE, Philadelphia, Pennsylvania,
Institute for the Study of Human Issues, 1976.
Reports a series of surveys on social change
that span ten years, and provides information

404

about Chilean value patterns in the 1960s and 1970s. (BPA)

Spence, Jack, SEARCH FOR JUSTICE: NEIGHBORHOOD COURTS IN ALLENDE'S CHILE, Boulder, Colorado Westview Press, 1979. Though the Unidad Popular failed to legislate a nationwide system of neighborhood courts staffed with lay judges, two decentralized courts did emerge. One employed professional judges with weekly informal court sessions for poor residents; the other was established illegally by a highly organized squatter settlement. Their contrasting strategies and processes provide insights into the general problem of decentralization of urban institutions. (BPA)

Stallings, Barbara, CLASS CONFLICT AND ECONOMIC DEVELOPMENT IN CHILE, 1958-1973, Stanford, California, Stanford Press, 1978. This account of the interplay of politics and economics in Chile in three successive administrations ending with the 1973 coup suggests that social class plays a major role in determining the outcome of economic policies in Latin America. The nature of the class alliance that controls the state apparatus in Chile, together with the actions of foreign capital, determines not only the type of economic policies followed, but their outcome as well. (BPA)

Steenland, Kyle, AGRARIAN REFORM UNDER ALLENDE, Albuquerque, University of New Mexico Press, 1978. Written in a pro-Allende vein, this study of the most thorough attempt at agricultural reform since the Cuban revolution describes the Chilean expropriations, their effects on production, and the social organization of the countryside. (FA)

Thiesenhusen, William C., CHILE'S EXPERIMENTS IN AGRARIAN REFORM: Land Economics, a quarterly journal devoted to the study of economic and social institutions, Madison, Milwaukee, University of Wisconsin Press, 1966.

Valenzuela, Arturo, POLITICAL BROKERS IN CHILE: Local Government in a Centralized Polity, Duke University Press, 1977. In this study of relationships between local governments, people, and the central government in Chile, Arturo

405

Valenzuela draws on a range of modern quantitative techniques, extensive field research, and
historical data to illuminate significantly the
Chilean political system during the Allende
regime. Chile has always fascinated observers
because it has not conformed to the general
pattern of Latin American politics. In a continent where rule by armed forces was the norm,
Chile developed institutions that provided
strong civilian leadership. Allende's Popular
Unity government attempted to bring about fundamental change within the framework of traditional Chilean institutions. The reaction to
this experiment ushered in military rule and
marked the most severe political breakdown in
Chile's history. (BPA)

Whitaker, Arthur P., THE U.S. AND THE SOUTHERN CONE:
Argentina, Uruguay, and Chile. 1977. Covers
their history from time of liberation to
present, including recent coup in Argentina.
(BPA)

Young, George F. W., THE GERMANS IN CHILE: Immigration and Colonization, 1849-1914, New York,
Center for Migration Studies, 1974.

Zammit, J. Ann, ed., THE CHILEAN ROAD TO SOCIALISM,
proceedings of an ODEPLAN--IDS round table,
March 1972, with cooperation from Gabriel Palma,
Austin, University of Texas Press; Sussex, England, Institute of Development Studies, 1973.
Available in both English and Spanish (La Via
Chilena al Socialismo), this book contains the
speeches and discussions given by an international and interdisciplinary group of academics
and Chilean government officials, including the
late President, Salvador Allende, at a Santiago
March 1972 Round Table, sponsored by the Chilean
National Planning Office and the British Institute of Development Studies. The second section
contains official Chilean documents and background papers on the recently deposed Popular
Unity government's program, its six-year plan
and regional development strategy, and an
analysis of the economy in 1971. No index.
(JEL)

Colombia

X-REF: AGRARIAN REFORM: Shaw, AGRICULTURAL CREDIT: McPherson, CHILE: Mutchler, EMPLOYMENT LABOR: Berry, Seers, Thorbecke, INCOME DISTRIBUTION PRINCI-PLES: Berry, RURAL DEVELOPMENT: Thirsk, TECH-NOLOGY: Ilo, URBAN DEVELOPMENT: Robin.

Adams, Dale W., LANDOWNERSHIP PATTERNS IN COLOMBIA, LTC Reprint No. 3, Madison, University of Wis-consin, Land Tenure Center, 1964.

Avramovic, Dragoslav, ECONOMIC GROWTH OF COLOMBIA: Problems and Prospects, report of a mission sent to Colombia in 1970 by the World Bank, Baltimore, Maryland, Johns Hopkins Press, 1972. An immense compilation of data and analysis of the country's population, employment, growth, capital requirements, external debt, regional and urban development, manufacturing and indus-trialization, general industry and special in-dustry studies, mining, power sources, agricul-ture (coffee and other crops), transport and communications, tourism, education, health, and various other aspects of the country's socio-economic life. Numerous statistical tables, maps, and charts. There is also a pre-invest-ment study, various projections, and recom-mendations for future action. No index. (JEL)

Berry, A., "Changing Income Distribution Under De-velopment: Colombia," Review of Income and Wealth, Vol. 20, No. 3, September 1974, pp. 289-316.

Berry, R. Albert, "Farm Size Distribution, Income Distribution and the Efficiency of Agricultural Production: Colombia," American Economic Re-view, Vol. LXII, No. 2, May 1972.

Berry, Albert, "Rural Poverty in Twentieth-Century Colombia," Journal of Inter-American Studies and World Affairs, November 1978.

Berry, Albert, "Open Unemployment as a Social Prob-lem in Urban Colombia: Myth and Reality," Economic Development and Cultural Change, Vol. 23, No. 2, January 1975, pp. 276-291.

Berry, Albert and Urrutia, Miguel, INCOME DISTRIBU-
TION IN COLOMBIA, New Haven and London, Yale
University Press, Economic Growth Center, 1976.
Study of the structure of income distribution
in Colombia, emphasizing the negative distributional impact of several aspects of the financial and exchange rate systems and policy.
Divided into two parts, Part I examines the
measurement of income distribution in the mid-
1960's--overall, rural, and urban--and its historical trends, also by sectors, while Part II
discusses the effects of certain types of previous government policy on income distribution.
Establishes a benchmark distribution for 1964
and estimates trends earlier and later. Concluding that Colombia's distribution ranks
among the most unequal, the author recommends
that "a greater emphasis on the financing of a
minimum per capita level of some services such
as health and the lower levels of education and
less emphasis on investment for infrastructure
might produce a substantial improvement in the
welfare of the poorer sectors of the population. Index. (JEL)

Bird, Richard M., "Coffee Tax Policy in Colombia,"
Inter-American Economic Affairs, Vol. 22, No.
1, Summer 1968.

Boyce, James E. and Lombard, Francois J., COLOMBIA'S
TREATMENT OF FOREIGN BANKS: A Precedent Setting Case? Washington, D.C., American Enterprise Institute for Public Policy Research,
1976.

Catanese, A. J., "Planning in a State of Siege: The
Colombian Experience," Land Economics, Vol. 49,
No. 1, February 1973. This article examines
the problems of national planning in a democratic and free enterprise country that has
fallen into a state of siege (partial martial
law). The author contends that a lack of confidence in the future of the country has cast
national planning in a frustrating role that
will lead to rising expectations and unmet
promises. Conclusions are drawn which suggest
national planning in democratic countries
should be constrained in terms of promises,
timing, and criticality of problems. (JEL)

Colombia, GUIDELINES FOR A NEW STRATEGY, Bogota, The
National Planning Department, 1972.

Diaz-Alejandro, Carlos F., FOREIGN TRADE REGIMES AND
ECONOMIC DEVELOPMENT: Colombia, A Special Conference Series on Foreign Trade Regimes and
Economic Development, Vol. IX, New York and
London, National Bureau of Economic Research;
distributed by Columbia University Press, 1976.
Analysis of Colombian foreign trade and payment
system in relation to development over the
period 1950-1972. The study begins with a
review of the major trends in Colombian foreign
trade and payments with some discussion of
events before and after the period 1950-72.
Next is a description of the commodity composition of minor exports and a discussion of
policy instruments used to encourage them.
Merchandise imports and different policy instruments used to repress and manipulate the demand
for imports are examined in detail. Also
examined are the Colombian efforts during 1965-
66 to eliminate administrative controls over
imports and other transactions. And lastly,
there is a review of major economic trends
between 1967 and 1973 and a discussion of the
possible effects of further liberalization on
efficiency, growth, income distribution, employment, stability, and national autonomy.
Index. (JEL)

Dorner, P. and Felstehausen, H., "Agrarian Reform
and Employment: The Colombian Case," International Labour Review, Vol. 102, No. 3, September 1970.

Egginton, Everett, and Ruhl, J. Mark, "The Influence
of Agrarian Reform Participation on Peasant
Attitudes: The Case of Colombia," Inter-American Economic Affairs, Vol. 28, No. 3, Winter
1974, pp. 27-44.

Flinn, William L., RURAL AND INTRA-URBAN MIGRATION
IN COLOMBIA: Two Case Studies in Bogotá, LTC
Reprint No. 92, Madison, University of Wiscon-
sin, Land Tenure Center, 1971.

Gauhan, Timothy O'Dea, "Housing and the Urban Poor:
The Case of Bogota, Colombia," Journal of
InterAmerican Studies and World Affairs, Vol.
19, No. 1, February 1977, pp. 99-124.

Gillis, Malcolm, and McLure, Charles E., "Taxation
and Income Distribution: The Colombian Tax
Reform of 1974," Journal of Development Economics, September 1978.

Havens, A. Eugene and Flinn, William L., eds., IN-
TERNAL COLONIALISM AND STRUCTURAL CHANGE IN
COLOMBIA, Praeger Special Studies in International Economics and Development, New York,
Praeger, 1970. Contains 14 sociological and
economic essays on land, education, mobility,
and the class structure, all as determinants
of, and obstacles to, Colombia's economic
change. No index. (JEL)

ILO, TOWARDS FULL EMPLOYMENT, A Programme for Colombia, prepared by an Inter-Agency Team organized
by the International Labour Office, Geneva,
International Labour Office, 1970.

Jallade, Jean-Pierre, PUBLIC EXPENDITURES ON EDUCA-
TION AND INCOME DISTRIBUTION IN COLOMBIA,
INTERNATIONAL BANK FOR RECONSTRUCTION AND
DEVELOPMENT, 1974.

Lipman, Aaron, THE COLOMBIAN ENTREPRENEUR IN BOGOTA,
Hispanic-American Studies #22, Coral Gables,
Florida, University of Miami Press, 1969. Is
the status, image, role, and ideology of the
entrepreneur in Colombia the same as, or different from, more technologically advanced
countries? This pioneer study in Colombian
industrial sociology explores the nature of the
entrepreneurial position and role in the particular milieu of that country. The author
spent 18 months in Colombia investigating the
situation and discussing with government officials, business executives, and social scientists their understanding of the business community and its problems. (BPA)

Lombard, Francois J., THE FOREIGN INVESTMENT SCREEN-
ING PROCESS IN LDCs, The Case of Colombia,
1957-1967, Boulder, Colorado Westview Press,
1979. The author examines the mechanisms a
less developed country must establish to regu-
late the entry of foreign investment. His
model identifies the historical, political, and
economic dimensions of screening. He applies
it to Colombia, one of the first countries to
set up a foreign investment board. (BPA)

410

Maullin, Richard, SOLDIERS, GUERRILLAS, AND POLITICS
IN COLOMBIA, Lexington, Massachusetts, Lexington
Books, 1973. This is a competent analysis of
an important subject: the nature of the impact
of guerrilla warfare movements upon the political orientation and strategic concepts of the
military professionals. (FA)

McPherson, W. W., and Schwartz, Michael, CROP INPUT
PRODUCTIVITY AND AGRICULTURAL CREDIT ON THE
NORTH COAST OF COLOMBIA, Economics Report 56,
Institute of Food and Agricultural Sciences, University
of Florida, Gainesville, Florida, 1973.

Nelson, Richard R.; Schultz, T. Paul; and Slighton,
Robert L.; STRUCTURAL CHANGE IN A DEVELOPING
ECONOMY: Colombia's Problems and Prospects,
Princeton, New Jersey, Princeton University
Press, 1971. Discusses both theoretical relationships and specific problems of development.
Includes such topics as family planning and
population growth, rural-urban migration,
dualism and its effects on urban income distribution, and the economic, demographic and
political constraints on the growth of the
modern sector. Index. (JEL)

Sloan, John W., "Colombia's New Development Plan:
An Example of Post-ECLA Thinking," Inter-
American Economic Affairs, Vol. 27, No. 2,
Autumn 1973.

Thirsk, Wayne, RURAL CREDIT AND INCOME DISTRIBUTION
IN COLOMBIA, Houston, Texas, Rice University,
Program of Development Studies, Summer 1974.

Thorbecke, Erik and Sengupta, Jati K., A CONSISTENCY
FRAMEWORK FOR EMPLOYMENT OUTPUT AND INCOME DIS-
TRIBUTION PROJECTIONS APPLIED TO COLOMBIA, De-
velopment Research Center of the International
Bank for Reconstruction and Development, Janu-
ary 1972.

Whiteford, Michael B., THE FORGOTTEN ONES: Colombian
Countrymen in an Urban Setting, Latin American
Monographs--Second Series, No. 20, Gainesville,
The University Presses of Florida for the
Center for Latin American Studies, University
of Florida, 1976. To the elite "all the world
is Popayán," but to those in the barrios (the
book studies Popayán's poorest barrio, Tulcán),
to those recently arrived from the country and

socially, economically and politically deprived, life is grim. The urbanization process is studied in detail: family life in the country and in town, social relations and political institutions, levels of living, and medical and religious institutions and practices. The "fight" with life, to conquer its many uncertainties and to break out of the circle of poverty, is constant. But they are also protesting against exploitation and neglect, with some tangible results. (BPA)

World Bank, ECONOMIC GROWTH OF COLOMBIA, see under Avramovic (above).

Costa Rica

X-REF: AGRARIAN REFORM: Shaw.

Bell, John Patrick, CRISIS IN COSTA RICA: The 1948 Revolution, Austin, University of Texas Press (for the Institute of Latin American Studies, 1971. The most thorough account yet available concerning the origins and role of the National Liberation Movement in Costa Rica and the rise of José Figueres to political preeminence.(FA)

DeWitt, R. Peter, Jr., THE INTER-AMERICAN DEVELOPMENT BANK AND POLITICAL INFLUENCE: With Special Reference to Costa Rica, New York, Praeger, 1977. Utilizing dependency theory as a conceptual framework, the author examines the influence of U.S. national interests on the Bank, and the Bank's impact on Costa Rican development. An interesting study. (FA)

Waisanen, F. B., and Durlak, Jerome T., A SURVEY OF ATTITUDES RELATED TO COSTA RICAN POPULATION DYNAMICS, Programa InterAmericano de Informacion Popular of the American International Association for Economic and Social Development, San Jose, Costa Rica, 1966.

412

X-REF: AGRARIAN REFORM: Alier, FOREIGN INVESTMENT: Baklanoff, MISCELLANEOUS: Kalecki.

Barkin, David P., and Manitzas, Nita R., eds., CUBA: The Logic of the Revolution, New York, MSS Information, 1973. This volume includes nine articles examining the political and socio-economic development of Cuba as a type within the family of developing nations. Articles discuss the origins of the Cuban revolution, the social orientation of the revolutionary movement, Cuban agriculture, problems of economic organization, efficiency and incentives, the distribution of consumption, developments in education, urbanization, spatial structure and urban reform, methods of government, and an analysis of what the Cuban revolutionary government has tried to do and how much it has achieved. (JEL)

Bender, Lynn Darrell, THE POLITICS OF HOSTILITY: Castro's Revolution and United States Policy, Hato Rey, Puerto Rico, Inter American University Press, 1975. Revision of U.S. policy toward Cuba, in the direction of reconciliation or accommodation, is argued in an emotionally and intellectually balanced manner by an observer whose conceptual model of U.S.-Cuban relationships is based on mutual hostility arising from an intense, self-perpetuating reactive process. (FA)

Benjamin, Jules Robert, THE UNITED STATES AND CUBA: Hegemony and Dependent Development, 1880-1934, Pittsburgh, Pennsylvania, University of Pittsburgh Press, 1977. Detailed and scholarly, this historical investigation throws much light on Cuban events since 1959. The frustration of the 1933 revolution and the lack of social structure and leadership that followed deprived the regimes of the 1940s and 1950s of any true legitimacy, thereby creating "an ideological vacuum that served as an important precondition for the decisive victory of a new generation of radical nationalists in the 1960s..." (FA)

Blasier, Cole and Mesa-Lago, Carmelo, eds., CUBA IN
THE WORLD, Pittsburgh, Pennsylvania, University
of Pittsburgh Press, 1979. Since the early
1970s Cuba has greatly expanded its participation in world affairs. What changes in its
leadership, economy, and armed forces explain
this increased participation? How do Cuban
ties with Puerto Rico, Jamaica, Africa, Israel,
and the socialist countries reveal Cuban
purposes and affect U.S.-Cuban rapprochement?
(BPA)

Bonachea, Ramón L. and San Martín, Marta, THE CUBAN
INSURRECTION, 1952-1959, New Brunswick, Transaction Books, 1974. The authors, one of whom
participated in the first phase of the Cuban
revolution, seek to modify the orthodox view
that rural guerrilla initiatives dominated
events, insisting instead that urban guerrilla
support contributed substantially to what was a
continued urban-rural movement. (FA)

Bonachea, Rolando E. and Valdes, Nelson P., eds.,
REVOLUTIONARY STRUGGLE: Volume I (1947-1958)
of the Selected Works of Fidel Castro, Cambridge, Massachusetts, MIT Press, 1972. A
useful and substantial collection of Castro's
numerous communications, from ten-line personal
letters to "History Will Absolve Me," preceded
by more than 100 pages of historical and biographical material. (FA)

Bonsal, Philip W., CUBA, CASTRO, AND THE UNITED
STATES, Pittsburgh, Pennsylvania, University of
Pittsburgh Press, 1971. A former U.S. Ambassador to Cuba has written an eloquent first-hand
account of Castroite Cuba and its relations
with its northern neighbor. An important
conclusion: "There seems...no prospect of any
fundamental change in Cuban-American relations
as long as Castro remains in power." (FA)

Brunner, Heinrich, CUBAN SUGAR POLICY FROM 1963 TO
1970, translated by Marguerite Borchardt and H.
F. Broch de Rothermann, Pitt Latin American
Series, Pittsburgh, Pennsylvania, University of
Pittsburgh Press, 1977. Analyzes the development strategy from 1963 to 1970, which was designed to stimulate Cuba's economy through the
expansion of sugar exports. Applies the development model within the planning framework and
looks at the implementation of planning within

the scope of the sugar economy. Finds in part
that "the (sugar) plan was overly optimistic in
the determination of its objectives," and that
the plan became truly significant only in 1969.
Assessing the sugar economy under the profit
criterion, however, finds that over the plan
period, Cuba produced significantly above the
theoretical break-even point. Bibliography;
index. (JEL)

Cardenal, Ernesto, IN CUBA, New York, New Directions,
1974. The Nicaraguan poet-priest, for whom the
practice of religion becomes the making of
revolution, provides an informal and generally
(but not invariably) praiseful first-hand
account of Castro's Cuba. (FA)

Clytus, John, with Rieker, Jane, BLACK MAN IN RED
CUBA, Coral Gables, University of Miami Press,
1970. A cry of disillusionment from an American Black who sought justice in Castro's Cuba.
(FA)

Collier, Simon, FROM CORTES TO CASTRO, New York,
Macmillan, 1974. Breadth of scope is the dominant characteristic of this very competent
treatment of Cuba, which encompasses geography,
history, race, economic and social development,
and political themes, culminating in "Latin
America, the West, and the World." (FA)

Dominguez, Jorge I., CUBA: Order and Revolution,
Cambridge, Harvard University Press, 1978.
This lengthy analysis of twentieth-century Cuba
reflects an admirable striving for evenhanded-
ness. Three principal chronological divisions
cover developments from independence to Machado
(1902-33); the Batista era (1934-58); and the
Castro revolution (1959-). The roles of the
social groups, and the economic aspects, agriculture in particular, are well covered. A
final chapter describes political culture. (FA)

Domínguez, Jorge I., "Sectoral Clashes in Cuban
Politics and Development," Latin American
Research Review, Vol. VI, No. 3, Fall 1971.

Farber, Samuel, REVOLUTION AND REACTION IN CUBA
1933-1960, Middletown, Connecticut, Wesleyan
University Press, 1976. Analyzing the Cuban
revolution and its structural background from a

revolutionary democratic-socialist perspective, the author defines the Castro regime, disapprovingly, as Bonapartist. Cuba is "a new totalitarian and bureaucratic state in which one man, with the aid of a small group of associates, controls the economic, social and political life in the country." (FA)

Fontaine, Roger W., ON NEGOTIATING WITH CUBA, Washington, D.C., American Enterprise Institute for Public Policy Research, 1975.

Gellman, Irwin F., ROOSEVELT AND BATISTA: Good Neighbor Diplomacy in Cuba, 1933-1945, Albuquerque, University of New Mexico Press, 1973. Close analysis of Cuban aspects of FDR's Good Neighbor Policy yield the conclusion that basic relationships were little altered during the 1933-1945 period; overt intervention ceased but more subtle means, economic influences in particular, were employed to achieve traditional U.S. purposes. (FA)

Gonzalez, Edward, CUBA UNDER CASTRO: The Limits of Charisma, Boston, Massachusetts, Houghton Mifflin, 1974. A useful and well-reasoned summary, sufficiently detailed for most purposes, of the revolutionary experience and its historical setting, concluding with an appraisal of the directions in which the present regime may evolve. Regrettably, there is no bibliography. (FA)

Gonzalez, Edward, "The United States and Castro: Breaking the Deadlock," Foreign Affairs, Vol. 50, No. 4, July 1972.

Gordon, Michael W., THE CUBAN NATIONALIZATIONS: The Demise of Foreign Private Property, Buffalo, New York, Hein, 1976. Castro's program of total nationalization of business enterprises is evaluated within the context of U.S.-Cuban relations, the Cuban economy, international law, and U.S. court decisions. (FA)

Halperin, Maurice, THE RISE AND DECLINE OF FIDEL CASTRO: An Essay in Contemporary History, Berkeley, University of California Press, 1972. The author, six years a resident of Cuba, describes the rise of Castro and adumbrates the decline of the Revolution. The period covered is 1959-1964; a companion volume will follow. The analysis is good and so is the extensive selection of speeches and documents. (FA)

Llerena, Mario, THE UNSUSPECTED REVOLUTION: The Birth and Rise of Castroism, Ithaca, New York, Cornell University Press, 1978. In this authentic and well-written analysis, the author (formerly a representative abroad of the Castro movement) attempts to explain "...how it was possible for an originally middle-class reform movement to be transformed by an unprincipled, charismatic leader and a handful of close associates into a full-fledged Marxist-Leninist revolution." Leading roles in this metamorphosis are attributed to the "unpremeditated and yet perhaps decisive" activity of radical liberals and intellectuals who had envisioned something entirely different. (FA)

Macaulay, Neill, A REBEL IN CUBA: An American's Memoir, Chicago, Quadrangle Books, 1970. An American who fought in Castro's Rebel Army describes his experiences and offers his interpretations of the Cuban revolution. (FA)

Mankiewicz, Frank, and Jones, Kirby, WITH FIDEL: A Portrait of Castro and Cuba, New York, Playboy Press, 1975. This is yet another of the attempts to evaluate revolutionary Cuba, in a basically sympathetic vein, through interviews and man-in-the-street techniques. The core of the volume reproduces 23 hours of interviews and talk sessions with Castro. (FA)

Matthews, Herbert L., THE CUBAN STORY, New York, George Braziller, New York, 1961. An early analysis of the revolution by a New York Times correspondent who interviewed Castro while he was still a guerrilla in the mountains, and who became one of his early admirers in the U.S. (Ed)

Mesa-Lago, Carmelo, AVAILABILITY AND RELIABILITY OF STATISTICS IN SOCIALIST CUBA, Pittsburgh, Pennsylvania, University of Pittsburgh, 1970. Latin American Research Review, Vol. IV, Nos. 1 & 2, 1969.

Mesa-Lago, Carmelo, CUBA IN THE 1970s: Pragmatism
and Institutionalization, Albuquerque, New
Mexico, University of New Mexico Press, 1974.
Analyzes the present stage of the Cuban revolution, 1970 to 1974, distinguished by the author
as being characterized by more pragmatic and
conventional, institutionalized, post-reform
Soviet system after experimentation with alternative systems of socialist organization.
Discusses the reasons underlying the change in
thinking and examines its effects on Cuban economic policy, government structure and function, policies directed at the Cuban society,
and foreign relations. Index. (JEL)

Mesa-Lago, Carmelo, THE LABOR SECTOR AND SOCIALIST
DISTRIBUTION IN CUBA, New York, Praeger; published for the Hoover Institution on War, Revolution and Peace by Praeger, 1968.

Mesa-Lago, Carmelo, ed., REVOLUTIONARY CHANGE IN
CUBA, Pittsburgh, Pennsylvania, University of
Pittsburgh Press, 1971. A collection of
original essays on post-1959 Cuba. Part I
("Polity") has articles on Cuban leadership and
ideology, the generation of political support,
the elimination of United States influence,
Cuba's relationship with the Soviet Union,
Cuba's attitude toward the rest of Latin
America, and on the political sociology of
Cuba's communism. Part II ("Economy") features
essays on central planning, business management
and financing, the issue of wages and labor
organization, Cuba's international economic
relations, and on Cuban economic policies and
growth. Part III ("Society") includes articles
on various types of inequality and classes,
Cuban education, the Church, theater and
cinema, literature, and the change from traditional to modern values. (JEL)

Nelson, Lowry, CUBA: The Measure of a Revolution,
Minneapolis, University of Minnesota Press,
1972. Written by a rural sociologist, this is
an attempt to evaluate the changes which have
taken place in Cuba during the Castro regime.
Attention has been devoted to the agricultural
sector, the issue of labor incentives and productivity, social achievements, the effect of
the revolution on Cuban culture, and the impact

418

of the new ideology on Cuban life in general.
Index. (JEL)

Nicholson, Jr., Joe, INSIDE CUBA, New York, Sheed
    and Ward, 1974. A New York Post reporter pro-
    vides an informal, man-in-the-street account of
    contemporary Cuba from a pro-revolutionary
    point of view. Emphasizing the achievement of
    economic equality, he concedes that basic civil
    liberties are lacking, but regards them as
    "secondary." (FA)

O'Connor, James, THE ORIGINS OF SOCIALISM IN CUBA,
    Ithaca, New York, Cornell University Press,
    1970. A laudatory explanation of Cuban devel-
    opments since 1959, rooted in the premise that
    only through socialism could ancient ills be
    overcome. (FA)

Perez, Loues A. Jr., ARMY POLITICS IN CUBA, 1898-
    1958, Pitt Latin American Series, Pittsburgh,
    Pennsylvania, University of Pittsburgh Press,
    1978. "Copiously documented work, based on 15
    years of research...fine pioneer monograph.
    (Perez) is the first to examine the historical
    evolution of the Cuban army as a political
    institution." (BPA)

Ratliff, William E., CASTROISM AND COMMUNISM IN
    LATIN AMERICA, 1959-1976, Washington, American
    Enterprise Institute/Stanford, Hoover Institu-
    tion, 1976. The author believes that the three
    major currents of hemispheric Marxist-Leninist
    theory are converging; and that the strife they
    engender is at a low point, because of changes
    on the international scene, countermeasures by
    local military governments, and shifting rela-
    tionships among the leading communist powers.
    (FA)

Ritter, Archibald R. M., THE ECONOMIC DEVELOPMENT OF
    REVOLUTIONARY CUBA: Strategy and Performance,
    Praeger Special Studies in International Eco-
    nomics and Development, New York and London,
    Praeger, 1974. Study of economic policy and
    performance in Cuba from 1959 to mid-1972.
    "Four dimensions of economic performance are
    considered; income distribution, employment,
    economic growth, and the reduction of economic
    dependence." Nine chapters include examination
    of the socioeconomic problems of prerevolution-

419

ary Cuba, economic transition of 1959-61,
distinct growth strategies in 1961-63 and 1964-
70, both institutional and human resource
mobilization strategies, and the 1970's development strategy. Bibliography; no index. (JEL)

Ritter, Archibald R. M., THE ECONOMIC DEVELOPMENT OF
REVOLUTIONARY CUBA: Strategy and Performance,
New York, Praeger, 1974. Detailed analysis,
carried through 1972, of economic progress as
affected by social and political objectives.
The references to decreases in overt employment
and increases in covert or low-productivity employment are worthy of note. (FA)

Smith, Robert Freeman, ed., BACKGROUND TO REVOLUTION,
THE DEVELOPMENT OF MODERN CUBA, New York,
Alfred A. Knopf, 1966.

Smith, Robert F., THE UNITED STATES AND CUBA, BUSI-
NESS AND DIPLOMACY, 1917-1960, New York, Bookman
Associates, 1960.

Suchlicki, Jaime, ed., CUBA, CASTRO, AND REVOLUTION,
Coral Gables, Florida, University of Miami
Press, 1972. The scholarship in these seven
essays devoted to political, social and economic structures in Cuba is solid and well
grounded. Three of them focus on the Soviet
presence in the Revolution. (FA)

Suchlicki, Jaime, CUBA: From Columbus to Castro,
New York, Scribners, 1974. An excellent treatment of all aspects and eras, with emphasis on
the twentieth century. Succinct and complete,
balanced, fair and lucid throughout. (FA)

Ward, Fred, INSIDE CUBA TODAY, New York, Crown,
1978. A journalist, aided substantially by his
own photographs, provides detailed day-by-day
descriptions of Cuban life, with an overview of
political and international analysis. The
treatment is well balanced. (FA)

Weinstein, Martin, ed., REVOLUTIONARY CUBA IN THE
WORLD ARENA, Philadelphia, ISHI Publications,
1978. A group of scholars analyze Cuba's
national security policies, its role in world
trade (especially in sugar economics), its

relations with the United States and the Soviet
Union, and its commitment of troops abroad.
(BPA)

Dominican Republic

Atkins, G. Pope, and Wilson, Larman C., THE UNITED
STATES AND THE TRUJILLO REGIME, New Brunswick,
New Jersey, Rutgers University Press, 1972. A
sound study of U.S.-Dominican relations during
the era of Trujillo, with appropriate reference
to pre-Trujillo developments. The analysis is
not parochial, and several conclusions are
applicable in regions far from the Caribbean.
(FA)

Bosch, Juan, THE UNFINISHED EXPERIMENT: Democracy
in the Dominican Republic, New York, Washington,
London, Praeger, 1965.

Galindez, Jesús de, THE ERA OF TRUJILLO: Dominican
Dictator, edited by Russell H. Fitzgibbon,
Tucson, University of Arizona Press, 1973. The
first appearance in English in commercial format, of this famous study associated with the
kidnapping and presumed murder of Galindez.
Competently edited, this version restores the
source documentation largely omitted in the
Spanish editions, condenses and, to an extent,
rearranges the narrative material. (FA)

Lowenthal, Abraham F., THE DOMINICAN INTERVENTION,
Cambridge, Massachusetts, Harvard University
Press, 1972. Two notable qualities distinguish
this work of high excellence from many of its
predecessors. It is marked by a judicious and
balanced tolerance, undefiled by cant and jargon, and by the richness of its sources. There
are also discerning comments on the wayward,
many-faceted process by which foreign policy is
determined. (FA)

Slater, Jerome, INTERVENTION AND NEGOTIATION: The
United States and the Dominican Revolution, New
York, Harper and Row, 1970. A valuable addi-
tion to the growing literature on the contro-
versial American intervention in the Dominican
Republic in 1965. The approach is judicious,

the tone temperate and the research soundly
based. (FA)

Ecuador

X-REF: UNITED STATES POLICY: Pike.

Fitch, John Samuel, THE MILITARY COUP D'ETAT AS A
    POLITICAL PROCESS: Ecuador, 1948-1966, Balti-
    more, Maryland, The Johns Hopkins University
    Press, 1977.

Gibson, Charles R., FOREIGN TRADE IN THE ECONOMIC
    DEVELOPMENT OF SMALL NATIONS: The Case of
    Ecuador, Praeger Special Studies in Inter-
    national Economics and Development, New York,
    Praeger, 1971. Studies the past, present, and
    future role and performance of the external
    sector in the economic development of Ecuador.
    Primary emphasis is given to "The effects of
    Alternative trade policies on Ecuadorian eco-
    nomic growth...." No index. (JEL)

Redclift, M. R., AGRARIAN REFORM AND PEASANT ORGANI-
    ZATION ON THE ECUADORIAN COAST, London, Athlone
    Press, 1978. An interesting and dispassionate
    description of changes, funded by oil revenues,
    in the agricultural structure of the coastal
    rice zone after the abolition of rice tenancy
    in 1970. The program was a significant element
    in the national development objectives. (FA)

Tokman, V. E., "Income Distribution, Technology and
    Employment in Developing Countries: An Appli-
    cation to Ecuador," Journal of Development Eco-
    nomics, Vol. 2, No. 1, March 1975.

El Salvador

White, Alastair, EL SALVADOR, New York, Praeger,
    1973. This broad description of nearly all
    aspects of the life of a largely ignored nation
    is particularly welcome because it is almost
    without precedent in the literature on the
    region. Statistics, maps and illustrations
    enhance its appeal. (FA)

422

Guatemala

Adams, Richard Newbold, CRUCIFIXION BY POWER:
Essays on Guatemalan National Social Structure,
1944-1966, Austin, University of Texas Press,
1970. A distinguished social anthropologist
analyzes in depth the circumstances of peasant
life, development and evolution, using the
structure and concentration of power on the
national level as a framework. A rewarding
study. (FA)

Fletcher, Lehman B.; Graber, Eric; Merrill, William
C.; and Thorbecke, Eric, GUATEMALA'S ECONOMIC
DEVELOPMENT: The Role of Agriculture, Ames,
Iowa State University Press, 1971. A study
carried out by the authors with the help of the
United States A.I.D. Mission in Guatemala and
the government of Guatemala. It "analyzes the
present role of agriculture in the economic development of Guatemala and suggests short- and
medium-term policies conducive to economic development." Treats in detail the structure and
the working of the agricultural sector. Index.
(JEL)

Roberts, Bryan R., ORGANIZING STRANGERS: Poor Families in Guatemala City, Austin, University of
Texas Press, 1973. An analysis of urban ills
in Guatemala City and their effect on social
change. The author concludes that urbanization
has done little to enhance the capacity of the
general public for political and economic
organization, and emphasizes absence of mutual
trust as a barrier to such a development. (FA)

Silvert, Kalman H., A STUDY IN GOVERNMENT: Guatemala
(1954), Philadelphia, Pennsylvania, ISHI, 1977.
This book analyzes both the national and local
governments, their policies, conceptions, and
expectations. (BPA)

Haiti

Leyburn, James G., THE HAITIAN PEOPLE, New Haven,
Connecticut, Yale University Press, 1966. A
story of growth of Haitian institutions out of
the backgrounds of slavery and of French coloni-

al life, and of their development through a
century and a half of freedom, independence,
and virtual isolation. (BPA)

Lacerte, Robert K., "The First Land Reform in Latin
America: The Reforms of Alexander Petion,
1809-1814," Inter-American Economic Affairs,
Vol. 28, No. 4, Spring 1975.

Moore, O. Ernest, HAITI: Its Stagnant Society and
Shackled Economy, New York, Exposition Press,
1972. Authoritative but less massively detailed
than the recent Rotberg study (see below), this
volume will be a useful introduction for students of the many-sided Haitian dilemma. An
index is lacking. (FA)

Morrison, Thomas K., "Case Study of a 'Least Developed Country' Successfully Exporting Manufactures: Haiti," Inter-American Economic
Affairs, Vol. 29, No. 1, Summer 1975.

Rotberg, Robert I., with Clague, Christopher K.,
HAITI: The Politics of Squalor, Boston, Massachusetts, Houghton, 1971. An exhaustive study,
researched expensively and in depth, covering
almost all internal aspects of Haitian life and
development. (FA)

Schmidt, Hans, THE UNITED STATES OCCUPATION OF HAITI,
1915-1934, New Brunswick, New Jersey, Rutgers
University Press, 1971. A well-researched
account of the long Marine occupation, based on
archival sources hitherto largely ignored. (FA)

Honduras

Checchi, Vincent and Associates, HONDURAS: A Problem in Economic Development, New York, The
Twentieth Century Fund, 1959.

Jamaica

X-REF: COMMODITIES: Girvan.

424

Higman, B. W., SLAVE POPULATION AND ECONOMY IN
    JAMAICA, 1807-1834, New York, Cambridge Univer-
    sity Press, 1976. Dr. Higman offers a detailed
    analysis of the economic structure of the slave
    society in Jamaica. He describes the slave-
    based economy of the period, the occupational
    distribution of the slaves and levels of
    productivity. This in-depth examination of the
    growth and decline of the slave population, its
    changing composition, the family structure of
    the slaves and patterns of mortality and fer-
    tility provides an important relationship
    between economy, demography and ecology. (BPA)

Jefferson, Owen, THE POST-WAR ECONOMIC DEVELOPMENT
    OF JAMAICA, Jamaica, Institute of Social and
    Economic Research, University of the West
    Indies, 1972. A comprehensive statistical and
    analytical study of the behavior of the Jamai-
    can economy in the post-war period. With data
    for the 1950-68 period, the author reviews the
    following factors and sectors: population,
    labor force, employment, national income and
    expenditure, agriculture, manufacturing, mining,
    tourism and foreign trade. Substantial data.
    Index. (JEL)

Walsh, B. Thomas, ECONOMIC DEVELOPMENT AND POPULA-
    TION CONTROL: A Fifty-Year Projection for
    Jamaica, Praeger Special Studies in Interna-
    tional Economics and Development, New York,
    Praeger, 1970. This study seeks to extend the
    concept of hastening modernization by reversing
    the cause-effect relationship with fertility
    decline by exploring (for a developing country)
    the implications of lower rates of population
    growth for several major economic growth vari-
    ables. No index. (JEL)

Mexico

X-REF: AGRICULTURAL DEVELOPMENT: Ladman, AGRICUL-
TURAL DEVELOPMENT: Puebla, DEPENDENCY: Ceceña,
FOREIGN INVESTMENT: Baklanoff, IMPORT SUBSTITUTION:
Sheahan, INCOME DISTRIBUTION PRINCIPLES: Looney,
van Ginneken, KENYA: Cole, MODERNIZATION: Kahl,
MULTINATIONAL CORPORATIONS: Council, Osborn, REGION-
AL DEVELOPMENT: Barkin, TECHNOLOGY: Ilo, Mason,
URBAN DEVELOPMENT: Ilo.

Alisky, Marvin, "CONASUPO: A Mexican Agency Which Makes Low-Income Workers Feel Their Government Cares," Inter-American Economic Affairs, Vol. 27, No. 3, Winter 1973.

Aspra, L. A., "Import Substitution in Mexico: Past and Present," World Development, Vol. 5, Nos. 1 & 2, January-February 1977.

Atkin, Ronald, REVOLUTION! MEXICO 1910-20, New York, Day, 1970. A colorful account of the dramatic revolutionary decade in Mexico, with well-selected pictures. (FA)

Bailey, David C., VIVA CRISTO REY! THE CRISTERO REBELLION AND THE CHURCH-STATE CONFLICT IN MEXICO, Austin, University of Texas Press, 1974. A complete account of a particularly dramatic chapter in the long tale of church-state conflict--the 1926-1929 rebellion that was churned up by fanatical enforcement of revolutionary anti-clerical laws. U.S. Ambassador Morrow's contributions to the settlement receive close attention. (FA)

Balan, Jorge, MEN IN A DEVELOPING SOCIETY, GEOGRAPHIC AND SOCIAL MOBILITY IN MONTERREY, MEXICO, Austin and London, University of Texas Press, 1973.

Baring-Gould, Michael Darragh, AGRICULTURAL AND COMMUNITY DEVELOPMENT IN MEXICAN EJIDOS: Relatives in Conflict, Ithaca, New York, Cornell University Dissertation Series #52, 1974.

Bazant, Jan, A CONCISE HISTORY OF MEXICO: From Hidalgo to Cárdenas 1805-1940, New York, Cambridge University Press, 1977. Jan Bazant has woven into a coherent whole the chaotic series of political and social upheavals that characterized Mexican history from the start of the struggle for independence through the completion of basic social reforms in 1940. The author's political narrative concentrates on the struggle of the landless peasants and peasants with inadequate land to meet their needs and the striving of the wealthy to acquire status, power and more land. Bazant shows the influence of socio-economic forces and how these factors have colored the development of Mexico. (BPA)

Beals, Ralph L., THE PEASANT MARKETING SYSTEM OF OAXACA, MEXICO, Berkeley, Los Angeles, London, The University of California Press, 1975.

Bennett, Robert L., THE FINANCIAL SECTOR AND ECONOMIC DEVELOPMENT: The Mexican Case, Baltimore, Maryland, The Johns Hopkins Press, 1965.

Brandenburg, Frank R., THE MAKING OF MODERN MEXICO, Englewood Cliffs, New Jersey, Prentice-Hall, Inc., 1964.

Brothers, Dwight S. and Solis, Leopoldo, MEXICAN FINANCIAL DEVELOPMENT, Austin, University of Texas Press, 1966. Separate chapters are devoted to the money and capital market, the formulation and execution of monetary and financial policies, and the nature of Mexican financial experience in both the public and private sectors. The final chapter, a review of Mexican experience since 1960, speculates on the future course of financial development and offers specific proposals. (BPA)

Cole, William E., and Sanders, Richard D., "Income Distribution, Profits and Savings in the Recent Economic Experience of Mexico," Inter-American Economic Affairs, Vol. 24, No. 2, Autumn 1970.

Cornelius, Wayne A., POLITICS AND THE MIGRANT POOR IN MEXICO CITY, Stanford, California, Stanford University Press, 1975. In Latin America, migration to urban areas has proceeded more massively than anywhere else, leading to problems of assimilation and socialization that have enormous political consequences. The author examines these phenomena in six communities linked to Mexico City, and provides a detailed and exhaustive analysis. (FA)

Derossi, Flavia, THE MEXICAN ENTREPRENEUR, DEVELOPMENT CENTRE STUDIES, Paris, Development Centre of the Organization for Economic Cooperation and Development, 1971.

Díaz-Guerrero, R., PSYCHOLOGY OF THE MEXICAN: Culture and Personality, Austin, University of Texas Press, 1975. This is a work with many insights, devoted to the effects of culture upon personality. The author, a Mexican professor of psychology, addresses such topics as

427

neurosis and family structure, interpersonal
relations, respect and status, the passive-
active dichotomy, and mental and social health.
(FA)

Fagen, Richard R., "The Realities of U.S.-Mexican
Relations," _Foreign_ _Affairs_, Vol. 55, No. 4,
July 1977, p. 685.

Fox, Robert W., URBAN POPULATION GROWTH IN MEXICO,
Inter-American Development Bank, Urban Population Growth Series Report No. 1, October 1972.

Glade, William R. Jr., and Anderson, Charles W., THE
POLITICAL ECONOMY OF MEXICO, Madison, Milwaukee,
and London, The University of Wisconsin Press,
1968.

Gonzalez Casanova, Pablo, DEMOCRACY IN MEXICO, New
York, Oxford University Press, 1970. The Director of the Institute of Social Research at
the University of Mexico examines social and
political life in his country since 1910, with
particular reference to power mechanisms and
the prospects for a wider democracy. (FA)

Griffiths, B., MEXICAN MONETARY POLICY AND ECONOMIC
DEVELOPMENT, Praeger Special Studies in International Economics and Development, New York,
Praeger, 1972. A case study in the use of
macroeconomic policy to achieve both economic
stability and economic growth. Analyzes the
role of monetary, fiscal, and balance of payments policies in the performance of the Mexican economy from 1940 to 1967, a period distinguished by high rate of economic growth and low
rate of inflation. Designs and tests an econometric model of the Mexican economy to show
that a conservative monetary policy has produced economic growth without marked inflation
in Mexico during the period studied. Bibliography; no index. (JEL)

Hansen, Roger D., THE POLITICS OF MEXICAN DEVELOP-
MENT, Baltimore, Maryland, Johns Hopkins Press,
1971. The author criticizes the Mexican Revolution for its failure to diminish the gap between rich and poor, and assigns the principal
blame to nineteenth-century, self-seeking
entrepreneurial attitudes of the traditional
Mexican elite. (FA)

Hellman, Judith Adler, MEXICO IN CRISIS, New York, Holmes & Meier, 1978. After taking pessimistic note of the factors reinforcing continuity, such as the hold of the PRI, capitalist development, the power of a bourgeoisie undaunted by Echeverria's addiction to "radical rhetoric and half measures," the author asserts that "nothing short of a major upheaval in the Mexican system could genuinely improve their (the masses) lot. (FA)

Herman, Donald L., THE COMINTERN IN MEXICO, Washington, Public Affairs Press, 1974. A competent analysis of the Communist movement in Mexico, and the issues it raised, from the founding of the Communist International in 1919 to the end of World War II. Communism's lack of success, then and thereafter, is contrasted with the natural advantages it has seemed to possess. (FA)

Johnson, Kenneth F., MEXICAN DEMOCRACY: A Critical View, New York, Praeger, 1978. Traces the evolution of the PRI (Institutional Revolutionary Party), showing how it became the dominant force in a "one-party democracy;" the analysis of the policies of recent administrations, major socioeconomic problems, and government corruption reveals that deep-rooted alienation and strains of protest underlie an outwardly stable system. (BPA)

Ladman, Jerry R., "A Model of Credit Applied to the Allocation of Resources in a Case Study of a Sample of Mexican Farms," Economic Development and Cultural Change, Vol. 22, June 1974, pp. 279-301.

Looney, Robert E., MEXICO'S ECONOMY: A Policy Analysis with Forecasts to 1990, Boulder, Colorado, Westview Press, 1978. Robert Looney identifies the forces underlying Mexico's high rate of economic growth in the 1960s and early 1970s in order to determine if economic expansion can be resumed in the 1980s. He differs from other writers primarily in that his analysis indicates that most of the favorable conditions associated with the growth of the 1960s are not self-limiting. The major conclusion of his study is that the prime sources of Mexico's postwar expansion are indefinitely sustainable, while many of the adverse side effects associated with that growth are remediable. (BPA)

Mabry, Donald J., MEXICO'S ACCION NACIONAL: A Catholic Alternative to Revolution, Syracuse, New York, Syracuse University Press, 1973. Observers of Mexican politics, absorbed by evolutions within the long-ruling Partido Revolucionario Institucional, often overlook the Catholic and reformist Accion Nacional, whose loyal opposition has been sustained continuously for a third of a century. This study, with its exposition of church-state conflicts, should be welcomed. (FA)

Mayer, Lorenzo, MEXICO AND THE UNITED STATES IN THE OIL CONTROVERSY, 1917-1942, Austin, University of Texas Press, 1977. Previously untapped Mexican and U.S. archival materials are used in this study of economic and political dependency. In order to establish its authority, the leadership of the Mexican Revolution had to take control of the most dynamic economic sector, the oil industry. But ambiguity remains: after the disputes with U.S. business and the U.S. government were resolved--did dependency decline or increase? (FA)

Meyer, Jean A., THE CRISTERO REBELLION: The Mexican People Between Church and State 1926-1929, Cambridge, Cambridge University Press, 1976. The great war of the Cristeros is inseparable from political conflict inside and outside Mexico, and from issues of agrarian reform and anti-clericalism. Professor Meyer's story concerns a war of religion, a peasant war, a guerrilla movement, agrarian reform, and the violent upheavals that these changes involved. (BPA)

Poulson, Barry W., and Osborn, T. Noel, eds., U.S.-MEXICO ECONOMIC RELATIONS, Boulder, Colorado, Westview Press, 1979. A collection of essays by both Mexican and U.S. economists. Not surprisingly, Mexican economists tend to see a dependent relationship on the U.S. as the basic source of Mexico's economic problems, while U.S. economists generally focus on the failures of economic policies pursued by the Mexican government and the implications of Mexican economic instability on the U.S. (BPA)

THE PUEBLA PROJECT, SEVEN YEARS OF EXPERIENCE:
1967-1973, Analysis of a Program to Assist
Small Subsistence Farmers to Increase Crop
Production in a Rainfed Area of Mexico, The
International Maize and Wheat Improvement
Center, 1973.

Quirk, Robert E., THE MEXICAN REVOLUTION AND THE
CATHOLIC CHURCH, 1910-1929, Bloomington,
Indiana University Press, 1973. Church-state
relations in Mexico, and the parallel roles of
both institutions as social centers or cores,
are traced up to the 1929 modus vivendi that
still defines the government's participation in
ecclesiastical matters. The volume reflects
thorough research. (FA)

Randall, Laura R., A COMPARATIVE ECONOMIC HISTORY OF
LATIN AMERICA, 1500-1914, Volume 1, MEXICO,
Monograph Publishing on Demand Sponsor Series,
Ann Arbor, Michigan, University Microfilms for
Columbia University, Institute of Latin American Studies, New York, 1977. Volume I of a
four volume study of Latin American history.
This volume treats chronologically the political history and economic conditions and policy
of Mexico, a subregion where most of the
original Indian elements do not survive in
current economic practice, although they were
of much greater importance in the early colonial
period.(JEL)

Reyna, José L., and Weinert, Richard S., eds., AU-
THORITARIANISM IN MEXICO, Philadelphia, Pennsylvania, Institute for the Study of Human
Issues, 1977. Focuses on the manner in which
the government has consistently reduced social
protest by integrating the masses into cor-
poratist organizations. It demonstrates how
Mexico can have a formally democratic structure
which operates in an authoritarian manner, and
complements that analysis by examining the role
of foreign capital. (BPA)

Reubens, Edwin P., "Illegal Immigration and the
Mexican Economy," Challenge, November/December
1978.

431

Reynolds, Clark W., THE MEXICAN ECONOMY: Twentieth-
Century Structure and Growth, New Haven, Connecticut, Yale University Press, Economic
Growth Center, 1970. An extensive review of
the history of Mexican economic growth from
1900 to 1965. Confined primarily to quantifi-
able aspects of this history, the book includes
eighty-five statistical tables and forty-six
appendix tables to present the nature and
consequences of structural change in Mexico
during the first half of the twentieth century.
It covers the agrarian revolution, land reform,
public policy, urbanization and the industrial
revolution, changing trade patterns and trade
policy, and public finance in post-revolution
Mexico. Appendices; bibliography; index.
(JEL)

Ross, John B., THE ECONOMIC SYSTEM OF MEXICO, Stanford, California, Institute of International
Studies, 1971. Traces the role of the public
sector in economic development of Mexico since
1940. Gives an account of government policy
towards the agricultural and industrial sectors; also treats the financial system, and
economic growth and human welfare. Concludes
that the Mexican economy is by and large a
mixed one and predicts that the future policy
will continue to be pragmatic. Bibliography;
index. (JEL)

Ross, Stanley R., ed., IS THE MEXICAN REVOLUTION
DEAD? Second Edition, Philadelphia, Pennsylvania, Temple University Press, 1975. The mo-
mentous developments in Mexico in the last
decade have prompted a new edition of this
highly popular text on the first nationalist,
social revolution of twentieth-century Latin
America. Carefully selected essays--all in
translation--analyze the Revolution's antecedents, characteristics, and the issue of its
continuance. A complete new section consisting
of five new essays and a prologue by the editor
examining the continuing debate on the Mexican
Revolution has been prepared. (BPA)

Ross, Stanley R., ed., VIEWS ACROSS THE BORDER: The
United States and Mexico, Albuquerque, University of New Mexico Press (for the Weatherhead
Foundation), 1978. These 17 essays and nine
commentaries approach the U.S.-Mexican border

areas as a single entity and cover every con-
ceivable aspect: psychology, politics, ecology, economics, culture, sex, migration, social
class, personality development, labor, and
health. There are many interesting gleanings.
(FA)

Ruiz, Ramon Eduardo, LABOR AND THE AMBIVALENT REVO-
LUTIONARIES IN MEXICO 1911-1923, Baltimore,
Maryland, Johns Hopkins Press, 1976.

Singer, Morris, GROWTH, EQUALITY, AND THE MEXICAN
EXPERIENCE, Austin, University of Texas Press
(for the Institute of Latin American Studies),
1970. Mexican history from 1939 to 1961 is
explored in an effort to discern the relationship between growth and equality. The conclusion: the concepts of equality and inequality
should be disaggregated. The analysis is technical. (FA)

Solís, Leopoldo, LA REALIDAD ECONOMICA MEXICANA:
Retrovisión y Perspectivas, México, Siglo
veintinuno ediciones, 1970. An empirically
oriented study of the growth of the Mexican
economy. Contains many statistical tables and
detailed discussion of trends in agriculture,
the industrialization process, income distribution, and factor productivity. Solís makes an
apologetic bow to the need for "examination of
the principal social and political aspects
which have shaped our development," but has
chosen to emphasize instead "more rigor in
economic analysis and better decision in the
application of economic policy." No index.
(JEL)

Stewart, John R. Jr., "Potential Effects of Income
Redistribution on Economic Growth: An Expanded
Estimating Procedure Applied to Mexico," Eco-
nomic Development and Cultural Change, Vol. 26,
No. 3, April 1978.

Toscano, Alejandra Moreno, and Anaya, Carlos Aguirre,
"Migrations to Mexico City in the Nineteenth
Century: Research Approaches," Journal of
Inter-American Studies and World Affairs, Vol.
17, No. 1, February 1975.

Vernon, Raymond, THE DILEMMA OF MEXICO'S DEVELOPMENT,
THE ROLES OF THE PRIVATE AND PUBLIC SECTORS,
Cambridge, Massachusetts, Harvard University
Press, 1963.

Vernon, Raymond, ed., PUBLIC POLICY AND PRIVATE
ENTERPRISE IN MEXICO, Cambridge, Massachusetts,
Harvard University Press, 1964.

Von Sauer, Franz A., THE ALIENATED "LOYAL" OPPOSI-
TION: MEXICO'S PARTIDO ACCIÓN NACIONAL, Albuquerque, University of New Mexico Press, 1974.
A reasonable and judicious account of the origins, political history, beliefs, and prospects
of the largest of the parties functioning in
the minor zone of the political spectrum unoc-
cupied by the official PRI. A surprising
development: the urban-based, more conserva-
tively oriented PAN, now in its 36th year, won
more than 38 percent of the Federal District
vote in the 1974 elections for deputies. (FA)

Watanabe, S., "Constraints on Labor-Intensive Export
Industries in Mexico," International Labour Review, Vol. 109, No. 1, January 1974.

Wellhausen, Edwin J., "The Agriculture of Mexico,"
Scientific American, (Food and Agriculture
Issue, Vol. 235, No. 3, September 1976, p. 128.

Wilkie, Raymond, SAN MIGUEL: A Mexican Collective
Ejido, Stanford, California, Stanford University
Press, 1971. Anthropological study of a collective community in north central Mexico.
Part I describes the economic, political,
social, and other changes in San Miguel prior
to 1936, and then focuses on the ejido period
from 1936 to 1953. Part II discusses changes
since 1953 in San Miguel and other collective
ejidos. Index. (JEL)

Wright, Harry K., FOREIGN ENTERPRISE IN MEXICO:
Laws and Policies, Chapel Hill, North Carolina,
The University of North Carolina Press, 1971.

Nicaragua

Strachan, Harry W., FAMILY AND OTHER BUSINESS GROUPS
IN ECONOMIC DEVELOPMENT: The Case of Nicaragua,
Instituto Centro-Americano Administracion de
Empresas. "Studies three large groups and several subgroups in Nicaragua; covers similar
groups in other parts of the world, and identifies both their positive and negative contributions to economic development. (BPA)

Panama

Looney, Robert E., THE ECONOMIC DEVELOPMENT OF
PANAMA: The Impact of World Inflation on an
Open Economy, Praeger Special Studies in International Economics and Development, New York
and London, Praeger, 1976. Examination of the
effect of the Panama Canal and the treaty with
the United States on the economy of the Republic of Panama. Adopts a two-gap macroeconomic
approach, which involves the estimation for an
assumed rate of growth of the difference between investment requirements and potential
saving and the difference between import requirements and potential export of goods and
services. After looking at economic trends
since the pre-World War II period, the author
considers demographic characteristics, trade
and the balance of payments, monetary and
fiscal policy, inflation, and growth. Bibliography; index. (JEL)

Mellander, G. A., THE UNITED STATES IN PANAMANIAN
POLITICS: The Intriguing Formative Years, Dan-
ville, Illinois, Interstate Printers and Publishers, 1971. This interesting account of the
U.S. presence in Panamian affairs in 1903-08
serves as useful background for current Canal
negotiations. (FA)

Merrill, William C. and others, PANAMA'S ECONOMIC
DEVELOPMENT: The Role of Agriculture, 1st edition, Ames, Iowa State University Press, 1975.

Rosenfeld, Stephen S., "The Panama Negotiations,"
Foreign Affairs, Vol. 54, No. 1, October 1975.

435

Study Mission to Panama, A NEW PANAMA CANAL TREATY:
A Latin American Imperative, printed for the
use of the Committee on International Relations, Washington, D.C., U.S. Government Printing Office, 1976.

Paraguay

Arnold, Adlai F., FOUNDATIONS OF AN AGRICULTURAL
POLICY IN PARAGUAY, Praeger Special Studies in
International Economics and Development, New
York, Praeger, 1971. Case study of the Paraguayan agricultural economy to determine causes
of its low per capita income--which lags behind
those of other Latin American countries.
Author presents descriptive historical data
from 1523 to 1954 on the land, the people, and
land tenure. Contains 37 Tables; no index.
(JEL)

Baer, Werner, "The Paraguayan Economic Condition:
Past and Current Obstacles to Economic Modernization," Inter-American Economic Affairs, Vol.
29, No. 1, Summer 1975.

Peru

X-REF: AGRARIAN REFORM: Alier, Lehmann, Shaw,
MULTINATIONAL CORPORATIONS: Ingram, Pinelo, URBAN
DEVELOPMENT: Robin, UNITED STATES POLICY: Pike.

Alba, Victor, PERU, Boulder, Colorado, Westview
Press, 1977. A Spanish journalist and professor of political science traces in considerable
detail the reasons for the emergence of the
Revolutionary Government of the Armed Forces in
1968 (including, among other reasons, the
desire of younger officers for APRA-like programs but without public participation); the
elements that slowly congealed impulses for
change; and the revolution's demise in 1975,
symbolized by the "coup within a coup." (FA)

Astiz, Carlos A., PRESSURE GROUPS AND POWER ELITES
IN PERUVIAN POLITICS, Ithaca and London,
Cornell University Press, 1969.

436

Baker, A. B., and Falero, F. J., "Money, Exports,
    Government Spending and Income in Peru, 1951-
    66," Journal of Development Studies, Vol. 7,
    No. 4, July 1971.

Chaplin, David, ed., PERUVIAN NATIONALISM: A Cor-
    poratist Revolution, New Brunswick, New Jersey,
    Transaction Books, 1976.

Collier, David, SQUATTERS AND OLIGARCHS: Authori-
    tarian Rule and Policy Change in Peru, Balti-
    more, Maryland, Johns Hopkins, 1976. Travellers
    arriving in Lima who are depressed and disillu-
    sioned by the dismal squatter communities rim-
    ming the city will be fascinated by this analy-
    sis of their function as safety valve, provid-
    ing free land, rent, etc., and as a bridge to
    the national political structure. Serving such
    important needs, they receive elite and state
    support which is "essential though often co-
    vert." (FA)

Coutu, Arthur J., and King, Richard A., THE AGRICUL-
    TURAL DEVELOPMENT OF PERU, New York, Praeger
    Special Studies.

Dickerson, Mark O., "Peru Institutes Social Property
    as Part of its 'Revolutionary Transformation',"
    Inter-American Economic Affairs, Vol. 29, No.
    3, Winter 1975, pp. 23-34.

Dye, Richard W., "Peru, the United States, and
    Hemisphere Relations," Inter-American Economic
    Affairs, Vol. 26, No. 2, Autumn 1972.

Fitzgerald, E. V. K., THE STATE AND ECONOMIC DEVEL-
    OPMENT: Peru Since 1968, New York, Cambridge
    University Press, 1976. This "occasional
    paper" from the Department of Applied Economics
    at Cambridge University provides a compact and
    technically oriented economic analysis of the
    "Peruvian Model," with particular emphasis on
    state action in support of development. Numer-
    ous tables and charts are provided. (FA)

Ford, Thomas R., MAN AND LAND IN PERU, Gainesville,
    University of Florida Press, 1962.

Fox, Robert W., URBAN POPULATION GROWTH IN PERU, IDB
    Technical Department, Report #3, Urban Popula-
    tion Series, 1972.

437

Goodsell, Charles T., AMERICAN CORPORATIONS AND PER-
UVIAN POLITICS, Cambridge, Harvard University
Press, 1974. A detailed and essentially balanced study with strong political emphasis.
The author concludes that corporate foreign
investors are neither complete economic imperi-
alists nor uniformly good citizens, and should
be accepted selectively by host governments.
(FA)

Handelman, Howard, STRUGGLE IN THE ANDES: Peasant
Political Mobilization in Peru, Austin, University of Texas Press, 1975. A thorough analysis
of rural unrest, peasant land movements, and
community political activity, with interesting
references to regional differences created by
variations in the extent of social and economic
modernization. There is extensive statistical
material and a copious bibliography. (FA)

Hilliker, Grant, THE POLITICS OF REFORM IN PERU,
Baltimore, Johns Hopkins Press, 1971. This
study, centering around the APRA party in Peru,
throws light on the relative lack of efficiency
of broadly based reformist parties in creating
change in Latin America. (FA)

Karsten, Rafael, A TOTALITARIAN STATE OF THE PAST:
The Civilization of the Inca Empire in Ancient
Peru, Port Washington, New York, 1969. Studies
of the sociological and psychological aspects
as well as the political and social organizations and intellectual life of the ancient Inca
Empire. (BPA)

Kuczynski, Pedro-Pablo, PERUVIAN DEMOCRACY UNDER
ECONOMIC STRESS: An Account of the Belaunde
Administration, 1963-1968, Princeton, New
Jersey, Princeton University Press, 1977.
Analysis by a former economic advisor of the
Belaunde administration of Peruvian economic
policies and their political context, with
emphasis on the crisis years of 1966-68. Tries
to explain why, after a period of promising
growth in the early 1960's, Peru "was unable to
come to grips with some of the basic problems
of development in a democratic context."
Bibliography; index. (JEL)

Lewellen, Ted C., PEASANTS IN TRANSITION: The
    Changing Economy of the Peruvian Aymara: A
    General Systems Approach, Boulder, Colorado,
    Westview Press, 1978. The peasant transition
    from a subsistence-agriculture economy to a
    money economy is one of the most significant
    and widespread phenomena of the 20th century.
    The Aymara Indians of the Lake Titicaca Basin
    in Peru are presently undergoing such a trans-
    formation. Drawing upon 13 months fieldwork
    and on the most detailed economic data ever
    gathered for this area, Professor Lewellen
    shows why and how the Aymara have entered the
    money economy and the effects of this rapid
    change on social structure, religion, kinship,
    and world view. Several principles that might
    apply to a general model of peasant transition
    are suggested on the basis of comparison of the
    Aymara with peasant groups in other parts of
    the world. The book is an important demon-
    stration of the viability of General Systems
    theory for anthropology. Among the surprising
    findings directly deriving from this approach
    is that the Aymara transition is a response not
    to inputs from the industrial sector, but to
    instabilities within the traditional Aymara
    economic system itself. (BPA)

Lowenthal, Abraham F., "Peru's Ambiguous Revolution,"
    Foreign Affairs, Vol. 52, No. 4, July 1974.

Lowenthal, Abraham F., ed., THE PERUVIAN EXPERIMENT:
    Continuity and Change Under Military Rule,
    Princeton, New Jersey, Princeton University
    Press, 1975. Contains ten essays by the editor
    and eleven additional social scientists, all
    with extensive recent field work experience in
    Peru. Discusses Peru's current process of
    change under military rule within the perspec-
    tive of major issues of its recent history.
    Topics covered include: Peru's "ambiguous rev-
    olution," the new mode of political domination,
    government policy and income distribution in
    1963-73, squatter settlements, rural trans-
    formation, land reform and social conflict,
    Peruvian education, direct foreign investment
    in Peru, new forms of economic organization--
    toward workers' self management, and ideo-
    logical politics. Appendix; index. (JEL)

Pearson, Donald W., "The Comunidad Industrial:
    Peru's Experiment in Worker Management," Inter-
    American Economic Affairs, Vol. 27, No. 1,
    Summer 1973.

Philip, George D. E., THE RISE AND FALL OF THE PERU-
    VIAN MILITARY RADICALS, 1968-1976, London, Ath-
    lone Press, University of London, 1978.
    (Atlantic Highlands, New Jersey, Humanities
    Press, distributor). In a short analysis of
    the Velasco government and its successor,
    stressing the various views concerning the
    origins and nature of the left-oriented mili-
    tary and the reasons for their decline, the
    author concludes that a number of major ini-
    tiatives were achieved, but that "the problem
    of participation is the Achilles' heel." (FA)

Pinelo, Adalberto J., THE MULTINATIONAL CORPORATION
    AS A FORCE IN LATIN AMERICAN POLITICS: A Case
    Study of the International Petroleum Company in
    Peru, New York, Praeger, 1973. The ascent of
    IPC into hemispheric legendry has been accom-
    panied by a flowering of articles, pamphlets
    and seminar papers devoted to the company's
    role in Peru. This short volume, based in part
    on interview sources, now adds further per-
    spectives. (FA)

Randall, Laura, A COMPARATIVE ECONOMIC HISTORY OF
    LATIN AMERICA 1500-1914, Vol. 4: PERU, (pub-
    lished for Institute of Latin American Studies,
    Columbia University), University Microfilms
    International. 1977.

Roemer, Michael, FISHING FOR GROWTH: Export-Led
    Development in Peru, 1950-1967, Cambridge,
    Massachusetts, Harvard University Press, 1970.
    An in-depth study of export-led growth in Peru
    through the fishmeal industry which would serve
    as an encouraging model for less developed
    countries with export oriented economies. By
    utilizing primary product-export industries,
    these countries can successfully stimulate
    rapid and sustained economic growth. Bibli-
    ography; index. (JEL)

Sharp, Daniel A., ed., U.S. FOREIGN POLICY AND PERU,
    Austin, University of Texas Press (for the
    Institute of Latin American Studies), 1972. A
    competent collection of studies covering the

main aspects of the interplay between post-revolutionary Peruvian developments and U.S. policy. The chapters devoted to American business interests and the role of the United States in the international lending agencies will be interesting to many. (FA)

Smith, G. A., INTERNAL MIGRATION AND ECONOMIC AC-TIVITY: Some Cases From Peru, Paper No. 14, Montreal, Canada, Centre for Developing Area Studies, McGill University, 1976.

Stephens, Richard H., WEALTH AND POWER IN PERU, Me-tuchen, New Jersey, Scarecrow Press, 1971. The characteristics, significance and increasing power of the Peruvian landed class are de-scribed with a fine understanding of cultural and psychological intangibles. Unfortunately, there is no reference to the impact of the 1968 revolution upon this elite. (FA)

Thorp, Rosemary and Bertram, Geoffrey, PERU, 1890-1897, GROWTH AND POLICY IN AN OPEN ECONOMY, New York: Columbia University Press, 1978.

Tullis, F. LaMond, LORD AND PEASANT IN PERU: A PARADIGM OF POLITICAL AND SOCIAL CHANGE, Cam-bridge, Harvard University Press, 1970. The author examines the possibilities of reform from below, through peasant and village initia-tive, as a means of effecting change in the Peruvian land-tenure system. (Sponsored by Harvard's Center for International Affairs.) (FA)

Van Den Berghe, Pierre L., and Primov, George P., INEQUALITY IN THE PERUVIAN ANDES: Class and Ethnicity in Cuzco, Columbia, University of Missouri Press, 1977. Despite the intimidating sociological jargon, there is much of interest here. Examining the Cuzco region, the authors find considerable social stratification and in-equalities, but also surprisingly high mo-bility, both among groups and individuals. "The elites have circulated;" however, "the base of the pyramid (the Indians) has remained relatively stable." (FA)

Webb, Richard Charles, GOVERNMENT POLICY AND THE
    DISTRIBUTION OF INCOME IN PERU, 1963-1973,
    Harvard Economic Studies, Volume 147, Cam-
    bridge, Massachusetts, Harvard University
    Press, 1977. Quantifies the impact of redis-
    tributive measures of the Belaúnde (1963-68)
    and Velasco (1968-75) governments, comparing
    the impact with the size of initial inequali-
    ties and with the impact of economic growth on
    the market distribution of incomes. Describes
    the distribution of income throughout the
    period and sketches a model that explains the
    principal features of that distribution. Also
    examines several of the specific policies of
    the two regimes. Index. (JEL)

Werlich, David P., PERU: A Short History, Carbon-
    dale, Southern Illinois University Press, 1978.
    A first-rate performance, balanced in tone,
    thoroughly detailed and yet well structured,
    beginning with colonial times and stressing
    post-World War I developments. Although the
    author portrays the "rightward retreat" after
    Velasco, the study ends with 1976 and thus
    necessarily omits description of the acceler-
    ating decline of the 1968 revolutionary experi-
    ment in the past two years. (FA)

Whyte, William Foote, and Alberti, Giorgio, "The
    Industrial Community in Peru," The Annals of
    the American Academy of Political and Social
    Science, Vol. 431, May 1977.

Whyte, William Foote and Alberti, Giorgio, POWER,
    POLITICS AND PROGRESS: Social Change in Rural
    Peru, New York, Elsevier, 1976. Peasant move-
    ments, currents of change in rural communities,
    and the links between national and local devel-
    opment are subjected here to multi-disciplinary
    analysis that draws upon anthropology, history,
    economics and politics. The areas considered
    include Cuzco, Junin, and the Chancay Valley.
    (FA)

Puerto Rico

Bergad, Laird W., "Agrarian History of Puerto Rico,
    1870-1930," Latin American Research Review,
    Vol. XIII, No. 3, 1978, pp. 63-41z

442

Clark, Truman R., PUERTO RICO AND THE UNITED STATES, 1917-1933, Pitt Latin American Series, Pittsburgh, Pennsylvania, University of Pittsburgh Press, 1977. The book remains a major step in establishing a tradition of serious historical research, which has until very recently been extremely deficient for Puerto Rico. (JEL)

Dipaolo, Gordon A., MARKETING STRATEGY FOR ECONOMIC DEVELOPMENT: The Puerto Rican Experience, University Press of Cambridge, Massachusetts, Series, New York and London, Dunellen; distributed in the U.S. by Kennikat Press, Port Washington, New York, 1976. Examines the problem of attracting foreign investment, often from multinational companies, to a relatively underdeveloped area, focusing on the Puerto Rican experience during the third quarter of this century, particularly its attempt to import investment capital from the United States. Bibliography; index. (JEL)

Holbik, Karel and Swan, Philip L., INDUSTRIALIZATION AND EMPLOYMENT IN PUERTO RICO, 1950-1972, Studies in Latin American Business, No. 16, Austin University of Texas, Bureau of Business Research, 1975. Gives an overview of trends in the Puerto Rican economy since the late 1940's, showing the transformation was in large part attributable to capital from the United States. Discusses reasons for the persistent and high unemployment rates among the uneducated, unskilled, and the young, the increased sensitivity to U.S. economic fluctuations; and demand for a wider range of public services. Bibliography; no index. (JEL)

Liebman, Arthur, THE POLITICS OF PUERTO RICAN UNIVERSITY STUDENTS, Austin, University of Texas Press (for the Institute of Latin American Studies), 1970. Unlike their activist Latin American peers, students at the University of Puerto Rico are moderate and career-oriented, reflecting a pragmatic and basically conservative society. (FA)

Lopez, Adalberto and Petras, James, ed., PUERTO RICO AND PUERTO RICANS: Studies in History and Society, New York, Wiley, John & Sons, Schenkman Publishing Co., 1974.

Maldonado, R. M., "The Economic Costs and Benefits of Puerto Rico's Alternatives," Southern Economic Journal, Vol. 41, Number 2, October 1974. This paper assesses the economic implications of Puerto Rico's political alternatives--continued commonwealth status, statehood, or independence. It is concluded, on purely economic cost-benefit grounds, that continuation of commonwealth status is in all likelihood the most advantageous political alternative for the island. (JEL)

Maldonado, R., "Education, Income Distribution and Economic Growth in Puerto Rico," Review of Social Economy, Vol. 34, No. 1, April 1976. This paper investigates the Puerto Rican income distribution experience within the context of the Kuznets and Adelman-Morris hypotheses during a period of rapid economic development. The results do not contradict the Adelman-Morris contention that expanded educational opportunities can successfully modify income distribution in a developing economy. The Kuznets hypothesis was found to be neither appropriate nor applicable. (JEL)

Maldonado, Rita M., THE ROLE OF THE FINANCIAL SECTOR IN THE ECONOMIC DEVELOPMENT OF PUERTO RICO, Federal Deposit Insurance Corporation, 1970. The author emphasizes the role of financial intermediaries in the savings-investment process. She discusses the impact of the financial sector on Puerto Rican investment and economic growth. The large volume of investment activity in Puerto Rico has led to one of the world's highest annual growth rates (of about 10 percent). Appendix; bibliography; no index. (JEL)

Mingo, J. J., "Capital Importation and Sectoral Development: A Model Applied to Postwar Puerto Rico," American Economic Review, Vol. 64, No. 3, June 1974. An open, dual, growth model, in which labor migrates to the capital-intensive sector in response to a wage differential, is used to explain the time paths of per capita income and net factor income paid to foreigners.

Reynolds, Lloyd G., and Gregory, Peter, WAGES, PRO-
    DUCTIVITY, AND INDUSTRIALIZATION IN PUERTO
    RICO, New Haven, Connecticut, Yale University,
    Economic Growth Center, 1965.

Rivera, Angel Quintero, WORKERS' STRUGGLE IN PUERTO
    RICO: A Documentary History, New York, Monthly
    Review Press, 1977.

Steiner, Stan, THE ISLANDS: The Worlds of the
    Puerto Ricans, New York, Harper and Row, 1974.
    Earthy and informal, pungent with the flavor of
    the barrio, these vignettes of Puerto Rican
    life in the island and in New York provide a
    kind of curbstone sociology. The political
    orientation is pro-Independentista. (FA)

Strassman, W. Paul, TECHNOLOGICAL CHANGE AND ECO-
    NOMIC DEVELOPMENT: The Manufacturing Experi-
    ence of Mexico and Puerto Rico, Ithaca, New
    York, Cornell University Press, 1968.

Wagenheim, Kal, PUERTO RICO: A Profile, New York,
    Praeger, 1970. A short but competent treatment
    of all phases of Puerto Rican life. The pre-
    dictions concerning the island's future status,
    suitably hedged, indicate the complexity of the
    many factors involved. (FA)

Weisskoff, Richard, A MULTI-SECTOR SIMULATION MODEL
    OF EMPLOYMENT, GROWTH, AND INCOME DISTRIBUTION
    IN PUERTO RICO: A Re-Evaluation of "Successful"
    Development Strategy, New Haven, Connecticut,
    Yale University, Economic Growth Center Dis-
    cussion Paper No. 174, March 1973.

Uruguay

Brannon, Russell H., THE AGRICULTURAL DEVELOPMENT OF
    URUGUAY, New York, Praeger, Special Studies,
    1967.

Taylor, Philip B., Jr., GOVERNMENT AND POLITICS OF
    URUGUAY, Tulane Studies in Political Science,
    Volume VII, New Orleans, Tulane University,
    1960.

Weinstein, Martin, URUGUAY: The Politics of Failure,
Westport, Connecticut, Greenwood Press, 1975.
A competent analysis of an interesting and
important subject: the economic, political,
and social decline of Uruguay over the last two
decades. (FA)

Venezuela

X-REF: URBAN DEVELOPMENT: Robin.

Allen, Loring, VENEZUELAN ECONOMIC DEVELOPMENT: A
Politico-Economic Analysis, Contemporary
Studies in Economic and Financial Analysis,
Vol. 7, Greenwich, Connecticut, JAI Press,
1977. Survey of Venezuelan development over
the period 1945-75. Topics include: the
evolution of democracy, petroleum policy,
economic policy; economic growth, the public
sector, human resources, money and banking,
trade, agriculture, petroleum development, and
industry. (JEL)

Bond, Robert D., ed., CONTEMPORARY VENEZUELA AND ITS
ROLE IN INTERNATIONAL AFFAIRS, New York, New
York University Press, 1977. Of the seven competent essays presented here, three trace the
connections between domestic aspects and foreign affairs and four analyze Venezuelan foreign
policy. The consensus is moderately optimistic, with an affirmation that the country is
playing "an essentially constructive and responsible role in world affairs." (FA)

Burggraaff, Winfield J., THE VENEZUELAN ARMED FORCES
IN POLITICS, 1935-1959, Columbia, University of
Missouri Press, 1972. Here is yet another
example of the fascination the Latin American
military seems to hold for North American
historians and political scientists. Evolutionary changes in the relationships between
the military and the rest of society are described, and the future is appraised, somewhat
warily. (FA)

Caracas, Agosto, VENEZUELA: Bases de una Política
Hidraúlica, Planificación Financiera, Adminis-
trativa y Legal, 1972.

446

Edmonston, Barry and Oechsli, Frank W., "Fertility
    Decline and Socioeconomic Change in Venezuela,"
    Journal of InterAmerican Studies and World
    Affairs, Vol. 19, No. 3, August 1977, pp. 369-
    392.

Friedmann, John, VENEZUELA: From Doctrine to Dia-
    logue, Syracuse, New York, Syracuse University
    Press, 1965.

Hassan, Mostafa E., ECONOMIC GROWTH AND EMPLOYMENT
    PROBLEMS IN VENEZUELA: An Analysis of an Oil
    Based Economy, Praeger Special Studies in
    International Economics and Development, New
    York and London, Praeger, 1975. Examines the
    relations between Venezuela's high rate of eco-
    nomic growth in the post World War II period
    and her simultaneous high rates of unemploy-
    ment. Part I analyzes the factors contributing
    to that economic growth--the oil industry,
    investment value, and the international environ-
    ment. Part II examines factors affecting
    unemployment such as capital-intensive pro-
    duction methods, labor policies, education, and
    agricultural development. The final part
    analyzes the Venezuelan planning process,
    assessing it in terms of its success in meeting
    growth and employment targets. Bibliography;
    index. (JEL)

Heaton, Louis E., THE AGRICULTURAL DEVELOPMENT OF
    VENEZUELA, Foreword by Lowell S. Hardin, Vol. 5
    of Bench Mark Studies on Agricultural Develop-
    ment in Latin America, Praeger Special Studies
    in International Economics and Development, New
    York, Praeger, 1969. Describes the condition
    and achievements of the Venezuelan agricultural
    sector, measures its recent progress, compares
    it with other sectors of the economy, and
    contrasts its progress with the slower advances
    of agricultural sectors in most other Latin
    American countries. Data through 1965 from
    official Venezuelan sources. No index. (JEL)

Kolb, Glen L., DEMOCRACY AND DICTATORSHIP IN VENE-
    ZUELA, 1945-1958, Hamden, Connecticut, Archon
    Books (in association with Connecticut College),
    1974. Acción Democrática and the era of Pérez
    Jiménez are examined as the background of a
    prognosis of Venezuela's political future that

447

appears to blend equal measures of pessimism and optimism. (FA)

Levine, Daniel H., CONFLICT AND POLITICAL CHANGE IN VENEZUELA, Princeton, New Jersey, Princeton University Press, 1973. The author traces an interesting development--the emergence of broadly based political parties with continuing structures and loyalties and their role in defining and regulating political life. (FA)

Liss, Sheldon B., DIPLOMACY AND DEPENDENCY: Venezuela, The United States, and the Americas, Salisbury, North Carolina, Documentary Publications, 1978. The impact of foreign relations and external factors on Venezuelan development is the subject matter, with emphasis on the role of the OAS and the influence of the United States. (FA)

Martz, John D. and Baloyra, Enrique A., ELECTORAL MOBILIZATION AND PUBLIC OPINION: The Venezuelan Campaign of 1973, Chapel Hill, University of North Carolina Press, 1977. The 1973 electoral victory of Acción Democrática is examined in unusual detail and depth, with use of interviewing techniques and a variety of modern analytical tools and concepts. (FA)

Martz, John D. and Myers, David J., eds., VENEZUELA: The Democratic Experience, New York, Praeger, 1977. A broad Venezuelan survey in three parts: the historical and social framework; the articulation of the main interest groups; and policy and performance in specific areas, including oil and foreign policy. The democratic-reformist prognosis is favorable for 10 to 12 years; after that, "prospects are problematic." (FA)

Michelena, José A. Silva, THE ILLUSION OF DEMOCRACY IN DEPENDENT NATIONS, Cambridge, Massachusetts, MIT Press, 1971. The author studies Venezuelan society in depth and predicts a possible revolutionary crisis by 1984 if structural changes are not successfully implemented. The analysis tends to be technical. (FA)

Petras, James F.; Morley, Morris; and Smith, Steven; THE NATIONALIZATION OF VENEZUELAN OIL, New York, Praeger, 1977. The nationalization of oil in Venezuela is analyzed in the context of the interaction of classes within the country, the responses of North American industry, and the policies of the U.S. government. (FA)

Powell, John Duncan, POLITICAL MOBILIZATION OF THE VENEZUELAN PEASANT, Cambridge, Massachusetts, Harvard University Press, 1971. In Venezuela, 1935 to 1958 marked the decline of traditional dictatorships and the emergence of stable democratic government. This study traces the formation of a successful alliance between the peasants and a small urban elite, provides an empirical structural-functional analysis of the alliance, and develops a provocative new view of peasant mobilization. (BPA)

Salazar-Carrillo, Jorge, OIL IN THE ECONOMIC DEVELOPMENT OF VENEZUELA, Praeger Special Studies in International Economics and Development, New York, Praeger, 1976. Examination of the Venezuelan oil industry, the main source of the country's growth, discussed in the context of peripheral countries with patterns of trade and leading sectors or main sources of growth based on primary-type exports. The author traces the impact of petroleum on the economic development of Venezuela from 1936 to 1973. Focuses on policies that underdeveloped countries can devise in order to "augment the contribution of a primary export activity to the economy and to use this contribution in the most effective way." No index. (JEL)

Taylor, W. C., and Lindeman, J., THE CREOLE PETROLEUM CORPORATION IN VENEZUELA, with the assistance of V. Lopez R., American Business Abroad Series, New York, Arno Press, 1976.

Tugwell, Franklin, THE POLITICS OF OIL IN VENEZUELA, Stanford, California, Stanford University Press, 1975. Forces leading to the end of the era of privately managed oil development are analyzed, with special emphasis on the years 1960 to 1975. The departure of the multinational corporation heralds the takeover of domestic petroleum bureaucrats, who will now be charged with the heavy responsibility of dis-

449

covering and bringing into commercial production new reserves in an unstable international petroleum system. (BPA)

Vallenilla, Luis, OIL: The Making of a New Economic
    Order: Venezuelan Oil and OPEC, New York,
    McGraw-Hill, 1975. From his vantage point as
    founder and director of the Venezuela Petroleum
    Technical Office, the author surveys the histo-
    ry of the Venezuelan industry, OPEC and the new
    international order, and the issues and strate-
    gies that will determine the future of the
    international petroleum sector. (FA)